SCRIPTA SIGNA VOCIS

Studies about
Scripts, Scriptures, Scribes and Languages
in the Near East,
presented to

J. H. HOSPERS

by his pupils, colleagues and friends.

Edited by

H. L. J. Vanstiphout, K. Jongeling,
F. Leemhuis and G. J. Reinink

Egbert Forsten Groningen 1986

CIP-GEGEVENS KONINKLIJKE BIBLIOTHEEK, DEN HAAG

Scripta

Scripta signa vocis : studies about scripts, scriptures, scribes and languages in the Near East, presented to J.H. Hospers by his pupils, colleagues and friends / ed. by H.L.J. Vanstiphout . . . [et al.]. – Groningen : Forsten
Met lit. opg.
ISBN 90-6980-008-X
SISO oost 830 UDC [003+80+82](32+33+35)
Trefw.: schrift ; Nabije Oosten ; studies / taal ; Nabije Oosten ; studies / literatuur ; Nabije Oosten ; studies.

ISBN 90 6980 008 X

Foreword

The inexorable march of time - and University regulations - have caused Hans Hospers to vacate his chair of Semitic Languages and Culture and Near Eastern Archaeology in the State University of Groningen on the first of March 1986. However well deserved this coming period of rest may be, it happens much to his and our regret. The reason for regret is not merely Hans Hospers' total devotion to teaching, or his incisive yet pluriform and open-minded research in Semitic writing and grammar, based upon the broadest possible interest in all things linguistic; these tasks he performed instinctively. The main reason is that he represents Semitic Studies in Groningen in a verily concrete and specific way.

Appointed in 1948, the very young Professor of Semitics had to shoulder, all by himself, a formidable task. It is typical for him that, instead of confining himself to one or two disciplines within Semitics, he tried to incorporate in his teaching and research the main branches of the wide and many-hued field of Near Eastern studies. Now, in 1986, his Institute of Semitics has a teaching staff of seven members, covering the distinct areas of General Semitics, Assyriology, Hebrew, Aramaic, Arabic, and Near Eastern Archaeology. This growth and thoughtful articulation has been decisevely influenced by Hans Hospers' broad knowledge, his catholic and protean linguistic interest, and not in the last place his splendidly human, radically democratic, and painstakingly courteous behaviour to pupils and colleagues alike. Also, his career is in a way exemplary for the evolution of Near Eastern studies and Semitics as a whole. In the nature of things it is still often the case that very large fields in Semitist Academic endeavour have to be in the hands of one or two scholars; at the same time any detailed study has to be put into true prespective by a knowledge of the wider cultural background in all its aspects, since we are dealing with cultures which are certainly akin to, and in many cases even seminal to, Western European culture, but which have their own distinct line of evolution. And so it has come about that in Near Eastern studies in general, and certainly in Semitics, the best specialists have often been generalists, and *vice versa*.Yet the huge expansion the Semitic field underwent in the 19nth and 20th centuries, illustrated by the exciting new discoveries of vast but completely forgotten linguistic areas which have been made with some regularity since 1850, also implies that these days truly general semitists are to be found almost exclusively in the field of linguistics - which happens to be the main preoccupation of Hans Hospers.

Thus it is perhaps symbolic that in order to honour him at the occasion of his 65th birthday, the editors have been able to gather such a varied collection of studies. Scripts and Scriptures, and therefore Scribes, have always fascinated the jubilary, and in good linguistic tradition he has always insisted on *l'arbitraire du signe*, or the way in which a sign can be said to signify in human language and in its crowning achievement: writing. The editors are especially glad and grateful because nearly every contribution treats one or another aspect of the everlastingly interesting and basic problem:in what way does the sign (linguistic, or literary, or symbolic) represent the voice (of language, of discourse, of cultural tradition)? Since moreover these 27 contributions are held together somewhat by the underlying presence of writing and writings - the most precious gift bequeathed to us by the Ancient Near East and a favourite subject with Hans Hospers - , they are perhaps at the same time descriptive of the exciting variety within Near Eastern studies, illustrative of the jubilary's many-sided interest, and indicative of the deep gratitude we feel towards him.

The editors further have the pleasant task to thank all contributors for the enthusiasm with which they responded, the publisher, Egbert Forsten, for his technical and other assistance and his patience, the Faculty of Letters of Groningen University for creating the conditions which made possible conception, gestation and birth of the book, and the bodies who generously gave grants towards its publication: The Groninger Universiteitsfonds and the Oosters Genootschap in Nederland. A special word of thanks must go to the typists, Mrs. J.Y. Horlings-Brandse and Mrs. A. Reinink-Sirag, for the courage, devotion and good humour with which they undertook an unfamiliar and difficult task under pressure of time, and to Drs. M. Vogelzang for her careful proofreading.

Groningen, Christmas 1985

K. Jongeling - F. Leemhuis - G. Reinink - H. Vanstiphout

Table of Contents

NOTE: The *abbreviations* used in text and notes are conventional and/or selfexplanatory in context. The bibliographical *sigla* are taken from *A Basic Bibliography for the Study of Semitic Languages*, ed. H. Hospers *et. al.*, Leiden 1973-1974, vol. 1, pp. 386-396; vol. 2, pp. xi-xii, or they are indicated at first occurrence; a few sigla, very common in the discipline concerned, are left unsolved. Museum or Library *signatures* are left unchanged.

Herkunft und Sinn des Namens *Aqht* im ugaritischen Material

K. Aartun, Oslo

Ein besonderes Problem in der Ugaritistik stellt immer noch die Frage nach Herkunft und Sinn der Namensform *Aqht* in der epischen Ueberlieferung dar. Wenn die gesamten in Frage kommenden sprachlichen wie sachlichen Momente in Betracht gezogen werden, kann die bisher nur vereinzelt gebotene Erklärung unter keinen Umständen als befriedigend angesehen werden. Die übliche Deutung vertritt nämlich, wie gezeigt werden soll, eine isolierte Betrachtung des Problems, wobei, wie sich herausstellt, mehrere wichtige sprachliche und sachliche Faktoren ausser Acht gelassen werden. Es hat folglich dieses Verfahren zu einer rein willkürlichen Lösung der Frage geführt. Aus guten Gründen bedarf deshalb der Name *Aqht* einer neuen Erklärung, die dem ganzen zu Gebote stehenden relevanten Material Rechnung trägt. Im Folgenden soll daher der Versuch gemacht werden, die etymologische Grundlage und den begründeten nominalen Sinn des Namens *Aqht* von allen erforderlichen Gesichtspunkten aus zu beleuchten. Das geschieht gezwungenermassen unter Berücksichtigung sowohl des ganzen sprachlichen Materials des Ugaritischen bzw. Semitischen als auch des literarisch gegebenen Zeugnisses d.h. des sachlichen Inhalts des Namens in der dichterischen Ueberlieferung aus Ugarit. Nach einer kurzen Präsentation des Forschungsstandes in diesem Punkt - mit kritischer Beurteilung der Argumentation - unterziehen wir zuerst die sprachliche, dann die sachliche Frage einer genauen Analyse.

Die erwähnte traditionelle Erklärung des Namens *Aqht* rührt her vom Herausgeber des Textes, Charles Virolleaud. Seine Lösung sucht er durch Argumente etymologischer und morphologischer Art zu stützen. Ausdrücklich vermerkt Virolleaud, *La légende phénicienne de Danel*, S. 96, zur Namensform: "Etymologiquement, le nom d'Aqhat paraît être la 3e p. Imparf. d'un verbe *qht*; comparer, peut-être *Aleyn* (= *a-ley-n!*) et, en tout cas *Aymr* (à lire *Ayammar* sans doute) dans III AB, A. - Voir aussi, dans A.T., *Qehât*, nom d'un des fils de Lévi"; ähnlich führt C.H. Gordon, *Ugaritic textbook*, S. 365, an: '*aqht* (1 Aqht: 1, etc.): Dnil's son; cf. Heb. *qĕhāṯ*". Vgl. dementsprechend auch F. Gröndahl, *Die Personennamen der Texte aus Ugarit*, S. 100.

Aus verschiedenen Gründen kann jedoch - wie oben präzisiert - diese namentlich von Virolleaud beanspruchte Erklärung nicht aufrechterhalten werden. Einmal wäre morphologisch betrachtet ein hier vorausgesetztes *a*-Präformativ für die 3. Person Singular Imperfekt des Verbs ugaritisch wie semitisch völlig isoliert. Diese Argumentation ist also ohne jede sprachliche Stütze und muss, wie es scheint, einfach auf einem Lapsus beruhen. Ferner entbehrt auch die Annahme einer selbständigen Wurzel *QHT* der notwendigen positiven Grundlage. Im vorhandenen Sprachmaterial des Semitischen ist nämlich eine derartige Wurzel nicht nachzuweisen. Die von Virolleaud und anderen zum Vergleich herangezogene alttestamentliche Namensform *Qᵉhāṯ* braucht - vom derivativen und strukturellen Gesichtspunkt aus betrachtet - eine ganz andere Erklärung. Diese Frage wird unten genauer behandelt. Uebereinstimmend mit dem hier Angeführten sieht die weit überwiegende Mehrzahl der Forscher, die sich mit dem Aqht-Gedicht befasst haben, gänzlich von der von Virolleaud und anderen gegebenen Lösung des Problems des Namens *Aqht* ab. In der Regel enthält man sich bei der Behandlung des Textes jeder Erörterung des Namens. So verfahren z.B. Th. H. Gaster, *Thespis. Ritual, myth and drama in the ancient Near East,* S. 257 ff.; H.L. Ginsberg, *ANET*², S. 149f.; G.R. Driver, *Canaanite myths and legends,* S. 134; J. Aistleitner, *Wörterbuch der ugaritischen Sprache,* S. 33; H.-P. Müller, *Magisch-mantische Weisheit und die Gestalt Daniels,* in *UF* 1 (1969), S. 89f.; A. Caquot und M. Sznycer, *Textes ougaritiques.* Tome I. *Mythes et légendes,* S. 429 u.ö.; M. Dijkstra und J.C. de Moor, *Problematical passages in the legend of Aqhâtu,* in *UF* 7 (1975), S. 171 ff.; N. Wyatt, *Atonement theology in Ugarit and Israel,* in *UF* 8 (1976), S. 425; und mehrere andere.

Gehen wir jetzt zur direkten sprachlichen Untersuchung des Namens *Aqht* über, so ist zunächst in betreff der Herkunft desselben die derivative sowie die morphologische Voraussetzung dieser nominalen Form gar kein Problem. Nach Ausweis des sprachlichen Befundes des Ugaritischen/Semitischen gibt es in der Tat überhaupt nur eine Möglichkeit, die sowohl die Etymologie als auch die Morphologie des Wortes restlos erklären kann, nämlich die Auffassung der Form als einer Femininbildung auf *-t* von der Wurzel *'QH*. Dies ist ausserdem auch die einzige Erklärung, die unter Bezugnahme auf den gesicherten sachlichen Sinn des Namens in dem betreffenden Gedicht positiv begründet werden kann. Als sprachliche Voraussetzung dieser Deutung erweisen sich unter anderen folgende Momente als wesentlich: Auf vergleichender Basis ist die Wurzel *'QH* des Semitischen, wenn auch nur sporadisch, literarisch nachweisbar. Gesichert ist diese durch die jüdisch-aramäische Ueberlieferung. Von dieser Wurzel ist jüdisch-aramäisch ein nominales Derivat, eine sogar mit dem ugaritischen Namen *Aqht* morphologisch vergleichbare Formbildung mit Femininendung *-ṯ*, vorhanden, nämlich *'aqhĕṯā* (neben *'aqwĕṯā*). Der Sinn dieser jüdisch-aramäischen Form(en) ist: "Einwurf, Protest". Dazu siehe genauer G.H. Dalman, *Aramäisch-neuhebräisches Handwörterbuch zu Targum, Talmud und Midrasch* (1967), S. 37; vgl. ferner J. Levy, *Wörterbuch über die Talmudim und Midraschim* I, S. 155. Dieses allerdings ganz isolierte sprachliche Zeugnis darf man natürlich nicht, wie bisher der Fall zu sein scheint, übersehen. Als solche verdient die Bildung - und zwar als überlieferter Teil der betreffenden Sprache - die gleiche Beachtung wie jede sonstige überlieferte Sprachform. Das bedeutet, dass dieselbe als vollgültiger Sprachbeweis behandelt werden muss. Verglichen mit dem ugaritischen Namen *Aqht* hat dies zur Folge: Nicht nur die zugrundeliegende Wurzel und morphologische Struktur, sondern auch - wie unten klargelegt werden soll - der belegte Sinn der Bildung befriedigen die grundlegenden Forderungen mit Bezug auf die sprachliche Erklärung des zu erörternden ugaritischen Namens: *Aqht*.

Vom Standpunkt der Namengebung aus fällt auf dieser Grundlage der Formtypus des Namens *Aqht* keineswegs aus der Reihe. Wie schon längst in einzelsprachlichen Studien zur Namengebung im Ugaritischen/Semitischen gezeigt, ist die Anwendung femininer Wortbildungen (Abstraktbildungen) als Männernamen (, die also ihrer Funktion entsprechend als Maskulinum konstruiert werden,) eine wohlbekannte Erscheinung. Als Analogien vergleiche man so zunächst aus dem ugaritischen Material Männernamen femininer Struktur wie *Ḥgbt* (309:28; CTA 131:28; KTU 4.55:28; Gröndahl, *Personennamen*, S. 135); *ᶜṮqbt* (321:II:27; CTA 119:II:27; KTU 4.63:27; Gröndahl, *Personennamen*, S. 113); *(Bn) Ḏqnt* (2023 rev. 11; KTU 4.422:40; Gröndahl, *Personennamen*, S. 197); *(Bn) Ḥlbt* (2117:12; KTU 4.617:12; Gröndahl, *Personennamen*, S. 135); usw. Siehe Gröndahl, *op. cit.*, passim. Unter den zahlreichen Entsprechungen aus den verwandten Sprachen vergleiche man der Kürze halber vor allem hebräische Typen dieser Art wie *'Ēlā* (Gn 36:41 u.ö.); *Bĕḵōraṯ* (1 S 9:1); *Baᶜănā* (2 S 4:2 u.ö.); *Bĕrīᶜā* (Gn 46:17 u.ö.); *Gĕnūḇaṯ* (1 K 11:20); *Ḥubbā* (1 Ch 7:34); *Pilhā* (Neh 10:25); *Śalmā* (Ru 4:20); *Sĕlōmīṯ* (2 Ch 11:20 u.ö.); usw. Zur ganzen Frage siehe schon M. Noth, *Die israelitischen Personennamen im Rahmen der gemeinsemitischen Namengebung*, passim (besonders das Namenregister S. 233 ff.). Hierher gehört auch die oben genannte hebräische Namensform *Qĕhāṯ* (Gn 46:11 u.ö.). Letztere ist eine Abstraktbildung mit Femininendung *-āṯ* < **-at* und Wegfall des ersten Radikals von der Wurzel *WQH* (zur Wurzel vgl. vor allem arabische Derivate von derselben Wurzel; dazu z.B. A. de B. Kazimirski, *Dictionnaire arabe-français* II, S. 1592) in analoger Weise wie z.B. *Qĕnāṯ* "n. pr. einer Stadt" (Nu 32:42

u.ö) von *WQN* (zur Wurzel vgl. gleichfalls besonders die arabische Dokumentation; siehe z.B. Kazimirski, a.a.O.). Für die Struktur der letztgenannten hebräischen Formen auf *-āṯ* < **-at* neben *-aṯ* (vgl. schon oben) statt zu erwarendem *-ā* < **-at*, wie auch analog z.B. *Bĕḵōraṯ* (statt *Bĕḵōrā*; siehe oben); *Šimʿāṯ* (statt *Šimʿā*; 2 K 12:22 u.ö.); *Šimrāṯ* (statt *Šimrā*; 1 Ch 8:21) usw. vgl. schon besonders H. Birkeland, *Akzent und Vokalismus im Althebräischen*, an mehreren Stellen; ferner ausführlich Aartun, *Althebräische Nomina mit konserviertem kurzem Vokal in der Hauptdrucksilbe*, in: *ZDMG* 117,2 (1967), S. 247 ff., besonders S. 262f., sowie id., *Noch einmal zum Problem der Haupttondehnung beim Nomen im Althebräischen*, in: *ZDMG* 131,1 (1981), S. 28 ff. Für weitere häufige Belege von männlichen Eigennamen femininer Struktur im Semitischen siehe bereits die einschlägigen Lexika; ferner besonders z.B. fürs Arabische die Verweise bei H. Reckendorf, *Die syntaktischen Verhältnisse des Arabischen*, an verschiedenen Stellen (siehe Index, S. 821); fürs Altsüdarabische G.L. Harding, *An Index and Concordance of Pre-islamic Arabian Namens* ..., passim; usw.

Gerade zur hier gegebenen sprachlichen Analyse stimmt nun ferner auch, wie oben erwähnt, der vom Inhalt des ugaritischen Epos geforderte sachliche Sinn des Namens *Aqht*. Dabei ist es für die richtige Fassung des Namens von besonderer Wichtigkeit sich die ererbten Prinzipien der Namengebung im alten Orient zu vergegenwärtigen. Nach altorientalischer Anschauung deckt sich, wie bekannt, der Name grundsätzlich mit der Person, dem Gegenstand usw., die/den er bezeichnet. Das heisst: Der Name bezeichnet immer ein Charakteristikum des Wesens, der Funktion usw. des Trägers, wird deshalb als identisch mit dem Träger selbst betrachtet. Beispielsweise wird von den alten Israeliten diese Ueberzeugung folgendermassen zum Ausdruck gebracht: 1 S 25:25 *'al-nā yāšīm 'ăḏōnī 'èṯ-libbō 'èl-'īš hab-bĕlīyaʿal haz-zè ʿal-Nāḇāl kī ḵi-šmō ken-hū Nāḇāl šemō u-nĕḇālā ʿimmō* "mein Herr errege sich nicht über diesen bösartigen Menschen, den Nabal; denn wie sein Name (d.h. wie er heisst), so (ist) er. Nabal (d.h. Tor) (ist) sein Name (d.h. heisst er) und Torheit (ist) bei ihm (d.h. voll Torheit ist er)". Dass der Name semitisch Identität mit dem Träger bedeutet, also nichts Äusserliches ist, wird vielfach auch ausdrücklich von den Arabern bestätigt. Dazu siehe genauer J. Wellhausen, *Reste arabischen Heidentums*, S. 199f., und die dort angeführten Daten. So legt auch im vorliegenden Fall - der traditionellen semitischen Voraussetzung zufolge - die blosse Existenz des Namens der Person *Aqht* ein sicheres Zeugnis für den Charakter und damit für das innerste Wesen, das Tun und Handeln u.s.w. dieser Gestalt ab. Dies hat dann inhaltlich zur Folge, dass innerhalb des Gedichtes die Stellung, das Benehmen, die Tätigkeit u.dgl. der *Aqht* benannten Gestalt dem semantisch gebundenen Sinn des

Namens derselben entsprechen muss. Wie aus dem Gedicht hervorgeht, ist das Vorhandensein dieser sachlichen Korrespondenz zwischen dem lexikalischen Sinn des Namens (vgl. oben) und der Funktion des Trägers/dem Inhalt des Gedichtes (vgl. unten) nur zu konstatieren. Dafür seien in Kürze folgende sachliche Argumente aus dem Epos zur Begründung angeführt: Dem Inhalt nach bildet die durch den Namen *Aqht* geprägte und gekennzeichnete Person als Sohn des Königs Dnil die Hauptgestalt der Erzählung. Daher wird auch dieses Epos ausdrücklich mit dem Kennzeichnen *lAqht* "mit Bezug auf Aqht" (1 Aqht:1; CTA 19:I:1; KTU 1.19.I.1; dazu ferner Aartun, *AOAT* 21,2, S. 31ff.) versehen. In Bezug auf die Thematik ergeben sich nachstehende Momente als bedeutsam. Der lang ersehnte Sohn des Königs Dnil, der den Namen *Aqht* trägt, steht in regem Verkehr mit der Göttin ᶜNt. Auf Anregung seines Vaters wird dem schon zur Jagd reifen Jüngling ein vom Schmiedegott Kṯr-und-Ḫss verfertigter herrlicher Jagdbogen überreicht. Wegen dieses Bogens kommt es dann zum Konflikt zwischen Aqht und der Göttin ᶜNt. Als letztere den kostbaren Bogen erblickt, entbrennt sie in Begierde nach ihm. Sie fordert von Aqht den Bogen und bietet ihm dafür Gold und Silber. Aqht jedoch geht auf das Angebot der Göttin nicht ein, empfiehlt ihr dagegen, dem Künstlergott die benötigten Materialien zu liefern, damit er einen anderen Bogen anfertige (2 Aqht/CTA 17/KTU 1.17:VI:16 ff.). Darauf verspricht die Göttin dem Aqht für den Bogen ewiges Leben. Aqht jedoch lehnt auch dieses Angebot entschieden ab und beschuldigt die Göttin des Betruges, Gleichmut gegenüber dem Tod bezeugend: "Den Tod des Jedermann werde ich sterben, und ich werde gewisslich sterben". Auch fügt er als ein zweites Argument mit Nachdruck hinzu: Der Bogen sei ein Bogen für Helden, also ein Männerbogen besonderer Art, passe daher nicht in der Hand eines Weibes; usw. (2 Aqht/CTA 17/KTU 1.17:VI:25 ff.). Das konsequent ablehnende Verhalten des Aqht der ᶜNt gegenüber wird ihm zum Verhängnis. Dafür muss er - durch die erfolgreich geplante Rache der Göttin - mit dem Leben bezahlen (3 Aqht rev. bzw. obv./CTA 18:I, :IV/KTU 1.18:I, :IV). Das tragische Schicksal des *Aqht*, der unabwendbare Untergang der - dem Namen gemäss - Einwürfe erhebenden Gestalt (!), ist Realität geworden. In anderen Worten: Der im Namen gelegene Hinweis auf den Sachbegriff (dazu vgl. oben) lässt auf diese Weise den Akt und Inhalt der Benennung der Person mit der im Gedicht ausgedrückten Tätigkeit derselben miterleben. Dadurch wird die Ueberzeugung gewährt, dass die Benennung mit Recht erfolgt ist und im vollen Umfang der Wortbedeutung gilt.

So entsprechen die kritischen Zwischenbemerkungen Aqhts resp. seine (verhängnisvolle) Bekundung lebhaften Missfallens über die Vorschläge der Göttin sachlich im ganzen dem durch den Namen *Aqht* gekennzeichneten Charakteristikum des Wesens, des Handelns usw. dieser Person. Die Frage nach der Herkunft und der Bedeutung des Namens *Aqht* darf somit auf der Basis der hier vorgeführten Beweisgründe als erledigt angesehen werden: *Aqht* (Personenname) < nominale Stammbildung mit Femininendung -ṯ (von *'QH*) "Einwurf, Protest".

The Peshitta of *Sapientia Salomonis*

H.J.W. Drijvers, Groningen

The long-standing controversy about the authorship of the Peshitta Old Testament has not yet led to solid and generally accepted conclusions. Some scholars believe that the Syriac version of the Old Testament was of Jewish origin, others adduce arguments for a translation made by Christians[1)]. In this debate the Peshitta of the standard Old Testament apocrypha that are part of the LXX and of the Syriac Old Testament has not played any significant rôle. It is generally assumed that, with the exception of Ben Sira, these books were translated from Geek into Syriac at an early date, i.e. before the end of the fourth century C.E.[2)]. Detailed research into the translation-techniques used, and into the religio-cultural milieu in which these translations were made and read is, however, practically non-existent[3)].
In this connection a comparison between the Peshitta version of *Sapientis Salomonis* and the extant Greek text in the LXX can yield some insight into the complicated cultural process which we call translation[4)].

The Wisdom of Solomon is a highly poetical text in praise of the rôle of divine wisdom in human life and experience, and describes its supernatural rôle in the ancient history of Israel, and in particular in its exodus from Egypt. Its nineteen chapters do not contain any historical and geographical detail that illuminate its date and place of origin. The whole work, written in the form of an *encomium*, can be divided into three parts, which all show a well-reflected concentric structure, are thematically very well linked, contain in widely separated passages the same themes and vocabulary, and form consequently a well-knit literary whole. The first part, chs. 1-6, is an address to the rulers of the earth describing wisdom as avenger of unjust acts, and also its benefits: salvation of the world and life. In the framework of this address the sinners and the righteous are opposed in a dramatic way, so that the rulers of the earth may understand what wisdom is and be instructed by it. (6,22-25) The second part of Wisdom, chs. 7-9, describes how the wise king, presented with the characteristics of king Solomon, has obtained wisdom, and what the qualities of wisdom are. It is a perfect image of God that governs the universe and has been His intimate since the beginning of creation. The author, the 'I', wishes wisdom as his bride and begs her of God, since wisdom is only obtained by prayer (ch. 9). This prayer forms the centre of the book and is the end of the *encomium*. The remaining chs. 10-19 that form the third part, are a recollection of man's history from the creation of Adam to the exodus from Egypt. These stories are meant as *exempla* for the reader or hearer and describe the blessings granted to Israel guided by divine wisdom in vivid contrast with the plagues that afflicted the idolators, Egyptians as well as Canaanites. These lessons have timeless value and meaning for God's people, since they demonstrate the power of God's wisdom, identified with His Word or Spirit, in world history and how 'in all things, Lord, thou didst magnify and glorify thy people, and didst not overlook them, standing by them at every time and place' (19, 22)[5].

This homogeneous treatise written in a highly poetical hymnical style has a special notion of wisdom. It is God's mirror, reflection, and image (7, 26), but not identical with God. The author assimilates it to the Spirit of God (1, 6-7; 7, 22, 9, 17) and with God's Logos (9, 1-2; 16, 12). Wisdom confers immortality on man (6, 17-19; 8, 17), because love of wisdom impels man to obey God's laws and to do justice. In all this the pseudepigraphical author of the Wisdom of Solomon shows his knowledge of contemporary philosophy, in particular of Stoicism, which formed an important component of Middle Platonism, with which an author probably came into contact through a good general education, without any special training in philosophy.

The Wisdom of Solomon is an exclusively Jewish work written by a well-educated and cultured sage, who speaks about the rôle of God's wisdom in Israel's history to a divided community, in which doubts about God's guidance had clearly emerged. It is usually assumed that the book was written in Hellenistic Egypt, probably at Alexandria, during the last decades of the 2nd century B.C.E., but other scholars argue for a date at the end of the 1st century B.C.E., or even the beginning of the 1st century C.E. and suggest Syria as its homeland[6]. Curiously enough there are no quotations from the Wisdom of Solomon in Jewish writers of the first centuries C.E. Its survival was probably due to Christianity, and the first explicit quotations are in the works of Clement of Alexandria at the end of the 2nd century C.E.[7].

The Peshitta version of Wisdom of Solomon was made from the Greek and shows some similarities with the Vetus Latina. The Peshitta is rather paraphrastic down to the end of ch. 10, but from there till the end "it would almost seem that another interpreter had taken the task in hand, who had little or no knowledge of Greek"[8]. For purposes of textual criticism the Peshitta version and in particular the last part of it is, therefore, almost valueless, although the textual transmission of the Peshitta of Wisdom is very consistent and the great majority of the mss. only disagree in very minor matters[9]. Are the substantial disagreements between the Peshitta of Wisdom and the Greek to be explained by the existence of another *Vorlage* of the Peshitta, by the translator's poor knowledge of Greek, or by some other cause? At first glance it is clear that the Peshitta of Wisdom is not a literal word-for-word translation of the Greek as is usual with Bible translations. The Syriac version can be labelled a *sensus de sensu* translation, an approach that tries to bring the meaning of the original to the reader or hearer[10]. How, then, did the Syriac translator understand the meaning of Wisdom of Solomon, and in what particular manner did he express his understanding of that text? The Peshitta of Wisdom contains a whole range of pecularities that betray the cast of mind of its translator and provide us with a clue to his religious and cultural milieu. A selection from the available material may illustrate this.

. . . .

The verses II, 12-13 are part of a long speech of the ungodly against the righteous, of whom they say:

12. But let us lie in wait for the righteous, because he is of disservice to us,
And he is opposed to our doings
And reproaches us with sins against the law,
And lays to our charge sins against our education.
13. He professes to have knowledge of God,
And calls himself servant (or: son) of the Lord[11].

The Peshitta reads:

12. Let us obstruct the righteous, because he is not kind to us,
For he withstands our doings
And reproaches us with works of the law
And reminds us of the sins of our boldness.
13. And he professes that knowledge of God is in him,
And says of himself: "A son of God am I".

In this context the righteous is pictured as the suffering servant of the Lord (Is 52:13ff.), oppressed by the wicked. Apart from some minor disagreements between the Syriac and the Greek a remarkable element of the Peshitta is the direct speech "A son of God am I" (*dbrh 'n' d'lh'*). The only literal equivalent of this phrase is found in the Syriac Gospel of St Matthew 27:43, part of the crucifixion episode, and in the Peshitta of John 10, 36, a dispute between Jesus and the Jews. Did the translator have the gospel text in mind, when he read this verse[12])?

The passage II, 19 belongs to the same speech against the righteous. The impious say:

With wanton violence (*hybrei*) and torture let us test him,
That we may know his reasonableness (*epieikeian*),
And judge of his endurance of evil (*anexikakian*).

The Peshitta version has interesting variants again:

With despise (*ṣ^c r'*) and torture let us test him,
That we may know the diligence of his humility (*mkykwth*),
and examine if there is evil in him.

The Peshitta interprets "reason" or "virtue" as the Christian virtue par excellence, humility (see Phil 2:3; Ephes 4:2; Col 3:12; II Cor 10:1 etc.), which is very frequent in the N.T. Peshitta and has ascetical overtones and connotations[13]). Endurance of evil is transformed into "if there is evil in him" (*'l' 'yt bh byšt'*). This particular examination is a set part of the trial of Jesus before Pilatus. Pilatus' wife calls Him a righteous one (Matthew 27:19 parr.) and the governor himself establishes that there is no evil to be found in Him by asking the rhetorical question: "What evil has He done"? (Mattew 27:23 parr.).

Chapter III gives a vivid description of the happy fate and rewards of the righteous.

III, 8. They shall judge nations and have dominion over peoples,
And the Lord shall reign over them for ever.

The Greek version means the reign of the righteous over the pagan nations and peoples, a well-known Jewish concept, but the Peshitta changes this to:

The nations will exalt and the peoples will rejoice
And the Lord shall reign over them for ever.

In this translation the righteous are no longer the Jews, but the pagan nations and peoples, which fundamentally changes the meaning of the whole book of Wisdom! The pagans are the true righteous and heirs of God's grace, which implies that the Jews are the wicked sinners. The minor disagreements between the Greek and the Syriac in vs. II, 12, already mentioned, suddenly become understandable. The righteous reproach the Jews "with works of the Law" (*b^c bdwhy dnmws'*) and remind them of the "sins of their boldness" instead of changing them "with sins against the law" and "sins against their education" (*paideia*), as the Greek version reads. The internal

Jewish dispute between righteous and impious is transformed into a debate between Jews and pagans, the latter being the righteous.

If this interpretation of the Peshitta of Wisdom III, 8 holds true, the same tendency can be detected in III, 10. The Greek version states:

III, 10. The impious shall receive punishment in accord with their plans.
They that heeded not the righteous and revolted from the Lord.

The Peshitta gives the following reading of this verse:

And the impious will receive dishonour in accord with their plans,
They that despised the Lord and forsook His righteous.

Contempt and dishonour are key notions in the Gospel's picture of the Jewish view and treatment of Jesus and His followers (Mark 12:4; John 8:49; Romans 1:26 etc.). The impious Jews will be despised, just as they despised the Lord and His righteous!

A feature typical of Syriac-speaking Christianity emerges in the Peshitta of Wisdom III, 15. The Greek version reads:

For the fruit of good labours in glorious,
And the root of understanding (*phronèseōs*) is infallible.

The Peshitta gives the following text:

Good labour has a renowned reward (*'gr' bḥyr' ll'wt ṭbt'*)
And the roots of chastity (*nkpwt'*) will not uprooted.

The ideal of the Greek sage *phronèsis* is changed into the characteristic monastic virtue of chastity[14].

Ascetic connotations also come to light in IV, 1-2. The Greek version praises the virtue of the righteous person, even when he or she does not have children, so that the reward for virtuous behaviour seems to be lacking (cf. III, 13ff.).

IV, 1. Better is childlessness with virtue, (*meta aretès*)
For there is immortality in its (i.e. virtue) remembrance,
Since it is recognized both with God and with men.

2. When it is present men imitate it,
And when it is gone they long for it,
And for ever it marches crowned in pomp, (*stephanèphorousa*)
Victorious in the contest for prizes that are undefiled.

The Peshitta on the contrary praises the condition of childlessness:

IV, 1. Good is childlessness in glory (*btšbwḥt'*)
For there is life in its (i.e. glory) remembrance
Since it is well known with God and with men.
2. When it is present they imitate it,
And when it is gone they long for it
And in this world (*bᶜlm' hn'*) it is wearing an adornment
and a crown (*tṣbyt' wklyl' lbyš'*)
And it manifests itself when it has won the contest (*'gwn'*)
of those that are undefiled.

Childlessness is identified with the ascetical unmarried state which already in this world implies a life in divine glory, when the ascetic has won the ascetical struggle and the crown. All the notions in this passage belong to Syriac ascetic vocabulary: *tšbwḥt'*[15], *klyl'*[16], and *'gwn'*[17]. It reminds us of the characteristic phrasing of the famous pericope Luke 20:34-38 in the Vetus Syra, where the *vita angelica* is located in the present world for those who live an ascetic unmarried life[18]. This is the acme of ascetic virtue, identical with divine glory[19]. The translation of Greek *aretè* into Syriac *tšbwḥt'* 'glory', is therefore only understandable in a milieu in which divine, immortal glory is the highest ideal of virtue.

Thus we see that the righteous as pictured in the Peshitta of Wisdom displays the characteristic features of Jesus and those who believe in Him and imitate His life. The same trait can be detected in IV, 14-16. The Greek of IV, 14 reads:

For his (i.e. the righteous) soul was well-pleased to God,
Therefore he hastened away from the midst of wickedness[20].

The Peshitta renders this verse as follows:

For his soul was well-pleasing to God,
And because he (i.e. the righteous) was just (*k'yn*)
He (God) quickly raised him (*'rymh*) from the midst of evil.

Vs. 15 says that the nations did not understand that God's grace is with his chosen, and vs. 16 in the Greek version is:

But the righteous when he is outworn shall condemn the
impious that are alive[21].

The Peshitta gives a different version of vss. 15 and 16:

15. But the nations saw and did not understand and did not have
an idea (*wl' smw brᶜynyhwn*)
Why in this way (*hkn'*) God's judgment and grace and mercy
are with His holy ones (*bḥsywhy*)
And God's visitation (*swᶜrnh*) with His chosen (*ᶜl gbwhy*)
16. He administers justice (*d'n*) to the righteous and destroys
(*mwbd*) the impious when they are alive.

The words 'in this way' in vs. 15 refer to God's raising of the righteous as recorded in vs. 14. This act implies His judgment and grace, and finally His doing justice to the righteous and destroying the sinners. Did the Syriac translator have in mind the crucifixion and resurrection of the righteous (cf. Luke 23:47) which involves God' judgment over the world and the separation of the righteous from the impious (cf. Matthew 25:31ff.)?

Chapter V records a new speech of the impious, now describing the bliss of the just, whose deliverance they had not expected:

V, 2. And they shall be astonished at the unexpectedness of his deliverance (*epi tōi paradoxōi tès sōtèrias*)

For the Syriac translator the deliverance of the righteous apprently is not an unexpected event, for he gives the following text:

And they shall be amazed when they will see his glory (*tšbwḥth*).

Such a translation fits into the already outlined pattern of the life and death of the righteous, which is understood as a record of Jesus' life-story. It is, therefore, in complete accordance with this pattern that the last vs. 23 of ch. V is totally different in the Syriac version from the Greek. The Greek text records the destruction of the impious through an earthly catastrophe:

V, 23. A breath of power shall rise up against them (i.e. impious),
And like a storm shall winnow them away,
And lawlessness (*anomia*) shall lay waste the whole earth
And ill-dealing (*kakopragia*) overthrow the thrones of potentates.

The Syriac translator had a more optimistic view of the outcome of the final struggle against the impious:

V, 23. And a formidable wind (or: spirit) will rise up against them,
And like a whirlwind shall winnow them away,
And it will destroy the whole earth of the impious,
And it will shatter the works of injustice,
The power of the potentates and their thrones.

Not lawlessness and ill-dealing will destroy the earth and its impious rulers, but a formidable wind, i.e. God's power, will end all earthly injustice, so that men shall see His glory.

Chapter VI is an address to rulers to learn wisdom and justice. In this context we are told:

VI, 6. For the lowest (*elakhistos*) is pardonable of grace,
But the mighty shall be mightily tested.

The Peshitta interprets *elakhistos*, a king with a very small reign, as a humble king, and equips him in this way with a characteristic ascetic virtue that will bring him mercy:

For a humble king (*mlk' mkyk'*) is near to mercy (*qryb lrḥmyn*).

A well-known concept in the Book of Wisdom is that divine wisdom gives immortality. So VI, 19 praises wisdom and tells us:

VI, 19. And immortality (*aphtharsia*) makes to be near unto God.

The Syriac translation introduces instead of immortality the concept of 'incorruptible deeds', which is a typical ascetic idea.

And incorruptible deeds bring near to God.
(*w*^{c}*bd' dl' ḥbl' mqrbyn lwt 'lh'*)

The Syriac Acts of Thomas frequently refer to 'work of corruption' (^{c}*db' dḥbl'*), which means sexual intercourse[22]. An ascetic life not tainted by any form of sexuality is the way par excellence to immortality and a paradisiacal life. Therefore 'incorruptible deeds' means the life of the ascetic.

Chapter VII is the life-story of the author speaking in the first person singular and telling how he obtained wisdom. The 'I', who resembles the wise king Solomon, says in VII, 4:

VII, 4. In swaddling clothes was I reared and with cares.
(*en sparganois anetraphèn kai phrontisin*)

The Peshitta translates this verse in the following manner:

In swaddling clothes I was carefully wrapped.
(*wb*^{c}*zrwr' yṣyp'yt 'tkrkt*)

This phrasing recalls the Peshitta and Vetus Syra of Luke 2:7 '.... and she (Mary) wrapped him in swaddling clothes ...' (*wkrkth b*^{c}*zrwr'*), and this association might explain when the translator linked swaddling clothes with wrapping and not with rearing, possibly mistaking the Greek verb *anatrephō* for *anastrephō*.

Chapter VIII continues the praise of wisdom, of whom the author says in VIII, 3:

She glorifies her noble birth as being one that has the converse of God (*eugeneian doxasei symbiōsin theou ekhousa*)
And the Lord of all things loved her.

The Peshitta has a remarkable translation:

There is joy and the glory of God in marriage with her,
Because God is her father and the Lord of all loves her.
(*ḥdwt' wtšbwḥt' d'lh' bšwtpwth*)

God is the father of Wisdom, His Spirit and intimate communion with her means joy and divine glory. The emphasis is put on human communion with God's wisdom instead of on wisdom's relationship with God. This is the concept of the (heavenly) wedding, the union of man with God's Spirit, a very characteristic element in Syriac religious symbolism. It brings incorruptibility, in fact immortality[23]. Therefore the Peshitta renders the Greek of VIII, 16:

Converse with her has no vexation

as:

There is no corruption in marriage with her.

Acquiring wisdom as bride means for the Syriac translator that he must subject himself to an ascetic life. That is expressed in the Peshitta of VIII, 21, where the Greek reads:

But knowing that I shall not otherwise acquire her unless God give her (*ouk allōs esomai egkratès*)

The Syriac interpreter changes this into:

But I knew that I could not subdue myself, unless God would grant me (that).

This encratite life is the highest form of knowledge, in Greek called *phrōnèsis*, where the Syrian has *nhyrwt'*, the condition of being enlightened[24]!

The chapters X - XIX, which contain a recapitulation of man's early history from the creation till the exodus, disagree in many points with the Greek version. Some of those disagreements show a peculiar tendency that betrays the religious outlook of the translator. Ch. XIV, 5-7 refers in the Greek version to Noah, the flood, and the ark, but without mentioning him by name.

XIV, 5. But thou willest that the works of thy wisdom should not be idle;
Therefore do men entrust their lives to even the slenderest timber,
And passing through the surge on a raft are come safely through.

6. For even in the beginning, when arrogant giants were perishing,
The hope of the world took refuge on a raft
And guided by thy hand left to the world the seed of a (new) generation.
For blessed is the wood by which righteousness comes.

The Peshitta renders these verses in a way that differs from the Greek in essential points:

XIV, 5. Because you wanted to make everything and your wisdom is not idle without works (*bṭl' mn ^{c}bd'*)
Therefore you granted to men that their souls (lives) be entrusted to a small piece of wood (*dnthymnn npšthwn bqys' z^{c}wr'*),
And they passed through heavy waves and were saved (*wḥyw*).

6. For in the beginning elected giants perished when they passed through(*'bdw w^{c}brw gnbr' gby'*),
Whose hope it was to settle themselves in the world.
They fled and did not left a seed of a (new) generation for ever
This providence is yours, which you created.
(*dylk hy hd' mdbrnwt' dbryt*)

7. Blessed is the wood from which the righteous appears.

Whereas the Greek text clearly refers to Gen 6:1-4, the story of the giants, and to Gen 6:5ff., the righteousness of Noah, the ark and the flood, the Peshitta suppresses all allusions to the deluge and relates these verses to the exodus from Egypt. This becomes particularly clear at vs. 6, where the elected giants stand for Pharaoh's elected army (Ex 14:7) which, whilst fleeing from Israel and the waters through which it passed, perished to the last man (Ex 14:25-28). This interpretation becomes even more plausible, since the Syriac word *gnbr'* means both 'giant' and 'warrior', whereas the Greek *gigas* only has the meaning giant. This is attributed to God's providence, as in Ex 14:31: And Israel saw that great work which the Lord did upon the Egyptians. The small piece of wood denotes, therefore, Moses' rod, which divided the waters of the Red Sea, so that the Israelites could pass safely through (Ex 14:16).

The exodus from Egypt was a source of manifold symbolism in early Christianity and patristic literature[25]. Egypt symbolizes idolatry and the demonic powers from which Jesus rescued Mankind, so that their reign in the world definitely came to an end[26]. They had hoped to settle in the world, but were forced to flee and did not leave the seed of a new generation! Idolatry is very circumstantially described in the preceding ch. XIII, so that the Christian exodus interpretation of the relevant verses in ch. XIV suggested itself to the Syriac translator. Just as Moses rescued the Israelites from slavery in Egypt, so Jesus rescued those who believed in him from the bonds of Satan; and just as Moses led his people to the promised land through the Red Sea, so Jesus through His crucifixion, brought the gift of life to those who believe in Him. This biblical typology occurs in fully fledged form with Aphraates in the fourth century C.E.[27]. Moses' rod consequently stands for Jesus' cross, a familiar theme in patristic literature[28]. Therefore the small piece of wood in the Peshitta of XIV, 5 most likely denotes the cross, particularly since it is characterized as God's gift to mankind in order to save their lives. This interpretation is corroborated by the Syriac phrasing of XIV, 7 which, unlike the Greek which speaks of the wood, i.e. the ark, as an instrument bringing about righteousness in the world, explicitly, mentions the righteous one who appears (or: is to be seen) on the wood (*mbrk hw qys' dzdyq' mnh mtḥz'*). This recalls Jesus hanging on the cross, of whom the centurion who looked phrasing at Him said: "Certainly this was a righteous man" (Luke 23:47). This kind of Christian typological interpretation of the exodus story is not uncommon in early Syriac literature; it occurs in Ode of Solomon 39 and probably in Ode of Solomon 24[29].

The last instance of highly tendentious translation and interpretation of the Greek Wisdom of Solomon by the Syriac translator is XVI, 10. This verse belongs to a context contrasting the plagues of flies and locusts (Ex 8:20-32; 10:1-20) with the healing of the Israelites from snake-bites (Num 21:4-9).

XVI, 10. Whereas thy sons not even the teeth of poison-darting serpents overcame,
For thy mercy came forth to meet them and healed them.

The Peshitta phrases this verse as follows:

Your sons, however, overcame the teeth and the heads of the dragons (or: of the dragon)
For your grace sent and healed them.

In this translation the text refers to Gen 3:15 and symbolizes man's victory over the serpent or dragon, i.e. mortality; this is a very common motif in early Syriac theology and a central element in the famous Hymn of the Pearl in the apocryphal Acts of Thomas[30]. The following verse 11 in the Syriac translation confirms this interpretation, by a reading totally unlike the Greek:

That they should remember your words, that you delivered them,
And hastened to give them rest (*w'strhbt 'nyḥt*).

"Overcoming the dragon" implies the return to the paradisiacal state, indicated in Syriac by the concept of rest (*nyḥ'*) which is the equivalent of Greek *anapansis*[31]. The Peshitta of Wisdom describes this final victory as a fact, which marks this translation as originating in a Christian milieu. For Jews the final victory must wait till the days of the Messiah[32].

. . . .

The value and weight of these examples from the Syriac translation of Solomon's Wisdom might be questioned, if each case were taken by itself as an isolated instance. Taken together, however, they display a consistent and coherent thought pattern forming a substantial argument for a Syriac translation made in a Christian milieu. The main trend of the Syriac version is the identification of God's Wisdom, or Logos, with Jesus Christ, the Righteous par excellence. When a man made to be a king is granted this divine Wisdom, at his request, and becomes one with Wisdom, he becomes righteous too and gains immortality[33]. The Syriac version of II, 13, 19, VII, 4 and XIV, 7 attests the influence of the Syriac Gospel text, either in the version of the Vetus Syra or of the Peshitta. The general character of the whole translation is redolent, moreover, of the influence of the gospel tradition.

The Christian circle to which this Syriac translation is due, had ascetic traits betrayed by characteristic ascetic terms like *mkykwt'* "humility", *nkpwt'* "chastity", *'gwn'* "contest", *klyl'* "crown", *ᶜbd' dḥbl'* "work of corruption". Acquiring divine wisdom, God's Spirit or Logos, implies an ascetic life, and asceticism is the way to immortality. A Greek term in this area is *'gwn' = agōn.* "struggle"[34]. Besides ascetic concepts we come across philosophical notions which the Syriac version preserved in the Greek form. In XI, 17 *hwl' = hylè* "matter", occurs; XIX, 18 mentions *'sṭwks' =* Greek *stoicheiois* "element". In Syriac literature the Greek term *hylè* "matter", is attested for the first time with Ephrem Syrus (d. 373 C.E.), who ascribed the use of this word to Bardaiṣan, the Aramaic philosopher of Edessa (154-212 C.E.)[35]. The term *stoicheion* "element", is used in the *Book of the Laws of Countries*, the Dialogue on Fate from Bardaiṣan's school, in the description of cosmology[36]. This brings us back to the end of the second or the first half of the third century C.E. as a possible date for the Syriac version of Wisdom of Solomon. In this milieu tinged with philosophy the statement that God created the world out of formless matter (*ex amorphou hylès*, Wisdom XI, 17) which is rendered in Syriac as *hwl' dl' ydyᶜ'* "matter without fixed form", was not yet considered heretical, as it was to be in later times, when Ephrem defended the *creatio ex nihilo* against his opponents[37].

The spiritual climate in which the Peshitta of Wisdom originated is furthermore characterized by an anti-Jewish tendency. The Jews are the impious sinners who persecuted the righteous, and their divine punishment is pictured in vivid colors.

The Christian doctrine which is most dominant, however, is a kind of Spirit Christology. God's Wisdom, His Word or Spirit which created the world, guided mankind through the course of history, and made it righteous and immortal, is the divine power in God's Son which appears on the Cross, and also in all his righteous sons. Salvation is being united with this divine Spirit of Wisdom which provides man with insight into God's plans, and restores his immortal, paradisiac, and royal condition. The closest parallels to this anthropological-Christological pattern are to be found in the Syriac version of the Apocryphal Acts of Thomas and in the Odes of Solomon[38]. These writings display the same philosophical and ascetic background which comes to light in the Peshitta of Sapientia Salomonis. We may assume that this Peshitta version of Wisdom was executed somewhere in the first half of the third century C.E., most likely at Edessa, which was the cultural and religious center of the Syriac-speaking area. Translation from Greek into Syriac and vice versa was common practice there. But the Syriac version of the Wisdom of Solomon cannot be considered a simple translation of one of the standard Old Testament apocrypha. In the process of translation it became a document of prime importance for the knowledge of third-century Syriac-speaking Christianity; it bears all the typical features of that branch of Christendom, and in particular of its typological understanding of sacred history. It should be added to the still small number of sources we possess for the knowledge of Early Syriac Christianity, and of the sophisticated and learned circles that formed part of it. They were responsible for the translation of the Wisdom of Solomon. They understood all the subtleties of the Greek text so well, that they could reinterpret its whole contents just by introducing seemingly minor changes or some major revisions in the text. In this way the Peshitta of the Wisdom of Solomon represents both Early Syriac Christianity's bonds and its break with Jewish tradition.

Notes

1) See for a survey of recent research J.H. Hospers, "The present-day state of research on the Pešittā (since 1948)" in *Verbum. Essays dedicated to H.W. Obbink*, Utrecht 1964, pp. 148-157; *id.* "Some remarks with regard to Text and Language of the Old Testament Peshitta" in *Von Kanaan bis Kerala* (*Festschrift J.P.M. van der Ploeg*), Neukirchen 1982, pp. 443-455. M.D. Koster, *The Peshitta of Exodus. The Development of its Text in the Course of Fifteen Centuries*, Assen 1977, pp. 164-212, denies the links between Peshitta and Targumim; see further S. Brock, "Jewish Traditions in Syriac Sources" in *JJS* vol. 30, 1979, pp. 212ff.
2) See S. Brock in *Theologische Realenzyklopädie* vol. 6, p. 184; *id.* in *JJS* vol. 30, 1979, p. 223; J. Reider, *The Book of Wisdom. An English Translation with Introduction and Commentary*, New York 1957, p. 7; J.A. Emerton, *The Peshitta of the Wisdom of Solomon*, (*SP-B*, vol. 2), Leiden 1959, does not give a date.
3) Cf. J. Holtzmann, *Die Peshitta zum Buche der Weisheit*, Freiburg i.B. 1903; Reider, *op. cit.*, pp. 7f.; in general S. Brock, "Greek into Syriac and Syriac into Greek" in *Journal of the Syriac Academy* vol. 3, 1977, p. 3; *id.* "Aspects of Translation Technique in Antiquity" ("Aspects") in *Greek, Roman and Byzantine Studies* vol. 20, Durham 1979, pp. 69-87 (repr. in *id.*, *Syriac Perspectives on the Late Antiquity*, London 1984).
4) The Peshitta of Sapientia Salomonis is quoted after the Leiden Peshitta edition, vol. 2, fasc. 5, Leiden 1979; The Greek text used is Septuaginta, ed. A. Rahlfs; I usually follow the English translation of Reider, *op. cit.*; see also D. Georgi, *Weisheit Salomos. Unterweisung in lehrhaften Form* (= *Weisheit*), Gütersloh 1980.
5) Cf. M. Gilbert, "Wisdom Literature" in *Jewish Writings of the Second Temple Period*, ed. M.E. Stone, Assen-Philadelphia 1984, pp. 301-312; A.G. Wright, "The Structure of the Book of Wisdom" in *Bibl* vol. 48, 1967, pp. 165-184; D. Georgi, "Das Wesen der Weisheit nach der 'Weisheit Salomos' " in *Gnosis und Politik* (= "*Gnosis*"), ed. J. Taubes, München-Paderborn 1984, pp. 66-81.
6) Cf. D. Georgi, *Weisheit*, pp. 395-397; Reider, *op. cit.*, 12ff.; Gilbert, *op. cit.*, p. 312.
7) Clement of Alexandria, *Paedagogus* 2,1,7; *Strom.* 2,2,6; 6,14,110; 6,15,120 and fragm. 23, ed. Staehlin, vol. 3, p. 202; cf. Gilbert, *op. cit.*, p. 313.
8) Reider, *op. cit.*, p. 7 quoting A.T.S. Goodrick, *The Book of Wisdom*, New York 1913.
9) Emerton, *op. cit.*, p. C.
10) Brock, "Aspects", p. 73.
11) The text contains a pun on Greek *pais* which means both child and servant; cf. Is 52:13ff.; see especially Reider's commentary *ad loc.*; since the Epistle of Barnabas this passage is considered a Messianic prophecy concerning the coming of Jesus: see Justin, *Dial. c. Trypho* XVII; Eusebius, *Praep. Evang.* XIII, 13; Clement of Alexandria, *Strom.* 5,24.
12) Both the Vetus Syra and the Peshitta of Matth 27:43 read *dbrh 'n' d'lh'*; the reading also occurs in the Peshitta of John 10:36, where the Vetus Syra reads *d'mr lkwn dbrh d'lh'*".. That he said to you that he is the Son of God", see F.C. Burkitt, *Evangelion da-Mepharreshe*, vol. 1, Cambridge 1904, p. 486.
13) Aphraates devoted his *Dem.* IX to the theme of humility, *Patrologia Sacra*, (= "*PS*"), vol.1, cols. 407-442, where the ascetical connection is quite clear.
14) On the close links between knowledge and chastity see Ephrem Syrus, *Hymn. de Eccl.* 28,9; *Carm. Nis.* 15,3; E. Beck, *Asketentum und Mönchtum bei Ephraem* (*Orientalia Christiania Analecta*, vol. 153), Rome 1958, pp. 353f.; P, Canivet, *Le monachisme syrien selon Théodoret de Cyr*, Paris 1977, pp. 255ff.; cf. Methodius,

Symposium 6,3, where *sōphrosyne* seems to be an equivalent of *hagneia*, see Ton H.C. van Eijk, "Marriage and Virginity, Death and Immortality" in *EPEKTASIS* (*Mélanges offerts à J. Daniélou*), Paris 1972, p. 222.

15) Especially in the Odes of Solomon *tšbwht'* "glory" is a divine quality of the ascetic believer; cf. *Ode of Solomon* 6,7; 13,2; 20,9; 29,2; 41,4.

16) For the crown see *Ode of Solomon* 5,12; 9,8-11,20,7; Aphraates, *De Monachis*, *PS* vol. 1, p. 248, col. 20.

17) The notion of "struggle" is central in Aphraates *Dem.* VII, *De Paenitentibus*, *PS* vol. 1, cols. 313-360; cf. R. Murray, "The Exhortation to Candidates for Ascetical Vows at Baptism in the Ancient Syrian Church" in *NTSt* vol. 21, 1974-1975, pp. 58-79; cf. H.J.W. Drijvers "Athleten des Geistes. Zur politischen Rolle der syrischen Asketen und Gnostiker" in *Gnosis*, pp. 113f.

18) Cf. P. Nagel, "Die Motivierung der Askese in der Alten Kirche und der Ursprung des Mönchtums" in *TU* vol. 95, Berlin 1966, pp. 34ff.

19) This union of ascetic virtue and divine glory is explicitly expressed in John 1:12-14 and in the current interpretation of these verses in Syriac exegesis, cf. Drijvers, *op. cit.*, pp. 113ff.; P. Nagel, *op. cit.*, pp. 55ff.

20) Reider's translation "he hastened him away" (*espeusen ek*) is rather forced, since *speudein* is never used with a person as object; I follow Georgi's interpretation: "eilte er (i.e. the righteous) hinweg".

21) Reidel's translation of IV,16: 'But the righteous that is dead ..." is not a correct rendering of Greek *kamōn*; I follow Liddell-Scott, s.v. *kamnō* 5: "in aor. part., of the dead, i.e. either *outworn*, or *those whose work is done*, or *those who have met with disaster*". Georgi's translation "Der Gerechte wird, wenn er *ausruht*, ..." is apparently a misinterpretation of "*those whose work is done*". A perfect parallel to the *Peshitta of Wisdom* IV,14 is found in *Ode of Solomon* 8,5 and 41;12; cf. J.H. Charlesworth, *The Odes of Solomon*, Oxford 1973, p. 43.

22) Cf. W. Wright, *Apocryphal Acts of the Apostles*, London 1871, p. *qpg*, 1.4 (t); p. 157 (v.); cf. the meaning of *aphtharsia* in Methodius of Olympus, Basil of Ancyra, and Gregory of Nyssa; see Van Eijk, *op. cit.*, pp. 221ff., esp. 226.

23) Cf. Wright, *op. cit.*, p. 157 (v.): ".. that this deed of corruption is despised by me, and the spoils of this wedding-feast that passes away , (is) because I am invited to the true wedding-feast". cf. H.J.W. Drijvers, *East of Antioch. Studies in Early Syriac Christianity*, London 1984, pp. 10ff. and the studies listed there.

24) Interesting is the Syriac phrasing of the preceding verse VIII,19: *ṭly' hwyt nhyr'* "I was an enlightened boy"; the concept of *nhyrwt'* means God-given insight in this connection; cf. *Ode of Solomon* 36,3 and 34,2 and H.J.W. Drijvers, "Early Forms of Antiochene Christology" in *After Chalcedon* (*Studies in Theology and Church History offered to Professor Albert van Roey*), Leuven 1985, p. 102. In contrast to the variegated Greek wording of Wisdom IV, 19-21 the Syriac is dominated by two notions, *nhyrwt'* and *ṭybwt'*.

25) See J. Daniélou, *Sacramentum Futuri. Etudes sur les origines de la typologie biblique*, Paris 1950, pp. 131-200.

26) See e.g. Irenaeus, *Demonstratio* 46 (*Sources Chrétiennes*, vol. 62, p. 105); in this connection it is not without interest that the same symbolic meaning of Egypt occurs in the *Hymn of the Pearl* in the *Acts of Thomas*; see Wright, *op. cit.*, pp. 239-240; cf. H. Kruse's lucid interpretation of this famous hymn in "The Return of the Prodigal" in *OrNS* vol. 47, 1978, pp. 163-214, esp. 196.

27) Aphraates, *Dem*. XII, 8, in *PS* vol. 1, col. 521; cf. Daniélou, *op. cit*., p. 161; R. Murray, *Symbols of Church and Kingdom* (= *Symbols*), Cambridge 1975, pp. 52ff.
28) Cf. G.Q. Reijners, *The Terminology of the Holy Cross in Early Christian Literature*, Nijmegen 1965, 109ff. (diss.).
29) See e.g. *Ode* 39,11: "On this side and on that the waves were lifted up, but the footsteps of our Lord Messiah stand firm". The exodus symbolism of *Ode* 39 is indirectly corroborated by the next *Ode* 40 which deals with milk and honey, i.e. the promised land, the next stage in Israels history. *Ode* 24 combines the motif of the deluge with the exodus symbolism, not uncommon in early Christian literature, as I hope to demonstrate in a forthcoming article.
30) Cf. Kruse, *op. cit*., pp. 199ff., where the Prayer of Kyriakos is also quoted.
31) See *Ode of Solomon* 3,5; 25,12; 37,4 and the frequent use of the verb *nwḥ* "to rest", and its derivates in the Odes of Solomon; cf. J. Helderman, *Die Anapausis im Evangelium Veritatis*, Leiden 1984.
32) The *Palestinian Targum* explicitly refers Gen 3:15 to the days of the Messiah.
33) *Wisdom of Solomon* 2,23; 8,13; 8,17; 9,17-18; In the Syriac tradition the first man, Adam, is considered a king, and consequently gaining immortality means restoration of man's royal status; cf. the *Hymn of the Pearl* describing the paradisiacal condition: "When I was young, a child still, dwelling in my kingdom, in my Father's house, ..."; cf. Murray, *Symbols*, pp. 304-306.
34) *'gwn'* or *'ygwn'* is frequently used in the New Testament Peshitta I Cor 9:25; Col. 2:1; 1 Thess 2:2; 1 Tim 6:12.; it occurs in Syriac literature for the first time in the Letter of Mara bar Serapion to his son, ed. W. Cureton, *Spicilegium Syriacum*, London 1855, p. 43,1.17; cf. A. Schall, *Studien über Griechische Fremdwörter im Syrischen*, Darmstadt 1960, p. 54; with ascetical connotations the term is frequently used by Aphraates.
35) Ephrem Syrus, *Hymni contra Haereses* XIV,7-8; *Prose Ref*. I,141,9-17; 122,13-17.
36) *Liber Legum Regionum* in *PS* vol. 2, col. 548, 11. 2, 23; col. 568, 1. 5; col. 572, 1. 5; cf. Schall, *op. cit*., p. 76f.
37) N. El-Khoury, *Die Interpretation der Welt bei Ephraem dem Syrer* (*Tüb. Theol. Stud*., vol. 6), Mainz 1976, pp. 65ff.
38) H.J.W. Drijvers, "Solomon as Teacher. Early Syriac Didactic Poetry", in *Proceedings of the IV Symposium Syriacum*, Rome 1986 (in the press).

^{c}Anat, Seth and the Seed of Prē^{c}

J. van Dijk, Groningen

Meije jo formannichfâldigje jierren fan lok,
meije jins moannen yn foarspoed forstrike,
jins dagen yn libben en biwâld
en jins ûren yn sounens.
(pAnast.III rt.4,7)

It may not always be easy for an Egyptologist to find a suitable subject for an article in honour of a Semitic scholar, but no such problems arise in the case of Prof. Hospers. Egyptian is one of the many languages he commands, and he has even taught it himself at the University of Groningen during the brief "interregnum" (1950-1952) between G. van der Leeuw and Th.P. van Baaren. It is with great pleasure, therefore, that I dedicate the following remarks to him, in grateful memory of the many happy hours spent "at the feet of Gamaliel", listening to his expositions on the comparative grammar of the Semitic languages or reading Hebrew ostraca under his guidance[*].

There are in existence, in the rich literary heritage given to us by the ancient Egyptians, two texts for which a Canaanite origin has been postulated. These have been or still are considered as Egyptianized versions or even "translations" of Canaanite myths. One of these is the story preserved in the so-called *^{c}Astarte Papyrus*, a badly damaged manuscript dating from the reign of Ḥoremḥeb and nowadays kept in the Pierpont Morgan Library, New York[1]. This text deals with the conflict between the Ennead, presided by Ptaḥ, and the insatiable Sea (*p3 y3m*), who keeps asking for more tribute and in fact seems to demand the rulership over heaven and earth. Ptaḥ sends his daughter ^{c}Astarte as a messenger to the Sea, but apparently she is unable to satisfy the ever increasing demands. At the end, just before the text breaks off, the god Seth appears, and from allusion in other (chiefly magical texts[2]) it is usually assumed that the Sea is finally defeated by this aggressive god, who elsewhere in Egyptian mythology is depicted as warding off Apophis, the monster of chaos[3]. The story has been compared to the Ugaritic mythological poem describing the battle between Ba^{c}al, who is often seen as a manifestation of Seth in New Kingdom Egypt, and Yamm, the Sea[4]. Although Posener has made an attempt to demonstrate that the Egyptian text is rooted in indigenous Egyptian mythology which has only been "modernized" by the introduction of foreign elements like the phrase *p3 y3m* instead of *w3ḏ wr*, or the Canaanite goddesss ^{c}Astarte[5], it is in my opinion hard to imagine that the Egyptian text could have been written without any knowledge of the Canaanite myth[6].

The other text, the one that will concern us here, is commonly known as the Story of ^{c}Anat and Seth. Contrary to the Astarte Papyrus, which, as far as can be judged from its tattered state, seems to have been an independent narrative, the ^{c}Anat story has come down to us only in the form of a "mythical precedent"[7] to certain magical spells. Each of the five sources presently known to us is damaged, but the two most important texts, though showing a number of variants, supplement each other, and a more or less complete story can be reconstructed from them. The sources are the following:

1. *pCh. Beatty VII* vs. 1,5-6,7; A.H. Gardiner, *Hieratic Papyri in the Britsh Museum, Third Series; Chester Beatty Gift*, London 1935, vol. I, pp. 61-65; vol. II, pls. 36-37. The papyrus, written in the reign of Ramesses II, originates from Deir el-Medîna[8]. Its main text contains a collection of spells against scorpions.
2. *pTurin*, without number; A. Roccati, "Une légende égyptienne d'Anat", in *RdE*, vol. 24, 1972, pp. 154-159, pl. 14; an additional fragment appears on a photograph illustrating Roccati's article "Les papyrus de Turin", in *BSFE*, vol. 99, 1984, pp. 9-27, pl. 4. The fragment dates from Dyn. XIX and derives from Deir el-Medîna. It may have been part of the ms. now known as *pTurin CG 54052*; see Roccati, "Tra i papiri torinesi", in *OrAnt* vol. 14, 1975, 245 [10]. The spell to which our fragment belongs was directed against the poison, presumably of a scorpion. The fragment corresponds to *pCh. Beatty VII* vs. 1,5-2,2.
3. *oUC 31942*, W. Spiegelberg, *Hieratic Ostraka and Papyri found by J.E. Quibell, in the Ramesseum, 1895-6*, London 1898, pls. I-I^A, nos. 1-2. A modified transcription based upon Spiegelberg's facsimile (not upon the original!) was given by Gardiner, *op. cit.*, vol. I, p. 62 n. 8. The ostracon is of Ramesside

date and was found in the south east corner of the mud-brick dependencies surrounding the Ramesseum[9]. There are drawings on the reverse[10]. Although line 1 of the ostracon corresponds to *pCh. Beatty VII* vs. 1,6, the rest of its text apparently contained a different version of the story.

4. *oDM 1591*; G. Posener, *Catalogue des ostraca hiératiques littéraires de Deir el Médineh*, vol. III/2, Cairo, 1978, pp. 77, pl. 45-45^{A}. A Ramesside ostracon containing short fragments of 16 lines, the first 8 of which correspond to *pCh. Beatty VII* vs. 1,5-2,3, though several phrases not found in the other sources occur. The remaining lines contain a version of the *Gliedervergottung* similar, but not identical, to *pCh. Beatty VII* vs. 2,5-5,7.
5. *oDM 1592*; Posener, *op. cit.*, p. 77, pl. 45-45^{A}. This tiny little fragment contains a few words corresponding to *pCh. Beatty VII* vs. 1,6 and 1,8. Stadelmann[11] has suggested that an episode from *pVatican 19a*, which relates of the poisoning of the god Seth[12], belongs to the same story. This is not very likely, because a) not a single phrase from the Vatican Papyrus can be linked with any of the known versions of the ^{c}Anat story listed above, and b) it is not Isis but Horus who after an initial refusal(?) cures Seth from the poison in the story of the Vatican Papyrus. The latter, though doubtless belonging to a group of related stories about Seth and the seed or poison[13], has therefore no place among the sources of ^{c}Anat and Seth.

The following translation of the story is based upon the version given by *pCh. Beatty VII*. The missing parts have been supplied from *pTurin* and put between brackets. In addition to this, phrases absent from both sources have been printed in italics. The notes to the translation are not meant to be exhaustive; further details concerning the interpretation will be given in the commentary.

[The Seed took a bath] on the shore (a) in order to purify herself (b) in the *Ḥmkt* (c). Then the Great God (d) went out for a walk and he [percieved her (and saw) her beauty because of (?) the girdle] of her buttocks (e). Then he mounted her like a ram mounts, he covered her like a [bull] covers (f). [*Thereupon the Seed* fl]ew up to his forehead, to the region of his eyebrows (g), and he lay down upon his bed in his house [*and was ill*. Hur]ried ^{c}Anat (h), the Victorious Goddess, the woman who acts like a warrior (i), who wears a skirt like men and a sash (?) like women (j), to Prē^{c}, her father. He said to her: "What is the matter with you, ^{c}Anat, Victorious Goddess, who acts as a warrior, who wears a skirt like men and a sash (?) like women? I have ended (my course) in the evening (k) and I know that you have come to ask that Seth be delivered from the Seed. [*Look*], let (his) stupidity be a lesson (to him) (l). The Seed had been given as a wife to the God Above (m), that he should copulate with her with fire after deflowering her with a chisel" (n). Said the divine Isis: "I am a Nubian woman (o). I have descended from heaven and I have come to uncover the Seed which is in the body [*of X son of Y*], and to make him go in health to his mother like Horus went in health to his mother Isis. X born of Y shall be (well), for as Horus lives so shall live X son of Y (...)".

(a) , var. *pTurin*  *ḫp/ḫa-pú*, a Semitic loanword doubtless to be connected with Ug. *ḫp* and Hebr. *ḥōp* "shore", "(river-)bank"[14]. The meaning is proven by *oDM 1591* which replaces *ḫp* by the Eg. equivalent *spt*. Roccati[15] has connected *ḫp* with a placename 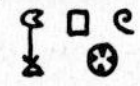 mentioned on a Dyn. XXI statue from a place near Tanis in the Delta, published by the late Labib Habachi[16], who compared it to "the district  " occurring on another statue from the same area. This does not testify against a Semitic derivation of the term, however; in fact the Delta toponyms, whether or not connected with the place where our story is situated, may well be derived from the same Semitic word.

(b) It is impossible to be sure whether some more specific meaning should be attached to the verb *w*^{c}*b*, which can mean "purify (oneself)" as well as simply "wash", "bathe"[17]. On the other hand, certain Near-Eastern parallels to be discussed later on suggest that the text may refer to the ritual purification following a woman's monthly period of impurity, see H. Behrens, *Enlil und Ninlil. Ein sumerischer Mythos aus Nippur*, Rome 1978, pp. 62-65 and the remarks of L.R. Fischer and F.B. Knutson, in *JNES* vol. 28, 1969, pp. 164-166, on washing (and subsequent dressing up) as a preparation for making love. Related passages in Egyptian texts, like the bathing beaty in the Love Songs of the Cairo Vase or the naked goddess in the Story of the Herdsman, also suggest that Seth is not just following his own lascivious nature, but that he is responding to an erotic signal of the Seed-goddess.

(c) The identification of *Hmkt* remains a mystery. Albright connected it with Ug. *Šmk* mentioned in *KTU* 1.10,II,9.12 as the name of a swampy area[18] where Ba^{c}al and ^{c}Anat meet[19]. But, apart from being linguistically difficult to explain, the equation is now completely obsolete, since the Egyptian story has no direct parallel in the Ugaritic episode concerning Ba^{c}al and ^{c}Anat (see the commentary below).

(d) Var. *pTurin*: "Seth", which proves that "the Great God" of the Ch. Beatty version is Seth, not Prē^{c} (Gardiner, *op. cit.*, vol. I, p. 62 nn. 3 and 7; Stadelmann, *SPGÄ*, p. 132 n. 2; cf. Roccati, *RdE* 24, 1972, p. 158).

(e) The translation follows *oDM 1591*, but the exact wording varies in the three sources: *pTurin* has *m33 sw Sth nfrw.s r p3 mr n pḥt.s*; *pCh. Beatty* reads [......] *ḥr pḥt.s*, whereas *oDM 1591* gives [......] *ḥr nfrw.s ḥr p3(y).s mr n* [.....]. For the meaning of *mr* ("Zeugstreifen, Binde", *Wb.* I 105,9), derived from a verb *mr* "to bind (together)", one may compare a phrase from the Ch. Beatty Love Songs: *bdš pḥt.s mr ḥry-ỉb d3 mnty.s nfrw.s* "her buttocks droop, her waist is girt, her thighs reveal her beauty"[20]. In Egyptian erotic art women are often shown dressed in nothing but a girdle tied around the waist or hips, see e.g. the famous Leiden fayence bowl[21] or the Turin Erotic Papyrus[22].

(f) See for the different versions of this line in various sources Roccati, *op. cit.*, 158. *^{c}mq* is a Semitic loan-word deriving from a root with the basic meanings "strong", "deep", "wise"[23]. In Akkadian in particular it denotes physical strength (as localized in the arms) and violence. Unlike the Egyptian usage[24], however, it is not employed as a fientic verb in Akkadian nor, as far as I am aware, in any of the North-West Semitic languages. A specialized sexual meaning of *^{c}mq* is also absent from the Semitic usages. Perhaps the closest parallel is a phrase from a Middle Assyrian text quoted in the *CAD*[25]: "If a man seizes (another) man's wife, *emuqama iṣṣabassi ittiakši* if he takes her by force and rapes her", but here the sexual activity is expressed by the verbs *ṣabātu* and *niāku*[26] and not by the adverb *emuqama* "by force". The Egyptian verb *^{c}mq* therefore does not necessarily imply that Seth is raping the goddess, i.e. that he is taking her against her will[27]; rather it stresses the vigourous nature of Seth's coition.

(g) Seth is immediately punished for his sexual indulgence, see the remarks on this passage by Te Velde, *Seth*, p. 37.

(h) Although constructed in a different way (*^{c}ḥ^{c}.n ^{c}nt ... ḥn.ti*), *pTurin* suggests that we should read [*ḥn*]*.in ^{c}nt* in *pCh. Beatty*.

(i) See Gardiner, *op. cit.*, vol. I, p. 62 n. 12 for this translation. The phrase refers to the well-known belligerous aspect of the goddess ^{c}Anat, not to her bi-sexual traits (thus Te Velde, *Seth*, p. 56, who translates "acting as a male"; cf. also W.F. Albright, *Yahweh and the Gods of Canaan*, London 1968, p. 112: "a man-like woman"; Helck, *Beziehungen*, p. 461: "Frau die wie ein Mann ist").

(j) It is difficult to ascertain the exact difference between the verbs *sd* and *bnd* which both refer to some kind of clothing. Unfortunately, the same must be said about the related nouns *sd* (Old Eg. *msdt*) and *bnd*. *Sd*, usually spelled *sdw* or *sdy* in Late Eg., seems to refer to the triangular loin-cloth[28] commonly worn by gods and men[29]. No exact meaning is known of *bnd* (also written *bdn*), but according to Janssen[30] the price to be paid for such a garment would indicate something small. Since the verb *bnd* can also mean "to tie", "wrap up" one might suggest that a *bnd* is a kind of sash tied around the waist to confine the garment underneath. A long ribbed sash of this type is often worn by royal ladies since the early Amarna Period[31], and also by goddesses in the period following Amarna[32]. On a statue group from Tanis ᶜAnat too is shown wearing such a sash[33]. The word *bnd* occurs as an Egyptian loan-word in the OT (*'abnēt*) with the meaning "sash" or "scarf"[34]. The word pair *sd/bnd* is found in other magical texts as well, see e.g. *pTurin 1993* vs. 5,8 (= Pleyte/Rossi 137,8): [*sd*].*kwỉ m Ḥr, bnd.kwỉ m 3st* "I am wearing a kilt like Horus and a sash like Isis"; similarly in *Cairo JE 37508*,8: *sd.kwỉ m Ḥr, bnd.kwỉ m* [*3st*] (?)[35]; *pLeiden* I 349 vs. 2,1: *sd.kwỉ m ṯḥnt, bnd.kwỉ m ᶜrᶜrwt* "I am dressed in fayence, I am wearing uraei for a sash". In the first two of these quotations it is noticeable that a male divinity (Horus) is opposed to a female one (Isis) in the same way as "men" and "women" are opposed in our text. In the magical texts, the reciter identifies himself with what may be called the prototypes of male and female deities, Isis and Horus, in order to unite within himself the all-embracing power of both. The same may be said of the phrase describing ᶜAnat in our text: in the mighty warrior-goddess the powers of man and woman are united. In Near-Eastern sources both ᶜAnat and her "double" ᶜAstarte are sometimes described or depicted as androgynous goddesses[36]. In Ugaritic texts ᶜAnat is said to "be like a man"[37] and to wear a beard and side-whiskers[38].

(k) See the commentary below.

(l) Taking *swg* as a nominal subject of the phrase *sb3 pw swg* "being stupid is a lesson/punishment". *Swg* "(be) foolish" is used as a noun in *ỉ y3 ỉḫ p3y.k swg* "hey, what is this stupidity of yours?", *pDM XI* rt. 4. The alternative rendering "it is a punishment for (his) stupidity"[39] would almost certainly require *sb3 pw n swg*. Roccati takes the following *t3 mtwt* as subject of a verb *swg* "inflict (punishment)"[40], but such a meaning of *swg* is unattested. In the short lacuna preceding *sb3* in pCh. Beatty one might read the enclitic particle *m.t* or sim.; pTurin begins with *ỉw.s*, which probably means that here again it had a different reading from *pCh. Beatty* (a verbal sentence with the preceeding *t3 mtwt* as subject: "she p[unished him for his foolish]ness" ?).

(m) *p3 nṯr ḥry* "the God Above" is usually taken as a designation of the Sun-god, see Gardiner, *op. cit.*, vol. I, p. 63, n. 4; A. Massart, *The Leiden Magical Papyrus I 343 + 345*, Leiden 1954, p. 67 (16); Stadelmann, *SPGA*, p. 133, n. 1; Helck, *Beziehungen*, p. 468. But in our text it is Prēʿ himself who is speaking and who would thus be referring to himself as *p3 nṯr ḥry*, whereas elsewhere he uses the 1st pers. sing. This is not impossible in itself, but it is not very likely either, especially since a comparison with other texts mentioning "the God Above" point in a different direction. The phrase occurs in three more places, all in magical texts with a clear Asiatic flavour. In *pLeiden* I 343 + 345 rt. 5,6 (= vs. 8,2-3) *p3 nṯr ḥry* definitely refers to the Moon-god. Here he appears together with "his wife Nikkal" (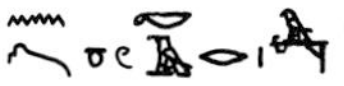, i.e. *Nkl*) and with "Reshep and his wife *'Itm*". The Mesopotamian lunar goddess Ningal was the consort of the Moon-god Nanna/Sin, and in Ugarit, where she was called *Nkl* (Nikkal), a mythological poem describes her wedding to the Moon-god Yarikh[41]. Since it is obvious that the author of this magical papyrus was quite familiar with Canaanite mythology[42], there can be little doubt that he knew these facts and that he used the phrase *p3 nṯr ḥry* with reference to the Moon-god. The God Above occurs again in the same papyrus in rt. 2,11 (= vs. 4,6), where he is mentioned in parallelism with Prēʿ. From this Gardiner[43] concluded that the God Above was identical with Prēʿ, especially since the phrase *ḫft wbn.f* is used in connection with *p3 nṯr ḥry*. But, as Massart rightly points out, the parallelism would rather indicate that two different deities are meant, and the verb *wbn* "arise" can be used not only for the sun, but also for the moon. A third text mentioning *p3 nṯr ḥry* is a rather obscure spell from *pHearst* (11,12-15) directed against the "Asiatic disease" (*t3 nt ʿ3mw*). It reads: "Who is wise like Rēʿ? Who is as wise as this god, who blackens his belly in order to seize the God Above? Even as Seth conjured the Sea[44], so will Seth conjure you, Asiatic disease! Then you will no longer wander about in the body of X son of Y". The meaning of the beginning of this spell is obviously difficult to grasp. With all reserve I would suggest an interpretation along the following lines: "the god who blackens his belly" is Rēʿ himself. Black is the colour of night and underworld, and Osiris, Rēʿ's nocturnal body, is called "the Black One (*km*)[45]. When Rēʿ descends into the underworld he makes himself "black", and he and Osiris unite. The visible proof of the united Rēʿ-Osiris is the moon. When Rēʿ makes himself black he "seizes" the God Above, i.e. the moon, his nocturnal manifestation[46]. Although *ḥry* "above" (not *p3 nṯr ḥry*!) is used in at least one isolated case with reference to the Sun-god[47], I think it is highly probable that in all of the texts discussed above the phrase *p3 nṯr ḥry* denotes the Moon-god.

(n) See the commentary.

(o) This rare designation of Isis is sometimes applied to Hathor in Ptolemaic texts[48], but, as Borghouts points out, in that case she is a fearful goddess[49]. On the other hand Nekhbet may be called a Nubian woman in her role of mother-goddess and divine wet-nurse[50]. In view of the fact that Isis is the mother-goddess *par excellence* in Egyptian religion, the epithet *Nḥsyt* may refer to this aspect of Isis. Maria Münster has suggested that Isis is called a Nubian woman in our text, because of the prominence of her cult in the NK temples of Lower Nubia[51]. In any case it is significant that she replaces the goddess Mut as wife and mother of Amun-Rē^{c}-Kamutef[52] in the temples of Ramesses II in ed-Derr, Abu Simbel and Wâdi es-Sebua. The ambivalence of the epithet *Nḥsyt* may reflect the two contrasting aspects of the goddess in the mythical complex of the Eye of Rē^{c}: as Rē^{c}'s daughter she is a fearful goddess who withdraws to Nubia and destroys his enemies, but after having been pacified by Shu or Thoth, she returns from Nubia in order to become Rē^{c}'s wife and mother who gives birth to him in her temple.

Since, as we have seen, the subject of the first line of the text is missing in *pCh. Beatty*, all commentators have invariably followed Gardiner in defining this subject as the goddess ^{c}Anat. This restoration was in itself a plausible one, not only because it seemed to make excellent sense, but also because it was suggested by a comparison with an episode from the Ugaritic myth of Ba^{c}al which relates how Ba^{c}al and ^{c}Anat mate as bull and cow[53]. On the other hand, none of the scholars who followed this line of thought[54] have made an attempt to connect the rest of the Egyptian story with the Ugaritic text, and this is not surprising, for it would be very difficult, if not impossible, to establish such a connection. In the Ugaritic poem the alledged mating of Ba^{c}al and ^{c}Anat results in the birth of a son, and when news of this is brought to Ba^{c}al he rejoices. In the Egyptian story Seth's copulation is an illicit act resulting in illness and punishment. No son is born to Seth - quite on the contrary: as I will try to demonstrate, the birth of a son is prevented by Seth's copulation.

After Roccati's publication of the Turin version of the story a comparison with the Ugaritic text is no longer possible, for here the subject of the first line is clearly stated as *t3 mtwt*, "the Seed". Despite this, however, the occurence of the Canaanite goddess ^{c}Anat and especially the elaborate description of her nature and appearance still invite us to look for Near-Eastern elements in the story, and such elements are not difficult to find. To start with the description of ᶜAnat, Helck has already mentioned a parallel in *KUB* XXXI, 69, 5ff., where the Hurrian goddess Šaušga is said to "dress herself like a man and like a woman" and to similar statements about Ištar[55]. In the Ugaritic Aqhat text the princess Pughat, in order to revenge the death of her brother Aqhat, "puts on be[neath] the dress of a hero" as well as his weapons, and "on top she puts on the dress of a women"[56]. Since she also paints herself with rouge from sea shells, a custom elsewhere ascribed to ᶜAnat, de Moor has rightly concluded that Pughat is deliberately disguising herself as the goddess ᶜAnat[57]. Another element in the Egyptian story familiar to several Near-Eastern texts is the motif of the bathing goddess inducing sexual contact. It occurs e.g. in the Ugaritic myth of Shachar and Shalim[58], where El goes out to the shore of the sea and perceives two women who represent Athirat and *Rḥmy*, i.e. ᶜAnat[59]. These goddesses are "raising themselves up" from the water "at the beginning of the bay(?)"[60]. Then El's "hand", i.e. his penis, "grows long as the sea" and he takes the women home and engenders Shachar and Shalim, the gods of dawn and sunset , and later a number of minor deities, the so-called "Gracious Gods". In the Sumerian myth of Enlil and Ninlil[61] a similar course of events takes place. Upon the advise of her mother the young goddess Ninlil bathes "in the pure stream Nunbirdu". As the mother had predicted, the god Enlil sees her and, although Ninlil objects that her vagina is too small, he takes her against her will, impregnating her with the Moon-god Nanna. Enlil is punished for this behaviour and sent to the underworld, but as Ninlil has followed him there he is able to engender three minor deities which will serve as substitutes for the Moon-god in order to release him from the underworld.

These parallels are certainly not without interest, but they are probably not very significant for the interpretation of the Egyptian story. The woman disguising herself as a male warrior and the bathing seductress may represent mere folktale motifs, "the building-blocks of any narrative"[62]. They belong to the narrative form of the myth, not to its underlying structure, and stories that share a common motif are therefore not necessarily relevant for their mutual interpretation. Moreover, the first of these motifs has been cast in a typical Egyptian phrase (see textual note (j) above), and the "bathing beauty" motif itself occurs not only in Ugaritic or Mesopotamian texts, but also in genuine Egyptian literature. It seems best, therefore, to return to the native ground of our story, and proceed to analyse it from a purely Egyptian point of view.

The bathing woman who seduces Seth is called *t3 mtwt* "the Seed". It can also mean "the poison", *sc.* of a snake or scorpion, and as in many magical texts, this double meaning is also implied here. But on the mythological level to be discussed now, the meaning "Seed" is prominent and this translation will be retained in the following. Roccati has already quoted another magical text in which *t3 mtwt* is personified and said to be able to appear as a snake, a dog, a human being and a crocodile[63]. As early as 1891 Marucchi recognized in *t3 mtwt* in the Vatican Magical Papyrus a *divinitas malefica muliebris*[64]; An interesting parallel for the role of the Seed-goddess in our text is provided by a passage from the Pyramid Texts which says that "the King has copulated with  *Mwt*"[65]. Later variants write this word as  [66] or  [67]. It is generally assumed that *Mwt* or *Mwyt* is a personification of semen[68]. In our story this goddess is said to have been given as a wife to the God Above, who, as we have seen, probably represents Osiris Lunus[69] as nocturnal incarnation of the Sun-god; in other words, the Seed-goddess is Prē^c's own wife, to be impregnated by his nightly "body" Osiris in order to give birth to him as the rejuvenated Rē^c-Harakhty. Like the King in the Pyramid Text the God Above copulates with the Seed-goddess, and he does this "with fire"[70], i.e. he impregnates her with fire. This further corroborates our interpretation of *p3 nṯr ḥry* as the nocturnal Sun-god, for it is precisely this god who begets himself with fire in the primaeval darkness of the Underworld. Texts which document this idea have been discussed elsewhere[71] and it is not necessary to repeat them here; suffice it to recall the vignettes and text of *La création du disque solaire* and the statement of several classical authors that the mother of the Apis bull was made pregnant by heavenly fire or by light emitted by the moon[72]. The seed cannot develop when it has not been joined with the light or fire of the Sun-god (or his nocturnal form), and this is the reason why the God Above has to copulate with the Seed "with fire"[73]. The Seed-goddess represents Rē^c's primaeval wife, she is identical with Hathor. In this admirable study on Hathor, Derchain has shown that this goddess represents *l'excitation sexuelle*, the libido of the Creator God, which is the source of his creative activity[74]. The Seed also behaves like Hathor, who often plays the role of a divine seductress. When Prē^c has retreated because his ability to rule the earth has been questioned, Hathor stands before him and exposes her vagina before his eyes. Then Prē^c laughs at her, gets up from his bed and resumes his responsibilities[75]. In Egyptian love songs the girl is often called "the Golden One", i.e. Hathor. In one of these songs the girl behaves in much the same way as the Seed-goddess in our text. After having addressed her lover as "my god" and "my lotus" she says to him: "It is my desire to descend (to the water) and bathe myself before your eyes. I will let you see my beauty (*di͗.i͗ m33.k nfrw.i͗*) through my robe of first class royal linen (...)"[76]. But as a divine seductress, Hathor does not direct her attentions exclusively to Prē^{c}. She is also the divine prostitute, the "woman who is a stranger", so often condemned in the wisdom texts. In the opposition Mut *versus* Hathor, Mut is the goddess of good women and Hathor the goddess of bad women[77]. This aspect she shares with Seth, who breaks the boundaries of regular sexuality, the god of bad men who do not care to distinguish between married and unmarried women[78]. Seth commits adultery with the wife of Prē^{c}. In a late mythological text the crimes of Seth are summed up before Rē^{c}: apart from leading Apophis to Rē^{c}'s sanctuary in Heliopolis and from cutting down the *išd*-tree from which the Sun-god arises in the morning, Seth has also "taken away the penis (*mṯ3*) of Tefnut"[79]. In this text Tefnut represents the primaeval wife of the Creator God Rē^{c}-Atum, who like Iusa^{c}as and Nebetḥetepet symbolizes the "hand" with which the god masturbated in order to impregnate himself[80]. By taking away the penis of this primaeval androgynous goddess, Seth frustrates Rē^{c}'s rebirth and resurrection, and this is exactly what he does in our story too. This is also the reason why Prē^{c} refers to the "evening" (*mšrw*), the time of sunset, when he has become an old man who is about to enter the realm of the dead, from which he can arise only by means of the Seed which will engender him again.

After the intervention of ^{c}Anat, Isis descends from heaven in order to uncover the Seed. The fact that the goddess is given the name of Isis and the epithet "Nubian woman" signifies that she is Rē^{c}'s mother. This is further indicated by the statement that she descends from heaven, for the mother of Rē^{c} who gives birth to him in the morning is usually called Nut, the sky-goddess.

Between the Seed (Hathor) and Isis stands ^{c}Anat. She plays a very interesting ambiguous role, which is quite in agreement with her character. Unlike the Seed, who has given herself to Seth, and Isis, who is Rē^{c}'s mother, ^{c}Anat is committed to both gods. She is Rē^{c}'s daughter, but Seth's wife. Thus she is the right person to intervene in the conflict between Rē^{c} and Seth, and she does so by asking Rē^{c} to release Seth from the Seed, for this is in the interest of both parties: the Sun-god will be able to ensure his resurrection and Seth will be cured from his illness. As consort of Seth, ^{c}Anat's role is similar to that of his Egyptian spouse Nephthys. Nephthys is sometimes called "the would-be woman without a vagina"[81] and, although exceptions occur in Egyptian mythology, she usually represents the childless woman who acts as wailing-woman and wet-nurse[82]. The same applies to ^{c}Anat. Like Nephthys, she is not a "real" woman, for she behaves and dresses like a man, and just like her Egyptian equivalent she is childless, for although she conceived a child, she was unable to give birth to it[83]. In Ugaritic mythology too she is the divine wet-nurse who does not bear a child herself, but suckles the child of another goddess[84]. On the other hand, ^{c}Anat is the daughter of Rē^{c}, and as such she may be compared with Sakhmet, the Eye of Rē^{c} who protects her father against those who take advantage of him when he has grown old and weak.

The three goddesses mentioned in the text, *t3 mtwt* (Hathor), ^{c}Anat and Isis, are three aspects of one and the same goddess who herself is an aspect of Rē^{c}. These goddesses are part of the "multiplicity of constitutive powers, roles and forms" of the divine person which Assmann has called a "constellation"[85]. Our text shows in a narrative form how one aspect (*ḫprw*) of this constellation, the divine prostitute, is transformed into its opposite, the divine mother. Between the two stands ^{c}Anat, who is a true mediator in the Lévi-Straussian sense of the term. She bridges the gap between the two opposites, sharing aspects of both. Rē^{c}'s primaeval wife (his hand, his penis, his seed) is an androgynous goddess, she belongs to the undifferentiated unity of the Creator God who was alone in the primaeval chaos[86]. This androgynous goddess who acts as a "strange woman" by committing adultery, is transformed into ^{c}Anat, who is a foreign goddess in the literal sense of the word and who is also characterized by a certain amount of androgyny, at least in outward appearance. On the other hand ^{c}Anat is the Eye of Rē^{c} who protects her father against his enemies, and as such she becomes Isis, the Eye of Rē^{c}, who returns from Nubia in order to become Rē^{c}'s divine queen, his spouse and mother. Thus ^{c}Anat bridges the gap between Hathor, the divine prostitute and Isis, the divine wife and mother, between undifferentiated unity and the structured duality of man and wife, between irregularity and chaos represented by Seth and order and regularity established by Rē^{c}.

Before closing this already too long discussion of the myth of ^{c}Anat, Seth and the Seed of Prē^{c}, three further aspects must be mentioned briefly. First, there is a remarkable similarity between the structure of our story and the myth of Osiris. It is well-known that a coherent account of this myth is lacking from Egyptian sources, and that such an account has to be reconstructed from allusions in various religious texts and from Plutarch's *De Iside et Osiride* (ch. 13-20). The episode which interests us here relates how Seth, after having killed Osiris, cut his body into pieces and scattered them all over the country. Isis, assisted by Nephthys, searches for them and manages to recover all of them except Osiris' penis, which had been eaten by a fish, a feature found in Plutarch but not in ancient Egyptian sources, which say that the penis was found as well[87]. In Plutarch's version Isis replaces the lost member by a new one. After having reassembled Osiris' body, Isis joins her husband and conceives posthumously Osiris' son Horus. The similarities between this myth and the ^{c}Anat story are shown in the following tabulation:

Osiris myth	*^{c}Anat myth*
Seth kills Osiris.	Rē^{c} is old and about to die.
Seth prevents Osiris' resurrection by cutting his body into pieces and making the penis lost.	Seth prevents Rē^{c}'s rebirth by robbing his seed.
Isis, assisted by Nephthys, recovers the pieces, including the penis (or: fashions a new penis) and,	Isis, assisted by ^{c}Anat, recovers the seed and,
becoming his wife and mother, gives birth to Osiris' reincarnation Horus.	becoming his wife and mother, enables Rē^{c} to be reborn in the morning.

In a penetrating study Jan Assmann[88] has made a distinction between "myth" (*Mythos*) and "mythical statement" (*mythische Aussage*). Myth, according to him, is an abstraction, a nucleus of actions and events, of heroes and fates, which form the basic thematic material shared by a group of mythical statements. The latter represent the concrete realizations of myth found in written or inscribed documents[89]. Following this distinction one may say that the Osiris and the ^{c}Anat stories are two divergent mythical statements of one and the same myth. Both are narrative realizations of a myth, which itself has a non-narrative structure, and which deals with the interrelations between Re^{c}-Osiris and his constellation and with the interactions between the opposite forces of chaos and order, which was one of the major concerns of ancient Egyptian religion.

A second remark regards the practical application of the mythical precedent told in our text. Elsewhere I have presented a case-study in Egyptian magic, in which I have tried to show how the magical spell operates and how the recitation of the spell influences in a favourable sense the process to which the patient is subjected[90]. Much of what has been said there, may be applied to our text as well. What remains to be shown is how the analogy between the mythical precedent and the actual situation of the patient is established in this case. We have already remarked that part of the analogy lies in the double meaning of the word *mtwt*, which indicates both the seed that harmed Seth and the poison of the scorpion from which the patient suffers. But for obvious reasons the patient is not identified with Seth. In the mythical precedent the seed is given back to Rē^{c}-Osiris, its rightful owner; the integrity of the god and his constellation is re-established, and it is with this god that the patient is identified. Just as Rē^{c} is reborn and Osiris is resurrected as Horus, so the patient will recover from the poison that threatens to kill him. When the patient is cured "the Sun will arise and the Inundation will flow and rituals will be observed in Heliopolis"[91]; in other words, cosmic order will be re-established. This analogy is realized by means of the deification of the members of the patient's body (*Gliedervergottung*), which Assmann has interpreted as an enumeration of the constellation and of the "*Sphäre des Seinigen*" of the god[92]. Thus the renewed integrity of the god is reflected by that of the patient, who will regain control over every part of his body despite of the scorpion's poison. The recitation of the mythical precedent and of the *Gliedervergottung* with its solemn, repetitive strain, influences the psychic attitude of the patient, and mobilizes his ability to overcome the poison's attack on his life[93].

Finally, we must return briefly to a problem mentioned earlier in this article, *viz.* the possible influence of non-Egyptian myths on our story. The occurrence of a few Semitic loan-words and of a Canaanite goddess does not mean very much in this respect, and, as we have seen, even the inclusion of some motifs known from other Near-Eastern stories is not necessarily of great importance. On the other hand, our story reveals a number of similarities, notably with the Mesopotamian myth of Enlil and Ninlil, which seem to go beyond these superficial resemblances. Both stories begin with a goddess (Ninlil, the Seed) who bathes, thereby revealing her attractions to a god passing by (Enlil, Seth), who has illicit sexual intercourse with her (against her will in the Sumerian myth; with her consent in the Egyptian story). Both gods are punished for their bad behaviour. In the Mesopotamian case, the result of Enlil's intercourse with Ninlil is the birth of the Moon-god Nanna, who is born in the underworld, from which he is set free by the subsequent birth of three minor divinities given as substitutes for the Moon-god, a feature probably invented to explain the periodical invisibility of the moon. In the Egyptian myth, the final outcome is that Rē^{c} is reborn with the help of his mother Isis, who recovers the lost seed of the Moon-god, Rē^{c}'s nocturnal form. How Isis manages to do this is not mentioned, but as the seed is located in Seth's forehead one may surmise that she operated in the same way as Thoth did in a related story from *The*

Contendings of Horus and Seth[94]. When Seth has swallowed the seed of Horus, Thoth makes it appear from Seth's head in the form of a golden disc. Before Seth can seize it, Thoth places it on his own head, and since Thoth is a Moon-god it is clear that this golden disc represents the moon[95]. In fact, one may wonder whether the myth of ᶜAnat and Seth does not also contain a level describing the (re)birth of the moon. This is suggested by a passage in the Coffin Texts discussed by Derchain and Te Velde[96], ascribing the periodical waning of the Moon-god to the temporary removal of his seed. If this interpretation is accepted, there would be a further parallel between the myth of Enlil and Ninlil on the one hand, and that of Seth and the Seed on the other: both would describe the birth of the Moon-god, and both would give an explanation for the waning and periodical invisibility of the moon.

Kirk, without whose wonderful study of ancient Near-Eastern and Greek myths this article could hardly have been written, has given an analysis of Enlil and Ninlil and of the related myth of Enki and Ninhursag[97]. According to him, the underlying meaning of these myths is that "the pursuit of fertility can be carried to excess; if it is so carried, it tends to result in infertility". They also reveal a moralistic statement, *viz.* that sexual excess and irregularity should be condemned because they are harmful and counterproductive. This again is certainly one of the underlying ideas in the Egyptian myth, and an idea quite familiar to us from Egyptian wisdom literature, with its emphasis on the concept of *maᶜat* and its constant warning to avoid excess in every aspect of life. Seth is punished for his sexual exuberance, and his irregular sexual behaviour does not result in fertility and birth, but in infertility and abortion[98]; it is only when cosmic and social order (*maᶜat*) has been restored that Rēᶜ is reborn.

Roccati has expressed the opinion that "there are no certain non-Egyptian elements in the story, even if it shows a certain familiarity with Canaanite motifs"[99]. After all that has been said in the preceding pages it would be difficult not to agree with this opinion. Certain non-Egyptian motifs are detectable in the story, but these have been incorporated in a genuine Egyptian myth expressed in purely Egyptian religious terms, and it is quite out of the question that the story represents an Egyptian translation or even an *interpretatio aegyptiaca* of a non-Egyptian myth. If on the other hand there exists a similarity between the Egyptian story and a Mesopotamian one, this similarity lies mainly in the underlying structure shared by these stories, i.e. in the "myths" themselves rather than in their divergent mythical realizations. Since the transmission of the mythical heritage of one culture to another is more likely to have taken place by means of narrative forms than by means of mythical abstractions, it seems best to assume that both myths arose from their own cultural setting, and that the Mesopotamian myth had no influence on the origin of the Egyptian story. After all, Egyptian and Mesopotamian civilizations, besides displaying many differences, have also much in common[100], and the similarities as well as the divergencies are reflected in the mythologies of these ancient cultures.

Notes

*) Abbreviations used in this article follow the standard accepted in Egyptology, see the *Annual Egyptological Bibliography*, Leiden 1947-- and the *Lexikon der Ägyptologie* (= LÄ), Wiesbaden 1972--. In addition to these note the following: Helck, *Beziehungen* = W. Helck, *Die Beziehungen Ägyptens zu Verderasiens im 3. und 4. Jahrtausend v. Chr.*, Wiesbaden 1971^2; Stadelmann, *SPGÄ* = R. Stadelmann, *Syrisch-Palästinensische Gottheiten in Ägypten*, Leiden 1967; Te Velde, *Seth* = H. te Velde, *Seth, God of Confusion*, Leiden 1977^2. This article has been written with financial support of the Netherlands Organization for the Advancement of Pure Research (Z.W.O.).

1) A.H. Gardiner, "The Astarte Papyrus", in *Studies presented to F.Ll. Griffith on his 70th birthday*, London 1932, pp. 74-85; *id.*, *Late-Egyptian Stories*, Brussels 1932, pp. 76-81. See Stadelmann, *SPGÄ*, pp. 125-131 for bibliographical references. More recent translations include E. Brunner-Traut, *Altägyptische Märchen*, Düsseldorf-Köln 1963, pp. 72-76, 268-269 and E.F. Wente, in *The Literature of Ancient Egypt*, ed. W.K. Simpson, New Haven/London 1972, pp. 133-136. Cf. also W. Kaiser, *Die mythische Bedeutung des Meeres in Ägypten, Ugarit und Israel*, Berlin 1962^2, pp. 81-91, 166-167; Stadelmann, art. "Astartepapyrus", in *LÄ* vol. 1, cols. 509-511.

2) *pHearst* 11,13; *pBerlin 3038* rt. 21, 2-3; *pLeiden* I 343 + 345 rt. 4, 12-13 = vs. 7,7.

3) Te Velde, *Seth*, pp. 99-108.

4) *KTU* 1.1-2; J.C.L. Gibson, *Canaanite Myths and Legends*, Edinburgh 1978, pp. 2-8, 37-45. Cf. Th.H. Gaster, "the Egyptian 'Story of Astarte' and the Ugaritic Poem of Baal", in *BiOr* vol. 9, 1952, pp. 82-85, 232.

5) G. Posener, "La légende égyptienne de la mer insatiable", in *AIPHOS* vol. 13, 1953, pp. 461-478.

6) Cf. Te Velde, *Seth*, p. 123; Stadelmann, *SPGÄ*, p. 130, and much more reluctantly, *id.*, in *LÄ* I, col. 510; J. Leclant, art. "Astarte", in *LÄ* I, col. 502, with nn. 57-58 speaks of a "traduction en égyptien de fragments de mythes [cananéens]".

7) G. van der Leeuw, "Die sog. epische Einleitung der Zauberformeln", in *Zeitschrift für Religionspsychologie* vol. 6, 1933, pp. 161-180.

8) Gardiner, *op. cit.*, vol. I, p. viii; G. Posener, in J. Černý, *Papyrus hiératiques de Deir el-Médineh*, vol. I, Cairo 1978, p. viii; cf. P.W. Pestman, "Who were the owners, in the 'Community of Workmen', of the Chester Beatty Papyri", in *Gleanings from Deir el-Medîna*. eds. R.J. Demarée and J.J. Janssen, Leiden 1982, pp. 155-172.

9) Spiegelberg, *op. cit.*, Introduction; J.E. Quibell, *The Ramesseum*, London 1898, p. 9 (14).

10) Information kindly supplied by Ms. Rosalind Hall, assistant curator of the Petrie Museum, University College, London. I learned too late about the present location of the ostracon to be able to use for the present article the excellent photographs sent to me by Ms. Hall, but I hope to return to the ostracon elsewhere. In the meantime it may be noted here, that Gardiner's transcription is certainly not an improvement upon the one published by Spiegelberg.

11) *SPGÄ*, pp. 131-133.

12) O. Marucchi, *Monuments Papyracea Aegyptia Bibliothecae Vaticanae*, Rome 1891, pls. 2-3; A. Erman, "Der Zauberpapyrus des Vatikans", in *ZÄS* vol. 31, 1893, pp. 119-124; E. Suys, "Le papyrus magique du Vatican", in *OrNS* vol. 3, 1934, pp. 63-87; B. de Rachewiltz, *Il papiro magico vaticano*, Rome 1954.

13) *pLeiden* I 349 vs. 2,9-10; *pCh. Beatty* I rt. 11,1-13,1.

14) W.F. Albright, *Archaeology and the Religion of Israel*, Baltimore 1946^2, p. 197, n. 39; Stadelmann, *SPGÄ*, p. 131, n. 4.

15) *RdE* vol. 24, 1972, p. 157.

16) L. Habachi, "A Statue Made for Ankhefenamun, Prophet of the House of Amun in Khapu and His Daughter", in *ASAE* vol. 47, 1947, pp. 261-282.
17) Cf. *Wb*. I, 280-282.
18) Ug. *'aḫ* = Hebr. *'aḥu*, for which an Egyptian derivation has been suggested, see T.O. Lambdin, "Egyptian Loan Words in the Old Testament", in *JAOS* vol. 73, 1953, p. 146, and J. Vergote, *Joseph en Égypte*, Louvain 1959, pp. 59-66. Others have approached it to Akk. *aḫu* "(river)bank)", see Ch. Virolleaud, in *Syria* vol. 17, 1936, pp. 156-158; B. Couroyer, in *RB* vol. 66, 1959, p. 588. The toponym *Šmk* has been connected with the Samachonitis mentioned by Josephus, modern lake Huleh, see Virolleaud, *loc. cit.*, and R. de Langhe, *Les textes de Ras Shamra-Ugarit et leurs rapports avec le milieu biblique de l'Ancien Testament*, Gembloux-Paris 1945, vol. II, pp. 209-217.
19) Albright, *op. cit.*, p. 197, n. 39.
20) *pCh. Beatty* I vs. C1, 5.
21) H.D. Schneider and M.J. Raven, *De Egyptische Oudheid*, 's-Gravenhage 1981, pp. 26, 105 (no. 102); A.J. Milward, in *Egypt's Golden Age: The Art of Living in the New Kingdom 1550-1085 B.C.*, Boston 1982, pp. 144-145 (no. 143).
22) J.A. Omlin, *Der Papyrus 55001 und seine satirisch-erotischen Zeichnungen und Inschriften*, Turin 1973.
23) See e.g. *CAD*, E, pp. 151-152, 156-162; *AHw*, pp. 213-214, 216-217; C.H. Gordon, *Ugaritic Textbook*, Glossary, no. 1874; *DISO*, p. 217.
24) In *pCh. Beatty VII* rt. 8,4 a verb ^{c}*mq* (written 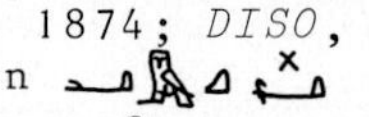) is used with reference to a scorpion, the object of ^{c}*mq* being its tail (hence Gardiner's suggestion "tuck together"). Whether a verb 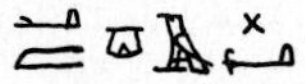 (*Edfou* IV, 34, 7-8), which, judging from its context, appears to mean "pluck" (of flowers), has anything to do with this meaning of ^{c}*mq*, as suggested by D. Meeks, *AL* 77.0646, seems highly dubious to me.
25) *CAD*, E. p. 156.
26) Cf. *CAD*, Ṣ., p. 12 (e, 2') and N, pp. 197-198, resp.
27) Stadelmann, *SPGA*, pp. 132-133 translates ^{c}*mq* as "Gewalt antun" and "vergewaltigen"; according to him Seth "zwingt die Göttin gewaltsam ihn zu Willen zu sein". Te Velde, *Seth*, p. 37 also speaks of "rape".
28) J.J. Janssen, *Commodity Prices from the Ramessid Period*, Leiden 1975, pp. 272-277.
29) *Wb*. IV, 365.
30) *op. cit.*, pp. 288-289.
31) C.Aldred, in *JEA* vol. 56, 1970, pp. 195-196.
32) See e.g. G. Thausing and H. Goedicke, *Nofretari. Eine Dokumentation der Wandgemälde ihres Grabes*, Graz 1971, *passim*.
33) Louvre AF 2576; P. Montet, *Les nouvelles fouilles de Tanis 1929-32*, Paris 1933, pls. 70-72.
34) Cf. B.H. Stricker, in *AcOr* vol. 15, 1936, p. 10; *id.*, in *OMRO* vol. 24, 1943, p. 30 n. 1; Lambdin, *op. cit.*, p. 146; A. Loprieno, in *AION* vol. 37, 1977, p. 128.
35) Cf. G. Daressy, "Stèle de Karnak avec textes magiques" in *ASAE* 17, 1917, pp. 194-196, who reads *sd.kwỉ m Ḥr,nd.kwỉ* (*sic*, J.v.D.) *m Ḥr* without indicating a lacuna at the end. The copy made for the Berlin Dictionary, quoted in the *Belegstellen* to *Wb*. I, 465,3 gives *sd.kwỉ m Ḥr,bnd.kwỉ m* [*Sth*]. The parallel in *pTurin 1993* suggests the restoration *bnd.kwỉ m* [*3st*].
36) See e.g. J.C. de Moor, in *UF* vol. 1, 1969, p. 171; J. Leclant, in *Syria* vol. 37, 1960, pp. 7-9; W.F. Albright, *Yahweh and the Gods of Canaan*, London, 1968, pp. 112-113; H. Gese, *Die Religionen Altsyriens, Altarabiens und der Mandäer*, eds. H. Gese, M. Höpfner, K. Rudolph, Stuttgart etc. 1970, pp. 158, 214.

37) *KTU* 1.3,V,27; cf. J.C. de Moor, *The Seasonal Pattern in the Ugaritic Myth of Ba^{c}lu*, Neukirchen 1971, p. 132.
38) *KTU* 1.6,I,3; so with De Moor, *op. cit.*, p. 193, despite the criticism of K. Aartun, in *WdO* vol. 4, 1968, pp. 286-287, and S.E. Loewenstamm, in *IOS* vol. 4, 1974, pp. 1-3.
39) Stadelmann, *SPGÄ*, p. 133; Helck, *Beziehungen*, p. 461; Albright, *op. cit.*, p. 112.
40) *op. cit.*, p. 157.
41) *KTU* 1.24; Gibson, *Canaanite Myths and Legends*, pp. 30-31, 128-129.
42) Cf. Stadelmann, *SPGÄ*, pp. 124-125, who suggests that the author had an onomasticon of Near-Eastern gods at hand.
43) A.H. Gardiner, "The goddess Ningal in an Egyptian text", in *ZÄS* vol. 43, 1906, p. 97.
44) Cf. note 2 above.
45) H. Kees, *Farbensymbolik in ägyptischen religiösen Texten*, Göttingen 1943, p. 418.
46) The same idea is probably meant in another magical spell (*pBM 10059*, 8,2) where seven gods are invoked "who bring the One Above of the Underworld and make him travel towards this ground (*i͗nyw ḥry n dw3t rdyw nm.f r s3t tn*)". The One Above of the Underworld is the moon as nocturnal Sun-god, who travels along the nightly sky towards the earth, the place where he will arise in the morning as the newly born Sun-god. Cf. my remarks on *CT* Spell 691 = *BD* 71 in *JEOL* vol. 26, 1979-1980, p. 21.
47) *KRI* II,197,10 = H. Ricke, G.R. Hughes, E.F. Wente, *The Beit el-Wali Temple of Ramesses II*, Chicago 1967, pl. 15: *pr.n.k ḥr t3 iw.k mi R^{c} ḥry sšb (?) 3ḫty* "When you (i.e. the King) come forth upon earth you are like Rē^{c} above who illumines (?) the Two Horizons". Another text in the same temple (*op. cit.*, p. 10 = *KRI* II,197,3), badly damaged, mentions "the rays of the light above (*stwt šw ḥry*)", but this is inconclusive, since *šw* can refer to the light of both sun and moon, see *Wb.* IV, 430,7-9.
48) *Wb.* II, 303,11.
49) J.F. Borghouts, *The Magical Texts of Papyrus Leiden I 348* (*OMRO* vol. 51), Leiden 1971, p. 151 with n. 2.
50) Cf. H. Brunner, *Die Geburt des Gottkönigs*, Wiesbaden 1964, p. 86, and Borghouts, *op. cit.*, p. 151.
51) M. Münster, *Untersuchungen zur Göttin Isis vom Alten Reich bis zum Ende des Neuen Reiches*, Berlin 1968, p. 180.
52) See on this role of Mut H. te Velde, "Towards a Minimal Definition of the Goddess Mut", in *JEOL* vol. 26, 1979-1980, pp. 3-9.
53) It should be noted, however, that this interpretation of the Ugaritic text is not beyond doubt. "A cow" is repeatedly mentioned and this cow "bears a bull to Ba^{c}al" (*KTU* 1.10,III,20-22), but it is by no means certain that this cow is actually identical with ^{c}Anat; rather it would seem that ^{c}Anat chooses a cow from "the inundated shore... teeming with old oxen" (*ʾah...mlʾat rʾumm*; cf. Gen 41:2,28 and Vergote, *Joseph en Égypte*, p. 59) and gives it to Ba^{c}al to bear him a son. The crucial passage describing Ba^{c}al's mating with the cow is much damaged. For another view see E. Lipiński in *Syria* vol. 42, 1965, pp. 45-73.
54) Albright, *Archaeology and the Religion of Israel*, pp. 197-198 n. 39; Stadelmann, *SPGÄ*, p. 133; Helck, *Beziehungen*, p. 461; *id.*, *Betrachtungen zur grossen Göttin und den mit ihr verbundenen Gottheiten*, Münich-Vienna, 1971, pp. 151-153.
55) Helck, *Beziehungen*, p. 461; *id.*, *Betrachtungen zur grossen Göttin*, pp. 105 and 125, n. 135.
56) *KTU* 1.19,IV, 206-208.
57) J.C. de Moor in *OrNS* vol. 37, 1968, pp. 212-215; see esp. p. 213, n. 1.
58) *KTU* 1.23, 30ff.
59) Cf. J.C. de Moor, *New Year with Canaanites and Israelites*, part 2, Kampen 1972, p. 18.

60) Following a suggestion made by G. Haaijer in his unpublished thesis *Een ritueel voor een sacrale maaltijd uit Ugarit. De tekst* CTA *23*, Groningen 1978, p. 30.
61) H. Behrens, *Enlil und Ninlil. Ein sumerischer Mythos aus Nippur*, Rome 1978; cf. S.N. Kramer, *Sumerian Mythology* (revised ed.), New York 1961, pp. 43-47. A similar incident occurs between Enki and the goddesses Ninmu and Ninkurra in the myth of Enki and Ninhursag, see Kramer's translation in *ANET*[2], pp. 38ff.
62) G.S. Kirk, *Myth. Its Meaning and Functions in Ancient and Other Cultures*, Cambridge etc. 1970, p. 93.
63) *pGeneva MAH 15274*; see Roccati, *op. cit.*, p. 157.
64) O. Marucchi, *Monumenta Papyracea Aegyptia*, p. 92.
65) *Pyr.* 123a (W).
66) E. Naville, *The Temple of Deir el-Bahari*, vol. 4, London 1901, pl. 110.
67) H.O. Lange and H. Schaefer, *Grab- und Denksteine des Mittleren Reiches*, vol. 2, Berlin 1908, p. 119 (CGC 20520).
68) *Wb.* II,53,11; R.O. Faulkner, *The Ancient Egyptian Pyramid Texts*, Oxford 1969, p. 38, n. 4; T.G. Allen, *The Book of the Dead or Going Forth By Day*, Chicago 1974, p. 187 n. 292; H. te Velde in *JEOL* vol. 26, 1979-1980, p. 4.
69) On Osiris and the moon see Ph. Derchain, in *La Lune: mythes et rites* (*Sources Orientales*, vol. 5). Paris 1962, pp. 44-46; J.Gw. Griffiths in *JEA* vol. 62, 1976, pp. 153-159.
70) The text adds: "... after deflowering her with a chisel", a phrase unknown to me from other sources. In any case it has nothing to do with ᶜAnat's alledged epithet "Mistress of the chisel" (Stadelmann, *SPGA*, p. 133, n. 2), for the passage in our text does not refer to ᶜAnat. Moreover, the connection of the "Mistress of the chisel" (found only in *pLeiden* I 343 + 345 vs. 3,7 = rt. 1,12) with ᶜAnat is itself highly dubious. The chisel is mentioned in magical texts as a weapon used to strike a demon on his head, see Massart, *op. cit.*, p. 55, n. 24. It is interesting to note that this use of the chisel survives in the Coptic Martyrdoms, see the refferences given by W.E. Crum, *A Coptic Dictionary*, Oxford 1939, p. 213, s.v. **ⲙⲁϫⲉ**.
71) J. van Dijk in *JEOL* vol. 26, 1979-1980, pp. 11-14.
72) R.O. Faulkner in *JEA* vol. 54, 1968, p. 44.
73) Cf. Te Velde, *Seth*, p. 52.
74) Ph. Derchain, *Hathor Quadrifrons. Recherches sur la syntaxe d'un mythe égyptien*, Istanbul 1972, pp. 45-49.
75) *pCh. Beatty* I rt. 3,9-4,3.
76) *oDM 1266 + oCairo CG 25218*, 8-9; see G. Posener, *Catalogues des ostraca hiératiques littéraires de Deir el-Médineh*, vol. II, 3, Cairo 1972, pl. 76, and the commentary by Ph. Derchain in *RdE* vol. 50, 1975, pp. 70-77.
77) Cf. H. te Velde, in *JEOL* vol. 26, 1979-1980, p. 8.
78) Te Velde, *JEOL*, pp. 55-56.
79) *TM* II,228,18ff., ed. J.-Cl. Goyon in *BIFAO* vol. 75, 1975, pp. 349-399. I do not believe it is necessary to emend the text as Goyon has suggested.
80) Cf. U. Verhoeven, art. "Tefnut" in *LÄ* VI, col. 298, with n. 24.
81) *Pyr.* 1273b.
82) Cf. H. te Velde, "Relations and Conflicts between Egyptian Gods, particularly in the Divine Ennead of Heliopolis, in *Struggles of Gods* (*Papers of the Groningen Work Group for the Study of History of Religions*), ed. H.G. Kippenberg, Berlin etc. 1984, p. 253.
83) *p mag. Harris* rt. 3,8-9.
84) Cf. JC. de Moor in *UF* vol. 1, 1969, p. 182, and *id.*, *New Year with Canaanites and Israelites*, part 2, p. 19, n. 62.
85) J. Assmann, *Liturgische Lieder an den Sonnengott*, Berlin 1969, pp. 339-352.
86) Cf. Te Velde, in *Struggles of Gods*, pp. 247-249.

87) J.Gw. Griffiths, *Plutarch's De Iside et Osiride*, Cambridge 1970, pp. 342-344.
88) J. Assmann, "Die Verborgenheit des Mythos in Ägypten" in *GM* vol. 25, 1977, pp. 7-43.
89) *op. cit.*, p. 38.
90) J. van Dijk, "The Birth of Horus according to the Ebers Papyrus" in *JEOL* vol. 26, 1979-1980, pp. 10-25.
91) *pCh. Beatty VII* vs. 6,2-3.
92) Assmann, *Liturgische Lieder*, pp. 347-349.
93) Cf. *JEOL* vol. 26, pp. 23-25, and the remark of P. Behrens, art. "Skorpion", in *LÄ* V, col. 988 (D).
94) *pCh. Beatty* I rt. 11,1-13,1.
95) Cf. Ph. Derchain, in *La Lune*, pp. 21-23, where allusions to this myth in other texts are mentioned.
96) *CT* Spell 310; see Derchain, *op. cit.*, p. 41; Te Velde, *Seth*, p. 43.
97) G.S. Kirk, *Myth. Its Meaning and Functions in Ancient and Other Cultures*, pp. 90-107.
98) Cf. Te Velde, *Seth*, pp. 28-29, 55.
99) Roccati in *RdE* vol. 24, 1972, pp. 158-159.
100) See e.g. H. and H.A. Frankfort *et. al.*, *Before Philosophy*, Harmondsworth 1949[2], pp. 238-241; S. Morenz, "Der Alte Orient. Von Bedeutung und Struktur seiner Geschichte" in *Summa Historica. Die Grundzüge der welthistorischen Epochen* (*Propyläen Weltgeschichte*, vol. 11), Berlin etc. 1965, pp. 25-64.

Man of Letters *v.* Man of Figures

The Seventh Night from al-Tawḥīdī's *al-Imtāʿ wa-l-muʾānasa*

G.J. van Gelder, Groningen

(I, 96) "When I returned to him[1] for another session he said: Today I heard you and Ibn ᶜUbayd[2] shout at each other in the palace; what was it all about? -- I answered: He was saying that accountancy (*kitābat al-ḥisāb*) is more useful, nobler, more closely connected with kingship, more needed by the ruler and more indispensable to him, than eloquent writing, the drafting of letters and the making of fair copies (*kitābat al-balāgha wa-l-inshā' wa-l-taḥrīr*)[3]. For the former is a serious matter, the latter mere fun: a lot of orotund prolixity, trumpery and swindling, is it not? Not so accountancy, collection, requisition and specification (*al-ḥisāb wa-l-taḥṣīl wa-l-istidrāk wa-l-tafṣīl*)[4]. Furthermore, accountancy is an art with a well-known starting-point, which leads strait to the goal; its benefit readily presents itself and its profit is quick in coming. But eloquence consists of ornamentation and tricks; it is like a *fata morgana* and the other like real water. The inferiority of eloquence also lies in the fact that those who practise it are considered foolish and stupid. From times of old, civil servants in caliphal palaces and councils of viziers used to say: 'O God, protect us from the folly of chancery officials, the stupidity of school-teachers and the inarticulateness of grammarians'. Chancery officials, school-teachers and grammarians are brothers, in spite of their differences, united as they are by inadequacy, held together by their (bad) habits and abounding in shortcomings, even though they live in different places and diverse circumstances. Think only of the fact, he said, that in a large kingdom one single chancery official would be sufficient, whereas a hundred accountants would not be enough! If the need for accountancy is more pressing, then the other art is essentially inferior. Moreover, the welfare of (I, 97) the masses and the élite depends on accountancy; that goes for young and old, high and low. Prudent and experienced people have always urged their sons and those in their care to learn accountancy, saying to them: 'Then you will have your bread and butter (*huwa sallat al-khubz*)'[5]. Everyone says so. Whoever expresses what he wants to say ungrammatically, with distorted or misplaced wording, yet makes himself understood and thus achieves his intention by informing the other, has done enough. Whatever exceeds that which is enough is superfluous, and what is superfluous is largely dispensable; but the basic principle is very much wanted. Also, one of its bad aspects is that those employed at the Chancellery are always under suspicion and charged with evil things: al-Ḥasan Ibn Wahb, for instance, or Ibn Thawāba and both their families[6].

-- That was a shocking scene, said the vizier. What did you answer? -- I said: He left our session only after having been thoroughly humiliated and made contemptible. Thus fares he who blames the moon for its spots and the sun for its eclipse, who holds on to falsehood and supports him who speaks falsely, who falsifies truth and upbraids him who speaks truthfully. I said: Listen; what you say could be accepted if the drafting and fair-copying of letters and eloquence were detached from the art of accountancy, collection, correction, making final accounts (? *ᶜamal al-jamāᶜa*)[7] and expense accounts (? *ᶜaqd al-mu'āmara*)[8]. But since they are connected with it, part of it, and comprising all of it, how then can your opinion be consistent and your claim granted? Do you not know that working in (I, 98) those departments where the employees are solely occupied with accountancy requires the writing of letters in every branch of what they describe and deal with? They cannot even begin their work if they do not first present these letters, which are hinged on eloquent communication, clear exposition and lucid argumentation. All this is found with the chancery official whom you denounced with your backbitting. The departments that I have in mind are well known and their activities well-defined. I will enumerate them for you, that you may know that you are wrong and straying from the truth.

They are[9]: the Army Department, the Treasury, the Office of Caliphal Decisions (or the Caliphal Cabinet, *dīwān al-tawqīᶜ wa-l-dār*) the Office of the Seal, the Archives (*dīwān al-faḍḍ*)[10], the Office of Coinage and Standards (*dīwān al-naqd wa-l-ᶜiyār*), the Mint (*dūr al-ḍarb*)[11], the Department of Torts (*dīwān al-maẓālim*), the Department of Police and Militia (*dīwān al-shurṭa wa-l-aḥdāth*), and subsidiary departments such as those of taxes on specific crops[12], financial reports, unusual events and dates (*bāb al-nawādir*[13] *wa-l-tawārīkh*), the administration of letters and the departmental sessions, and so forth and so on.

An accountancy official must know about the different types of revenue so that, after levying and collecting them, he can work at his computations on them. But he can levy taxes only by means of eloquent letters with cogent arguments and employing various subtleties. Among these (sources of wealth)[14] are *fay'* -- that is:

land conquered by unconditional surrender -- , land conquered by conditional surrender, the cultivation of virgin land, fiefs, the leader's share of the booty, payment of a fixed part of the crops (*al-muqāsama*), taxes (*waḍā'i^c*), (I, 99) poll-tax paid by non-Muslims, charitable gifts (*ṣadaqāt*) consisting of camels and large or small cattle, 'fifths' of spoils, minerals, treasure-troves, buried money and what comes from the sea, tithes exacted from passing merchants, found property, stray animals, legacies without heirs, and money paid as a charitable gift -- and all the other things one needs to know about in official correspondence according to the customary prescriptions and the normal procedures, such as when an agreement is composed concerning the improvement of the Postal Service, or the distribution of irrigation water, or a letter concerning buildings (or: cultivation, *fi l-^cimāra*) and the restoration of its deficiencies, or concerning the estimation of the yield of crops and threshing, or concerning buckets, water wheels and water scoops (*al-dawālī wa-l-dawālīb wa-l-gharrāfāt*), or concerning *al-qalb wa-l-qisma* (?)[15], or the assessment of early vegetables, or land-measuring, or water-dividing dams (*al-ṭarāz*), or poll-tax paid by 'émigrés' (*al-jawālī*)[16], or the collecting of prescribed alms, or the 'opening' of land-taxes (*iftitāḥ al-kharājāt*)[17], and all the other kinds of letters such as are written by accountants.

Now when you say: 'All this (viz. eloquence, etc.) can be dispensed with', you are presumptuous and you lie. For if money circulates and flows abundantly and accrues in plenty to the various departments, then this is either mostly due to eloquence, or more evidently effected by accountancy, or by both in equal measure. In no circumstance is a civil servant perfect, or deserving of the name 'civil servant', unless he takes (I, 100) all this upon himself, combining it with some principles of jurisprudence mixed with their applications, and verses of the Koran joined with a sound understanding of them, and many different bits of information on all kinds of subjects, so that he is well-prepared when he needs them; as well as proverbs, apt lines of verse, striking passages in prose, well-known experiences and memorable sessions; together with a hand-writing like cast gold and a diction like embroidered tissue. Therefore one rarely finds anyone who is perfect in this art. Our friends said: We believe that all this was combined only in Ja^cfar Ibn Yaḥyā[18]; for his writing (*kitābatuhu*) was that of the Sawād (i.e. that of Iraq), his eloquence that of Saḥbān[19], his art of government Greek, his education (erudition and good manners, *ādāb*) Arab, and his character Iraqi[20].

Do you not see that accountancy is submerged by the flood of all these subjects? Furthermore, you must know that an eloquent man lets his intellect dictate his eloquence, which he derives from a sound discernment. Accountancy plays no part in this. If someone were to think that government is hinged upon accountancy, he is right; but it comes after the eloquence of the letter-writer, because the ruler commands, forbids, cajoles, orates, argues, rebukes[21)], threatens promises, warrants, raises hopes, gives assurance of expectations, eliminates harmful matters, lets his subjects taste the sweetness of justice and wards off from them the bitterness of oppression. Then he raises taxes. And when he does so, he needs accountancy in order to know the total returns; he has the work divided among his accountants, in order to ensure against any mistakes.

Now look and see how different is the status of the two arts, and how one of the two can be more excellent. If you were fair you would realize that the art (of governing) combines both things, i.e. accountancy and eloquence. One cannot just split an art into two halves and proclaim one half to be nobler than the other.

(I, 101) As for your words: 'one of the two arts is mere fun, the other serious' -- there you let yourself say a bad thing about eloquence indeed. It is serious: it gathers the fruits of reason, because it declares the truth to be true and falsehood to be false, as things ought to be. Proclaiming falsehood as true or truth as false may happen for diverse purposes or a concurrence of circumstances[22)], on account of the good and evil things that this world is never free from: pride and submissiveness, obedience and disobedience, justice and iniquity, unbelief and belief. Necessity calls for someone who practises eloquence, who lays down rules of wisdom, who is capable of clear exposition and oratory. One is defined by reason, the other by practice[23)].

As for your words: 'letter-composing is an art that has no known principles, whereas accountancy has a well-known starting-point': that is a stupid lie[24)]. For its starting-point is reason, its pathway is expression in spoken words and its fixed abode is in writing. By your words you prove that you yourself lack insight in this noble starting-point, this ethereal first principle[25)].

As for your saying that 'eloquence is mere ornamentation, resembling a *fata morgana*': we have made it sufficiently clear to you. If it is not enough, you are in need of more clear evidence.

As for your saying that 'those who practise it are considered foolish': that is a horrid thing to say. If only you knew the truth you would not have uttered a word of what you said, for in doing so you revile the pious former generations at the beginning of Islam. If an eloquent man must be called foolish when he is an intelligent being, then someone who cannot express himself properly ought to be called intelligent when he is stupid; and that is absurd[26)].

(I, 102) As for your saying: 'chancery officials, schoolteachers and grammarians are brothers in their inarticulateness': it is only from teachers, scholars and grammarians that people learn, even though on rare occasions one may find among them one who is not proficient.

As for your saying that 'one single chancery official would be sufficient': there you are right. That is to say that the power of this single person is equivalent to that of many individuals, and that all these individuals cannot counterbalance this single person. It is an argument against your point of view, not in favour of it. But it remains for you to understand that you are more in need of shoe-makers than of perfume vendors: this does not show that a shoe-maker is nobler than a perfume vendor, or a perfume vendor lowlier than a shoe-maker. There are fewer doctors than tailors, and we need them[27)] more; it does not follow that a doctor is lowlier than a tailor.

As for your saying: 'people have always urged their sons to learn accountancy saying: "Then you will have your bread and butter": it is as you say, because it is generally needed, for young and old. The noblest people require the noblest arts. The highest ranking person is the sovereign; he needs someone who is eloquent, who can make drafts and fair copies of letters. For he is the tongue that he speaks with, the eye he sees with, the confidant from whom he derives opinions and insight in all affairs. It is not fitting that, in this quality, he should have partners, for he carries secrets, is told things that should remain concealed, and to him are imparted the innermost thoughts.

As for your saying: 'whoever expresses whatever he wants to say ungrammatically, with distorted wording, yet makes himself understood, has done enough': how can this judgment be correct and this view be accepted? The meaning of what is said changes when the desinential inflection (*al-iᶜrāb*) is different, just as its function (*al-ḥukm fīh*)[28] changes when the nouns are different, and the denotation (*al-mafhūm*) changes when the verbs are different, and just as the sense (*al-maᶜnā*) is altered when the particles (*al-ḥurūf*) are different. A certain man in al-Rayy[29)], a nobly situated, high-ranking and self-important person, once said: 'Sit down and dine on me (*tataghaddā binā*)'[30)]. He meant to say 'and dine with me (*tataghaddā maᶜanā*)'. Look at the absurdity he produced with his words (I, 103) and how he, in his ignorance, missed the mark. There are many similar instances that are not hidden from you, nor are you above them (? *li-hādhā naẓā'ir ghayr khāfiya ᶜalayk walā sāqiṭa dūnak*).

The nobility of eloquence is sufficiently shown by the fact that you could only run it down by means of eloquence. Only through its power could you hit upon things to speak against it. See how you have found in its being independent in itself a means to belittle it and to belittle other things beside it[31] -- an extraordinary and strange thing!

As for your saying: 'one of its bad aspects is that those who practise it are under suspicion and mentioned discreditably': this deserves no answer. The sun is not harmed by the barking of dogs. It were better to safeguard one's tongue from such words. God, the Exalted One, said: 'And when the ignorant address them, they say: "Peace"'[32]. ᶜUmar Ibn al-Khaṭṭāb -- may God be pleased with him -- said: 'Even though a man were straighter than an arrow-shaft, someone will be found who slanders him'. The families of Ibn Wahb and Ibn Thawāba were too noble, too virtuous and too intelligent to be suspected of what (even) base slaves, stupid people, the rabble and riff-raff would not be suspected of. In fact, we have heard these things only in the circle of Ibn ᶜAbbād[33], from him and those who curry his favour[34] and seek to ingratiate themselves by such stories. Because he envies them their craft he incites those people to tell these lies about them. It is strange that he seems to think that lying about others can dispel the truth about himself. It would be more fitting and more decorous if he kept his tongue, his circle, his 'school' (*madhhabahu*) and his fatherhood (? *ubuwwatahu*) clear of it. But whenever good fortune and power have no intellect to rule them, no prudence to guard them, nor firm religion or straight path, they do everything by halves; one is forsaken by them and not supported by them. God save us from a good fortune that turns into affliction! Welcome to an affliction that engenders vigilance and purifies any shortcomings! But who can drink without getting drunk and inebriated? Who, being drunk, can be reasonable? And who, sobered up, is not left with a hangover that splits the head and eases the way for the Whisperer[35]?

(I, 104) -- That, said the Vizier, was a good rebuttal for someone with such presumptions and who behaves like that. How did you do it? Why don't you have a chat with the head of some Department or other? Why are you content with your present situation[36]?

-- I am a man, I answered, who is dominated by his love of well-being. I am gladly content with little things.

-- You hint at laziness, said the Vizier, when you speak of 'love of well-being', and at lowliness when you say you are happy with insignificant things.

-- If I can achieve well-being only through lowliness, I replied, and comfort only through laziness, then welcome to them both.

-- Everyone, said the Vizier, has his own view, his choice,

his habits, a place where he grew up, and his own intimate and familiar friends; he would be distressed if he were forcibly removed from it all; he would be frightened if he were compelled to live in other circumstances. I think it must be the middle of the night.

-- Possibly, I said.

-- Good night, he said. There is one question I have kept back from you; I shall bring it up another time, if God wills.

Then I left".

This seventh night in *al-Imtāᶜ* is flanked by two well-known disputes: the discussion of the supperiority of the Arabs over the non-Arabs[37)] and the debate between the grammarian and the logician[38)]. In all three debates the opponents are unevenly matched: the superiority of the Arabs is defended most eloquently by a non-Arab; the blundering logician has no chance against the grammarian. Similarly, the 'accountant' is not given a fair opportunity to play a convincing Socrates *vis-à-vis* al-Tawḥīdī's Gorgias.

The contrast between *balāgha*, 'eloquence', and *ḥisāb*, 'computation, arithmetic', might suggest that the dispute is one of the Arts vs. the Sciences[39)]. But it is not that. It is, first of all, a comparison of two types of civil servants, the accountant and the chancery scribe. Al-Tawḥīdī grants that both are necessary and complementary in a well-functioning government. That the accountant gets the worst of it is the result of al-Tawḥīdī's one-sided presentation of the arguments provoked perhaps by the spiteful and not very adroit attack by Ibn ᶜUbayd -- if his words are recorded truthfully by al-Tawḥīdī.

At the same time, the inclusion of the debate in *al-Imtāᶜ* is itself a playful provocation. Al-Tawḥīdī dedicated his book to his friend Abū l-Wafā' al-Būzjānī, one of the greatest of Arab mathematicians[40)]; the author, moreover, of *al-Manāzil fīmā yaḥtāj ilayh al-kuttāb wa-l-ᶜummāl min al-ḥisāb*, 'The Stations; or, All that Civil Servants and Financial Administrators Ought to Know about Arithmetic'[41)]. In his dedication al-Tawḥīdī quotes, with obvious approval, at some length the advice given to him by Abū l-Wafā', in the course of which he warns him '... not to become enamoured of diction (*lafẓ*) at the expense of sense (*maᶜnā*), nor *vice versa*; keep aloof from specialists in eloquence and letter-composition (*aṣḥāb al-balāgha wa-l-inshā'*), for their art lacks a number of things for which other people are blamed. You are not one of them, so do not resemble them, do not follow their methods, do not weave on their loom ...'[42)].

The defence of these very specialists in eloquence must be read in the light of this passage: the defence is partly undermined from the beginning. Al-Tawḥīdī followed the advice of his friend in more than one way. Although his style is highly eloquent, it is very different from the ornate rhymed prose current among the professional epistolographers of his time. Moreover, at the end of the nightly session he reaffirms his aloofness from a career as a chancery official. Rather than fawning upon the head of some Department, to ask for a job, as the vizier suggested, he remains poor: the last part of *al-Imtāᶜ* is formed by a letter addressed to Abū l-Wafā' in which he begs him for help: 'rescue me from beggary ... how much longer must I eat dry morsels and wilted vegetables, and wear patched clothes ...?[43]). Apparently, for Abū l-Wafā' *ḥisāb* had indeed turned out to be *sallat al-khubz*, and this argument in favour of learning accountancy adduced by Ibn ᶜUbayd is, as it happens, the only one that al-Tawḥīdī readily accepts. A passage in a treatise against the *kātib*s, *Dhamm akhlāq al-kuttāb*, attributed to al-Jāḥiẓ, points at the paradox that 'those most noble among them earn the lowest salaries ...; the Head of the Chancellery earns one tenth of the salary of the Head of the Land Tax Department, and a letter-writer (*muḥarrir*) whose handwriting represents the beauty of caliphal letters, earns a fraction of the salary of a copyist in the Land Tax Department'[44]).

The victory of eloquence is qualified in yet another sense: in order to be perfect -- indeed, to deserve the name at all -- a civil servant (*kātib*) must have a truly encyclopaedic knowledge; at least, this is implied in al-Tawḥīdī's words. Small wonder, then, that perhaps only one man ever met with this condition. But there were at least some who claimed competence in both fields: Abān al-Lāḥiqī (d.c. 200/815), a well-known poet, described himself as a *kātib ḥāsib, adīb khaṭīb*[45]).

Summing up, the debate has one unambiguous and unqualified victor: Abū Ḥayyān al-Tawḥīdī, speaking for no one but himself. His proficiency in the dispute seems to serve successfully as a plea for preferment, comparable to the function, perhaps, of the Middle English debate of *The Owl and the Nightingale*[46]). But the supreme moment of al-Tawḥīdī's victory occurs when he spurns the preferment when it is offered[47]).

Notes

1) The vizier Abū ʿAbd Allāh al-Ḥusayn Ibn Aḥmad Ibn Saʿdān, executed in 375/985, at the order of the Buyid ruler Ṣamṣām al-Dawla. Abū Ḥayyān al-Tawḥīdī (who died at an advanced age after 1010, perhaps as late as 414/1023), one of the greater writers of Arabic prose, wrote *al-Imtāʿ wa-l-muʾānasa* about a thousand and one years ago, in 984 or 985 (see Marc Bergé in *BEO* vol. 29, 1977, p. 59); it consists of the description of thirty-nine nightly sessions in the company of the vizier (The editors count forty nights; but compare vol. 1 pp. 159 and 195 with p. 198, note). Each night is devoted to one or more of a wide-ranging variety of subjects, including philosophical, religious, linguistic, biological and literary themes. The work was edited by Aḥmad Amīn and Aḥmad al-Zayn (3 vols., Cairo 1939-1953). On al-Tawḥīdī, see e.g. the article 'Abū Ḥayyān al-Tawḥīdī' by S.M. Stern in *EI*2 and the many studies on him by Marc Bergé, such as his *Pour un humanisme vécu: Abū Ḥayyān al-Tawḥīdī. Essai sur la personalité morale, intellectuelle et littéraire d'un grand prosateur et humaniste arabe* (Collection IFEA), Damascus 1977.
2) A civil servant (*kātib*) mentioned several times in *al-Imtāʿ* (i, 48, 61, ii, 9, 146, 192, 201, iii, 74). Perhaps he is identical with Abū (sic) ʿUbayd, a Christian *kātib* mentioned by al-Tawḥīdī in his *Mathālib al-wazīrayn* (= *Mathālib*), ed. Ibrāhīm al-Kaylānī, Damascus s.d., p. 93 (he is praised for his eloquence!). Both here and in *Imtāʿ*, i, 61 the *kātib* gives his opinion of the style of Ibn ʿAbbād (on whom see note 33).
3) On the difference between *inshāʾ* and *taḥrīr*, see Abū ʿAbd Allāh Muḥammad Ibn Aḥmad al-Khwārazmī, *Mafātīḥ al-ʿulūm* (= *Mafātīḥ*), ed. G. van Vloten, Leiden 1895, p. 78.
4) The exact meanings are not clear to me. On the various kinds of *kātib*, see for instance al-Bayhaqī, *al-Maḥāsin wa-l-masāwīʾ*, Beirut 1970, pp. 418-420 (the same in al-Tanūkhī, *al-Faraj baʿd al-shidda*, Cairo 1955, pp. 241-243, translated by A.F.L. Beeston in *Journal of Arabic Literature* vol. 2, 1971, pp. 4ff., Ibn ʿAbd Rabbih, *al-ʿIqd al-farīd*, vol. 4, Cairo 1948-1953, pp. 176-178), Abū Ṭāhir al-Baghdādī, *Qānūn al-balāgha*, in *Rasāʾil al-bulaghāʾ*, ed. Muḥammad Kurd ʿAlī, Cairo 1954, pp. 428-430; and cf. *BEO* vol 14, 1952-1954, pp. 149f.), al-Khwārazmī, *op. cit.*, pp. 53ff.; Isḥāq Ibn Ibrāhīm Ibn Wahb, *al-Burhān*, Cairo 1969, pp. 254-362. The 22nd *maqāma* by al-Ḥarīrī contains a dispute on the merits of the 'accountants' *v.* the 'composers' or 'scribes of composition' (see Th. Chenery's translation in *The Assemblies of al-Ḥarîri*, vol. 1, London 1867, pp. 229ff.).
5) Literally, it is a 'bread-basket'; perhaps to be connected with the expression *salat al-khayr* that appears in al-Tanūkhī, *op. cit.*, p. 240 (al-Bayhaqī, *op. cit.*, p. 417 has *sallat al-dunyā*, and al-Sharīshī, *Sharḥ Maqāmāt al-Ḥarīrī*, Beirut 1979 (repr.), vol. 2, p. 195: *surrat al-dunyā*, in the correponding place).
6) Al-Ḥasan Ibn Wahb, *kātib* and poet, was arrested, fined and imprisoned in 229/844. Several of his relations had high positions. For a genealogy and survey, see H. Ritter, *Die Geheimnisse der Wortkunst*, Wiesbaden 1959, pp. 6-8. Aḥmad Ibn Muḥammad Ibn Thawāba died in 277/890 or 273/886, see *EI*2, s.v., on him and his family. On both families, see also D. Sourdel, *Le vizirat ʿabbaside de 749 à 936*, Damas 1959-1960, index.
7) Cf. *Mafātīḥ*, p. 56; C.E. Bosworth, "Abū ʿAbdallāh al-Khwārazmī on the technical terms of the secretary's art" in *JESHO* vol. 12, 1969, p. 124.
8) Cf. *Mafātīḥ*, p. 56; Bosworth, *op. cit.*, p. 126.
9) The names and the order of the following list is almost exactly identical with that in *Ṣanʿat al-kitāba* by Qudāma Ibn Jaʿfar (d. after 320/932), see Badawī Ṭabāna, *Qudāma Ibn Jaʿfar wa-l-naqd al-adabī*, Cairo 1954, p. 86. Qudāma's work was known to al-Tawḥīdī,

see *Imtāᶜ*, ii, 145. On the various *dīwān*s see e.g. *EI*², s.v.; F. Løkkegaard, *Islamic Taxation in the Classical Period with special reference to circumstances in Iraq*, Copenhagen 1950, index.
10) See *EI*², s.v. 'Dīwān', p. 325b, Løkkegaard, *op. cit.*, pp. 150f.
11) Qudāma's list has *al-nuqūd wa-l-ᶜiyār wa-l-awzān wa-dīwān al-ṣarf*.
12) *bāb al-ᶜayn*; see the note of the editors of the *Imtāᶜ*.
13) The editors suggest reading *taqādīr* 'estimates'.
14) On the *wujūh al-amwāl*, see e.g. Abū Bakr Muhammad Ibn Yaḥyā al-Ṣūlī, *Adab al-kuttāb*, Cairo 1341/1922, pp. 198 ff., Isḥāq Ibn Ibrāhīm Ibn Wahb, *op. cit.*, pp. 307ff., A. Ben Shemesh, *Taxation in Islam* vol. 2, Leiden-London 1965, passim.
15) I do not know the meaning of these terms in this context.
16) See *EI*², s.v. 'djawālī' and 'djizya' esp. p. 561a.
17) *Mafātīḥ*, p. 60; Bosworth, *op. cit.*, pp. 134f.
18) The famous Barmakid vizier, executed by Hārūn al-Rashīd in 187/803.
19) Saḥbān Ibn Wā'il, proverbially eloquent pre-Islamic orator.
20) Al-Sawād "the dark land", is the cultivated part of al-ᶜIrāq (Lower Mesopotamia); but here the implied distinction between *sawādī* and *ᶜirāqī* escapes me.
21) Reading *yuᶜannif*, with the errata by Muhammad Kurd ᶜAlī.
22) The editor has *li-aghrāḍ takhtalif wa-aghrāḍ ta'talif*; I prefer to read *wa-aᶜrāḍ ta'talif*.
23) *Wa-hādha huwa ḥadd al-ᶜaql wa-l-ākhar ḥadd al-ᶜamal*: presumably the true representation of facts is contrasted with diverging from the truth, for practical reasons, as described. Alternatively, eloquence is associated with reason and intellect, accountancy with practical affairs.
24) *kharifta*; Muḥammad Kurd ᶜAlī prefers *kharaqta* (errata).
25) *hādhā l-awwal al-laṭīf*: the neo-Platonic connotations are clear, as often in al-Tawḥīdī's writings.
26) The logic of this passage does not seem quite impeccable.
27) "them" is ambiguous; apparently the tailors are meant.
28) On *ḥukm* as a term used by the grammarians, see *EI*², s.v.
29) Possibly Ibn al-ᶜAmīd or Ibn ᶜAbbād; see below, note 33.
30) Read, with the errata, *tataghaddā* instead of *tataghadhdhā*.
31) A pun (*fī stiqlālihā ... yuqilluhā*).
32) Koran 25:64.
33) The famous vizier and man of letters, d. 385/995. Against him and his predecessor Ibn al-ᶜAmīd al-Tawḥīdī wrote his infamous *Mathālib* (or *Akhlāq*) *al-wazīrayn*, a masterpiece of prose invective, any copy of which was certain to bring bad luck to its owner, according to Ibn Khallikān, *Wafayāt al-aᶜyān*, vol. 5, Beirut 1972, p. 113. Ibn ᶜAbbād "used to invent all sorts of sordid and obscene stories about the Thawāba family" (*Mathālib*, p. 122).
34) *yaḥuṭṭ fī hawāh*; the emendation made by the editors (*yakhbiṭ fī hawāh*) is justly rejected by Muṣṭafā Jawād (see appendix to vol. 3).
35) *al-Waswās*: the Devil; or any delusion, anxiety, obsession or melancholy.
36) Literally, "with these clothes", not necessarily a metaphor. *Kātib*s usually wore the *durrāᶜa* or the *ṭaylasān*. See *EI*², s.v. 'kātib', Ibn al-Mudabbir, *al-Risāla al-ᶜadhrā'*, ed. by Zakī Mubārak, Cairo 1931, pp. 8f., M.M. Ahsan, *Social Life under the Abbasids (170-289 AH / 786-902 AD)*, London - New York 1979, pp. 29, 40, 55, etc.
37) The sixth night, cf. summaries in *Islamica* vol. 2, 1926-1927, pp. 380-390 by D.S. Margoliouth; in *Ar* vol. 19, 1972, pp. 165-176, by Marc Bergé, and in Ilse Lichtenstadter, *Introduction to Classical Arabic Literature*, New York 1974, pp. 353-357, by J. Damis.
38) The eight night, cf. *JRAS* 1905, pp. 79-129 (D.S. Margoliouth), *Ar* vol. 25, 1978, pp. 310-323 (Taha Abderrahmane).
39) Thus e.g. Bergé in *BEO* vol. 25, 1972, p. 98, n., and p. 102.
40) See *EI*², s.v. "Abū '1-Wafā' al-Būzadjānī"; Fuat Sezgin, *Geschichte des arabischen Schrifttums*, vol. 5: *Mathematik*, Leiden 1974, pp. 321-325.

41) For a list of contents see Ibn al-Nadīm, *al-Fihrist*, ed. G. Flügel, Leipzig 1871-1872, p. 283; F. Woepcke in *JA*, 1885, pp. 246-250. A similar work is the subject of Cl. Cahen, "Quelques problèmes économiques et fiscaux de l'Iraq buyide d'après un traité de mathématiques" in *AIEO* vol. 10, 1952, pp. 326-363 (republished in Cl. Cahen, *Les peuples musulmans dans l'histoire médiévale*, Damas 1977, pp. 366-403).

42) *Imtāᶜ*, i, 10.

43) *Imtāᶜ*, iii, 226, 227.

44) Al-Jāḥiẓ, *al-Rasā'il*, ed. by ᶜAbd al-Salām Muḥammad Hārūn, Cairo, s.d., vol. 2, p. 205. The authorship of al-Jāḥiẓ is uncertain.

45) Ibn al-Muᶜtazz, *Ṭabaqāt al-shuᶜarā'*, ed. ᶜAbd al-Sattār Aḥmad Farrāj, Cairo 1968, p. 202; cf. S.A. Bonebakker, "Early Arabic Literature and the term *adab*" in *Jerusalem Studies in Arabic and Islam* vol. 5, 1984, p. 401. On the encyclopaedic knowledge required of the complete *kātib*, see e.g. ᶜAbd al-Ḥamīd Ibn Yaḥyā, *Risāla ilā l-kuttāb*, in *Rasā'il al-bulaghā'*, ed. Muḥammad Kurd ᶜAlī, Cairo 1954, p. 225 (cf. Rosenthal's translation of Ibn Khaldūn's *Muqaddima*, vol. 2, Princeton 1967, pp. 30 f.); Ibn Qutayba, *ᶜUyūn al-akhbār*, vol. 1, Cairo 1925, pp. 44 f.; al-Ghazālī, *Counsel for Kings (Naṣīḥat al-mulūk)*, transl. F.R.C. Bagley, London 1971, p. 114; C.E. Bosworth, "A *maqāma* on secretaryship: al-Qalqashandī's *al-Kawākib al-durriyya fī'l-manāqib al-Badriyya*" in *BSOAS* vol. 27, 1964, pp. 291-298.

46) Kathryn Hume, *The Owl and the Nightingale: The Poem and its Critics*, Toronto - Buffalo 1975, pp. 5, 119, 131 f.

47) This article is dedicated (without any plea for preferment or remuneration) to Prof. Dr. J.H. Hospers. The *munshi'*, the *muᶜallim* and the *naḥwī* are brothers, says Ibn ᶜUbayd, in their deplorable use of language. Hans Hospers combines in his person the qualities of the *naḥwī*, as a linguist who knows not only linguistics but languages, the *muᶜallim*, teacher, and the *munshi'* ('moonshee'), letter-writer, as Head of Department in a world where men of letters and accountants are more at variance with each other than ever before. As for *rakāka*, he is the living refutation of Ibn ᶜUbayd.

Signum Ignis Signum Vitae

Lamps in Ancient Israelite Tombs

C.H.J. de Geus, Groningen

Hans Hospers will always remain my teacher and mentor, even though I have been a member of his staff now for almost a quarter of a century. I have vivid memories of Professor Hospers in the old Workroom for Semitic Studies, high up in the Academiegebouw, the central building of the University of Groningen. Among glass show-cases displaying archaeological finds, shelves of books written in exotic scripts, pale and bizarre but undoubtedly very bright students and - of course - the mummy, there above the Aula sat the Semitist of Groningen. Hospers gave his lectures from amidst the antiquities, as if he himself formed a part of them. Only a few weeks passed by before I realized that this first impression, that had in fact been strengthened by the stories of older students, was nevertheless totally wrong. In the first place Professor Hospers turned out to be much, much younger than his appearance suggested, but in addition it became clear that he had a sparkling sense of humour and a lively and inquiring mind, that had nothing to do with mummies. Finally it soon became evident that Hospers did indeed take his seat among the archeological miscellanea and was supposed to teach about them - which he faithfully and scrupulously did - but that his interest in these dead objects was in fact very slight.

Although I was very pleased at the beginning of the 1970's when we were able to move into the spacious Institute for Semitic Studies in the Oude Boteringestraat, I was very sad to have to leave behind the beautiful oaken show-cases, each with glass at the top and three deep drawers underneath. As a result of this it was no longer possible to keep all of the collection available for display, so part of it was put away 'for the meantime' in boxes in the loft. For many years I have tried to establish a modern storage system that would make available also the less spectacular items of the collection, such as the sherds, but my efforts have always been thwarted. This sherd collection was collected largely by myself, but also includes material collected by Han Drijvers in Palmyra and especially a few

boxes with large sherds that were collected by the founder of our institute, Professor Dr. F.M.Th. de Liagre Böhl, from what was formerly Palestine. For De Liagre Böhl had participated in the excavation of Shechem under the direction of Ernst Sellin, in the years 1926, 1927 and 1928[1]. During those years Böhl also visited other excavations that were then in progress, notably that of W.F. Albright who was then digging in the far south at Tell Beit Mirsim, and that of E. Grant at Beth-Shemesh, to the west of Jerusalem at the foot of the Judaean hills. A memento of each of these visits still exists in the form of a box of sherds.
In addition, the collection of the Institute for Semitic Studies includes a group of eighteen earthenware lamps, almost without exception late Judaean. Fifteen specimens are marked with the letters '*B S*', which should probably be interpreted as 'Beth-Shemesh'. They must have been acquired or bought by Böhl. In view of the good state of preservation of most of the lamps it may be presumed that they come from rock-cut tombs, and probably from the series of late Judaean tombs that had been found already in 1911-1912 by D. Mackenzie, and that were studied once again, if I presume correctly, in 1928 by Grant. It is also well possible that these lamps did not come from regular excavations at all, but that they were bought by Böhl from the local population. In that case the origin of the lamps is unknown. In any case they form a fine series, like the series of water decanters or jugs, that Böhl also brought to Groningen. Fortunately, these jugs are on display.

It is well known that intact objects made of earthenware mainly come from tombs. For in the layers of a Palestinian settlement mound (*tell*) the pressure increases to such an extent that ewers, pots or lamps almost always collapse, if indeed they had not been broken already by the original devastation or catastrophe. Fortunately, complete specimens are often found that can be restored into whole objects. But the intact objects that are to be seen in museums and that are still offered for sale by dealers originate almost without exception from tombs. Moreover, the ancient tombs that were hacked out of the rock can conveniently be excavated clandestinely. In these burial chambers, such as those that were customary in Israel in the Bronze Age and the Iron Age, a relatively high proportion of objects have been preserved intact, because the problem of 'pressure' did not occur there.
In view of the type of the lamps, it is clear that they did not come from Böhl's excavation at Shechem[2]. It is certainly not so that lamps belong to the most frequently occurring finds in the excavation

of a settlement. Lamps were by no means as often a normal household item as we might think. Unfortunately, most of the excavation reports give very few precise numbers, and furthermore it is often impossible to ascertain from excavation reports exactly where, in which room, a ewer or lamp was found. In most cases the only objects described in publications were those that could be restored into whole specimens. In any case that was how the situation used to be. In later publications a more or less reliable indication of *locus* is given. Seeing that by far the greatest quantity of earthenware is found in the form of sherds, probably broken already in ancient times, it is still impossible to say how many lamps belonged to the average inventory of an average household. On the basis of the specimens that can be restored and the recognizable fragments, we may assume that this number was fairly small, certainly if we compare the lamps with the huge numbers of jugs or cooking pots[3)]. Consequently one gets the impression that in ancient Israel most activities ceased in the early evening when darkness fell, to be resumed the following morning in daylight. Notwithstanding, in Tenach it is assumed that lamps were present in every house[4)]. Also the numerous and popular metaphors with the word *nēr* are suggestive of the same. An archaic form *nīr* is even used exclusively figuratively, namely for the comparison of a living dynasty to a burning lamp[5)]. Seeing that Palestinian archaeologists undeniably show a preference for excavating larger houses of the four-room type[6)], the relatively small number of lamps that are found in excavations could be partly explained by the use of much more expensive bronze lamps precisely in these houses. Bronze objects are found far less often, because the metal kept its value and usefulness, even when the object itself was broken.

The illuminating effect of a lamp could be increased by having more than one spout, or by placing the lamp higher up, preferably on some kind of supporting stand. Such stands have been found, made out of earthenware as well as bronze. Such a stand is called *menōrā* in Hebrew. Since the stand does not have any function without the accompanying lamp on top of it, in Tenach the term *menōrā* is also used for the combination of stand with lamp. The list of items: bed, table, stool, *menōrā* in 2 Kings 4:10 indicates that a *menōrā* is regarded as a piece of furniture. Seeing that we are concerned here with the house of a well-to-do farming family, it may be presumed that the author has a bronze combination in mind. Ordinary earthenware objects, like the water decanter that was undoubtedly also present, were simply not mentioned.

In reconstructions of Israelite houses, one often sees a niche in the wall of the living room. In this niche there stands a lamp. This can be seen, for example, in the well known reconstruction of an Israelite house in the Ha'areẓ Museum in Tel Aviv. Since Israelite houses are never to be found with any walls still standing, this situation is purely hypothetical and has never been found in reality. We may assume that the niches were similar to the lamp-niches that are found in burial chambers (see below) and also in the wall of the great water tunnel of Gibeon[7)].

If we now confine ourselves from here on to the Iron Age tombs, we see once again that lamps belonged to the normal inventory of grave objects. We find the lamps in two contexts:
1) as burial finds, sometimes in remarkably large numbers;
2) as an architectonic detail in the design of the tombs.
Three examples will serve as illustrations.

A. David Ussishkin has published four tombs from the surroundings of Tel ᶜEton, 18 km southwest of Hebron[8)]. These are typical family tombs, cut out of the rock, dating from the Iron Age. The tombs contain the following standard elements: behind the tomb opening there are a few steps down, so that one descends into the tomb. After the two to four steps one enters a central burial chamber. Tomb 1 has two chambers, one behind the other. In the front chamber on the left and the right side an *arcosolium* is present in the side walls, in the back chamber an *arcosolium* is also present in the back wall, as well as on each side; therefore in total there are five *arcosolia*. In the back chamber there is a hole that served as a repository for bones and pottery, if there was no longer any room in the *arcosolia* for new interments. Tomb 2 has one large central burial chamber with four *arcosolia*, two on each side, one right behind the other. This tomb has been made with considerable technical precision. In front of the actual tomb opening there was still a short *dromos*. Tomb 3 was made much more roughly. Here too there are five *arcosolia*. Tomb 4 is the smallest: three *arcosolia* along the three walls of a small burial chamber. In tombs 1, 2 and 3 architectonic elements were found that are indicative of lamps: in tomb 1 on each side of the entrance a kind of supporting structure had been cut out and roughly hewn into the shape of a lion's head. These supporting structures are flat on top so that a lamp could be placed on them. On each side of the passage into the second chamber similar crudely made lion's heads are also present. Here too the top is flattened, and this flattened surface extends into a niche in the rock face: a distinct lamp-niche. In the elaborately made tomb 2 each *arcosolium* is provided with a lamp-niche in one of the side-walls (at the head- or foot-end). This tomb is oriented approximately sout-north. In the case of the first pair of *arcosolia* the lamp-niches are present in the sout walls, in the case of the latter pair, further back, the lamp-niches have been made in the north walls. In tomb 3 only one lamp-niche is present, situated in the right wall, exactly between two *arcosolia*. All four tombs had been plundered by the local villagers, i.e. all complete and sellable objects had been removed. Nevertheless, five lamps were found, in a fragmentary state: two from tomb 1, one from tomb 2 and two from tomb 3. All of the lamps had soot on the spout and had therefore been used. Two lamps (from grave 1 and 3) belong to the younger Judaean type with the high, solid foot[9].

B. Biran and Gophna published an undisturbed tomb that was found on the land of kibbutz Lahav , also in southern Judah[10]. In this context 'undisturbed' means: not disturbed by grave robbers. The ancient Israelite custom of interring the dead in family tombs with only a limited number of benches or *arcosolia*[11], caused serious disturbance of older burials, as will be made clear by the example of this tomb at Lahav. The tomb was found with the sealing-stone still *in situ*. The central burial chamber is small: 3 x 2.5 metres. There is only one bench against the back wall, 1.60 m wide, half a metre higher than the floor of the central chamber. On the bench there was thus room for two bodies. Indeed, two skeletons were found on top of it. On the left side of the bench a repository hole had been cut out. In the course of time this repository had become so filled, that at the edge of the bench a low wall of loose stones had been built up, so that behind it on the repository even more remains of earlier burials could be kept. On the bench, in addition to the two skeletons there were 27 objects, while on the floor of the burial chamber more than 100 objects were found, including fragments of five skulls. Apart from the bones, in the repository[12] there were numerous intact and restorable items of earthenware and bronze objects, including 34 bronze bracelets or anklets. In this tomb the total number of complete objects found was 350, of which 281 were made of earthenware. The total number of lamps found in this tomb amounted to 40: 15 in the repository, 25 elsewhere in the tomb. It is remarkable that all the lamps from the repository have a round (convex) or slightly flattened base, while the lamps from the burial chamber all have a flattened foot. The contents of the repository are clearly older than the rest of the inventory of the tomb. The most important find from the repository was that of the 16th lamp: a bronze specimen. This was standing next to an earthenware specimen, each in a small niche cut out when the repository was made. This repository hole thus did not belong to the oldest form of the tomb. It was made only when the tomb became too full and when it was no longer possible to simply move earlier burials into a corner. To make it possible to place the bones in the repository with some show of reverence, the two lamps were put in the niches. They probably already belonged to the tomb inventory. A remarkable find in the burial chamber was that of two iron two-pronged forks, comparable to the well known iron three-pronged forks from tombs at Lachish and Beth-Pelet. The inventory of this tomb spans a period lasting in all from the 9th to the 6th century B.C.

C. The third example is the tomb that in the meantime has become known as the tomb of Ḥami'ohel. So far this is the only undisturbed Iron Age tomb found in Jerusalem. It is a family tomb cut out from the west slope of Mount Zion in Jerusalem[13]. It was found in the course of road works when the modern road to Bethlehem was being widened. The name comes from a seal found in the tomb[14], and is completely arbitrary, since in this tomb the remains of no fewer than 43 individuals were found. Clearly we are concerned here, too, with a family tomb. The tomb consists of an oblong central burial chamber oriented north-south, in this case perpendicular to the entrance. Along the south and east wall (the back wall) there is a continuous bench. In the southeast corner the wall of the tomb curves round, and consequently the bench also. Left of the entrance, in the northern wall of the large oblong burial chamber, is a passage into a second chamber, which thus lies to the north of the first one. This northern chamber has a continuous bench along all three walls. Between these benches the burial chamber is so narrow as to be little more than a passage-way between the benches. In the first burial chamber, on the southern bench, the intact skeleton of the last interment was found. The skeleton was lying on its back, with the head towards the west. A second skeleton, from an earlier interment, lay behind the first, and had clearly been moved backwards. This second skeleton was lying with the head towards the east. On the eastern part of the bench, towards the back back wall of the tomb, no entire skeletons have been preserved, but the position of a number of skulls and long bones indicates that there too skeletons had been lying in an extended position. This burial position is in fact well known, especially around Jerusalem. A number of benches and *arcosolia* of Iron Age tombs around Jerusalem are provided with head-rests or hollows for the head to lie in. In a number of cases these occur alternately. The tomb has no repository. Remains of older interments were collected, and the skulls and long bones had been placed neatly on the floor of the grave, against the vertical face of the bench. It is remarkable that the row of skulls continues into the northern burial chamber, but that on the benches no human remains were found. Some pottery was found, also two iron arrowheads and the previously mentioned seal, but no bones. Were these benches used for the preparation of the bodies of the deceased, for washing, anointing or enshrouding? In connection with the subject of this contribution, the fascinating thing about this complete tomb is that all the skulls of the last interments, that were still lying on the benches, were consistently accompanied by an earthenware lamp. Only in the southeast corner, where the bench curves round, there stood two lamps together without any skulls. It is probable that these served primarily to illuminate the tomb.

Lamps thus belong to the normal inventory of tombs in Judah and Central Israel[15)]. Just as was the case in the houses, here too lamps are found relatively less frequently as the tombs become larger and more elaborate. This also applies to the lamp niches. Most of the monumental Iron Age tombs around Jerusalem, namely those on the land of the *École Biblique*[16)], do not have any lamp niches. Here too, as in the grander houses, bronze lamps on stands would have been used. The question that now arises is what could have been the function of the lamps in the tombs. I am somewhat hesitant to put this question, because so far no comprehensive study at all has been made on the subject of which objects are found in tombs and what their function was there. The lamps are only one element of the whole assemblage. But at the same time they form a very remarkable element, because they occur much more abundantly in tombs than in houses. Concerning those tombs for which the inventory of grave-goods has been preserved partly or wholly, one does not get the impression that the prominent Judaeans - for whom most of the burial chambers would have been intended - were customarily buried with their weapons, tools or instruments. The only personal belongings that we find are ornaments and seals. Also the typical earthenware female figurines, notably found in Jerusalem in alsmost every room of a dwelling[17)], hardly occur at all in tombs. There is thus a clear difference between the inventory of a house and that of a tomb.
The occurrence of lamps in tombs could be explained in different ways:

I Lamps were needed to illuminate the tomb during the actual burial and the preceding preparations

II Lamps may have played a role in the burial rites

III The deceased was provided with lamps, in the expectation that he would be entering a dark realm of the dead

IV There is always the possibility that the custom of placing lamps in tombs was so ancient and traditional that its original meaning was hardly understood anymore.

From the material presented here it is evident that the first explanation is insufficient. It does explain the presence of a number of lamps, but not why so many lamps were put in the tombs. Moreover the opening of most of the tombs is large enough to let in sufficient light to permit working in daylight at least in the first burial chamber. That lamps already present were used for this purpose during subsequent burials is almost self-evident. It is noteworthy that in the case of tomb 1 at Tel ᶜEton the lamps were placed next to the entrance, where daylight would certainly have provided enough illumination. On the other hand, the images of lions suggests that an apotropaic effect may have been intended. That explanation II could play a role in this connection is possibly evident from the occurrence of the iron forks in a number of tombs. It is generally assumed that these forks served to spike pieces of meat out of large pots (I Sam 2:13-14). Their presence in tombs could indicate that on the occasion of the burial a sacrificial or funeral meal was provided, probably in the immediate vicinity of the tomb. In the actual tombs there was not enough room. In a number of cases the remains or a part of this meal may have been given to the deceased, together with the fork used to spike it. On the other hand, the possibility cannot be excluded that the forks were provided as grave-goods to persons who had used them during their lifetime, thus to Levites and/or priests.

Ussishkin too has wondered whether the occurrence of the lamps and the lamp-niches could have something to do with a burial rite[18]. He thinks that "at the time of the burial a lamp was lit in memory of the deceased"[19]. In any case, the use of lamps in tombs fits in well with the biblical phraseology in which the life of man is compared to a burning lamp: Prov 20:27; 24:20. In tomb 1 with the *arcosolia* Ussishkin moreover found traces of a fire in all of the *arcosolia*, without any of the bones showing any traces of burning. He refers to the text 2 Chron 16:14, where the burial of Asa, King of Judah, is described: "... and (they) laid him in the bed which was filled with sweet odours and divers kinds of spices prepared by the apothecaries' art: and they made a very great burning for him".

The place of the lamps in the Jerusalem tomb suggests that lamps were always provided when a burial took place. Also the place of the lamp-niches in tomb 2 at Tel ᶜEton is indicative of this. I have already proposed that the deceased needed the lamp in the realm of the dead, and an extra argument in favour of this idea is the fact that lamps are also found in a few simple individual tombs dating from the Iron Age. Here we are concerned with a few simple cist graves from Lachish and Tel Zeror[20]. Unfortunately, no further details are given in the literature. But it is self-evident that it is senseless to reverently place a burning lamp in tombs that were filled up immediately afterwards. I have already pointed out that the life of man can be compared to a burning lamp. Similarly, death can be compared to the extinction of a lamp (2 Sam 21:17; Isa 42:3, 43:17). At the same time, the realm of the dead was certainly expected to be a place of darkness and gloom (Ps 143:3; Job 10:21-22, 38-17 *ṣlmwt* (!); cf. also Job 17:13). The texts concerned have already been collected by N.J. Tromp[21].

It can therefore be assumed that the three first explanations are applicable to some extent, but that especially the third one was decisive. Lamps were placed near the head of the deceased as a symbol of the ephemerality of life, but also to provide him with light on his journey to the realm of everlasting darkness. The presence of lamps in Israelite tombs illustrates something about their ideas concerning life and death.

Finally, it was known precisely in ancient Israel that also the world of the living can be dark. Therefore the word *nēr* also has a function in another metaphor, namely with God's Word and Law, which are a light for mankind. This simile is incorporated in the motto of our University: *Lucerna pedibus meis verbum tuum et lumen semitis meis* (Ps 119:105).

Notes

1) M.A. Beek in F.M.Th. de Liagre Böhl, *Opera Minora*, Groningen-Jakarta 1953, pp. x-xvi. For the excavations of Shechem by E. Sellin, cf. K. Jaroš, *Sichem* (*Orbis Biblicus et Orientalis*, vol. 11), Göttingen 1976; but see also my review of this work in *BiOr* vol. 39, 1982, pp. 206-207.
2) Sellin's excavations at Shechem were partly financed with Dutch funds. The greater part of Böhl's Shechem collection has found its way to the Rijksmuseum voor Oudheden, Leiden.
3) H.J. Franken, *Grondstoffen voor de materiele cultuur in Palestina en omliggende gebieden* (*Palaestina Antiqua*, vol. 1), Kampen 1982. Also R. Amiran and A. Eitan, "Notes on the functions of pottery-mending in excavations" in *PEQ* vol. 98, 1968, pp. 99-103.
4) The only study of the ancient Palestinian earthenware oil lamps is the one by R. Houston Smith, "The Household Lamps of Palestine in Old Testament Times" in *BiAr* vol. 27, 1964, pp. 2-31, 101-124 and vol. 29. 1966, pp. 2-27. The relevant Bible passages as well can be found in this study. Smith, however, treats the lamps only as such. Typological developments are discussed, but hardly their distinct functions and never their archaeological contexts (houses, tombs *etc.*). Much shorter but also much more up to date is the survey by Helga Weippert in *BRL*^{2}, Tübingen 1977, pp. 198-201.
5) 2 Kings 15:4; 11:36; 2 Kings 8:19 // 2 Chron 21:7. In Ps 132:17, the word *nēr* is used with this meaning.
6) C.H.J. de Geus, *De Israelitische Stad* (*Palaestina Antiqua*, vol. 3), Kampen 1984, especially chapter 5.
7) J.B. Pritchard, *The Water System of Gibeon* (*Museum Monographs*), Philadelphia 1961. Along the stairway to the spring and at the spring itself there are nine lamp niches. See plan on fig. 3 and photograph on fig. 11.
8) D. Ussishkin, "Tombs from the Israelite Period at Tell ^{c}Eton" in *Tel Aviv* vol. 1, 1974, pp. 109-127).
9) The 'official' name is: high disc base.
10) A. Biran and R. Gophna, "An Iron Age Burial Cave at Tell Ḥalif in *IEJ* vol. 20, 1970, pp. 151-169.
11) The use of the terminology 'bench' or *arcosolium* is not always consistent in archaeological publications. I use the word 'bench' when the ceiling of the burial chamber continues over the raised part of the floor alongside one or more walls, on which the body or bodies was or were laid, but the word *arcosolium* when this is not the case. Even when the separate ceiling over the big niche in the side-walls has not the form of an arch.
12) The publication does not inform us about the exact number of individuals of whom the remains were found on the floor or in the repository. Nor is any further anthropological information given, as to sex, age, health or general condition. It is therefore impossible to relate the number of burials to the number of lamps found in the tomb.
13) D. Davis and A. Kloner, "A Burial Cave of the Late Israelite Period on the Slopes of Mt. Zion" in *Qadmoniot* vol. 11, 1978, pp. 16-20 (in Hebrew). See now B. Arensburg and Y. Rak, "Jewish Skeletal Remains from the Period of the Kings of Judaea" in *PEQ* vol. 117, 1985, pp. 30-34.
14) The seal has the form of a scaraboid, and was carved out of bone. The seal bears the name of its owner and of her father. The composition is in three registers: the upper line has *l ḥ m y ' h l*; the middle one is a divider in the form of a beautiful fish. The bottom line reads: *b t m n ḥ m*..
15) Going northwards, the number of Iron Age tombs diminishes. There are hardly any Iron Age tombs from Galilee.
16) A publication of these tombs by G. Barkai is forthcoming in the *Biblical Archaeology Review*.
17) The City of David Excavations of the Hebrew University, Jerusalem. Oral communication by Prof. Dr Y. Shiloh.

18) *op. cit.*, pp. 123-126.
19) *op. cit.*, p. 125.
20) O. Tuffnel, *Lachiš*, vol. III (*The Iron Age*), London 1953. Tombs 132 and 189. K. Ohata, *Tel Zeror*, vol. II, Tokyo 1967, pp. 36-41. Tomb I at T. Zeror contained 3, tombs II and III 4 lamps each. Tomb 132 at Lachis also contained three lamps.
21) N.J. Tromp, *Primitive Conceptions of Death and the Netherworld in the Old Testament*, Rome 1969; esp. pp. 142-144.

Languages in Contact

The Case of Akkadian and Sumerian

G. Haayer, Groningen

The syntactic structure of a language at a given point in history is often the resultant of an internal diachronic development in that language and contact with another language[1]. The basic word order in Semitic Languages, and particularly in Akkadian, illustrates this process and provides a good example of the problems involved.

Most Ancient Semitic Languages - Hebrew, Aramaic, Ugaritic and Arabic - have V(erb) - S(ubject) - O(bject) as their basic word order. From this observation the convenient conclusion may be drawn that Proto-Semitic was a VSO type language. Virtually all Semitists seem to agree on that. However, there are at least two Semitic languages that manifestly do not have VSO basic word order.

The first is Amharic, a Semitic language spoken in Southern Ethiopia. Amharic in contrast to its parent language Ge'ez and its northern sisters Tigre and Tigrinya shows SOV basic word order[2]. It is generally agreed that this deviation from the general pattern results from syntactic interference of the neighbouring Cushitic languages, which have SOV basic word order. It is well known that long and intimate contact between languages may result in drastic changes in their phonology, morphology and lexicon. Syntactic changes in languages also are often due to interference of another language. Amharic is a clear example. The language is to a very large extent desemiticized, as may be seen on all levels of grammar and lexicon. We only mention here the rather unsemitic order of Adjective and Noun and the prenominal Genitive, obviously developed under Cushitic influence[3].

The second non-VSO Semitic language is Akkadian. Like Amharic it has SOV basic word order. Assyriologists take it for granted that this is due to the syntactic interference of the SOV language Sumerian[4]. Akkadian and Sumerian had been in close contact for probably a millennium before Sumerian ceased to be a living language at the end of the third millennium BC[5]. This contact has been very intimate, as can be judged from the vast amount of lexical borrowings of Akkadian words into Sumerian and vice versa. The question of whether Sumerian is responsible for SOV word order in Akkadian or not, is not as easy to answer as one might believe. It is quite possible that Akkadian had SOV word order before it came in contact with Sumerian only if we reject the latter possibility, and assume that Proto-Semitic was a VSO language, then we can safely hypothesize that Sumerian interference *caused* Akkadian to be a SOV language.

Evidence for the VSO hypothesis

However, what evidence do we have that Proto-Semitic was VSO? Not very much: in fact this assumption is solely based on the fact that most Semitic languages are VSO. This by no means constitutes a proof; rather it remains a mere plausibility. The oldest Akkadian data are the personal names from the tablets of Fara and Abū Ṣalābikh[6)]. Quite a number of these names belong to the type of 'sentence-names' e.g. the name *Iš-dup-Il* "God preserves (life)". These names put the verb in initial position followed by the subject. If we can accept proper names as evidence for basic word order, Akkadian of the Fara period would seem to have VSO word order. This would point to VSO word order for Proto-Akkadian and Proto-Semitic. However, there are good reasons not to accept proper names as evidence. First of all the occurence of such forms in Akkadian personal names must be taken as part of the formation of the Akkadian proper names, but not necessarily as an exemplary part of the Akkadian language, since the formation of proper names does not always follow the syntactic or morphological structure of the language[7)]. There is an even more compelling objection to the use of proper names from Fara and Abū Ṣalābikh as evidence. The scribes of the Fara period were using a peculiar writing system, in which it was not necessary to write the signs in the sequence demanded by grammar. A name written with the signs IŠ, DUB and IL occurs on the tablets as *iš:dup:il*, *il:dup:iš* and *il:iš:dup*, etc. From these spellings two meaningful names can be reconstructed: *iš-dup-il* which points to VSO and *il-iš-dup* which points to SOV word order. The fact that the same complex is to be read as *iš-dup-il* in Old Akkadian does not compel us to read it the same way in earlier periods.

The second oldest recorded Semitic language is Eblaic. As far as can be judged from the meagre data concerning word order, there is no clear evidence for an original VSO word order. Both VSO and SOV are attested and one might wonder whether Eblaic was in a transitionary stage, changing from either SOV to VSO or from VSO to SOV[8)]. Eblaic personal names often show VS word order but, as we have noted above, this can not be accepted as evidence. In any case, SOV word order is attested in Ebla and it is highly unlikely that Sumerian interference is responsible for this phenomenon, though an other unknown SOV language might have triggered the change from VSO to SOV. We simply do not know. Thus far the only evidence for the VSO hypothesis remains the fact that most Semitic languages do have VSO basic word order, but all these languages are younger than Akkadian and Eblaic.

In fact the VSO hypothesis for Akkadian is even highly unlikely. The majority of Akkadians lived outside the Sumerian speaking area, which was confined to Southern Babylonia. This would leave unexplained why the northern variants of Akkadian are SOV as well. Therefore I would like to present some argument in favour of the hypothesis that Proto-Semitic was SOV.

Evidence for the SOV hypothesis

An interesting theory favouring the SOV hypothesis was put forward by the American linguist T. Givón[9)]. The main purport of his theory is that the information about original word order is hidden in the sequence of subject and object agreement morphemes bound to the verb. His theory is based upon three assumptions. The first is that verb agreement affixes invariably develop diachronically from pronouns. The second is that bound morphemes invariably derive from independent, free morphemes. The third is that, once a sequence of words becomes fused together as a sequence of bound morphemes within a single word, the order of the morphemes is thereafter not subject to change. We may apply these assumptions to the Semitic verb. In Semitic the prefix conjugation (imperfect) is older than the suffix conjugation (perfect), which is a nominal sentence in origin. The prefix conjugation subject agreement prefixes *ju*, *ja/tu*, *ta*, etc. are dirived from independent personal pronouns, as Gelb has shown in his Sequential Reconstruction[10)]. Combining Givón's basic assumptions with Gelb's reconstructions, we can readily see that a verbal form such as *juštamhiru* reflects SOV word order. The form was analysed by Gelb as follows: *ju+šø+ta+møhir+u* i.e. "he (*ju*) caused it (*ša*) to be (*ta*) received (*mahir*)"[11)].

Givón's theory was heavily critized by B. Comrie, who argued mainly against Givón's claim that his assumptions could be generalized to all languages[12)]. Comrie's objections are certainly correct, because in many languages verb agreement affixes do not develop from pronouns (first assumption) and bound morphemes do not necessarily derive from independent words, but can be borrowed from other languages as well. In Semitic however, both subject and object agreement affixes derive from independent pronouns, so we may accept Givón's theory in spite of Comrie's scepticism.

Apart from the evidence provided by Givón's theory, there are other indications in favour of the SOV hypothesis. These indications may be extracted from the development of the Akkadian case system. The triptotic case system of Old Akkadian is a late development as Gelb has demonstrated[13]. It was preceded by a diptotic case system, which itself derived from an older postpositional system in Early East Semitic and Proto-Semitic[14]. Remnants of the old postpositions are attested in all Semitic languages, but especially in Akkadian and Eblaic the postpositional system is still productive, as can be seen in Old Akkadian where the locative postposition *-um* and the dative/terminative *-iš* are frequently used. The prepositional systems of both Akkadian and Eblaic differ considerably from the systems used in Arabic, Hebrew, Aramaic and Ugaritic[15]. This leads to the suspicion that prepositions had not developed in Proto-Semitic, and that they came into being rather late. On the basis of this observation we may posit that Proto-Semitic was basically a postpositional language. This observation is important, because it is a universal tendency that SOV languages strongly prefer postpositions[16].
Another characteristic of postpositional languages is that they often have an ergative system in contrast to prepositional languages that prefer to have a nominative/accusative system. Most ergative languages have SOV basic word order[17]. The combination of ergativity and postpositions in a single language points almost invariably to SOV basic word order. Are there any positive indications that suggest ergativity for Proto-Semitic? In order to answer this question we need to know the characteristic properties of an ergative language. One of the most characteristic features found in case marking in ergative languages is that the ergative case is often identical with another case, most often the genitive or instrumental, sometimes the locative or dative. In Sumerian, for instance, the ergative case is marked by the postposition -e, which is identical to the locative-terminative -e, and is in origin a deictic pronoun. In Akkadian the later nominative case ending *-um* is identical with the old locative postposition *-um*, or rather I assume they are identical. According to Gelb the nom. *-um* is to be distinguished from the locative *-ūm* by vocalic quantity. However, evidence from Arabic shows that the vowel is short; e.g. in *ba*ᶜ*du* and *taḫtu* the *u* is short and this *u* certainly derives from the Proto-Semitic locative postposition *-um*. Late plene spellings that indicate a long *ū* in *ūm* are not conclusive for the simple reason that it points to a late and secondary differentiation between the nominative and the locative[18]. The first to suggest that the identity of the locative and the nominative points to ergativity in Proto-Semitic was

Diakonoff[19]. I agree with him in this matter.

On the basis of these observations, the development of the Akkadian case system can be schematized as follows[20]:

Proto-Semitic	*East Semitic*	*Proto-Akkadian*	*Old Akkadian*
Ergative-postpositional	Ergative-postpositional	Nom/Acc. diptotic	Triptotic + mimation
⟶ Development of Prepositions ⟶			
Ergative *-∅* ↗	Ergative *-um* ⟶	Nominative *-um* ⟶	Nominative *-um*
Locative *-um* ⟶	Locative *-um* ⟶	Locative *-um* ⟶	Locative *(-um)*
Absolutive *-∅* ⟶	Absolutive *-∅* ↗	Accusative *-a* }	⟶ Accusative *-am*
Connective *-a* ⟶	Genitive *-a* ⟶	Genitive *-a* }	⟶ Genitive *-im*
Dative *-iš* ⟶	Dative *-iš* ⟶	Dative *-iš* ⟶	Terminative *(-iš)*

From this evidence it seems safe to conclude that Proto-Semitic (and Early East Semitic) was a postpositional ergative language which changed to a prepositional language with a nominative/accusative case system. As a consequence it lost its original agglutinating character and became a synthetic language. As we saw above, languages which are both postpositional and ergative have a strong tendency to have SOV basic word order[21]. Since Proto-Semitic seems both postpositional and ergative, it very likely had SOV basic order as well.

If this should be correct, Akkadian was a SOV language from the very beginning. The question must now be answered why Akkadian remained SOV, while the other Semitic languages changed to VSO.

In order to solve this problem, it should be noted that the change from ergativity to accusativity, and the subsequent change from a postpositional to a prepositional system, are largely responsible for the transition SOV > VSO. It is a universal tendency that prepositional languages prefer a basic word order that differs from SOV. Prepositional languages are usually SVO or VSO. Thus the development of prepositions often results in a change in word order. This is exactly what happened in West, North and South Semitic.

The fact that Akkadian did not change to VSO must have been caused by interference from Sumerian, which exercized a conserving influence on Akkadian. Occasional deviations from SOV word order in Akkadian may be viewed as signals of a tendency towards VSO. Sumerian prevented Akkadian from deviant behaviour and in this sense Sumerian is the conservator of Akkadian sentence structure and not its instigator as has been assumed until now.

The case of Akkadian and Sumerian shows that linguistic interference often obscures the underlying historical development of a language.

Both linguists and philologists should be aware of such pitfalls. Professor Hospers, to whom I dedicate this modest contribution, initiated me in the complex field of Comparative Semitics. I would like to thank him for his stimulating lectures, his generous guidance and the sound advice he has given me for so many years.

Notes

1) For the problems of language contact and the processes and mechanisms involved see the classic Introduction by U. Weinreich, *Languages in Contact*, The Hague 1966.
2) A useful survey of the Ethiopic Languages is: W. Leslau, "Characteristics of the Ethiopic Language Group of Semitic Languages", in *Linguistic Analyses. The Non-Bantu Languages of North-Eastern Africa* (*Handbook of African Languages*, part 3), ed. A.N. Tucker and M.A. Bryan, London 1966, pp. 593-613. The northern Ethiopic Languages have a rather free word order. They are apparently in a transitionary stage.
3) See Leslau, *op. cit.*, p. 593 and pp. 612-613.
4) See W. von. Soden, *Grundriss der akkadischen Grammatik*, Rome 1952, p. 183: "Das Prädikat steht in Akk. unter dem Einfluss des sumer. Satzbaus in der Regel am Ende des Satzes". But note the relativizing remark by J.S. Cooper, "Sumerian and Akkadian in Sumer and Akkad" in *OrNS* vol. 42, 1973, pp. 239-246, esp. p. 243, n. 6: "While most of these suggested examples (i.e. final position of the Akkadian verb) are plausible, the arguments for Sumerian interference rather than strictly internal development is in no case conclusive".
5) For this see J.S. Cooper, *op. cit.*
6) For a discussion of these names see R.D. Biggs, "Semitic Names in the Fara Period" in *OrNS* vol. 36, 1967, pp. 55-66. A list of the Abū Ṣalābīkh names is published by Biggs in *Inscriptions from Tell Abū Ṣalābīkh* (*OIP*, vol. 99), Chicago 1974, pp. 34-35. The date of the Fara texts is discussed by W.W. Hallo in *OrNS* vol. 42, 1973, pp. 228-238.
7) See I.J. Gelb, *MAD* II[2] p. 142.
8) For the syntax of the Ebla texts, see D.O. Edzard, "Syntax der Ebla-Texte" in *Studies on the Language of Ebla*, ed. P. Fronzaroli, (= *Studies*) Firenze 1984, pp. 101-116 and esp. pp. 115-116.
9) See Talmy Givón, "Topic, Pronoun and Grammatical Agreement", in *Subject and Topic*, ed. Ch.N. Li, New York 1976, pp. 149-185 and esp. pp. 183-184.
10) Gelb, *AS*, vol. 18, 1969, pp. 187 ff.
11) Gelb, *AS*, vol. 18, 1969, p. 200.
12) Bernard Comrie, "Morphology and wordorder reconstruction: problems and prospects" in *Historical morphology (Trends in Linguistics, Studies and Monographs*, vol. 17), ed. J. Fisiak, The Hague 1980. pp. 83-96.
13) See Gelb, *AS*, vol. 18, 1969, pp. 83 ff. and also pp. 73 ff.
14) For this see K. Petráček, "Les categories flexionnelles en Eblaite", in *Studies*, p. 44 and B. Kienast, "Die Sprache von Ebla und das Alt-Semitische", in *La Lingua di Ebla*, ed. L. Cagni, Napoli 1981, pp. 90 ff.
15) See H. Limet, "Le système prépositionnel dans les documents d' Ebla", in *Studies*, pp. 59-70 and esp. the scheme on p. 70.
16) For the theory of language universals and universal tendencies one is referred to B. Comrie, *Language Universals and Linguistic Typology*, Oxford 1981. Comrie gives a detailed discussion of the merits and limitations of language universals as proposed by J. Greenberg and others.
17) The problem of ergativity, syntactic typology and universal grammar is discussed by F. Plank in *Ergativity. Towards a Theory of Grammatical Relations* (= *Ergativity*), ed. F. Plank, London 1979, pp. 3-36. This volume contains a number of very important articles on ergativity and various ergative languages including an extensive bibliography.
18) For a discussion and literature, see Gelb, *AS*, vol. 18, 1969, pp. 96 ff.

19) I.M. Diakonoff, *Semito-Hamitic Languages. An Essay in Classification*, Moscow 1966, pp. 58-59.

20) The model given here is a simplified representation of a far more complex historical process. In a future study I will give the full details.

21) See R.L. Trask, "On the Origins of Ergativity", in *Ergativity*, pp. 384 and 392-393.

Frustula Epigraphica Hebraica

J. Hoftijzer, Leiden

In the second part of the third Lachish letter (ll. 13-21) the addresser informs the addressee about two subjects: a) the journey of a high-ranking officer, Konyahu, to Egypt (ll. 13-18), and b) a letter sent to a certain Shallum (ll. 19-21)[1]. In this article I want to tackle some problems concerning both subjects.

1. Konyahu and his journey. A first difficulty here is this: what is the object of the infinitive *(l)qḥt* in l. 18? If one takes, with Albright a.o. the *mzh* in this line as a noun indicating "provisions, rations", there is no problem: *mzh* must be the object[2]. This interpretation, however, is not self-evident. Albright based it on his interpretation of the *mzy* in Dt 32:24[3], and on a comparison with the *mzw-* in Ps 144:13 and with the noun *mzwn*[4]. He translated the *mzy rᶜb* and its parallel *lḥmy ršp* in Dt 32:24 respectively as "rations of famine" and "food of pestilence", taking *lḥmy* as a noun and not as a passive participle of the Qal[5]. If this interpretation were correct, it would be peculiar to find in a letter a word indicating "provision" which, otherwise, has only once been attested, and that in a poetical text. Moreover, this interpretation of the *mzy* in Dt 32:24 depends on that of *lḥmy*; this is in my opinion less probable because, although *lèḥèm* occurs often in classical Hebrew, there is no attestation of its plural form anywhere (in the two instances in which *leḥum* is attested, Zeph 1:17 and Job 20:23, it is also singular). The noun *mzwn* cannot be adduced as a help, because it must be derived from a root *zwn*[6], from which a noun *mzh* cannot be made. Against this background an interpretation of *mzh* as "provision, rations" seems uncertain, to say the least[7]. It seems better to retain for the *mzh* in l. 18 the interpretation already given by the editor of the text: *mizzè* = from here[8]. (Cf. also the combination of a form of *lqḥ* with *mšm*: Gen 24:7, 27:9,45, 28:2,6, Dt 19:12, 2 Sam 14:2, 1 Kings 9:28, etc. and with *mzh* in Jer 38:10). If one accepts this interpretation of *mzh*, the problem about the object of *(l)qḥt* again arises. The original editor solves this by taking *w't-hwdwyhw bn 'ḥyhw w'nšw* (ll. 16-18) as

the object not of *šlḥ* (l. 18) but of *(l)qḥt*[9]. The question is whether in classical Hebrew a grammatical object belonging to an infinitive can precede this infinitive and if so, whether it can also precede the finite verbal form if this precedes the infinitive. To the best of my knowledge, an object belonging to an infinitive, and preceding it, is rare in classical Hebrew[10]. The instances known to me are: Lev 19:9 (cf. however Lev 23:22), 21:21, Dt 28:56, Judg 9:24 (chiasm), 2 Sam 11:19 (probably a good example), Is 49:6 (chiasm), Esth 3:13, 8:11, Neh 10:37, 2 Chr 31:7,10. Among these instances, half of which belong to the post-exilic period, there is only one in which the object in question also precedes the finite verbal form: Lev 21:21 (*'t lḥm 'lhyw l' ygš lhqryb*)[11]. Against this background the interpretation of Torczyner and others of ll. 16-18 of our ostracon cannot be excluded[12]. So the interpretation of Lemaire, who takes *w't hwdwyhw* up to and including *'nšw* as *casus pendens* and prefers an interpretation in which its corresponding pronominal suffix after *lqḥt* is deleted, is not necessary[13].

Still, I think another interpretation deserves consideration. The Qal of *lqḥ* can be used not only to indicate taking people from somewhere (cf. e.g. Jer 38:10: *qḥ bydk mzh šlšym 'nšym*), but it can also be used to indicate fetching provision, food, materials etc. (cf. Gen 6:21, 45:19, Ex 5:11, Neh 5:2, etc.; also Arad-ostracon xii 1, xvii 3f.)[14]. If we want to interpret *(l)qḥt* in l. 18 in the latter way, retaining our interpretation of *mzh*, we have to take *w't hwdqyhw* up to and including *'nšw* as the object of *šlḥ* (l. 18), and to suppose that the object of *(l)qḥt* is not mentioned *espressis verbis*. Of course an object may be deleted when it has been mentioned before in the direct context (for instances with forms of *lqḥ*, cf. e.g. Gen 23:13, 24:51, 27:13 (object mentioned in v. 9), 14 (idem), 31:32, 33:11, Ex 22:10, 32:4). The question is whether the object of *lqḥ* may be omitted, although it has not been previously mentioned in the direct context. In my opinion, this is possible in instances where the nature of the object is more or less self-evident. Cf. Gen 3:22; in this passage God is described as considering the real possibility that Adam will stretch out his hand *wlqḥ gm m*^{c}*s hhyym w'kl*... The object is not mentioned here *expressis verbis*, neither is it present in the direct context. Yet its nature is still clear. Nor is the object mentioned in Job 1:21: the words expressing Job's acquiescense in his fate are: *YHWH ntn wYHWH lqḥ*; and yet here also its nature is clear. So we have, in my opinion, to consider the <u>possibility</u> that in l. 18 the object of *(l)qḥt* is not mentioned *expressis verbis*. In this case the logical object of *(l)qḥt* would be "provisions". Probably the addresser of the third Lachish letter, a subordinate of his addressee, a high-ranking officer, finds himself in a military outpost[15]; in such a post there could be stores of flour, wine and oil as especially attested in the Arad-ostraca[16]. What the addresser tells the addressee, provided my suggestions are correct, is that Hodavyahu, following Konyahu's instructions, has fetched provisions from the stores of the outpost[17]. This would fit the context very well. In ll. 13-16 the addresser speaks of a rumour that Konyahu has gone to Egypt (or: will go/wants to go/is on the point of going)[18]. A piece of information about some of Konyahu's subordinates having fetched provisions from the addresser's outpost would fit this picture very well. These provisions could be used as rations for the journey[19]. Does the fact that the addresser speaks of Konyahu's going down to Egypt (and not of his being sent to Egypt) perhaps indicate that one has to do with personal initiative on the part of Konyahu? In any case, one cannot assume without further argumentation that it is certain that he went on an official mission[20]. One might wonder whether on an official mission the addresser would have used a formula which allows two quite different interpretations. For people, and also detachments army, going down to Egypt on their own initiative in order to escape trouble at home, one can point to e.g. Jer 41:17, 42:14ff., 43:5ff., texts set in a period more or less contemporary with our ostracon.

2. The letter sent to Shallum. There can be no doubt that the Qal of *bw'* can be used with *spr* (meaning "letter, document") as a grammatical subject, cf. 2 Kings 5:6, 10:2,7, Neh 6:17 (also 2 Chr 21:12, where *mktb* is subject); also there are instances where *spr* is the object of a Hiphil of *bw'* (2 Kings 5:6, Esth 6:1, Neh 8:1 (compare v. 2), 2 Chr 34:16)[21]. The real problem of the lines in question is the interpretation of the compound preposition *m't* (l. 20), closely related to which is the problem of the role of the prophet in this letter.

In those instances where a *m't*-phrase functions on clause level in a verbal clause with a verbal form indicating some type of movement we find the following situation[22]. If the subject of such a clause indicates a human(/living) being, the *m't*-phrase mostly has a local-separative function (cf. Gen 26:31, 38:1, 44:28, Dt 2:8, Josh 22:9, Judg 19:2, 1 Kings 11:23, 18:12, 20:36, 2 Kings 4:5, 5:19, 8:14, Jer 3:1, 9:1. Also there are some instances where the verbal form indicates that something or someone is being moved and where a human(/living) being is the object: Gen 8:8, 26:27, Jer 40:16. In none of these instances can the deity or person indicated by the noun phrase or the name preceded by *m't* be considered as being the originator of the action expressed in the verbal form[23]. There is one exception: Jer 51:53 (*m'ty yb'w šddym*): here the "I" (= God) clearly is the originator of the action described in the clause; He is the one who will cause it to happen[24]. However, if the subject in such a clause type is an object, a certain substance or a phenomenon of some type (and not a human/living being), we find a different situation. Then the *m't*-phrase does not (primarily) have a local-separative function, but it indicates the originator (prime mover) of the action described in the clause. Cf. e.g. Num 11:31 (*wrwḥ ns^{c} m't YHWH*); here it is clearly meant that God is the originator of the fact that the wind burst forth (cf. also Num 16:35); Micha 1:12 (*yrd r^{c} m't YHWH*), where it is clearly intended that God is the originator of the fact that evil has come to Jerusalem; Is 51:4 (*twrh m'ty tṣ'*): God is indicated as the one who will give the law; Jer 23:15 (*m't nb'y yrwšlm yṣ'h ḥnph lkl-h'rṣ*) obviously means that the prophets in Jerusalem are the originators of wickedness coming forth in the whole land (cf. also vv. 13, 16); Ez 33:30 (*hdbr hywṣ' m't YHWH*) clearly must mean that God is the originator of the word coming forth (i.e. the word in question is His, cf. *dbryk* in v. 31)[25]. For the *m't* in 1. 20 this means, that in all probability the prophet is the originator of the carrying of the letter to Shallum which means that he has sent it of his own accord. The probability of this interpretation may also be argued from 2 Chr 21:12 (*wyb' 'lyw mktb m'lyhw hnby'*), where the document which reached the addressee was clearly sent by the prophet (in this text no *m't*-phrase is used, but a *mn*-phrase)[26]. This means that all those interpretations of our ostracon, in which the prophet is considered to be "only" a go-between or an intermediary, are less probable[27].

Such an interpretation of *m't*, however, confronts us with other problems. The letter in question is called *spr ṭbyhw*. An interpretation in which *ṭbyhw* is not taken as *nomen rectum* but as the first word of a relative clause, is less probable for a type of text such as this and for a type of relative clause, which in that case has to be presupposed: *ṭbyhw ... hb'* (Hiphil perfect) *'l šlm ... m't hnb'*[28]. It is probable that *spr ṭbyhw* means a letter/document written by (or: according to instructions of) Tobiyahu; cf. the (*sp*)*r hmlk* (w...) *spry hśr*(*m*) in Lachish letter 6 11. 3f. (= KAI 196) - clearly letters written by or according to instructions of kings and officials. Provided our interpretation of *m't* is right, the only possible interpretation seems to be that an unnamed prophet sent Shallum a letter written by Tobiyahu, servant of the king. The possibility of this is proven by Lachish letter 6, where the addresser (a subordinate of Yaush) refers to the fact that Yaush has sent him letters from the king and from the officials, letters which were not originally destined for his (= the addresser's) eyes. Note furthermore that the addresser of Lachish letter 3 is sending Tobiyahu's letter to his addressee[29). This interpretation of the background of the letter possibly also helps in interpreting another problem, namely the interpretation of the words *l'mr hšmr* (11. 20f.). By many interpreters *hšmr* is taken to be either the summary of the contents of the letter or the first word of the letter[30). However, if it was sent by someone who was not the original addresser - and probably to someone who was not the original addressee -, the word *hšmr* could very well be the message accompanying the letter sent to Shallum; in other words, a kind of comment on it. Such a possibility is again evidenced by Lachish letter 6, where one finds a comparable formula: *šlḥ 'dny '(t sp)r hmlk (w't) spry hšr(m l'm)r qr'n'* (11. 3ff.). As we already saw, this also concerns letters sent to someone who is not the original addressee. The words *(l'm)r qr' n'* (this restoration is quite probable) indicate the message accompanying the letters and clearly not their first word or their contents[31). If we take *hšmr* to be an accompanying message, also another problem could be solved. In this case one need not answer the question why the addresser of Lachish letter 3 should quote the summary (or the first word) of a letter which he, in any event, did send to his superior[32), and which could be identified by the name of his original addresser.

Provided my interpretation is correct, the prophet sending this letter from Tobiyahu on to Shallum added a warning to it[33). The exact relation of this warning to the contents of Tobiyahu's letter cannot be established, because we do not know them. But to Yaush, who received Tobiyahu's letter, knowledge of the accompanying message cannot have been devoid of interest. We do not know how the addresser came into the possession of the letter which reached Shallum. A further problem is the fact that the addresser does not mention the name of the prophet whereas he mentions other people's names. It has been suggested that it was not necessary for him to do so, because the addressee knew who was meant[34); another possibility is that the addresser only wanted to indicate that this letter, with its accompanying message, was sent by someone who was a *prophet*, and whose *name* he did not know, or did not think important. In such instances classical Hebrew may use the article[35). This also could explain why, in this case, no name is mentioned.

I am glad to have the opportunity to express in this way my sincere and high appreciation of an esteemed colleague, whom I admire for his learning and for whose friendship I am thankful.

Notes

1) For a publication of this letter cf. e.g. *KAI* 193; J.C.L. Gibson, *Textbook of Syrian Semitic inscriptions* (= *SSI*), vol. 1, *Hebrew and Moabite inscriptions*, Oxford 1971, pp. 38ff.; and D. Pardee, *Handbook of ancient Hebrew letters* (= *Handbook*), Chicago 1982, pp. 81ff.
2) Cf. W.F. Albright, "A supplement to Jeremiah, the Lachish ostraca" in *BASOR* vol. 61, 1936, pp. 10-16 (on pp. 12ff.); *id.* "The oldest Hebrew letters the Lachish ostraca" in *BASOR* vol. 70, 1938, pp. 11-17 (on p. 14); cf. also J. Hempel, "Die Ostraka von Lakiš", in *ZAW* vol. 58, 1938, pp. 126-139 (on p. 131); R. de Vaux, "Les ostraca de Lachis" in *RB* vol. 48, 1939, pp. 181-206 (on pp. 189f., 193); K. Elliger, "Zu Text und Schrift der Ostraka von Lachis" in *ZDPV* vol. 42, 1939, pp. 63-89 (on p. 68). The reading *myh* instead of *mzh* (cf. especially Albright, "The Lachish letters after five years" in *BASOR* vol. 82, 1941, pp. 18-24 (on p. 20)) is less probable, cf. e.g. D.W. Thomas, "Ostracon III 13-18 from Tell-Duweir" in *PEQ* vol. 80, 1948; pp. 131-136 (on p. 133).
3) Cf. Albright, *op. cit.* in *BASOR* vol. 61, p. 13.
4) Cf. Albright, "A reëxamination of the Lachish letters" in *BASOR* vol. 73, 1939, pp. 16-21 (on p. 19 n. 23).
5) Cf. Albright, *op. cit.* in *BASOR* vol. 61, p. 13.
6) Cf. e.g. *BDB*, p. 266a, *KBL*[3], p. 535b.
7) The *mzw-* in Ps 114:13 which must indicate something like a garner, cannot act as a counterpoise. Cf. also H.P. Müller, "Notizen zu althebräischen Inschriften" in *UF* vol. 2, 1970, pp. 229-242 (on p. 240). I still prefer to interpret the *mzy* in Dt 32:24 as a nominal derivative (with passive meaning) of a root *mzw/y* meaning something like "to squeeze" (cf. also *CAD* s.v. *mazû* (II)). For the nominal form having a passive meaning, cf. corresponding types quoted in H. Bauer-P. Leander, *Historische Grammatik der hebräischen Sprache des Alten Testaments*, Halle a.S. 1922, par. 61 e'''.
8) Cf. H. Torczyner, *Lachish I, The Lachish Letters* (= *Lachish I*), London-New York-Toronto 1938, p. 59. This interpretation is followed by most interpreters, cf. e.g. U. Cassuto, "Ancora sui primi quattro ostraci di Lākīš" in *RSO* vol. 16, 1936, pp. 392-394 (on p. 393); *id.*, "Die Ostraka von Lakisch" in *MGWJ* vol. 83, 1939, pp. 81-92 (on p. 87); H.P. Müller, *op. cit.* in *UF* vol. 2, p. 240; A. Lemaire, *Inscriptions hébraîques*, vol. 1, *Les Ostraca* (= *IH* 1), Paris 1977, pp. 104f.; Pardee, *Handbook*, p. 84.
9) Cf. H. Torczyner, *Lachish* I, p. 51 n. 2, 58. This interpretation is followed by many interpreters, cf. e.g. Thomas, *op. cit.* in *PEQ* vol. 80, p. 134; H. Michaud, *Sur la pierre et l'argile. Inscriptions hébraîques et Ancien Testament* (= *Pierre*), Neuchâtel-Paris 1958, p. 98; H.P. Müller, *op. cit.* in *UF* vol. 2, p. 240; Pardee, *Handbook*, p. 86 (*w't hwdwyhw* .... object to *šlh lqḥt*).
10) Cf. S.R. Driver, *A treatise on the use of the tenses in Hebrew*, Oxford 1892[3], par. 208, 3ff.; Gesenius-Kautzsch-Cowley, Oxford 1910[2], pp. 456f. n. 2. I cannot agree with C. Brockelmann, *Hebräische Syntax*, Neukirchen 1956, par. 122 i, who says: "Das akkusativische und das präpositionelle Objekt treten gern vor den Infinitiv".
11) The first half of the verse (*l' ygš lhqryb 't-'šy YHWH*) makes an interpretation of the *ygš* in the second half as Hiphil (against Tiberian vocalization) less probable.
12) The examples given by Torczyner (*Lachish* I, p. 58) to prove his interpretation are insufficient (cf. also Albright, *op. cit.* in *BASOR* vol. 70, p. 14).
13) Cf. Lemaire, *IH* 1, pp. 101, 104f.
14) The Arad ostraca are quoted from Y. Aharoni, *Arad inscriptions*, Jerusalem 1981.
15) Cf. e.g. Gibson, *SSI*, vol. 1, p. 33; Lemaire, *IH* 1, pp. 141f.

16) Cf. e.g. Aharoni, *op. cit.*, p. 142ff.
17) Albright, *op. cit.* in *BASOR* vol. 82, p. 2, n. 14, also supposed that *(l)qḥt* was used here without object. But it is, in my opinion, not necessary to interpret *lqḥ* as "to buy" in order to make its use without object understandable. For *lqḥ* with the meaning "to fetch" (something from military stores), cf. also the two Arad instances mentioned above. For an interpretation (without argumentation) which resembles mine cf. Gibson, *SSI*, vol. 1, p. 39.
18) For the *possibility*, that *yrd* has to be interpreted as a Qal imperfect cf. also Pardee, *Handbook*, p. 88.
19) For an interesting text about the distribution of rations for a journey of an official cf. the sixth letter of the Arsham-correspondence (cf. G.R. Driver, *Aramaic Documents of the fifth century BC*, Oxford 1957[2], pp. 27f. (this document is nearly two centuries younger than our ostracon)).
20) For authors who assume that Konyahu went on an official mission of some sort cf. e.g. K. Elliger, "Die Ostraka von Lachis" in *PJB* vol. 34, 1938, pp. 30-58 (on p. 55); J.W. Jack, "The Lachish letters, their date and import" in *PEQ* vol. 70, 1938, pp. 165-187 (on p. 173); S. Yeivin, "Masaᶜam hahisṭori shel mikhteve Lakhish" in *BJPES* vol. 6, 1938-1939, pp. 1-7 (on p. 3); B. Chapira, "Les lettres de Lakiš" in *RES* 1941-1945, pp.105-173 (on p. 116); D.W. Thomas, *op. cit.* in *PEQ* vol. 80, p. 135, n. 5; H.L. Ginsberg, "An aramaic contemporary to the Lachish letters" in *BASOR* vol. 111, 1948, pp. 24-27 (on p. 24); Röllig, *KAI*, *ad. loc.*; Gibson, *SSL* vol. 1, pp. 34f.; Lemaire, *IH* 1, pp. 107f.; Pardee, *Handbook*, p. 88. For studies on the history of Judah which are based on the same supposition, cf. e.g. B. Oded, "Judah and the exile", in *Israelite and Judaean history*, ed. J.H. Hayes and J.M. Miller, London 1977, pp. 435-488 (on p. 472); S. Hermann, *Geschichte Israels in alttestamentlicher Zeit*, München 1980[2], p. 346. However, J.A. Montgomery, "The new sources of knowledge" in *Record and Revelation* ed. H.Wh. Robinson, Oxford 1938, pp. 1-27 (on p. 24) says that Konyahu went to Egypt "in flight presumably".
21) Theoretically it is possible to combine *hb'* with *ṭbyhw* and not with *spr ṭbyhw* (cf. especially U. Cassuto, "I primi quattro ostraci di Lakiš" *RSO* vol. 16, 1936, pp. 163-177 (on p. 173); idem, *op. cit.* in *MGWJ* vol. 83, p. 87). However, it seems to me to make less sense in the context to indicate, that the letter sent by the addresser, was from a man who came to Shallum with a message.
22) I leave *m't-pny*-phrases out of discussion.
23) The same is true for clauses of a corresponding type in which *mᶜm*-phrases occur instead of *m't*-phrases: Gen 26:16, Ex 8:7, 25, 26, 9:33, 10:6, 18, 11:8, Lev 25:41, Dt 15:16, Judg 9:37, 1 Sam 10:2, 9, 14:17, 2 Sam 1:2, 3:26, for instances where the verbal form indicates that something or someone is being moved and where a human or another living being is the object, cf. Dt 15:12, 13, 18, Jer 34:14.
24) Another exception could be I Kings 5:14.
25) Cf. also *Arad ostracon V* 2f., *VI* 2ff. The same is true for clauses of a corresponding type in which *mᶜm*-phrases occur instead of *m't*-phrases: 2 Sam 15:28 (*ᶜd bw' dbr mᶜmkm lhgyd ly*), here clearly is meant that "you" are originators of the coming of the message, i.e. that they will send the message; Is 28:29 (*gm z't mᶜm YHWH sb'wt ys'h*), here clearly is meant that God is the originator of the *z't* (the situation as described in vv. 27f.). For a corresponding function of *m't*-phrases cf. e.g. also those functioning on clause level in verbal clauses with a verbal form of the root *hyh* or functioning as core constituent (as so-called predicate) in nominal clauses: I Kings 1:27, 12:24 (= 2 Chr 11:4), Jer 7:1, 11:1, 18:1, 21:1, 26:1, 27:1, 30:1, 32:1, 34:1, 8, 12, 35:1, 36:1, 37:17, 40:1, Hab 2:13, Zech 7:12, Ps 109:20, 118:23, Esr 9:8 (for clauses of a corresponding type in which a *mᶜm*-phrase occurs instead of a *m't*-phrase, cf. 1 Kings 12:15 (cf. 2 Chr 10:15),

Ps 121:2). I have left out of this discussion *m't*-phrases and $m^{c}m$-phrases occurring in verbal clauses with a verbal form of the semantically related roots *swr*, ^{c}*br*, *pnh*, *nṭh* and *mwš*: these phrases always have a local-separative function: Dt 29:17, 1 Sam 16:14, 18:12, 2 Sam 7:15, 1 Kings 11:9, 22:24 (2 Chr 18:23), Is 54:10.

26) In this test it is also clear that Eliyahu is responsible for the contents of the document.

27) For such interpretations, cf. e.g. Albright, *op. cit.* in *BASOR* vol. 61, p. 13; *id.*, *op. cit.* in *BASOR* vol. 73, p. 19, n. 24; *id.*, *op. cit.* in *BASOR* vol. 82, p. 21; *id.* in *ANET*, Princeton 1969, pp. 320-322 (on p. 322); Hempel, *op. cit.* in *ZAW* vol. 58, p. 132; J. Pedersen in a review in *AcOr(K)* vol. 18, 1940, p. 150; Michaud, *Pierre*, p. 99, cf. however also below; D.W. Thomas, "Letters from Lachish", in *Documents from Old Testament Times*, ed. D.W. Thomas, London-Edinburgh 1958, pp. 212-217 (on p. 215); *id.* "Again 'The prophet' in the Lachish Ostraca" in *Von Ugarit nach Qumran. Beiträge zur alttestamentlichen und altorientalischen Forschung Otto Eissfeldt ... dargebracht* (= *BZAW*, vol. 77), ed. J. Hempel and L. Rost, Berlin 1958, pp. 244-249 (on pp. 244, 246ff.); J.G. Février, "Ostraca, Sceaux et Cachets" in *SDB*, vol. 6, Paris 1960, cols. 948-963 (col. 953); Röllig, *KAI, ad. loc.*; K. Galling, *Textbuch zur Geschichte Israels*, Tübingen 1968^{2}, p. 76, n. 8; Gibson, *SSI*, vol. 1, p. 41. The interpretation which I propose also implies that our text does not give insight into a delivery system for official letters, as proposed by Elliger, *op. cit.* in *PJB* vol. 34, pp. 45f. (cf. also D.W. Thomas, *'The Prophet "in the Lachish Ostraca"* (= *Prophet*), London 1946, pp. 17f., 23). It also implies that the interpretation of *nb'* in our letter as "messenger" (an interpretation based on the interpretation of *m't* as indicating mediation) cannot be sustained, against H.P. Müller, *op. cit.* in *UF* vol. 2, pp. 240ff. The solution suggested by Michaud, *Pierre*, p. 99, that the prophet was only the originator of the sending of the letter, but also of it being written by Tobijahu, is going too far in my opinion: cf. also the examples quoted above.

28) For an interpretation with a relative clause which is not introduced by *'šr* or any other conjunction, cf. e.g. R. Dussaud, "Le prophète Jérémie et les lettres de Lakish" in *Syria* vol. 19, 1938, pp. 256-271 (on p. 267); J. Reider, "The Lachish letters" in *JQR* vol. 29, 1938-1939, pp. 225-239 (on p. 235); H. Michaud, "Le témoignage des ostraca de Tell Douweir concernant le prophète Jérémie" in *RES*, 1941, pp. 42-60 (on pp. 50, 54); Ch.J. Jean, "Inscriptions sémitiques" in *SDB*, vol. 4, Paris 1949, cols. 384-417 (col. 414). One finds this interpretation already with Torczyner, *Lachish* I, pp. 52, 59. For a description of the types of relative clauses which can or need not be introduced by any conjunction, and in which type of text they occur, cf. Gesenius-Kautzsch-Cowley, par. 155e ff.

29) This interpretation, while not conflicting with the interpretation of *m't* given above, implies that the use of *m't* in a context like this does not *necessarily* indicate that the prophet wrote the letter. Against Torczyner, *Lachish* I, pp. 59f.; Dussaud, *op. cit.* in *Syria* vol. 19, p. 267f.; A. Vincent, "Les lettres de Lachis" in *Journal des Savants*, 1939, pp. 61-68 (on pp. 65, 68); Michaud, *op. cit.* in *RES*, 1941, p. 54. It is less probable that "Tobijahu's letter" could be interpreted as being the letter written by him as a scribe or brought by him as messenger against Lemaire, *IH* 1, p. 105. In itself it is also possible that *spr ṭbyhw* is not a status constructus group, but that *spr* is grammatical object, *ṭbyhw* is subject and that we have to interpret *hb'* as Hiphil perfect (instead of as article + participle Qal): a letter Tobijahu has brought (for this possibility, cf. Torczyner, *Lachish* I, p. 59. This clause order (OSV) is, however, extremely rare, especially in prose, cf. e.g. Gesenius-Kautzsch-Cowley, par. 142f, P. Joüon,

Grammaire de l'Hébreu biblique, Rome 1947[2], par. 155o. For this reason it seems preferable to take *spr ṭbyhw* as a status constructus group.

30) Cf. e.g. Albright, *op. cit.* in *BASOR* vol. 61, p. 13; Dussaud, *op. cit.* in *Syria* vol. 19, p. 267; Hempel, *op. cit.* in *ZAW* vol. 58, p. 132, Montgomery, *op. cit.* in *Record and Revelation*, p. 25; K. Galling in a review in *OLZ* vol. 42, 1939, p. 366; A. Vaccari, "Le lettere di Lachis" in *Bibl* vol. 20, 1939, pp. 180-199 (on p. 190); de Vaux, *op. cit.* in *RB* vol. 48, p. 193; Michaud, *Pierre*, pp. 98f.; Thomas, *op. cit.* in *BZAW* vol. 77, p. 247 n. 18; Röllig, *KAI ad. loc.*; Gibson, *SSI*, vol. 1, p. 41; H. Reviv, *Ketovot mitqufat hameluka beyisra'el*, Jerusalem 1975, p. 80; Lemaire, *IH* 1, pp. 105f.; Pardee, *Handbook*, p. 85.

31) Elliger, *op. cit.* in *PJB* vol. 34, p. 51, has rightly drawn attention to the remarkable parallel between Lachish letter 3,11. 19-21 and Lachish letter 6,11. 3-5.

32) Cf. l. 21. I will not go into the use of the perfect in those instances (*šlḥh*, l. 21); cf. on this subject recently D. Pardee, "The 'epistolary perfect' in Hebrew letters", in *Biblische Notizen* vol. 22, 1983, pp. 34-40.

33) This seems to be the most probable interpretation of *hšmr* (cf. 1 Sam 19:2, cf. also 2 Kings 6:9), and the one which fits the situation best. The imperative as such could also have a more "innocent" meaning: be quiet, do not be excited (cf. Is 7:4).

34) Cf. e.g. Elliger, *op. cit.* in *PJB* vol. 34, pp. 46, 55; Chapira, *op. cit.* in *RES* 1941-1945, p. 117; Thomas, *Prophet*, pp. 18f.

35) Cf. e.g. Gesenius-Kautzsch-Cowley, par. 126r.

La préposition *L* dans 1 Samuel 16:7

B. Jongeling (†), Groningen

Dans le seizième chapitre du premier livre de Samuel on nous raconte que David, fils cadet d'Isaï, est oint roi futur d'Israël par le prophète Samuel. D'abord tous les fils plus âgés d'Isaï, dont le premier-né est Eliab, passent devant Samuel. Quand Samuel voit celui-ci il pense: "Certainement, l'oint de l'Eternel est ici devant lui"[1]. Mais *YHWH* lui fait savoir: "... l'homme regarde à ce qui frappe les yeux, mais l'Eternel regarde au coeur"[2]. Le texte hébreu a ici: *H'DM YR'H L^{c}YNYM WYHWH YR'H LLBB*. La question qui nous occupe ici est de savoir quelle est la signification de la préposition *L* dans *L^{c}YNYM* et dans *LLBB*.

Le verbe *R'H* figure plus de 1200 fois dans l'Ancien Testament[3], mais je n'ai trouvé que trois endroits où il semble être construit avec la préposition *L*, à savoir 1 Sam 16:7, Psaumes 64:6 et Lament 3:34-36. Le verbe *R'H* ayant un complément d'objet est normalement suivi d'un accusatif, indiqué ou non par la *nota accusativi 'T*. On rencontre aussi *R'H* avec la préposition *B*. Dans cette combination *R'H* signifie "voir avec joie" ou "voir avec douleur"[4]. La préposition *L* connaît beaucoup de nuances de signification. Joüon dit: "Le *L* exprime l'idée de relation (par rapport à) avec une grande variété de nuances. Ainsi il exprime la possession (comp. le *L auctoris* ...) et supplée le génitif ...; il indique l'auteur de l'action ... Il s'emploie pour la causalité, la finalité, la norme (selon)"[5]. Dans l'hébreu postérieur le *L* est souvent employé pour indiquer l'accusatif. Je cite encore Joüon: "Dans la langue postérieure principalement, on trouve assez souvent *L* employé comme exposant de l'accusatif du nom objet déterminé"[6]. Dans une note l'auteur ajoute: "L'emploi du *L* comme exposant de l'objet déterminé est dû sans doute, en grande partie, à l'influence de l'araméen"; il est vrai qu'il remarque ensuite: "mais certains emplois hébreux du *L* tendaient au même résultat ..."[7]. En effet, la préposition araméenne peut souvent avoir les mêmes significations qu'elle a en hébreu mais, autrement que dans cette dernière langue, l'emploi comme *nota accusativi* y est normal. La plupart des commentaires que j'ai consultés comprennent le *L* de

LLBB en 1 Sam 16:7 comme indiquant le complément direct: "*YHWH* voit le coeur", tandis qu'on explique le *L* de *L*^{c}*YNYM* comme voulant dire "selon" ou quelque chose de semblable[8]: "l'homme voit selon les yeux", ce qui signifie: "en accord avec les yeux", "selon la norme des yeux". Ce que les yeux de l'homme voient c'est là la réalité, la vérité. La traduction de Segond 'ce qui frappe les yeux" n'est pas littérale mais elle est essentiellement correcte. Le mot ^{c}*YNYM* ne peut pas être le complément direct de *YR'H*, et le *L* ne peut donc pas indiquer l'accusatif. L'homme voit ce qui est visible pour ses yeux, ses yeux sont sa mesure, son critère. Mais pour connaître une personne ou quelque chose, il y a encore d'autres facteurs qui jouent leur rôle.

Dans la deuxième moitié de la phrase en question le *L* est généralement compris comme *nota accusativi*: "*YHWH* voit (ou: regarde) le coeur". *LBB* est alors l'objet du deuxième *YR'H*. On donne donc une interprétation tout à fait différente aux deux parties de la phrase. Dans la première partie les ^{c}*YNYM* sont les yeux du sujet, dans la deuxième partie le *LBB* est le *LBB* de l'objet. Et dans cette dernière partie le *L* est compris comme indiquant le complément direct: "*YHWH* voit le coeur", c'est-à-dire: *YHWH* tient compte d'autres facteurs, Il ne voit pas seulement l'extérieur, Il voit aussi l'intérieur. Grammaticalement cette interprétation n'est pas tout à fait impossible. Surtout dans l'hébreu postérieur le *L* peut en effet indiquer l'accusatif.

En Lament 3:34-36 on trouve trois infinitifs avec *L* tandis que la fin de ce passage comporte: *'DNY* (ou: *YHWH*) *L' R'H*. Segond traduit: "Le Seigneur ne le voit-il pas?" Il est possible que les infinitifs forment le complément direct du verbe *R'H*. H.J. Kraus écrit: "Die Infinitive mit *L* streben alle dem bestimmenden Satzglied 36b zu"[9]. Dans son commentaire sur les Lamentations C.F. Keil remarque: "Wäre die Behauptung von *Böttcher* in s. Aehrenlese: dass *R'H* nie mit *L* construirt vorkomme, begründet, so könte (sic!) man die Infinitive mit *L* in dem Sinne: anlangend das Zertreten aller Gefangene u.s.w. als Object von *R'H* fassen. Allein die Behauptung ist nicht richtig, sie wird durch 1 Sam 16,7: *H'DM YR'H L*^{c}*YNYM YHWH YR'H LLBB* widerlegt"[10]. Mais Keil ne s'arrête pas ici à l'interprétation de *YR'H L*^{c}*YNYM*, où le *L* ne peut guère indiquer l'accusatif. Cependant dans son commentaire sur les livres de Samuel Keil donne la traduction suivante du passage discuté: "denn der Mensch sieht auf die Augen und Jehova sieht aufs Herz". A cette traduction il ajoute: "Die Augen im Gegensatz zum Herzen sind Bild der äussern Gestalt"[11]. Il faut admettre que Keil est conséquent. Evidemment il comprend ^{c}*YNYM* comme objet du premier *YR'H*, et qu'il interprète oui ou non la préposition comme indiquant l'accusatif, pour lui les ^{c}*YNYM* sont les yeux de celui qui est vu

et non pas de celui qui voit. Cette interprétation ne me semble guère admissible. Je préfère comprendre la phrase comme je l'ai exposé ci-dessus: "l'homme voit selon ses yeux, selon la norme de ses yeux", c'est-à-dire: il ne voit que l'extérieur. Quant aux infinitifs de Lament 3:34-36 on peut les prendre comme complément du *R'H* qui suit, mais on peut aussi les interpréter comme des infinitifs tout court[12)] et penser que *R'H* n'a pas de complément exprimé. De toute façon on ne peut pas, comme le fait Keil, citer 1 Sam 16:7 pour prouver que *R'H* se construit avec *L*.
Dans le Psaume 64:6 on lit: *YḤZQW LMW DBR R^c YSPRW LṬMWN MWQŠYM 'MRW MY YR'H LMW*. Segond traduit: "Ils se fortifient dans leur méchanceté; ils se concertent pour tendre des pièges; ils disent: Qui les verra?" H.J. Kraus rend la dernière partie par: "sie denken: "wer sieht uns schon"...[13)]. Kraus préfère lire, avec le texte syriaque et Jérôme, *LNW* au lieu de *LMW*[14)]. Après avoir mentionné la lecture du texte syriaque et de Jérôme l'éditeur des Psaumes dans BHK^3 (F. Buhl†) écrit: "*prb recte*"; H. Bardtke (†) note dans BHS: *l LaNû cf Syr. Hier*". A mon avis cette modification n'est pas nécessaire. On pourrait rapprocher *LMW* de *MWQŠYM*[15)], mais on pourrait aussi penser que la phrase commence à la troisième personne et continue également ainsi, comparer ma remarque sur Job 11:4 dans *"L'expression MY YTN dans l'Ancien Testament"*, *Vetus Testamentum* 24, 1974, pp. 32-40 (voir la page 36 note). Quelle que soit l'interprétation que l'on donne au Ps 64:6 il nous reste encore le problème de la construction de *R'H* aussi bien dans le Psaume nommé que dans Lament 3. Quant à ce dernier endroit j'ai déjà dit ci-dessus que *R'H* n'a peut-être pas de complément exprimé. Mais si l'on veut maintenir les infinitifs précédents comme objet du verbe on peut considérer que les Lamentations sont tardives, voir les notes 6 et 7. Et pour le Psaume je cite encore H.J. Kraus: "Für die Erklärung der Abfassungszeit fehlt jeder eindeutige Anhaltspunkt"[16)] [17)] [18)].
Quoi qu'il en soit, il me semble guère possible de prouver à l'aide de Ps 64:6 et de Lament 3:34-36 que le *L* de 1 Sam 16:7 indique l'accusatif.

Aussi aimerais-je proposer une autre solution. Il me semble que le deuxième *L* (*LLBB*) doit être compris dans le même sens que le premier (*L^{c}YNYM*), et qu'il faut traduire: "*YHWH* voit selon (la norme) le (du) coeur". Pour l'homme les yeux sont la norme selon laquelle il voit et juge, pour Dieu c'est le coeur.
Il nous reste encore une question à examiner: le coeur de qui est envisagé? Dans la traduction traditionnelle il s'agit du coeur de David qui sera oint roi d'Israël. Il faut alors comprendre la prépo-

sition *L* de *LLBB* comme indiquant l'accusatif ou bien dans le sens de : concernant (le coeur). Il n'est pas tout à fait impossible de comprendre le texte de cette façon. Mais la difficulté est alors que *^{c}YNYM* est pris comme les yeux du sujet tandis que *LBB* est compris comme le coeur de l'objet. C'est pourquoi je préfère prendre *LBB* comme le coeur du sujet. C'est-à-dire : Dieu voit selon son propre coeur. Ce n'est pas le coeur de David (ou de quelque autre personne) qui décide de la dignité royale, mais c'est le coeur de Dieu. David est élu non pas parce que son coeur est meilleur que celui d'une autre personne, mais parce que le coeur de Dieu l'a choisi. Ainsi David est l'homme de 1 Sam 13:14: "L'Eternel s'est choisi un homme selon son coeur (*KLBBW*)"[19].

Notes

1) Traduction de L. Segond, *La Sainte Bible*, Paris-Bruxelles 1954.
2) *id.*
3) D. Vetter dans *Theologisches Wörterbuch zum Alten Testament*, vol. 2, ed. Jenni-Westermann, München-Zürich 1976, p. 694.
4) Voir les dictionnaires.
5) P. Joüon, *Grammaire de l'hébreu biblique*, Rome 1947, par. 133d.
6) Joüon, *op. cit.*, par. 125k.
7) Joüon, *loc. cit.*
8) Voir cependant, plus loin, l'opinion de C.F. Keil.
9) H.J. Kraus, *Klagelieder (Threni) (Biblischer Kommentar AT)*, Neukirchen 1956, p. 48.
10) C.F. Keil, *Biblischer Commentar über den Propheten Jeremia und die Klagelieder (Biblischer Commentar über das AT*, vol. 3, ed. C.F. Keil-Fr. Delitzsch), Leipzig 1872[2], p. 599. Keil omet le *W* devant *YHWH*.
11) C.F. Keil, *Biblischer Commentar über die prophetischen Geschichtsbücher des Alten Testaments (Biblischer Commentar über das AT*, vol. 2), Leipzig 1864[2], p. 124.
12) Cf. Joüon, *op. cit.*, par. 1241,m.
13) H.J. Kraus, *Psalmen I (Biblischer Kommentar AT)*, Neukirchen 1960, p. 445.
14) Kraus, *loc. cit.*
15) Kraus, *loc. cit.*: "*LMW* ("auf sie") würde sich im Textzusammenhang auf die Fallen beziehen. Besser: *LaNû* (mit Syr Hie)".
16) H.J. Kraus, *op. cit.*, p. 446.
17) Parfois *LMW* = *LW*, voir Joüon, *op. cit.*, par. 103f. Quelques auteurs comprennent le mot dans ce sens.
18) C.A. Briggs, *The Book of Psalms (International Critical Commentary)* Edinburg 1907-1909-1925, p. 79, écrit: "*LMW* as obj. of *YR'H* is unexplained and improb. It should go with *'MRW*. It has been misplaced". Trad.: "Who can see?" Calvin, *Commentaire aux Psaumes*, *ad. loc.*, rapproche *LMW* de ceux qui tendent les pièges.
19) Traduction de L. Segond.

K and variants in Punic

K. Jongeling, Leiden

J. Friedrich and W. Röllig in their grammar of Phoenician and Punic give a short discussion on the use of original consonant signs to denote vowels in later Punic[1]. After the treatment of the supposed two different systems of vowel notation[2], the authors conclude this section with the following remark:

> "Sonstige seltener vorkommende Schreibungen scheinen einfach aus der völligen Unsicherheit über die Verwendung der Zeichen für die verstummten Laryngale erklärbar, z.B. *HDN* für *'*adōn* "Herr" Np 3, 1, *PNʿ BʿL* für **panē Baʿal* "Angesicht des Baʿal" 992, 1. 1834, 2. 2005, 1. 2992, 1. 3363, 1f., KAI 97, 1, *Š'ŠM* für **šiššīm* "sechzig" Np 123, 2, *QLH* für **qūlō* "seine Stimme" Eph. 1, 41 oben 3, *K'* 2595, 6. 3390, 3 usw., *Kʿ* Np 7, 1. 8, 1 usw., *KH* Np 36, 5. 112, 4 und *KḤ* JA 1917/2, 37 b, 4 für **kī* "denn" usw. Vgl. ferner in lat. Wörtern: *ʿKSNDRʿ* "exedra" KAI 129, 2, *YHLYʿ* "Julia" KAI 122, 1, *NPTḤN* "Nyptan" KAI 140, 1 und *Q Wʿ R Ṭ Ḥ* "Quarta" ebd."[3].

This remark calls for some close scrutiny, the more so since not all the examples are equally felicitous. One might ask why the Berber name Nyptan is mentioned as a Latin word[4]. Also, would it not have been more appropriate to transscribe *HDN* as **adūn*, since the loss of *'* in pronunciation is discussed by the authors in an earlier section of their grammar[5], where the first syllable of *LDN* for historical *L'DN* is correctly represented by **la-*, and the development /ō/>/ū/ has also been mentioned earlier[6]? Perhaps it would even have been preferable to transscribe *LHDN* as **ladūn*, which then ought to have been discussed in connection with other instances of the use of *H* for /a/. Then again one might be surprised by the representation **baʿal* - with anaptyctic vowel - for *BʿL*, since the development in Phoenician-Punic must have been /baʿl/>/bal/[7]. But these are minor points, and much more important is the really unavoidable observation that it seems hardly possible to explain *K'*, *Kʿ*, *KH*, *KḤ* as mere orthographical variants of *K* = /kī/[8], among other things because an expected **KY* has so far not been attested.

In the first place it is advisable to get a more complete picture of the geographical distribution of *K* and variants. This conjunction is frequently used in the sterotyped formula *K ŠM*^{c} *QL'* "because he heard his voice", and variants, in the numerous votive texts that remain in North Africa and adjacent territories; therefore the very few and dubious other examples of *K* were left aside. Because the number of occurrences is so high, detailed references are only given for the smaller groups of texts.

a) Distribution of *K*:

Carthage	346 times on a total of	348 instances[9]
Lepcis Magna N	2	2[10]
Sousse	6	6[11]
Tunisia OU[12] N	1[13]. . . .	5
Arseu	1	1[14]
Constantine	67	95[15]
Constantine N	9	18[16]
(Constantine+	76	113[17])
Malta	3	3[18]
Sicilia	3	3[19]
Sardinia	3	3[20]
Pyrgi	1	1[21]
Spain	1	1[22];

b) Distribution of *K'*:

Carthage	2[23]. . . .	348
H. Medeine N	1	1[24]
Constantine	22	95
Constantine N	8	18
(Constantine+	30	113)

c) Distribution of *KḤ*:

H. Maktar N	2	12[25]
Tunisia OU N	1[26]. . . .	5
Constantine	2[27]. . . .	95 (resp. Const.+ 113)

d) Distribution of *KH* (or read *KḤ*?):

Tunisia OU N	1[28]. . . .	5

e) Distribution of *K*^{c}:

H. Maktar N	10	12
Tunisia OU N	2[29]. . . .	5
Constantine	4[30]. . . .	95
Constantine N	1[31]. . . .	18
(Constantine+	5	113)

Instead of *K* and variants in a few cases another conjunction is found, ending in *-N*. This conjunction is attested in four texts; in all instances the complete word is repeated:

f) *KḤN KḤN:*

H. Maktar N	2[32].	3

g) *K^{c}N K^{c}N:*

H. Maktar N	1[33].	3
Tunisia OU N	1[34].	1

It is obvious that the normal form of the conjunction is *K* (used in 100 % of the instances in Lepcis Magna, Sousse, Arseu, Malta, Sicilia, Sardinia, Pyrgi and Spain, and also, what is more important, in 99 % of the numerous instances in the texts from Carthage[35]; the only significant deviations occur in H. Maktar (and Tunisia OU, cf. note 12) and Constantine. In Constantine *K* is used in 65 % of the instances, in Tunisia OU 20 %, and in H. Maktar *K* is not yet attested. The distribution of the deviating forms, i.e. *K'*, *KḤ*, *KH*, *K^{c}*, also is worthy of note: of the 33 instances of *K'*, 30 are found in texts from Constantine, whereas the texts from H. Maktar (together with the texts from unknown but Tunisian origin) are in favour of the forms ending in -*H* (-*Ḥ*) and -^{c}. Such forms are attested a few times in Constantine, but not in the so much larger group of texts from Carthage. The same preference for *Ḥ* and ^{c} in H. Maktar (and Tunisia OU) can be detected in the spelling of the reduplicated longer conjunction. Although certainty is impossible here, this phenomenon makes it probable that *KḤ/K^{c}* and *KḤN/K^{c}N* are closely related.
Another interesting feature of the list is that most of the forms in which a laryngeal occurs, are found in texts in Neo-Punic script. Among the 512 examples of *K* only 12 are found in Neo-Punic texts, whereas among the forms with laryngeal 30 are found in Neo-Punic texts, i.e. 50 %; the other examples are mainly from Constantine (28), and only twice is a form with laryngeal attested in Carthage. As laryngeals in these later texts often indicate vowels, we will have to establish which vowel is meant by *'* in texts from Constantine, and by ^{c} and *Ḥ* in H. Maktar.
In Constantine *'* is used as a vowel-letter as indication of the suffix of the 3rd person sing. after nouns and verbs: *QL'* "his voice" and *BRK'* "blessed him" occur passim; in both words the realisation of the vowel has been /ō/, cf. the transcriptions of these words in Greek script, in an inscription from Constantine[36]: *koulō* resp. *barakhō*; in the same text *samō* is found, which pronunciation is reflected several times by the spelling *ŠM'* for historical correct *ŠM^{c}*[37]. However, *'* is found indicating /ē/, thus e.g. in the ending of the construct state of a masculine plural noun, cf. *PN'/P^{c}N'*[38] (for older *PN*) which is rendered in the just mentioned text in Greek script by *phane*[39]. This use of *'* for both /ō/ and /ē/ is attested in most later Punic texts[40].

In H. Maktar ^{c} usually indicates /a/ when used as a vowel-letter, cf. *B^{c}T*, for normal *BT*[41], "daughter", *ND^{c}R*[42] "vow", *N^{c}DR*[43] "he vowed", *^{c}BN*[44], for original *'BN*, "stone" etc.; *Ḥ* is not extensively used in H. Maktar as a vowel-letter, but it may be supposed that it could be used for /a/ like ^{c}; cf. *BḤL ^{c}MN*[45], which might be explained as a simple lapsus for *B^{c}L ḤMN*, cf. however from outside H. Maktar *BḤL ḤMN*[46], which was probably pronounced /bal amūn/, a pronunciation also indicated by the text in Greek script from Constantine, where this name is rendered by *bal amoun*[47]; cf. further some words spelled with historically correct *Ḥ*, which are several times attested with ^{c} instead, indicating the usual pronunciation: *ḤMŠ*[48] // *^{c}MŠ*[49] "five", *ḤMŠM*[50] // *^{c}MŠM*[51] "fifty", *BḤYM*[52] // *B^{c}YM*[53] "during his/her life", *ḤW'*[54] / *ḤW^c*[55] // *^{c}W'*[56] / *^{c}Ẉ^c*[57] "he/she lived", cf. also *^{c}WḤ*[58], *TḤT*[59] // *T^{c}T*[60] "under"; whether in *TNḤ*[61], instead of normal *TN'*[62], *Ḥ* indicates /ō/ or /a/ cannot be ascertained, as the spelling *ṬN^c* is also attested[63]. From outside H. Maktar the personal name *NPTḤN*[64] may be compared, where *Ḥ* indicates /a/ as is proven by the Latin parallel text, which offers *Nyptanis*; in the same text the personal name *Quarta* occurs, but the Neo-Punic text is damaged in the corresponding place, the reading being given as [*Q*] *W^{c}R*[*Ṭ*] *Ḥ* or --*H*. Perhaps the use of *H* for /a/ is also to be compared, cf. *HBN*[65] for historically correct *'BN*[66] "stone"; the pronunciation is secured by the spelling *^{c}BN* (v. supra).

Apart from the indication of vowels as occurring in later Punic and Neo-Punic texts, our most important source for the study of the vocalization of Punic is the Poenulus by Plaute, in which several Punic words and sentences and one longer text in Punic are preserved. In this longer text the conjunction under discussion has been preserved. In the second version of this text[67] it is written *co*, which form has been compared by Sznycer to the variant forms *K'*, *K^c*, *KḤ*, *KH* in the later Punic texts[68]. This comparison shows beyond doubt that in the case of *K'* the pronunciation must have been /ko/, not /ke/ with a front vowel as might be supposed from a comparison to Hebrew *kī*. In the first version of this text[69] the conjunction appears as *chy*. The relative frequency of *y* and the digraphs *ch* and *th*, as well as the form of the name of the son of Hanno's former host (*agorastocles*) are in favour of a Greek original of this first version of Hanno's speech. If this is correct the vowel in the conjunction *chy* was originally written *u* (= *upsilon*). In several other instances *upsilon* seems to have been used to represent /ĕ/[70], and there is no reason to postulate, as did Sznycer and others[71], a pronunciation /ki/ on the evidence of *chy*. One is tempted to regard the spelling with ^{c} and

Ḥ/H, i.e. with vowel-letters normally representing /a/, as an attempt to render /ĕ/ (see however also below p. 98). It is difficult to give a historical explanation of the form of the conjunction /ko/ - /ke/. Sznycer[72] rather easily remarks that in Phoenician the pronunciation of the conjunction probably was /ki/, and that the change /ki/ > /ko/ is a later development in Punic. As this would be the only example of a sound-change /i/ > /o/ in Punic, this explanation seems to be unsatisfactory. Before we proceed with our remarks on the internal situation in Phoenician and Punic it seems advisable to have a look at some cognate languages, to see whether information of a comparative kind can be of any use.

In Hebrew the same conjunction is attested in the form /kī/[73]; the same form can be supposed for Moabite (spelled *KY*), Aramaic (also spelled *KY*), and most probably also Ugaritic, where the conjunction is normally written *K*, but at least once *KY* is attested[74]. In Akkadian *kî* is also attested, with an alternative form *kê*[75], used as conjunction ("when, as soon as, after, if, in case, whether, that, because, according to, as, just as") as well as preposition ("like, in the manner of, as, according to, instead of")[76]. Related to this *ki* is most probably the Arabic conjunction *kay* "that, in order that"[77], which seems to be unrelated to the element *kay-* in *kayfa* "how"[78], cf. however also Akkadian *kî/kê* "how"[79]. Also in several non-Semitic Afro-Asiatic languages comparable particles are to be found, cf. e.g. Egyptian *k3*[80], and perhaps also Berber *akka*[81]. The difficult matter of the presumed relationships between these words cannot be described in a satisfactory way without taking into account several other words, and/or morphemes, in which a so called "deictic *k*" is attested. There is e.g. the pronominal element indicating the 2nd person in the suffix pronouns, the element *-ku/-ki* attested in the pronoun of the first person sing. in Akkadian, *anaku*, Hebrew, *anoki* (cf. Phoenician *'nk*), also attested in Egyptian, cf. Coptic *anok*, etc. Prominent among these words we find the preposition *ka-* "as, like" in Hebrew, Aramaic, North- and South-Arabian. The same original **ka*, used in an accented position as adverb, developed > **kā*, Hebrew *kō* (also in the reduplicated form *kākā*) "thus", Aramaic *kā* "here, now". It seems probable that /ko/ in Punic has to be related to this particle. For its use as a conjunction one may compare the relation between Hebrew *k*^{e}*mō* (< **kamā*) used as variant form of the preposition, "as, like", and Arabic *kamā*, used as a conjunction introducing verbal sentences (cf. also the situation in Akkadian, where *kî*, with palatal vowel, as in the conjunction *kî*, is used as preposition)[82].

If this reasoning is correct, and Punic *K'* is to be explained as /ko/ < *kā* < *ka*, then one might propose another explanation for the forms attested in H. Maktar *K^{c}*, *KḤ*. As was remarked above, the most probable reading for these forms is /ka/, and perhaps this /ka/ might be understood as the older form of this conjunction without the lengthening of /-a/ attested in Constantine (/ĕ/ in the Poenulus-form *chy*, is easier to explain as a shortening of /-a/ than as shortening of a long /-ō/. In other parts of speech, the same phenomenon is attested elsewhere in Punic, cf. *nadōr*[83], *ND'R*[84] (= /n(-)dor/), *NDWR*[85] (= /n(-)dor/), to *N^{c}D^{c}R*[86] (= /nadar/)[87]. Related to this /ka/ is the longer form /kan/, used in H. Maktar (*K^{c}N K^{c}N*, *KḤN KḤN*). Perhaps this word is to be compared to Hebrew *kēn* "thus"[88], with the same variation of vowels as in Hebrew *kî* versus Punic /ka/ (palatal vowel versus central vowel); cf. also, with central vowel, Akkadian *akanna*, *kanna*, adv. "thus"[89], resp. *akanna*, adv. "here"[90]. In Phoenician *kn* is attested, as an adverb "thus"[91], possibly pronounced /ken/ (for which pronunciation one is referred to *chen* in the Poenulus, where however only *chem* is attested[92])[93]; but this adverb *kn* is, of course, only indirectly related to /kan/. Since the only attestations of /kan/ are from late texts, possibly reflecting a special dialect of Punic as spoken in H. Maktar, it is impossible to say whether this /kan/ existed in earlier stages of the language or is to be explained as an innovation in (some form of) Punic. A comparable problem arises in connection with *K*, conjunction, in Phoenician and older Punic. Although it remains possible that in all instances, also in Phoenician, *K* represents /ko/, resp. /ka/, it is perhaps more probable that /ko/ - /ka/ only occurs in Punic, and that *K* in Phoenician should be read /ki/[94].

Notes

1) J. Friedrich - W. Röllig, *Phönizisch-Punische Grammatik* (*Analecta Orientalia*, vol. 46; = *FR*), Roma 1970^{2}, pp. 41-44.
2) If the second system of vowel notation, as described in *FR* p. 44, really exists, then at least some of the examples should be dismissed as inadequate; cf. e.g. *QL*^{c}, which is quoted as proof of the use of ^{c} for /o/, without reference to the rest of the text in which it occurs (P. Berthier - R. Charlier, *Le sanctuaire punique d'El-Hofra* (= *EH*), Paris 1952-1955, no. 151), whereas the word directly following *QL*^{c} is *BRK'*, in which ' is used to represent /o/; two systems of vowel notation in the same text is improbable, and cf. *N'DR* from NP 79, the reading of this word is extremely uncertain, but rather *NDR* than *N'DR*.
3) *FR* p. 44.
4) On this type of Berber personal names, cf. the author, *Names in Neo-Punic Inscriptions* (= *NNPI*), Groningen 1984 (diss., pp. 57ff.
5) *FR* p. 12f.
6) *id.*, p. 30f.
7) Cf. *FR* pp. 37, 94; the examples quoted for anaptyctic vowels in the neighbourhood laryngeals, *id.*, *ibid.*, are unconvincing: Greek *baal* originates from a Jewish author used to the form /ba^{c}al/, whereas *-a* in Greek *zera* must be explained as representation of /^{c}/, which explanation is given by Friedrich and Röllig, p. 38, only as a secondary possibility; in the spelling ^{I}*ba-'a-lu*, *'a* probably is meant for an audible laryngeal closing the syllable, for which the syllabic writing system of Akkadian did not have a proper sign; the only case in which anaptyxis can be made probable is in a double-closed syllable ending in /-r/, cf. *QBR* (< /qabr/) // *QB*^{c}*R*, *QB'R*, *NDR* (< /nidr/) // *ND*^{c}*R*, *SKR* (< /sikr/) // *SK*^{c}*R*, ^{c}*SR* (< /^{c}asr/) // ^{c}*S*^{c}*R* (for references cf. *DISO* s.v.).
8) The same explanation can be distilled from A. van den Branden, *Grammaire Phénicienne*, Beyrouth 1969, p. 121.
9) The material is from CIS i.
10) *KAI* 119 line 8; 129.
11) *KAI* 98; *Revue Africaine* vol. 88, 1947, p. 38, T9; p. 39 no. 3; p. 41 no. 24; p. 43 no 288; p. 44 no. 289.
12) OU = origin unknown; the texts of unknown, but Tunesian, origin used in this study were probably found in H(enchir) Maktar.
13) Punica xvii (= *JA* vol. xi, 10, 1917, pp. 31-38) 10.
14) P. Schröder, *Die Phönizische Sprache*, Halle 1869, p. 265 no. 5.
15) An overview of the inscriptions from Constantine known in the beginning of this century is to be found in Chabot's Punica xviii (= *JA* vol. xi, 10, 1917, pp. 38-79); many more texts were published in 1952 in *EH*.
16) Cf. note 7; the letter after some place names refers to the Neo-Punic inscriptions from that place; for a survey of Neo-Punic inscriptions, cf. *NNPI* pp. xvff.
17) Sub Constantine+ we have combined the Punic and Neo-Punic material from that town.
18) M.G. Guzzo Amadasi, *Le iscrizioni Fenicie e Puniche delle colonie in Occidente* (*Studi Semitici*, vol. 28; = *ICO*), Roma 1967, Malta-Pu 1, 1bis, 4.
19) *ICO* Sicilia-Pu 1, 5, 10.
20) *ICO* Sardinia-Pu 17, 34, 39.
21) *ICO* App. 2.
22) *ICO* Spagna-Pu 16.
23) CIS i 2592, 3390.
24) *KAI* 159 line 7.
25) For a survey of Neo-Punic texts from H. Maktar, cf. *NNPI* pp. xviii-xix; the texts containing *KḤ* are to be found in Punica xii (= *JA* vol. xi, 9, 1917, pp. 145-166) 3, 11.
26) Punica xvii 11.

27) Punica xviii ii 105, *EH* 251.
28) Punica xvii 3; apart from this text (= NP 112), *FR* p. 44 also quotes NP 36 (Punica xii 3) where the reading *KḤ* is given by Chabot.
29) Gesenius *Monumenta*, tab. 22 lviii (NP 8), *NNPI* p. 12 (NP 9).
30) Punica xviii ii 125, RES 1931, *EH* 101, 182.
31) *EH* 104.
32) Punica xii 6 and 9, on the reading cf. *NNPI* p. 5.
33) Punica xii 8; Chabot reads $P^{c}N$ $K^{c}N$; lapsus for $K^{c}N$ $K^{c}N$ or read $K^{c}N$ $K^{c}N$, cf. *NNPI* p. 5.
34) Punica xvii 2.
35) The reading K^{c}, tentatively proposed in CIS i ad 4440, is less probable, read rather *M* lapsus for *K*.
36) *KAI* 175, cf. also *FR* pp. 48, 49.
37) Cf. also *FR* pp. 59f.
38) For *PN'* cf. e.g. in Punic script: RES 1537, 1562, Punica xviii ii 73, 102, *EH* 16, 17, 54, 81 etc., and in Neo-Punic Script Punica xviii ii 26, *EH* 24, 270; for $P^{c}N'$cf. e.g. in Punic script: Punica xviii ii 63, 88, *EH* 4, 80 etc., in Neo-Punic script: Punica xi (= *JA* vol. xi, 8, 1916, pp. 483-520) 35bis, xviii i 31, ii 86, *EH* 21, 271, 277.
39) Cf. also *FR* p. 105.
40) Cf. *FR* p. 43.
41) $B^{c}T$ is attested in Punica xii 3; the same person is mentioned again in Punica xii 5 where the affiliation is expressed by *BT*.
42) Punica xii 3, 10.
43) Punica xii 10.
44) Punica xii 20, 22, 24, 28, 31, *KAI* 134.
45) *Cahiers de Byrsa* vol. 8, 1958-1959, p. 31.
46) CIS i 1165, *EH* 187.
47) Cf. also *NNPI* p. 116 and p. 133.
48) M. Lidzbarski, *Handbuch der Nordsemitischen Epigraphik*, Weimar 1898, p. 436 C 8 (for this text cf. also Chabot, Punica iv (= *JA* vol. xi, 7, 1916, pp. 87-103) A 6).
49) Punica xii 23, 28, xv 3, *KAI* 135.
50) Punica iv D 4.
51) Punica xv 3.
52) *KAI* 152.
53) *KAI* 134.
54) Lidzbarski, *Handbuch* p. 436 C 8 v. supra note 48).
55) Punica xii 28.
56) Punica xii 23, 24 etc.
57) Punica xii 22, *KAI* 149.
58) Punica xii 33.
59) Lidzbarski, *Handbuch* p. 436 C 8 (v. supra), Punica iv A 8.
60) Punica iv A 7.
61) Punica xii 27, 32.
62) Punica xii 14, 15, 16 etc.
63) *KAI* 150; cf. also *FR* p. 60 with note 1.
64) *KAI* 140.
65) Punica iv A 7, E 7, xii 25, *KAI* 151.
66) Punica xii 14, 16, *KAI* 133 etc.
67) For the Punic passages in the Poenulus, cf. M. Sznycer, *Les passages Puniques en transcription Latine dans le "Poenulus" de Plaute* (= *PPP*), for the text of the second version, see *ibid.*, p. 114, l. 941.
68) Sznycer, *PPP*, pp. 120f.
69) *ibid.*, p. 46, l. 931.
70) Cf. e.g. Greek *bun* in *KAI* 175, which represents rather /ben/ than /bin/ (and which cannot be explained as /bun/ as is done inadvertently by Gordon, *Ugaritic Textbook* (*Analecta Orientalia*, vol. 38) Roma 1965, p. 373 sub no. 481), Greek *ly* in the same text (cf. *FR* p. 34); the examples adduced in *FR* p. 34 to show that *y* may be

used for /i/ remain uncertain; the first *ys* in Poenulus, l. 935, is perhaps to be explained as the Punic equivalent of Hebrew *yēš*, rather than Hebrew *'īš*, whatever the correct explanation is, however, one may assume that the vowel underwent reduction > /e/.

71) Sznycer, *PPP*, pp. 56, 121, *FR* p. 34.
72) Sznycer, *ibid*.
73) It seems unnecessary to give references for the following words from different Northwest-Semitic languages; cf. e.g. *DISO*.
74) Cf. *UT*, Glossary s.v. *k*.
75) Cf. *CAD* s.v.
76) Cf. also Von Soden, *GAG*, p. 165, 170.
77) On this relationship, cf. also Brockelmann, *GVG* vol. 1, p. 74.
78) J. Barth, *Sprachwissenschaftliche Untersuchungen zum Semitischen* I, Leipzig 1907, p. 17.
79) Cf. *CAD* s.v.
80) Cf. A. Erman - H. Grapow, *Wörterbuch der Aegyptischen Sprache*, Band 5, Leipzig 1931, p. 84; R.O. Faulkner, *A concise Dictionary of Middle Egyptian*, Oxford 1972, p. 283, "so, then", possibly related to the verb *k3i*, cf. e.g. A.H. Gardiner, *Egyptian Grammar*, Oxford-London 1950[2], p. 181; cf. perhaps also *kw*, a particle preceding a verbal used as an imperative, cf. E. Edel, *Altägyptische Grammatik*, vol. 2 (*Analecta Orientalia*, vol. 34 (39), Rome 1958/1964, p. 431.
81) Cf. e.g. J.-M. Dallet, *Dictionnaire Kabyle-Français*, Paris 1982, p. 388: *akka* "ainsi, de cette façon, comme".
82) Cf. also the uncertainty in 2 Sam 16:10 ketīb *KY*, qerē *kōh*.
83) *KAI* 175.
84) CIS i 3992, 4475.
85) CIS i 2522.
86) Punica xvii 1.
87) Cf. e.g. J. Friedrich in *ZDMG* vol. 107, 1957, p. 286; *FR* p. 60, and also M. Sznycer, "La vocalisation des formes verbales dans l'écriture Néopunique" in *Actes du Premier Congrès international de linguistique Sémitique et Chamito-Sémitique 1969*, The Hague-Paris 1974, p. 209ff., esp. p. 212.
88) A relationship of Hebrew *kēn* (< **kin*) with the root *kwn*, seems less probable.
89) Cf. *CAD* s.v. *akanna A*.
90) Cf. *CAD* s.v. *akanna B*.
91) Cf. *DISO* s.v.
92) Cf. Sznycer, *PPP*, pp. 84f.
93) Cf. also *FR* p. 124.
94) Differences between Phoenician and Punic of what might be called a dialectal type are known, of course, cf. e.g. the suffix indicating the 3rd p. m. sg. *-M*, which is almost exclusively attested in Punic (where also *-Y* (*-Y'*) and *-'* are found), against Phoenician where *-H*, *-W* and *-Y* are used; cf. *FR* pp. 47f.

The Origin of the Mandaic Script

A. Klugkist, Groningen

Because of the special forms of its characters the old Mandaic script is one of the most interesting middle Aramaic scripts[1]. About the origin of this script different theories have been developed, most of them concerning the question of the origin of the Mandaean sect in south Mesopotamia and Khuzistan, of which descendants are still living in the southern Iraq-Iran border area.

Fifteen years ago, three scholars made a detailed study of the origin of the Mandaic script, namely: P.W. Coxon[2], J. Naveh[3] and R. Macuch[4]. In particular they paid attention to the possible relations of this script to other middle Aramaic scripts, like that of the Elymaeans and the Characenians in southern Mesopotamia and that of the Nabataeans in Palestine. On comparing all these scripts they came to different conclusions.

P.W. Coxon is of the opinion that "the Mandaean script in its earliest attested form appears already to have adopted features of cursive writing, whereas the Elymaean group has adhered to the archaic lapidary script". His conclusion is that "the corpus of the comparative evidence points to the primacy of the Elymaean over against the Mandaean forms of the letters and that the latter seem to be stylized reductions of the older Elymaean orthography"[5].

R. Macuch, on the contrary, takes the view that the Mandaic script is older than the southern Mesopotamian script of Elymaea and also that of Characene. He even asserts that the latter scripts are influenced by and dependent on the former. His view is that the Mandaic script was already in use in south Mesopotamia in the second century A.D. and that the Elymaic and the Characenian script branched off from the Mandaic script. Moreover Macuch thinks that there are good reasons to believe in a western origin of the Mandaean sect. According to him the roots of Mandaeism are to be sought in Jewish circles in Palestine. By migration the Mandaean belief and the Mandaic script must have been imported from Palestine into south Mesopotamia. This would also explain the resemblance ("genuine associations") between Mandaic and Nabataean characters.

J. Naveh thinks it exaggerated to speak of direct relations between the Mandaic and Nabataean scripts. He denies Macuch's assertion that the Mandaeans took over the use of ligatures from the Nabataeans, remarking that ligatures are natural by-products of well-developed cursive scripts. He concludes: "Though there is no conclusive evidence, it seems likely that the Mandaeans adopted a ligatured formal script and stabilized it. At any rate palaeographic criteria support neither the theory of a western origin of the Mandaeans nor the existence of the sect in Khuzistan in the second century A.D."[6]. Although Naveh has written several times about the Mandaic script[7], he has not essentially changed his view.

Analysis of the old Mandaic script

Before we deal with the letters of the old Mandaic alphabet by comparing them with the letters of several other middle Aramaic scripts (see fig.) we would like to remark first of all that there are no important differences between the old Mandaic letters used on incantation bowls and those used on lead rolls. Taking into account the different materials (pottery and lead), the conclusion is justified that the old Mandaic script shows a remarkable unifomity.

alef The circular, oval or triangular shape of the old Mandaic *alef* is fairly typical of the middle Aramaic scripts. Only on the Characene coins and in some Elymaic and Nabataean inscriptions similar *alef* shapes are found. The old Mandaic and the Characene *alef* are linked at the foot, while the Nabataean variant is linked at the top.

bet The old Mandaic *bet* resembles the Elymaic *bet*, although in the latter the joining line generally extends from top right to bottom left. But also in Mandaic the central joining line often varies in position (to bottom left, to bottom right, vertical), sometimes even within one text. Similar *bet* shapes however can also be found in other middle Aramaic scripts, as our figure shows.

gimel The old Mandaic *gimel* has a unique form. For this manner of writing no clear parallels in other middle Aramaic scripts exist.

dalet Here the downstroke to bottom left is characteristic. The Elymaic *dalet* and some Palmyrene forms of *dalet* also have a leftward downstroke, although written somewhat different. Compare the *dalet* in the Avroman parchments.

he The *he*, often difficult to distinguish from the *alef*, has a form for which no clear parallels can be found. Although there is some resemblance with the Elymaic and the (old) Syriac *he*, it is not justified to conclude with Naveh that the "Mandaic *he* also developed from Elymaic"[8]. Macuch writes in his article "Anfänge der Mandäer" that: "... finales *-h*, dass allein als Suffix der 3. P. Sg. gebraucht wird, und sich nur als Entwicklung des finalen nabatäischen *-h* erklären lässt, kommt in den elymäischen Inschriften in einer verschiedenen Form vor". Further on he writes: "Das finale mand. *-h* wurde also in die elymäische Schrift nicht übernommen"[9].

Two critical remarks must be made here. In the first place it is hard to understand why the Elymaeans - if they had taken over the Old Mandaic script as Macuch wants us to believe - by exception restrained themselves from adopting the old Mandaic *he* for the representation of the 3. P. Sg. Scripts are not taken over in such a selective way. In the second place it goes too far to see a similarity between the old Mandaic and the Nabataean *he*.

waw The old Mandaic *waw* must be regarded as a stylistic reduction of the cursive Imperial Aramaic *waw*. In other middle Aramaic scripts the *waw* is more elaborate. There are no reasons to assume a special relation with Elymaic or Nabataean *waw* shapes. It is noteworthy that the Mandaic *waw* can be linked with other characters on both sides.

zayin, yod In my opinion these characters too are simple representations of their cursive Imperial Aramaic equivalents, which is also the case with the *zayin* and the *yod* in most other middle Aramaic scripts. The similarity of the middle Aramaic forms of *zayin* and *yod* must therefore in the first place be explained by parallel development.

ḥet The old Mandaic *ḥet* finds its nearest parallels in the (old) Syriac and the Characenian *ḥet*. Similar *ḥet*-forms can be found in some northern Mesopotamian middle Aramaic scripts, such as in Hatra.

ṭet This letter has a unique form, although some Characenian forms show some resemblance to it. Macuch's statement that the dependence of this letter on its Nabataean equivalent is clear from both Coxon's and Naveh's comparative charts is incorrect, even if the position of the Nabataean letter is turned 90° as Macuch wants[10].

kaf The old Mandaic *kaf* has a form which more or less resembles the cursive Imperial Aramaic *kaf* and the *kaf* as it appears in several middle Aramaic scripts, but it attracts the attention by the typical way in which it is written: a long stroke upwards to the left makes it possible to connect this letter with other ones. This is also the case with the old Mandaic *nun*, *pe* and *ṣade*. A related way of writing can be observed in the Characenian and Elymaic script, but here the connecting stroke does not make such a sharp angle (except Characenian *n*).

I want to explain this different way of writing of the above mentioned letters by regarding the Elymaic and Characenian script as belonging to a monumental or lapidary type of script and the old Mandaic script as belonging to a cursive one. This, however, does not mean that for this reason it is possible to conclude that the Elymaic and the Characenian script is older than the Mandaic script and that the Mandaic script stands in a dependent relation to the former two, as Coxon[11)] says. The opposite statement of Macuch is likewise unfounded[12)].

lamed The old Mandaic *lamed* has a form which can also be seen in several other middle Aramaic scripts. Here, too, I think there is a parallel development from the cursive Imperial Aramaic script.

mem The old Mandaic *mem* does not look like the Nabataean *mem* and I cannot understand Macuch's assertion of the opposite[13)]. Closer parallels can be found in the old Syriac and Palmyrene script. The Characenian *mem* has a corresponding form. The Elymaic *mem* in general has the form of a cross.

nun See my remarks about the *kaf*.

samek The old Mandaic *samek* looks like the Elymaic and Characenian *samek*. Macuch[14)] thinks that this letter is also of Nabataean origin, which is denied by Naveh[15)].

Although there are some *samek* forms in Nabataean inscriptions that show some similarity with the old Mandaic *samek*, it is not right to conclude a special relationship between both scripts on account of this, because similar forms of *samek* are also met in other middle Aramaic scripts like the Jewish Aramaic script of Palestine and Babylonia, the script of the Avroman parchments and that of the Nisa ostraca.

I therefore think that in this case too it is better to assume a parallel development of middle Aramaic forms from cursive Imperial Aramaic forms.

ᶜayin The Mandaic *ᶜayin* closely resembles the (old) Syrian *ᶜayin* and - to a lesser degree - the cursive Palmyrene *ᶜayin*. Also in other middle Aramaic scripts like that of Hatra and Assur similar forms can be found. The Elymaic *ᶜayin* has a different form which resembles the monumental Palmyrene *ᶜayin* and which is also usual in the Nabataean script.

pe, ṣade See my remarks about the *kaf*.

qof In other middle Aramaic scripts there are no forms of *qof* which fully correspond with the old Mandaic *qof* except on some Syriac magic bowls. I think that these are incidental cases of Mandaic influence on the Syriac script of the magic bowls.

reš In old Mandaic texts the *reš* is sometimes difficult to distinguish from the *dalet*. Remarkable is the relatively smooth styling of this letter, compared with other middle Aramaic *reš*-forms. Also here the leftward downstroke is characteristic.

šin The old Mandaic *šin* has a unique form which does not occur in other middle Aramaic scripts, except for the Characenian *šin*, some *šin*-forms on Syriac magic bowls and the *šin* in the inscriptions of Garni and Hassan-Kef[16]. In my opinion this is an illustration of the fact that in geographically different places of the middle Aramaic language area parallel developments of Aramaic letter forms took place. It is clear that in these cases one cannot speak of special relations.

tau According to Macuch[17] the old Mandaic *tau* is the same as the Elymaic. This is clear (and this is also the case with the Characenian *tau*). The Mandaic and Elymaic *tau* are in his opinion of Nabataean origin. This is denied by Naveh[18]. Coxon[19] writes that the old Mandaic and Characenian *tau* is paleographically similar to the cursive Palmyrene and Nabataean *tau*-forms, while the Elymaic *tau* is compared by him with the lapidary Palmyrene and Nabataean *tau*.
It is true that the old Mandaic *tau* resembles some (but not all) Nabataean - and Palmyrene - *tau*-forms. But some old Syriac *tau*-forms are also similar. And on the Persis-coins and in Jewish Babylonian and Palestinian texts related *tau*-forms occur. So one certainly cannot speak of an exclusive relationship between old Mandaic and Nabataean *tau*.

ḏ- Finally I would like to discuss the Mandaic relative particle *ḏ-*, which is also found in Elymaic inscriptions but in no other Aramaic dialect[20]. The relative particle *ḏ-* is graphically represented by the ligature of *z* + *y*. Macuch considers *ḏ-* as an independent Mandaean invention, which is borrowed by the Elymaeans. He thinks that this ligature "bears incontestable proof that the Elymaean inscriptions are nothing else but Mandaic in both script and language"[21]. Naveh, on the contrary, says that without any doubt old Mandaic *ḏ-* developed from Elymaic *zy* "and not the other way round"[22]. My opinion is that neither Macuch's nor Naveh's thesis can be proved. Also unprovable is a third possibility, namely that both scripts originated from a common prototype. One can only say that the exclusive use of *ḏ-* in Mandaic and Elymaic shows that both languages and scripts stood in a close relation to each other.

Conclusions

It is evident that the old Mandaic, the Elymaic and the Characenian script are closely related to each other. These scripts must be considered as one group or script-tradition. The differences in the forms of their letters are mainly determined by the fact that the old Mandaic script has a cursive style, while the Characenian script can be described as semi-cursive (or semi-monumental) and the Elymaic could be considered as monumental (or lapidary). However, it cannot be denied that the monumental Elymaic script also shows cursive character-traits. I think that for Elymaic inscribed texts most probably cursively written texts served as examples.

This is no exception: we can notice that in several Aramaic texts monumental or lapidary forms alternate with cursive forms. One of the clearest examples is the Palmyrene script[23)]. A cursive or monumental way of writing and likewise the use of (semi-)ligatures do not automatically tell us something about the stage of development of a script. The use of ligatures is inherent to cursive scripts. Which way of writing or which type of script is used (cursive or monumental) is primarily a question of function. Mixed script types prove that no clear lines can be drawn here. This does not only apply to Semitic scripts but to scripts in general.

So, taking into account that there are several examples of cursively and monumentally styled scripts which are simultaneously used in one and the same region and in one and the same place, I think it impossible to decide which of the three scripts (old Mandaic, Elymaic and Characenian) is dependent on or has originated from the other two.

Coxon is right when he states that it is impossible "to substantiate claims for the historical presence of the Mandaean sect in southern Mesopotamia in the second century A.D. on the basis of script analysis", but it is untrue that "the corpus of the comparative evidence points to the primacy of the Elymaean over against the Mandaean forms of the letters and that the latter seem to be stylized reductions of the older Elymaean orthography"[24)]. Furthermore the assertion that "die mand. Buchstaben am meisten den nabatäischen entsprechen ..." and that "... ihre Ähnlichkeit nicht weiter bewiesen zu werden braucht" is unjustified. But it also goes too far to write that "there is no connection at all between the Nabataean and the Mandaic scripts" as Naveh[26)] does.

On the basis of script analysis one can only state that the old Mandaic, Elymaic and Characenian scripts are the representatives of one group, one script-tradition, which existed in the second/third century A.D. in southern Mesopotamia and Khuzistan. Some old Mandaic letters may resemble Nabataean letter forms, but compared with other middle Aramaic scripts one connot speak of a special resemblance or an exclusive relationship between both scripts. In our script analysis we saw that there are also several resemblances and similarities between Mandaic letters and letters of the (old) Syriac, the Palmyrene and other middle Aramaic scripts. Like these other scripts, the old Mandaic script is not an original script, but a script that originated from the encounter of several middle Aramaic script traditions which have the cursive Imperial Aramaic script as their common background.

I think we have to acknowledge that the development of middle Aramaic scripts is complicated. The history of their development cannot be traced with certainty. And it seems that the more material becomes available the more complicated the picture is. Or, as R. Dussaud states: "La réalité est généralement plus complexe que ne le laisse entrevoir la pénurie de notre documentation. Dès que nos renseignements deviennent plus nombreux, les solutions simples sont dépassées"[27].

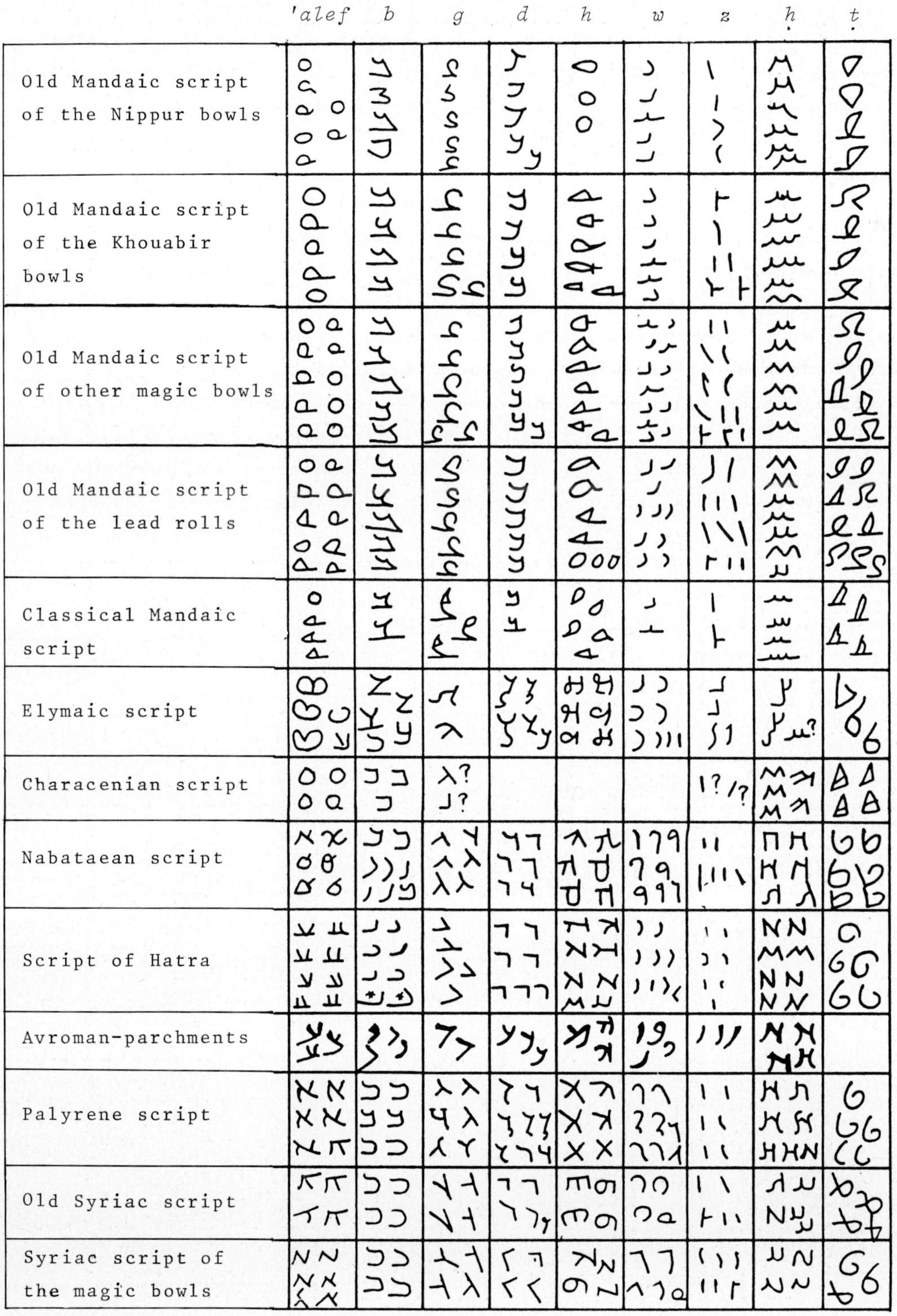
'alef
b
g
d
h
w
z
ḥ
ṭ
Old Mandaic script of the Nippur bowls
Old Mandaic script of the Khouabir bowls
Old Mandaic script of other magic bowls
Old Mandaic script of the lead rolls
Classical Mandaic script
Elymaic script
Characenian script
Nabataean script
Script of Hatra
Avroman-parchments
Palyrene script
Old Syriac script
Syriac script of the magic bowls

Fig. 1

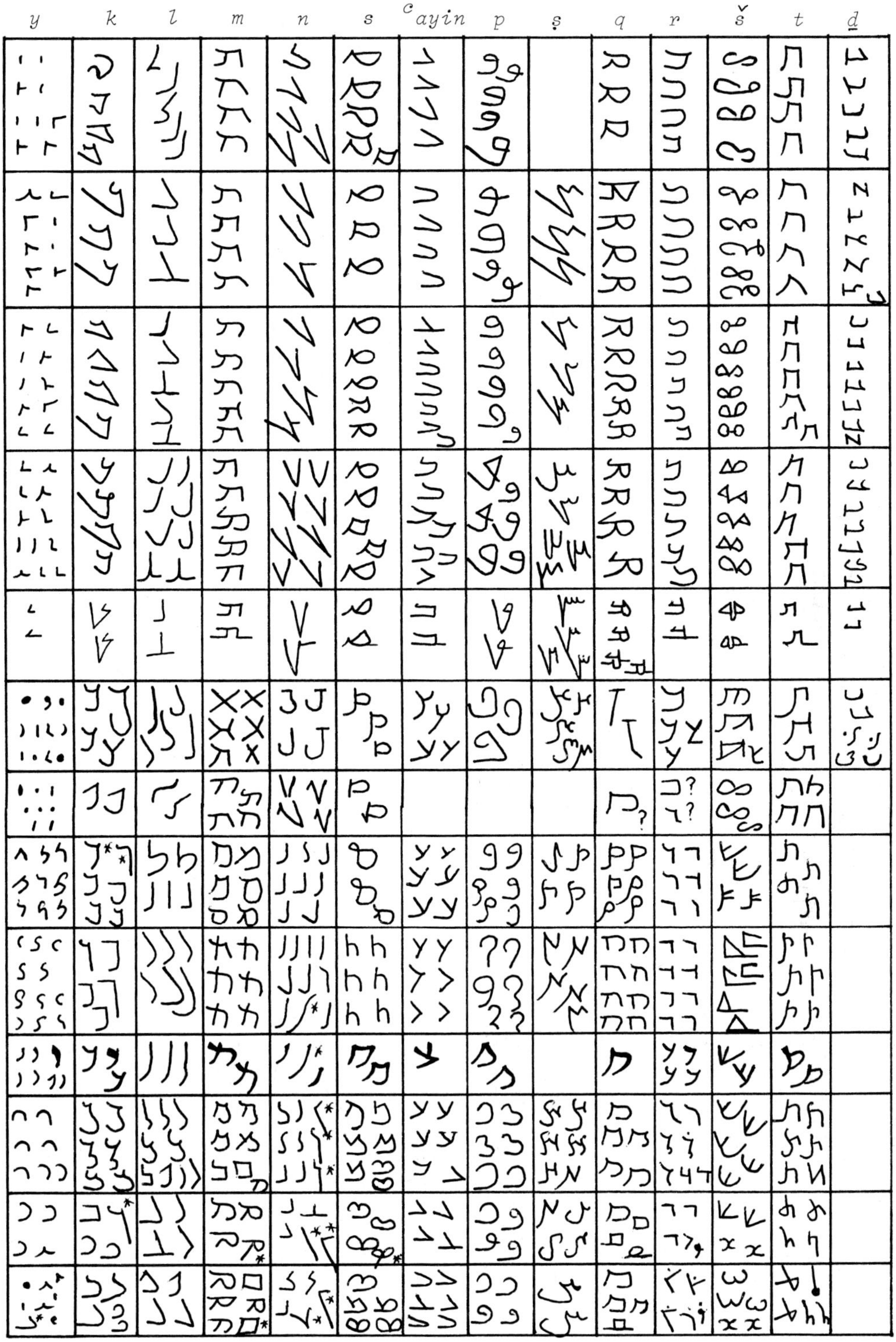

Fig. 2

Notes

1) On the middle Aramaic scripts see my *Midden-Aramese schriften in Syrië, Mesopotamië, Perzië en aangrenzende gebieden*, Groningen 1982 (diss.).
2) P.W. Coxon, "Script Analysis and Mandaean Origins" in *JSS* vol. 15, 1970, pp. 16-30.
3) J. Naveh, "The Origins of the Mandaic script" in *BASOR* vol. 198, 1970, pp. 32-37.
4) R. Macuch, "The Origins of the Mandaeans and their script" in *JSS* vol. 16, 1971, pp. 174-192. See also his articles "Anfänge der Mandäer" in *Die Araber in der Alten Welt*(= *AAW*), vol. 2, pp. 76-191, and "Altmandäische Bleirolle" in *AAW*, vol. 4, pp. 91ff.
5) Coxon, *op. cit.*, p. 29.
6) Naveh, *op. cit.*, p. 37.
7) For example: J. Naveh, *Early history of the Alphabet. An introduction to West Semitic epigraphy and palaeography*, Leiden 1982 pp. 132f.
8) Naveh, *op. cit.*, p. 36.
9) Macuch, *op. cit.* in *AAW* vol. 2, p. 144.
10) Macuch, *op. cit.* in *JSS* vol. 16, 1971, pp. 180-182.
11) Coxon, *op. cit.*, p. 26.
12) Macuch, *op. cit.*in *JSS* vol. 16, 1971, p. 185.
13) Macuch, *op. cit. ibid.* p. 183/4.
14) Macuch, *op. cit. ibid.* p. 188.
15) Naveh, *op. cit.*, p. 37.
16) See my *Midden-Aramese schriften*, pp. 240-241.
17) Macuch, *op. cit.* in *JSS* vol. 16, 1971, p. 188.
18) Naveh, *op. cit.*, p. 37.
19) Coxon, *op. cit.*, p. 29.
20) The reason that *d-* is not found in the Characenian inscriptions is most probably their brevity and illegibility.
21) Macuch, *op. cit.* in *JSS* vol. 16, 1971, p. 187.
22) Naveh, *op. cit.*, p. 36.
23) See my article "The importance of the Palmyrene script for our knowledge of the development of the late Aramaic scripts" in *Aramaeans, Aramaic and the Aramaic Literary Tradition*, ed. M. Sokoloff, Bar-Ilan 1982, pp. 142-168.
24) Coxon, *op. cit.*, p. 29
25) Macuch, *op. cit.* in *AAW* vol. 2, p. 145.
26) Naveh, *op. cit.*, p. 33.
27) R. Dussaud, "L'origine de l'alphabet et son évolution première d'après les découvertes de Byblos" in *Syria*, vol. 25, 1946-1948, p. 67.

Some Significant Composition Techniques in Deuteronomy

C. Labuschagne, Groningen

The purpose of this contribution is to demonstrate that the book of Deuteronomy is a numerical composition and to illustrate some of the most significant rhetorical techniques used to compose its text. A 'numerical composition' can be defined as a literary work of which the structure is essentially and fundamentally governed by certain numbers, such as *7, 10, 11, 13, 17* and their multiples, which I suggest to call *structure numbers*.

The structural use of numbers

The primary function of these numbers is to give structure to the text, i.e. to function as a technical device for determining the number of words in the text as a whole in its larger units, its pericopes, subsections, verses, sentences and clauses. It will be shown that a great variety of compositional formulae and models were used which have one thing in common and that is that they are all governed by the same limited number of undoubtedly symbolic numbers. We do not intend to study the symbolic aspects of these numbers here, since we are primarily concerned with their structural use. We should distinguish clearly between on the one hand the purely technical use of numbers as a device to give structure to the text and on the other hand the symbolic function of numbers to 'deepen' a text and to give it an extra dimension. The study of the structural use of numbers is an exact and objectively controllable matter of which the truth and accuracy can be checked by everyone. To determine their symbolic function precisely, however, is a different matter. Our knowledge of this is dependent upon post-biblical Jewish tradition and must remain tentative, at least for the time being until further study sheds new light on this particular aspect of numbers in biblical times. It would be a worthwhile undertaking to probe more deeply into the symbolic function of numbers. There is nothing mysterious about this, since it is something that can be investigated, but we have to distinguish sharply between number symbolism as a device for deepening a text and number mysticism as a later product of the fantasy, which

is a matter we need not take seriously here.
What concerns us here is the phenomenon of numerical compositions and the structural use of numbers, matters not unknown to classical and medieval scholars[1)], but up till now little known among biblical scholars and generally ignored by most. It was the Austrian scholar C. Schedl who has recently called the attention of the biblical scholarly world to the structural use of numbers in biblical texts[2)].
My own independent rediscovery of this phenomenon stems from my research with regard to the divine speech formulae in the Pentateuch[3)].
Schedl's work, especially his logotechnical method for text analysis inspired me to continue research in this field[4)] and to submit the book of Deuteronomy to a complete numerical structural analysis[5)]. The results of this analysis, to my mind and in my judgement, have established beyond any doubt that Deuteronomy in its present form is a meticulously constructed numerical composition. There is no doubt concerning the importance of this discovery: it has far-reaching consequences for our insight into the use of the Hebrew language (its grammar and syntax), the structure of the book, the delimitation and structure of its various component parts, the way in which it was composed, more particularly the use made of certain rhetorical techniques. Among such techniques the structural use of numbers is of paramount importance.
In addition to the evidence previously advanced concerning the structural role of certain numbers, in particular *10*, *17* and *26*, in the phrasing of certain stereotyped terms, more specifically the formulae introducing and referring to the divine speeches, and in the general structure of these speeches (*10* in Deut 1-3; *10* in Deut 4-26 and *10* in Deut 27-34)[6)]. I shall now try to give the reader, more particularly my friend and colleague J.H. Hospers, an impression of the new evidence. What follows here is not more than an impression, since it is impossible to present the overwhelming amount of evidence here in detail.

Logotechnical analysis of texts

In order to enable the reader to follow my presentation of the compositional formulae and models, I first must say something about my logotechnical method of text analysis step by step. The first step is to decompose the text verse by verse on the basis of a careful syntactical analysis into its smallest syntactical units and to write them separately in a column. Then the words in the syntactical units and the verses are counted in order to find the total number of words in the different verses and in a) the first half of the verse, i.e. before the *'atnāḥ*, b) the second half of the verse, c) the main clauses and d) the subordinate clauses[7]. The compositional formula of the verse, based on the *parallelismus membrorum* with the *'atnāḥ* as versedivider[8], can now be established, as well as the formula used for the syntax. The next step is to delimitate the group of verses forming a structural unit with the help of the masoretic structuring devices *pārāšā petūḥā* and *setūmā* (as far as they are present) and on the basis of the contents. The third step is to establish the compositional formula of such a structural unit, which is always made up of one or more of the structure numbers (or their multiples) mentioned above, with a distinct preference for *17* and *26* and their multiples. This means that the occurence of these numbers in the compositional formulae can be used as a criterion for determining the limits of a structural unit. These formulae are a great help in determining the exact delimitation and very often serve to correct wrong delimitations of the text. Moreover, there is a striking tendency to use the same formula for different purposes: to give structure to the syntax (with regard to the main and subordinate clauses), to the *parallelismus membrorum* (the division of the verse by means of the *'atnāḥ*) and often also to the contents, as we shall demonstrate presently. The next step is to find and apply relevant criteria for analysing the contents in order to establish the number of words used in the categories: narrative/dialogue, prohibition/command/motivation, singular/plural, and the different acting subjects, e.g. YHWH, Moses, Israël, the enemies. The last steps are devoted to the assessment of the number of words in larger literary units and the counting of the number of 'larger' and 'smaller' units and verses in the book and to the discovery of all possible numerical structures.

Let us illustrate what has been said above with some examples, starting with the first structural unit of the speech of Moses, 1:6-8, of which I present a complete logotechnical analysis:

				MC	*SC*	*Contents*	
6. *YHWH 'èlōhēnū dibbèr 'ēlēnū beḥōrēb*	11	5	I	5		*Intro-duction*	6
lēmōr		1	II		I		
rab-lākèm		2	III	2		YHWH's com-mand to Israel	14
šèbèt bāhār hazzè		3	IV		3		
7. *penū*	23	1	V	1!			
ūseʿū lākèm		2	VI	2!			
ūbō'ū har hā'èmōrī we'èl-kol-šekēnāw		6	VII	6!			
bāʿarābā bāhār ūbaššefēlā						*Geogra-phical*	14
ūbannègèb ūbeḥōf hayyām		6	VIII		6		

'èrèṣ hakk^{e}na^{ca}nī w^{e}hall^{e}bānōn	3 IX	14	3	*appo-*	
^{c}ad-hannāhār haggādōl n^{e}har-p^{e}rāt:	5 X		5	*sition*	
Vss. 6-7	(*34* =	16+I+*17*)		(6+14+14)	
	=	*17* + *17*			
8. *r^{e}'ē*	1 I	1!		YHWH's	
nātattī lifnēkèm 'èt-hā'ārèṣ	4 II	4		com-	
bō'ū	1 III	1!		mand	
ūr^{e}šū 'èt-hā'ārèṣ	20: 3 IV	3!		based	20
'^{a}šèr nišba^{c} YHWH la'^{a}bōtēkèm	4 V		4	on his	
l^{e}'abrāhām l^{e}yiṣḥāq ūl^{e}ya^{ca}qōb	3 VI	"11"	3	pro-	
lātēt lāhèm: ūl^{e}zar^{c}ām 'ah^{a}rēhèm	4 VII		4	mise	
Vs. 8	(20 =	9 + 11)		(20)	
Total: Vss. 6-8	54 =	25+I+28		6+14+14+20	
	=	*26* + 28		28 / *26*	

The compositional formula for the syntax of the first sub-section vss. 6-7, is *34* = *17* + *17* and that of the whole pericope is 54 = *26*+28. This final formula also serves to give structure to the *parallelismus membrorum* (with *'atnāḥ*) as verse divider:

vs. 6a	*6*	
b		5
vs. 7a	*15*	
b		8
vs. 8a	*5*	
b		15
	26 +	28 = 54.

The compositional formula is used even a third time, to give structure to the contents:

- Introduction to YHWH's speech (vs. 6, underlined)	*6*	
- Command concerning the journey to the land		14
- Description of the land		14
- Command to take possession of the land	*20*	
	26 +	28 = 54.

Thus we get the following picture of the compositional formula being used three times:

- Total = MC + SC = a + b = Possess + Go to land

  54 = *26* + 28 = *26*+28 = *26* + 28.

The dominance of *17* and *26* is quite evident. The number *17* is also present in the number of words phrased in the 3rd person singular form with YHWH as subject:

- vs. 6a (underlined) 6 }
- vs. 8 (underlined) 11 } *17*

In yet another way can it be made explicit, namely in the so-called Menorah-model of vs. 8 - see below.

The pericope has *17* clauses: ten in the first subsection (vss. 6-7, I-X divided into 4 + 6, the Decalogue-model) and seven in the second (vs. 8, I-VII, composed according to the Menorah-model[9], of which more examples will be given presently). These *17* clauses have their counterpart at the end of the first half of Moses' speech (1-6 - 2:1) where there is a distinct caesura (-S- in *BHS*) after the last pericope, 1:44 - 2:1, which also has exactly *17* clauses. The two sets of *17* clauses function as an *inclusio* which stresses the unity of 1:6 - 2:1. Other examples of this *inclusio* technique by means of *17* clauses (7+10 in a chiastic figure!) are, e.g. 3:18-29 and 5:1-22:

3:18-20	7 + 10 = 17		5: 1-5	7 + 10 = 17
3:26-29	10 + 7 = 17	and	5:17-22	10 + 7 = 17.

The pericope under discussion, 1:6-8, is dominated by the number *7* in the number of words in various categories:

- the introductory *lēmōr*[10] and YHWH's speech	*49 (7x7)*
- the imperative (!) clauses	*14 (2x7)*
- the subordinate clauses (with *'ašèr* and Inf.)	*14 (2x7)*
- the command to go to the land	*14 (2x7)*
- the description of the land	*14 (2x7)*.

For a similar phenomenon we may compare 8:7-10, where we find:

- in the opening sub. clause (vs. 7a)	7 words
- in the last main clause (vs. 10b)	7 words
- the word *'èrèṣ* (cf. 11:8-12!)	7 times
- the fruit of the land (vs. 8)	7 kinds
- the total number of clauses	14 (2x7).

Incidentally, like in 1:6-8, the compositional formula is used three times: for the syntax, for the *parallelismus membrorum* and for the contents (criterion: 'acting subject'):

- Total	=	MC + SC	=	a + b	=	YHWH/land	+	Israel
55	=	29 + *26*	=	*26* + 29	=	*26*	+	29.

This dominance of the number *7* can be found in many instances, but in 1:19-22 it is very conspicuous. There the composition formula, *77* = *49* + *28*, i.e. *(11x7)* = *(7x7* + *(4x7)*, occurs twice, first in the syntactical structure: 77 = 49MC + 28SC and second in the structure of the contents:

- Moses' address to the people (20b-21) 28 }
- Narratives (19-20a and 22): 25 + 24 = 49 } 77.

The dominance of *7* is also very noticeable in 2:26-37, which has *175*

(*7*x*25*) words and in which many multiples of *7* occur in the different categories: *56*, *77*, *98*, *119*. In 2:16 - 3:29 we count *770* (*7*x*10*x*11*) words and in 3: 1-10 and again in 3:11-17 *119* (*7*x*17*) words.
There are numerous examples of the dominance of the number *11*, especially in contexts dealing with the realisation of the promise of land:

- in 2:2-8a the divine speech has *55* } 121 words
- in 2:8b-15 the divine speech has *66* }
- in 2:16-25 the divine speech has *121* words
- in 3:1-7 we count a total of *110* words
    - the main clauses have *55* words
    - the sub. clauses have *55* words
    - the narrative consists of *88* words
    - the divine speech has *22* words
- in 3:18-22 Moses cites *55* words
- in 3:23-29 we count a total of *99* words
    - in the main clauses *55* words
    - in the sub. clauses *44* words

The Menorah-model

Returning to the passage under discussion, 1:6-8, we will now have a closer look at the Menorah-model in vs. 8, a very popular compositional model. The seven clauses are phrased so as to make the number *17* explicit in the 6 'outer' clauses and to focus special attention upon the clause in the centre of the structure (*ūr*^{e}*šū 'èt-hā'ārèṣ*) which is always of paramount importance in the context. As a further example of a small Menorah-model let us take 5:1, where we get a similar type of structure:

Deut 1:8 Deut 5:1

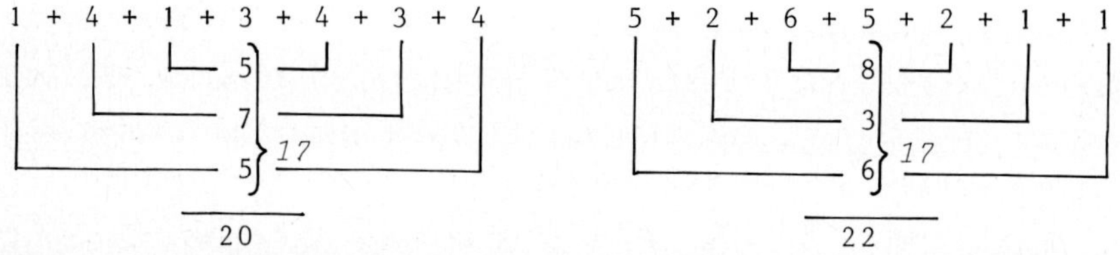

Here again the words at the centre are brought into focus and at the same time the number *17* is made explicit. For other examples of this type, see e.g. 5:28 and 6:4b-6, but there are also other types, for the discussion of which I have to refer to my Deuteronomy commentary. However, I cannot withhold from the reader the ingenious structure of the *22* words in 7:13, which has not only a Menorah-model but also contains the *7+4*-pattern to be discussed presently. Deut 7:13 has:

- 4 verbs describing God's promises
    - 11 words naming the *7* blessings
- 7 words about the land.

The *11* words in the centre, naming the *7* blessings are arranged in a Menorah-structure (with 'your wine' in the centre):

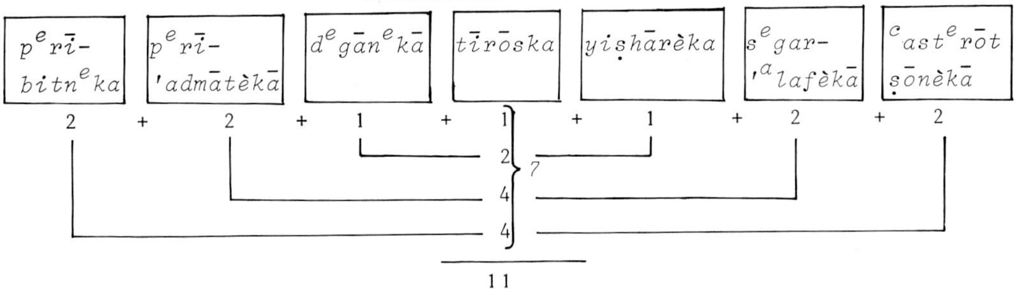

in which the *7+4*-pattern can once more be made explicit!

As an example of a larger Menorah-model let us examine Deut 7 and its content. This chapter is situated exactly in the centre of the seven 'major' literary units in chapters 4-11:

Units	Verses
I (4:1-43)	*43* (*17+26*)
II (4:44 - 6:3)	42 (6x*7*)
III (6:4-25)	22 (2x*11*)
IV (7:1-26)	*26* (2x*13*)
V (8:1 - 9:6)	26 (2x*13*)
VI (9:7 - 10:11)	34 (2x*17*)
VII (10:12 - 11:32)	*43* (*17+26*)

Units I and VII with *43* verses each serve as an *inclusio*. Unit IV, chapter 7, in the centre, has exactly *26* verses.
A closer study of this chapter has revealed the following Menorah-model based upon its smaller literary units and their number of words:

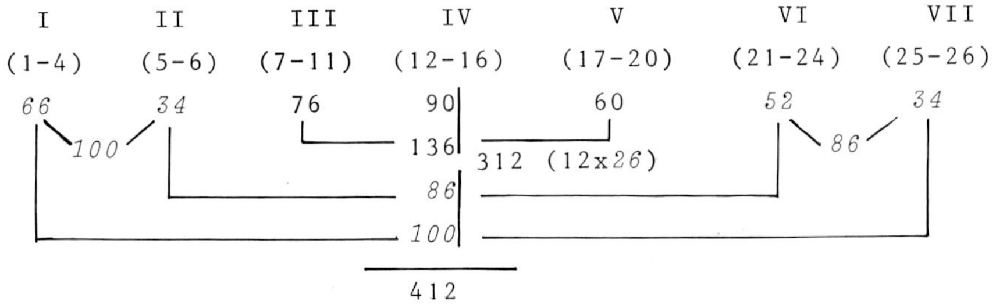

The numerical pattern speaks for itself. At the same time we have a magnificent concentric pattern, which cannot be discussed here any further because of lack of space.

The concentric structure and the *7+4*-pattern

Let us rather turn to another example of a large Menorah-model: the Decalogue-pericope (4:44 - 6:3 - without the superscription: 5:1 - 6:3), to illustrate the concentric structure, and at the same time the *7+4*-pattern. The literary unit 5:1 - 6:3 is delimitated in *BHS* by a *pārāšā pᵉtūḥā* at the beginning and at the end (the Decalogue itself, vss. 6-21, is divided by eleven instances of *pārāšā* *s*^{e}*tūmā* into *10* parts, vs. 21 being split in two to obtain this). On the basis of a logotechnical analysis the following structure presents itself in the first part (vss. 1-22):

I	(1-5)	Prologue
II	(6-11)	Prohibitions
III	(12-14)	Commandment
IV	(15)	Paraenesis
V	(16)	Commandment
VI	(17-21)	Prohibitions
VII	(22)	Epilogue

The second part, 5:23 - 6:3, has four literary units, consisting of three speeches of which the last one has two distinct parts:

I	(23-27)	Israel's reaction (Speech 1)
II	(28-31)	YHWH's reaction (Speech 2)
III	(32-33)	Moses' reaction (Speech 3a)
IV	(6:1-3)	Moses' reaction (Speech 3b).

Here we meet for the third time the unmistakable *7+4*-pattern, a very popular structuring pattern in the Pentateuch and particularly in Genesis, of which I have found a great number of examples[11]. The major literary units before and after the Decalogue-pericope have the same pattern, but in the following way:

I	(4:1-4)	I	*(6:4-9)*
II	(4:5-8)	II	*(6:10-15)*
III	(4:9-10)	III	*(6:16-19)*
IV	(4:11-14)	IV	*(6:20-25)*
V	(4:15-20)	I	(7:1-4)
VI	(4:21-24)	II	(7:5-6)
VII	(4:25-28)	III	(7:7-11)
I	*(4:29-31)*	IV	(7:12-16)
II	*(4:32-35)*	V	(7:17-20)
III	*(4:36-40)*	VI	(7:21-24)
IV	*(4:41-43)*	VII	(7:25-26).

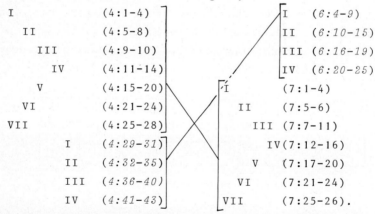

The chiastic arrangement is obvious, a well-known, frequently used rhetorical device: 7 + 4 = 11
4 + 7 = 11

The Decalogue-pericope with its *7+4*-pattern is wedged in within the framework of this chiasm.

The numerical chiasm

What has not been known until now is that there are also *numerical* chiasms. I have detected numerous examples of this compositional model in the first eleven chapters. The idea behind the numerical chiasm is that the text is divided into four blocks: horizontally by the caesura between the verses or groups of verses and vertically by the different diachronic categories of the text, the *parallelismus membrorum* due to the *'atnāḥ* as verse divider, the syntactic division between main and subordinate clauses, etc. At least two diagonally situated blocks should have the same number of words, and what is so remarkable about these chiasms is that they show a distinct tendency to make the numbers *17* and *26* or their multiples explicit, as we shall illustrate presently. We get the following models, of which I give some examples from Deut 1-11:

abba-model: Deut 3:1-4

	MC+SC=Total
vss.1-2	*17*+22=*39*(*26*+13)
vss.3-4	22+*17*=*39*(*26*+13)
	39+*39*=*78*(3x*26*)

abba-model: Deut 7:2b-6:

	Command+Motivation=Total
vss.2b-4(Sing.)	20+14=*34*(2x*17*)
vss.5-6(Plur.)	14+20=*34*(2x*17*)
	34+*34*=*68*(4x*17*)

For examples of the modifications of this perfect chiastic model see 6:1-3 (*abbb*-model), 7:21-24 (*abaa*-model) and 8:11-16(*aabb*- model).

abbc-model: Deut 5:28-31:

	MC + SC = Total
vss. 28-29	23 + 19 = 42
vss. 30-31	19 + 7 = *26*
	42 + *26* = *68*(4x*17*)

abbc-model: Deut 4:29-31:

	MC + SC = Total
vss. 29-30	12 + 14 = *26*
vss. 31	14 + 3 = *17*
	26 + *17* = *43*

For further examples of this model, see 1:16-18; 2:31-37; 3:11-14; 4:5-8; 5:32-33; 6:16-19.

abca-model: Deut 3:8-10:

	MC + SC = Total
vs. 8	14 + 3 = *17*
vss. 9-10	8 + 14 = 22
	22 + *17* = *39*

abca-model: Deut 3:21-22:

	a + b = Total
vs. 21	6 + 20= *26*
vs. 22	2 + 6 = 8
	8 + *26*= *34*

Other instances of this model are 1:46 - 2:1; 3:8-10; 6:4-9; 7:7-11 and 9:1-6.

Conclusion

These examples of the different numerical composition techniques used in Deuteronomy must suffice to demonstrate that Deuteronomy is a numerical composition and that the numbers *7*, *10*, *11*, *13*, *17* and their multiples give structure to the text. Having presented instances of the most important and frequently used rhetorical devices, we do not claim to have mentioned them all and to have treated the subject exhaustively. We have not referred, e.g., to two compositional models discovered by C. Schedl, the Minor and Major Tetraktys which have as compositional formula *55* = *23* + *32* and *54* = *18* + *36* respectively of which there are at least 13 instances in 1-11[12)]. Neither have we discussed the structural use of numbers mentioned in the text, as e.g. in the case of the *38* years referred to in 2:14, where the whole pericope (2:8b-15) with its 114 words has the structure: 38+38+38=114. Lack of space forced us also to refrain from discussing the interesting and very frequently found Decalogue-model (4+6=10) which we have mentioned only in passing. Finally, nothing has been said about the farreaching consequences of the discovery of the structural use of numbers, but matters such as these are discussed extensively in my commentary.

Notes

1) Cf. E.R. Curtius, *Europäische Literatur und Lateinisches Mittelalter*, Bern-München 1973[8], pp. 491-498, under the heading 'Zahlenkomposition'. For further literature see my contribution to the Van Selms memorial volume, C.J. Labuschagne, "On the Structural Use of Numbers as a Composition Technique. Psalm 79: An Example of a Numerical Composition" in *JNSEL* vol. 12, 1985 (in the press) and cf. also my article "Neue Wege und Perspektiven in der Pentateuchforschung" in *VT* vol. 36, 1986 (in the press).
2) See C. Schedl, *Baupläne des Wortes. Einführung in die biblische Logotechnik*, Wien 1974, with his other books and articles cited on pp. 30f.; cf. further *id.*, *Rufer des Heils in heilloser Zeit. Der Prophet Jesajah Kapitel I-XII logotechnisch und bibeltheologisch erklärt*, Paderborn 1973; *id.*, *Als sich der Pfingsttag erfüllte. Erklärung der Pfingstperikope Apg. 2,1-47*, Wien-Freiburg-Basel 1982; *id.*, *Zur Christologie der Evangelien*, Wien etc. 1984. For the rediscovery of the Koran as a numerical composition see C. Schedl, *Muhammad und Jesus. Die christologisch relevanten Texte des Korans neu übersetzt und erklärt*, Wien etc. 1978.
3) See C.J. Labuschagne, "The Pattern of the Divine Speech Formulas in the Pentateuch. The Key to its Literary Structure" in *VT* vol. 32, 1982, pp. 268-296; see also my "Additional Remarks on the Pattern of the Divine Speech Formulas in the Pentateuch" in *VT* vol. 34, 1984, pp. 91-95; cf. P.R. Davies and D.M. Gunn, "Pentateuchal Patterns. An examination of C.J. Labuschagne's theory" in *VT* vol. 34, 1984, pp. 399-406; and my reply "Pentateuchal Patterns: A Reply to P.R. Davies and D.M. Gunn" in *VT* vol. 34, 1984, pp. 407-413.
4) See C.J. Labuschagne, "The Literary and Theological Function of Divine Speech in the Pentateuch" in *VTS* vol. 36, 1985, pp. 154-173 and also "Divine Speech in Deuteronomy" in *Das Deuteronomium. Entstehung, Gestalt und Botschaft* (*Bibliotheca Ephemeridum Theologicarum Lovaniensium*, vol. 68), ed. N. Lohfink, Leuven 1985, pp. 111-126.
5) See my forthcoming (1986) commentary on Deuteronomy in the Dutch series *De Prediking van het Oude Testament*, ed. A. van Selms, A.S. van der Woude and C. van Leeuwen.
6) See the article "Divine Speech in Deuteronomy" cited above in note 4.
7) Subordinate clauses are clauses introduced by conjunctions, clauses in apposition to main clauses and clauses containing infinitives.
8) The term 'parallelismus membrorum' as used here, should not be confused with the original meaning of the term in connection with poetic texts. Prose texts have two halves too! When there is no *'atnāḥ*, the other strongest *distinctivus* in the verse functions as verse-divider, which depends upon the syntactical structure.
9) See C. Schedl, *Baupläne* ...(cf. note 2 above), p. 172, for the beautiful Menorah-structure of the *26* words of Deut 5:14.
10) We have discovered that *lēmōr* has an ambivalent position with regard to the categories of main and subordinate clauses: it can belong to the *main clause*, since it is a *sign* introducing direct narration, but in some cases it stands on its own as a separate *subordinate infinitive clause*. The details are discussed in my commentary on Deuteronomy.
11) See the articles referred to in note 3 above.
12) Cf. C. Schedl, *Baupläne* ..., pp. 40f., pp. 242f., who mentions Deut 5:13-15. I have discovered the *Minor* in 1:9-15; 3:18-20; 5:6-11, 23-27; 6:10-15; 8:1-6, 7-10; and the *Major* in 1:23-28; 3:26-28; 5:24-27; 7:7-11 and 9:1-4.

An Early Witness for a Fronted /g/ in Aramaic?

The Case of the Tell Fekherye Inscription

F. Leemhuis, Groningen

The only Semitic language in which the Proto-Semitic *g*[1] normally has become a *j*, as is well-known, is Arabic. Or more precisely: the Proto-Semitic phoneme *g*, usually considered as a voiced velar plosive, has in Classical Arabic developed into a voiced palato-alveolarised affricate *j*[2].
Also in modern Arabic dialects etymological *g* is usually fronted. Of course different realisations of the phoneme do occur and have occurred: the *g* in Egyptian Arabic as well as in other ancient and modern dialects of Arabic is well-known[3]. And, inversely, modern realisations of etymological *g* as *j* (or its variants) in a few eastern Neo-Aramaic dialects as well as in some modern South Arabian dialects have been noted[4].
In the ancient Semitic languages variant pronunciations may be supposed to have existed, but they are difficult to attest, due to the simple fact that exact pronunciations of early Semitic sounds have scarcely been recorded for us by competent contemporaries. It is mainly by reasoning from transcriptions in other languages and/or from "mistakes" in orthography that some light may be shed on the actual pronunciation of a given phoneme at a given time[5]. In the following I hope to show that in one early case - the language that is reflected in the Aramaic part of the bilingual inscription of Tell Fekherye - a fronted pronunciation of the *g* may be considered as a distinct probability.
It is an honour and a pleasure to dedicate these lines to Hans Hospers, the teacher to whom I owe all but the beginning of my training as a Semitist, and the scholar who always liberally shares his wide experience and knowledge in Semitics and related as well as unrelated fields.

The bilingual Akkadian-Aramaic inscription of Tell Fekherye in the upper Ḫābūr region, south of Ras al-ᶜAyn in north-eastern Syria, which was discovered in 1979 and of which the *editio princeps* appeared in 1982[6], has already received much attention from scholars. One of

the reasons is that the Aramaic part shows quite a few peculiarities that give this inscription a place of its own among the Ancient Aramaic inscriptions that are known to us so far[7].
Although there is still some discussion about the time of execution of the inscription, a date somewhere in the ninth century B.C. is considered as most plausible[8]. It is therefore probably the oldest of the known inscriptions in Ancient Aramaic.

The inscription actually consists of two parts: A, an older part (lines 1-18 of the Akkadian and lines 2-12a of the Aramaic), apparently copied from an older statue of the dedicator, king Hadad-Yis^{c}ī, and B, a younger part (lines 19-38 of the Akkadian and lines 1 and 12b-23 of the Aramaic) that was joined to A as a complement on his recently discovered statue "which he placed before Hadad of Sikan". Also from the point of view of the language, Akkadian as well as Aramaic, the two parts are distinct from each other[9].
Both Aramaic parts show a language that is apparently a variant of Early Standard Aramaic (ESA). However, the inscription as a whole has some peculiarities which set it somewhat apart from ESA, but both parts also show some traits that set them apart from each other so that it may be characterised as follows[10]:

1. The entire inscription is fundamentally in agreement with ESA.
2. Part A shows a more than average conformity with ESA.
3. Part B shows a more than average conformity with Mesopotamian Aramaic.

Moreover, whereas A is dependent upon the Akkadian text, in B the Aramaic text and the corresponding Akkadian text appear to be mutually dependent and both also show the same "taste" for the colloquial[11].

The most striking fact that distinguishes the entire inscription from the rest of ESA is the peculiarity that the Proto-Semitic interdental ṯ is written with an *s* (*samekh*) and not with a *š* (*šīn/śīn*) as in the other known ESA inscriptions or with a *t* as in Imperial Aramaic. So we find such forms as *ḥds* ('new, anew' l. 11), *ysb* ('to dwell', ll. 5 and 16) and *swr* ('cow', l. 20). Also the name of the king, who dedicated his statue to Hadad of Sikan, Hadad-Yis^{c}ī, actually written as *hdys^{c}y*, which is rendered in the Assyrian as *adad-it'i*, contains an *s* for an etymological interdental ṯ[12].
Now, whatever may have been the precise realisation of etymological ṯ[13] in the rest of ESA, it was apparently felt that the *šīn/śīn* of the Phoenician alphabet that was adopted was the nearest approximation. That we are dealing in such cases with graphic "Canaanisms" seems highly unlikely[14]. Why should such "Canaanisms" have been adopted in

these cases and not, for instance, in the case of such words as *'rq* and *nbš*? Be this as it may, the Tell Fekherye inscription clearly deviates from the ESA convention with respect to the notation of the etymological interdentals. And although one may wonder if such a convention really existed in a rigid form at least at such an early time[15], the deviation is so systematic that it is probably due to more than a whim or a deficient training of the scribe.
This deviation may be explained by the fact that the scribe, or possibly the scribes, in the region of the upper Ḫābūr considered the *s* to be the best approximation of their pronunciation of etymological *ṯ*. I think that there is a simple explanation for this fact: the choice of *s* to represent etymological *ṯ* must mean that the pronunciation of the etymological *ṯ* was more to the front than in the rest of ESA, because whatever may have been the precise pronunciation of *s* it may be considered fairly certain that *s* prepresents a sibilant that is more frontal than *š*. It should be remarked in this respect that this means that etymological *ṯ* was probably never pronounced as an interdental in ESA, but as a sibilant. In all probability, however, this sibilant did not sound the same as the respective etymological sibilant. For ESA apart from the upper Ḫābūr region we may think of a difference between an apical *š* for etymological *ṯ* and a predorsal *š* for etymological *s* and for the region of the upper Ḫābūr the same kind of difference for *s*. Such a difference, which in view of the limitations of the Phoenician alphabet could not be expressed graphically, would account for the fact that only etymological *ṯ* could shift more to the front, to become a *t* in Imperial Aramaic. In the Aramaic of the Tell Fekherye inscription this shift to the front apparently had not yet gone so far as to have become already indistinguishable from *t* as in later Imperial Aramaic, but the process had started.
This becomes all the more likely if we consider the fact that the name Mat^{c}ī which is written *mt^{c}y* in a Tell Halaf Aramaic tablet from the end of the seventh century B.C.[16] contains the same root as we find in Hadad-Yis^{c}ī: apparently by then the shift was completed in the region of the Upper Ḫābūr.
Something like this, of course, was only to be expected. It proves the essential correctness of the view of R. Degen in his *Altaramäische Grammatik* that the shift in graphic representation of the (etymological) interdentals must have its cause in a shift in their pronunciation[17].

There is another phenomenon in connection with an etymological interdental that deserves to be discussed here. If the *q* in ESA in such words as *'rq* and *mrq* really is the reflection of an attempt

to approximate the pronunciation of a phoneme that represented a Proto-Semitic interdental emphatic *ḍ*, which by now may be considered as sufficiently certain, then it entails that the ESA realisations of both phonemes must have had something in common; at least one element of articulation of both phonemes must have been similar. Velarization of the voiced interdental *ḍ* would make the choice of the symbol of the voiced velar *q* quite understandable.
Still there is a problem here. This problem is not the supposed lateral character of *ḍ* , which is suggested by such transcriptions of the name of the god Ruḍā' in Akkadian as *rulda'u* or in Greek as *Orotalt* and the like[18], because these may simply be cases of allophones or of local and temporal limitations of an overspecialised phoneme[19]. Neither is the problem whether the emphatic character of *ḍ*, which made it possible that it could be represented by *q*, was originally glottalisation or velarisation[20].
The problem lies with the realisation of *q*. Was *q* really a velar and if so what was the difference in pronunciation with *g*, which is often also considered to have been a voiced velar plosive? The difference between the two then would have been that *q* was an emphatic[21], whereas *g* was not, but what then was the emphatic co-articulation? Surely it was not velar. The question actually is a moot one. A look at the earliest accurate description of Semitic sounds, the one of Sībawaih, may help to sort things out.

Sībawaih's chapters that deal with *idġām* (the contraction and assimilation of consonants into geminates) start with an enumeration of what he considers the 29 fundamental consonants of Arabic[22], to which he adds 6 allophones that are considered correct and 7 others that are considered incorrect. One of the divisions of the 29 consonants is according to their respective *maḫraj* or point of articulation. What concerns us here are the points of articulation of the *qāf* and the *ḍād* which is the Arabic equivalent of Proto-Semitic *ḍ*.

The *qāf* comes "from the hindmost part of the tongue and the part of the palate that is above it"[23]: a (post)velar. A co-articulation e.g. a glottal one is not mentioned. As H. Blanc has pointed out by referring to Sībawaih's practical prescription of how to distinguish *q* from *k* the former must have been either a uvular or extreme post-velar [q] or a [G] that is its voiced counterpart[29]. The problem with the old Arabic *q* is that according to Blanc's interpretation of Sībawaih's system, which to me seems very plausible, it was both isolated and overdifferentiated. Consequently, allophones developed which missed one (or more?) of its many features. "In particular, the combination of voicing, full occlusion and extreme postvelar articulation, viz., [G], is, in the absence of phonemic symmetry or other bolstering factors, basically unstable"[25]. This instability has led to shifts in the realisation of *q* in the diverse forms of Arabic. "Most commonly, either voicing has been given up (*qāl* dialects) or articulation has shifted forward (*gāl* dialects)"[26].

The *ḍād* comes "from between the beginning (i.e. the hindmost part) of the rim of the tongue and the neighbouring molars"[27]: a laterodental. Interestingly enough it appears that the *ḍād* may be articulated by pressing the whole front part of the tongue to the corresponding part of the palate and the alveoli. It even may be considered as belonging to the *ḥurūf al-ṯanāyā*: the dentals[28].

Important in the present discussion is what constitutes, according to Sībawaih, the special character of the *ḍād* and the other so-called emphatics that set them apart from all other consonants. It is *iṭbāq*, the definition of which implies that the point of articulation is, as it were, extended by raising the tongue towards the palate so that "the sound is restricted to (the space that is thus formed from) what is between the tongue and the palate (and which extends) as far as their points of articulation"[29]. In short: The emphatics have a (post)velar co-articulation. This simple fact makes it, of course, understandable why a *q* could and can sound as an emphatic: its point of articulation is the same as that of the co-articulation of the emphatics.

Sībawaih is quite explicit about this co-articulation of the four Arabic emphatics: "These four have two places (of articulation) from the tongue .... and if it were not for emphasis (*iṭbāq*), the *ṭā'* would become a *dāl*, the *ṣād* a *sīn*, the *ẓā'* a *ḏāl* and the *ḍād* would go out of the language, because there is nothing besides it that has its (other) place (of articulation)"[30]. The exceptional character of the *ḍād* is clear: it has no non-emphatic counterpart. The reasons for this isolated position may be easily guessed from Sībawaih's remarks: Although (originally?) belonging to the group of dentals it has apparently shifted backwards. With hindsight we may also conclude that Sībawaih's remark about the *ḍād* disappearing altogether from the language if it did not have its (post)velar co-articulation is very acute indeed. This isolated and overdifferentiated *ḍ* like the above mentioned *q* is basically unstable[31] and shifts are as it were built in: Either the primary articulation shifts forward, so that it starts to resemble the *ṣ*, or it shifts backwards and because of its (post) velar co-articulation the resemblance with a (post)velar becomes more pronounced.

For the Aramaic of the upper Ḫābūr region of the ninth, eighth and seventh centuries B.C. we may guess that *q* was also on the move or at least had acquired a considerable "band width". That this probably was indeed the case may be concluded from such spellings in the contracts of El-manānī of the name *Ḥzg* in stead of *Ḥzq* and *ḥzg* for *ḥzq*[32]. Apparently at least an allophone of *q* existed that had an articulation more to the front[33]. It may be added that it is just an articulation more to the front of the *q* that makes a rendering of etymological *ḏ̣* by *ᶜ* in Imperial Aramaic intelligible.
There is, of course, no certain proof that such an articulation more to the front already existed at the time of execution of the Tell Fekherye inscription, but there is a strong indication that it did. The indication is not the probable loan-word *'dqwr*, because this could be a representation of *adagūru* as well as of *diqāru*[34]. The indication is an indirect one.
From Arabic we know that the articulations of *q* and *g* are interrelated in that (the beginning of) a shift to the front in the pronunciation of *q* exerted pressure on the pronunciation of *g*[35]. The point made by Blanc is that Arabic shows that *g* does not necessarily become fronted, "but pressures are evident: *q* is either moving back towards *ġ* or is becoming fully devoiced, or *g* is beginning to move forward, or both tendencies are evident"[36].

This would not bring us much further, were it not for the fact that the anomalous form *ygtzr* (l. 23) may be considered as probable proof for at least a fronted allophone of *g*.
The meaning of the form presents no difficulty. Line 23: *wmwtn šbṭ zy nyrgl 'l ygtzr mn mth* clearly means: and may pestilence, the plague of Nergal, not cease from his land. The Akkadian version of this curse makes clear that *'l ygtzr* means *lā ipparrasū* and thus that the form is a reflexive/passive with a meaning 'to cut itself off, to cease'.
The infixed *t* in an ESA verb is anomalous insofar as only one such form seems to be fairly certain until now: the conjecture [*yš*]*tḥt* (Sefire I A 32). There are two possible ways to deal with such a form. The infix *t* may be considered as a tG with metathesis[37] or as a regular Gt[38]. If the form *ygtzr* were a Gt then this would be the first certain attestation of this verbal stem in Aramaic[39] and thus a simple reference to Ugaritic, Phoenician and Moabite is not enough, especially not since the other certain *t*-stems that are known from ESA only show a prefixed *t*[40]. Of course, the conjecture [*yš*]*tḥt* is fairly certain, but this form, if the conjecture is right, may be easily explained as a tG with the *š-t* metathesis[41], that is familiar from other forms of Aramaic. The problem with the form *ygtzr* is that

at first sight it does not seem to fall within the usual, phonetically determined, terms for metathesis.

However, if g was <u>fronted</u> then the case is different, because if *g* is moving forward because of the pressure of a forward moving *q*, the resulting instability is resolved in that "Fronted *ǰ* is often more neatly paired with *š* as [ž] or [ǧ]"[42]. In other words, a metathesis in *ygtzr* would be nothing special if it had been generated by a fronted allophone of *g*. The formation of such an allophone may, moreover, in this special case have been yet more stimulated by the second root consonant. As long as no certain forms with infixed *t* that cannot be explained by metathesis are discovered, this seems the most plausible explanation of the form. This then entails a shift to the front of both *q* and *g*. This is the more probable, because it fits in with another tendency towards fronting: the beginning of the shift to the front of the etymological interdentals, which finally led to their replacement in Aramaic by the corresponding dentals, that as was argued above may be posited for the local form of Aramaic in Sikan at the time of the execution of the Tell Fekherye inscription. We may assume that such a fronted variant of *g* existed only dialectally and perhaps even in the dialects where it existed it was only a temporary phenomenon in a period when other sound changes, especially if tending to the front, were taking place. In a new stabilised situation a fronted *g*, or its fronted allophones, could shift (and in the case of Aramaic apparently had shifted) backward again. Even in Arabic there are reasons to believe that the non-fronted *g* of e.g. Cairene Arabic is the result of a backward shift[43].
The Aramaic of the Tell Fekherye inscription and especially that of part B has been characterised as essentially ESA with some traits that are dialectal (Mesopotamian Aramaic), some that are anticipatory and some that are independent[44]. A fronted *g* or a fronted allophone of *g* apparently belongs to the latter.

Notes

* This contribution was incited by the stimulating lecture on the Tell Fekherye inscription by J.C. Greenfield on 19 December 1984 at the Institute of Semitics and Archaeology of the Near East of the University of Groningen. Besides Prof. Greenfield I would like to express my thanks to my colleagues W.J. van Bekkum, G.J.H. van Gelder, G.J. Reinink and H.L.J. Vanstiphout for the discussions and remarks that helped to shape my thoughts and to Mrs. S. van Gelder-Ottway who improved the English of this contribution.

1) For the sake of convenience the conventional system of phonemic transliteration as in S. Moscati *et. al.*, *An Introduction to the Comparative Grammar of the Semitic Languages*, Wiesbaden 1969, is adopted except that for Arabic *ǰ* is used.

2) S. Moscati *et. al.*, *op. cit.*, p. 37, par. 8.38, and p. 38, par. 8.42.

3) H. Blanc, "The Fronting of Semitic *g* and the *qāl-gāl* Dialect Split in Arabic" in *Proceedings of the International Conference on Semitic Studies held in Jerusalem, 19-23 July 1965*, Jerusalem 1969, pp. 7-37, on p. 7.

4) H. Blanc, *op. cit.* p. 7, n. 2; C. Brockelmann, *Grundriss der vergleichende Grammatik der Semitischen Sprachen*, vol. 1, Berlin 1908, p. 208.

5) S. Moscati *et. al.*, *op. cit.*, pp. 22-23, pars. 7.1-7.3.

6) A. Abou-Assaf, P. Bordreuil and A.R. Millard, *La statue de Tell Fekherye et son inscription bilingue assyro-araméenne*, Paris 1982.

7) Apart from the *editio princeps* see for instance a.o. S.A. Kaufman, "Reflections on the Assyrian-Aramaic Bilingual from Tell Fakhariyeh" in *Maarav* vol. 3, 1982, pp. 136-175; F.M. Fales , "Le double bilinguisme de la statue de Tell Fekherye" in *Syria* vol. 60, pp. 233-250, and J.C. Greenfield - A. Shaffer, "Notes on the Akkadian-Aramaic Bilingual Statue from Tell Fekherye" in *Iraq* vol. 45, 1983, pp. 109-116 and "Notes on the Curse Formulae of the Tell Fekherye Inscription" in *RB* vol. 92, 1985, pp. 46-59.

8) See e.g. J.C. Greenfield - A. Shaffer, "Notes", p. 109, F.M. Fales, *op. cit.* p. 23, and S.A. Kaufman, *op. cit.*, pp. 139-142.

9) See F.M. Fales, *op. cit.*

10) In this I follow the analysis of F.M. Fales, *op. cit.*, pp. 241-245.

11) F.M. Fales, *op. cit.*, p. 250.

12) See *editio princeps*, p. 44.

13) The posited interdental character is as far as I can see largely based on etymological comparison with Arabic. The only thing that can be said with any certainty about the etymological interdentals in the early Semitic languages is that they were probably fricatives with a point of articulation somewhere in the frontal regions of the mouth.

14) See R. Degen's convincing treatment of this question in his *Altaramäische Grammatik*, Wiesbaden 1969, pp. 32-36.

15) After all, the corpus of ESA texts is not yet so vast that new inscriptions especially from fringe areas may not substantially modify the present conclusions about conventional orthography etc.

16) See the reference in the *editio princeps* p. 60. See also E. Lipiński, *Studies in Aramaic Inscriptions and Onomastics* (= *SAIO*), vol. 1, Leuven 1975, pp. 126 and 131-132. The name occurs also in a cuneiform text from the archive of El-manāni in the form *ma-te-e*^{c}*-i*.

17) R. Degen, *op. cit.*, pp. 33-34. It may be clear, however, that I disagree with Degen's statement:"Zum aa. Lautsystem [..] gehören noch interdentale". It does not follow from his reasoning. The conslusion should be that the etymological interdentals remained phonetically distinct from etymological *š*, *z* etc.

18) See e.g. the recent article of E. Lipiński, "The god 'Arqu-Rashap in the Samallian Hadad Inscription" in *Arameans, Aramaic and the Aramaic literary tradition*, ed. M. Sokoloff, Ramat-Gan 1983. pp. 15-21.

19) In Arabic lateralisation as an original element is considered probable. H. Fleisch has in fact in a masterstroke combined the available evidence and defined it as a "lateralized velarized interdental fricative", see art. *Ḍād* in *EI*[2]. However, it is well known that in present-day Arabic not all elements of this putative original character have survived and as with the other emphatics its emphasis lies in velarization.
20) See S. Moscati *et. al.*, *op. cit.*, pp. 23-24, par. 8.2.
21) See S. Moscati *et. al.*, *op. cit.*, p. 37, pars. 8.38 and 8.39. R. Degen's elegant solution is that he simply presents *g* as a voiced palatal and *q* as an emphatic velar, without however presenting the grounds for doing so, see R. Degen, *op. cit.* p. 37, par. 14. Probably he saw no reason to posit another articulation for *g* than the one that is considered normal for Aramaic, cf. e.g. S. Segert, *Altaramäische Grammatik*, Leipzig 1975, p. 84, par. 3.2.3.4.3.
22) *Kitāb Sībawaih*, *bāb* 565 (*al-idġām*), *Le livre de Sībawaihi*, ed. H. Derenbourg, Hildesheim 1970 (repr. of Paris 1881-9), vol. 2, pp. 252-255; in the Būlāq edition, vol. 2, pp. 404-407. I have mainly used the new edition of ᶜAbd al-Salām Muḥammad Hārūn, 5 vols., Cairo 1967-77. See also H. Fleisch, *Traité de philologie arabe*, vol. 1, Beyrouth 1961, pp. 207-230. In the following, references to Sībawaih will be only to the D(erenbourg) and the B(ūlāq) edition. In the new Cairo edition the page numbers of the Būlāq edition are added *in margine*. In passing it may be noted that in the Cairo edition (vol. 4, p. 433, l. 12) a curious case of "haplologische Zeilenellipse" occurs which seems to be caused by the words *ma fuwaiqa* which are printed in B, vol. 2, p. 405, l. 10, exactly above the same words in the following line. As a result the *maḫraj* of the *lām* has disappeared.
23) Sībawaih, D vol. 2, p. 453/B vol. 2, p. 405.
24) H. Blanc, *op. cit.*, p. 17-18.
25) H. Blanc, *op. cit.*, p. 30.
26) H. Blanc, *ibid.*
27) Sībawaih, D vol. 2, p. 453/B vol. 2, p. 405. On p. 425/404 also an incorrect allophone, the weak *ḍād* is mentioned which has as its main characteristic that it may be articulated with only one side of the tongue. The description itself remains somewhat obscure, but probably its tendency to approach the *ẓā'* is implied see Fleisch, *op. cit.*, p. 217.
28) Sībawaih, D vol. 2, pp. 470-1/B vol. 2, p. 420.
29) Sībawaih, D vol. 2, p. 455/B vol. 2, p. 406. It is significant that this further precision is found in the chapter that deals with *idġām* of letters of the tip of the tongue and the teeth.
30) Sibawaih, D vol. 2, p. 455/B vol. 2, p. 406.
31) In this respect the situation in Ya'udic Aramaic is revealing. Apparently a conventional notation of etymological *ḍ* is in the making so that mostly it is written as *q*, but there is still some fluctuation so that also *ṣ* and *g* are used. The notation by *g*, incidentally, shows that for Ya'udic Aramaic *g* still must have been a velar. Cf. e.g. P.-E. Dion, *La langue de Ya'udi*, Editions SR 1974, pp. 96-97.
32) Tell Ḥalaf tablet 1 l. 13 and tablet 5 l. 7. See E. Lipiński, *SAIO* , pp. 122-123 and p. 141. Cf. also F.M. Fales, "A list of Assyrian and West Semitic women's names" in *Iraq* vol. 41, 1979, p. 64, attesting the name *Ḫa-zu-ga-a* in Neo-Assyrian for Aramaic *Ḥazūqa*.
33) Although not widespread, the pronunciation of etymological *q* exactly as an etymological *g* is recorded in contemporary Arabic, see H. Blanc, *op. cit.*, p. 28. The same probably is the cause of such pairs as are mentioned on p. 55 in my "Qur'anic *siǧǧīl* and Aramaic *sgyl*" in *JSS* vol. 27, 1982, pp. 47-56.
34) If *'dqwr* in l. 3 of the Tell Fekherye inscription is indeed a transcription of the Assyrian *adaguru* as the editors (p. 29)

presume, it is another indication of at least the "band width" of the *q*. However, on p. 74 the editors note that "*'dqwr* pourrait aussi refleter l'akkadien *diqāru*, bol destiné aux aliments". In that case the initial *aleph* could have its origin in the elision of the *i* of the first syllable. Nevertheless it is noted also that in the Judeo-Aramaic form *dqwr'* it is not present. I am inclined to agree with the implicit opinion of the editors that, on the basis of the Aramaic form, *adaguru* is the stronger candidate.

35) H. Blanc, *op. cit.*, pp. 28-30. This was also A. Martinet's opinion, who is quoted by Blanc on p. 9 n. 7, as follows: "Mais avant même que ce stade avait été attaint (viz., full shift of *q* to [g]), le *g* ancien avait dû commencer à prendre ces distances".

36) H. Blanc, *op. cit.*, pp. 29-30.

37) So *editio princeps*, p. 37.

38) So S.A. Kaufman, *op. cit.*, pp. 150 and 173. It would seem that J.C. Greenfield - A. Shaffer in *RB*, p. 50, share this opinion.

39) As long as no other certain Gt forms are attested in Aramaic reference to Rosenthal's conjectural reading of ll. 24-25 of Sefire I C (as S.A. Kaufman, *op. cit.*, p. 173 does) is too meagre evidence.

40) See R. Degen, *op. cit.*, p. 67. In this respect it may be noted that the form *ytšm*^{c} in Sefire I A 29 may be easily explained as a pseudo-correct form if tG forms with metathesis were recognised as such by the scribe!

41) The more so because metathesis is primarily a sporadic sound change (cf. W.P. Lehmann, *Historical Linguistics*, New York 1973^2, pp. 166-168). This is another reason why exactly in ESA we find also the example of the form *ytšm*^{c} (Sefire I A 29) without metathesis. Cf. n. 40 above.

42) H. Blanc, *op. cit.*, p. 30.

43) H. Blanc, *op. cit.*, pp. 10, 23, 27.

44) e.g. F.M. Fales, *op. cit.*, pp. 242-244.

Scribes d'Ugarit et de Jérusalem

E. Lipiński, Leuven

Rois, dignitaires, prophètes, psalmistes, tous ces personnages de l'ancien Proche-Orient ne nous sont connus que grâce aux scribes. A.L. Oppenheim avait écrit avec raison que le scribe est la figure centrale de la civilisation cunéiforme[1)], et l'on pourrait étendre cette affirmation à toute l'antiquité proche-orientale. Certains de ces scribes étaient parfaitement conscients de leur importance, comme le montre la bénédiction que le scribe Šarruwa n'a pas hésité à écrire à son intention au bas du récit autobiographique d'Idrimi, roi d'Alalakh[2)]: "Puissent les dieux du ciel et de la terre maintenir en vie et protéger le scribe Šarruwa qui a écrit (le texte de) cette statue. Que Šamaš, seigneur de ce qui est là-sus et ci-bas, le purifie; que le Seigneur des mânes le renvoie".

C'est l'ouvrage magistral de M. Dandamayev sur les scribes néo-babyloniens qui nous a suggéré de reprendre le dossier des scribes d'Ugarit, déjà étudié par A.F. Rainey, W.J. Horwitz et M. Heltzer[3)], et de le compléter des informations fournies par la Bible et l'épigraphie sur les scribes hiérosolymitains, dont certains ont fait notamment l'objet d'une étude de T.N.D. Mettinger[4)]. Notre propos n'est cependant pas le même que celui des auteurs que nous venons de citer. En effet, ce n'est pas l'exercice de la profession scribale qui nous intéresse en premier lieu, mais plutôt la prosopographie et l'anthroponymie des scribes.

I. - Scribes d'Ugarit

Les textes d'Ugarit édités à ce jour contiennent au moins une quarantaine de noms de scribes, dont la plupart sont mentionnés dans les textes akkadiens. Certains de ces scribes - et d'autres sans doute - peuvent apparaître aussi dans les textes en cunéiformes alphabétiques, mais l'absence du titre de "scribe" (*spr*) ou du patronyme empêche de les identifier. Nous avons cru utile de dresser la liste alphabétique des scribes connus nommément, en donnant chaque fois les références aux textes et en signalant, si c'est possible, la période ou le règne durant lequel leur activité est attestée. En outre, nous indiquons la provenance probable du scribe s'il ne semble pas avoir résidé à Ugarit. L'ordre suivi est celui de l'alphabet latin.

1) ^{c}Abdi-^{d}[ ][5].

RS 19.78,17 (*PRU* VI,52): ARAD-DINGIR[ ].

2) ^{c}Abdi-^{c}Anat.

RS 16.129,19 (*PRU* III, p. 33): ^{m}ARAD-*a-na-ti*.

RS 16.178,21 (*PRU* III, p. 148): ^{m}ARAD-*an-ti*. ^{c}Ammištamru II.

3) ^{c}Abdi-Ḫamān.

RS 16.348, rev. 6' (*PRU* III, p. 163): ^{m}ARAD-*ḫa-ma-nu*. ^{c}Ammištamru II.

4) ^{c}Abdi-NINURTA[6].

RS 14.16 (*PRU* III, p. 237).

5) ^{c}Abdi-Yaraḫ.

RS 8.213,35 (*Syria* 18, 1937, p. 247):^{m}ARAD-^{d}XXX.

RS 17.86 + 241 + 208,19 (*Ugaritica* V, 159): [^{m}ARAD-^{d}X] XX. Šarelli[7].

6) 'Abi-milku.

RS 17.388,27 (*PRU* VI,50): ^{m}AD-LUGAL.

7) 'Aḫi-Yaraḫ.

RS 17.232,17 (*PRU* IV, p. 239): ^{m}PAP-^{d}XXX.

8) $^{a\text{-}lim}$ALIM$_{x}$-SAG[?], maître-scribe de Šipṭi-A.UM.

RS 22.439,IV,14' (*Ugaritica* V,163).

9) Ana-Tešub, fils de 'Iršeyānu.

RS 17.325,22 (*Ugaritica* V,161): ^{m}*a-na*-^{d}IM. Šarelli.

10) Attani-purli-anni, grand-prêtre, chef des pasteurs, maître-scribe de 'Ilu-milku.

AO 16.636,VI,55-56 = I AB (*CTA* 6 = *KTU* 1.6): *'atn.prln*. Niqmaddu II.

11) Burqānu.

RS 8.145,32 (*Syria* 18, 1937, p. 246): ^{m}*bur-qa-nu*.

RS 17.251,27 (*PRU* IV, p. 237): ^{m} *bur-qa-nu*. ^{c}Uzzinu, préfet d'Ugarit.

RS 19.66,23 (*PRU* V,116 = *KTU* 3.8): *brqn*.

12) Buṣmānu[8].

RS 15.116,II,29 (*PRU* II,39 = *KTU* 4.183): *bṣmn*.

13) [$^{?}$Ebinn]a'e[9].

RS 17.251,17 (*PRU* IV, p. 236):[ ]?-*'e-e*. Karkémish.

14) Eḫli-Tešub.

RS 18.21,34 (*PRU* VI,45): [^{m}]*eḫ-li*-^{d}IM. Niqmaddu IV[10].

15) Ḫūṣānu, père de Yaṣirānu.

RS 15.138 + 16.393 B,25 (*PRU* III, p. 102): *ḫu-ṣa-nu*. Niqmepa^{c}.

RS 16.153,7 (*PRU* III, p. 147): *ḫu-ṣa-na* (gén.). ^{c}Ammištamru II.

RS 16.206,10 (*PRU* III, p. 106): *ḫu-ṣa-na* (gén.). Niqmepa^{c}.

RS 16.239,4 (*PRU* III, p. 79): *ḫu-ṣa-na* (gén.). Ar-Ḫalba.

RS 16.285, rev. 8' (*PRU* III, p. 107): *ḫu-ṣa*. Niqmepa^{c}.

16) 'Ili-SANGA$^{?}$, fils de Šapaš-milku.

RS 16.114, rev. 14' (*PRU* III, p. 34): ^{m}DINGIR-SANGA$^{?}$.

17) 'Ili-Šapaš.

RS 17.36,17 (*Ugaritica* V,7): ^{m}DINGIR-^{d}UTU.

18) 'Iltaḥmu.

RS 15.140,26 (*PRU* III, p. 136): ^{m}*ìl-taḫ-mu*. ^{c}Ammištamru II.

RS 16.353,34 (*PRU* III, p. 115): ^{m}*ìl-taḫ-mu*. ^{c}Ammištamru II.

RS 17.88, rev. 5' (*PRU* VI,37): ^{m}*ìl-taḫ-mu*.

RS 17.299, rev. 2' (*PRU* IV, p. 182): ^{m}*ì l-taḫ-mu*.

RS 17.356,21 (*PRU* VI,38): ^{m}*ìl-taḫ-mu*.

RS 17.358,17' (*PRU* VI,39): ^{m}*ìl-taḫ-mu*.

RS 18.265,4' (*PRU* VI,41): ^{m}*ìl -taḫ-mu* .

RS 19.128, rev. 8' (*PRU* VI,32): ^{m}*ìl-taḫ-mu*. ^{c}Ammištamru II.

19) 'Ilu-milku / 'Ili-milku de Šūbānu, disciple d'Attani-purlianni et 'déchiffreur' du roi Niqmaddu II[11].

AO 16.636,VI,54 = I AB (*CTA* 6 = *KTU* 1.6): *'ilmlk*. Niqmaddu II.

A 2777, tr. lat. g. = II AB (*CTA* 4 = *KTU* 1.4): [*'ilmlk*]. Niqmaddu II.

A 2751, tr. lat. g. = II K (*CTA* 16 = *KTU* 1.16): *'ilmlk*.

RS 6.198 = AO 18.889 (*Syria* 16, 1935, p. 188-193): ^{m}DINGIR-LUGAL. Probablement reine 'Aḫat-milki. Lettre assyrienne.

RS 17.61,22 (*Ugaritica* V, 9): ^{m} DINGIR-LUGAL.

RS 17.67, rev. 15' (*Ugaritica* V,10): ^{m}DINGIR-LUGAL.

Syria 12, 1931, pl. XLVI + XLVIII, colophon: [^{m}DINGIR-]LUGAL, ou [^{m}UTU-]LUGAL, ou peut-être [^{m}AD-]LUGAL.

20) 'Ilu-rāmu.

RS 18.500,20 (*PRU* VI,30): ^{m}DIN GIR-*ra-mu*. ^{c}Ammištamru II.

21) Karrānu.

RS 15.119, rev. 20' (*PRU* III, p. 88): ^{m}*kar-ra*. Niqmepa^{c}.

RS 16.207,18 (*PRU* III, p. 109): ^{m}*kar-r*[*a*]. Niqmepa^{c}.

RS 16.284,20' (*PRU* III, p. 99): ^{m}*kar-ra-nu*.

22) Lāṭ-Dagan[12].

RS 17.28,28 et sceau (*PRU* IV, p. 110): ᵐ*La-aṭ*-ᵈKUR. Tili-šarruma, fils du roi de Karkémish; scribe probablement originaire d'Emar.

23) Munaḥḥimu, fils de Yarīmu.

RS 15.145,22 (*PRU* III, p. 123): ᵐ*mu-na-ḫi-mu*. ᶜAmmištamru II.

RS 15.147, rev. 20' (*PRU* III, p. 125): [ᵐ*mu-na-ḫi-mu*]. ᶜAmmištamru II.

RS 15.190, 8' (*PRU* III, p. 137): ᵐ*mu-na-ḫi-mu*. ᶜAmmištamru II.

RS 16.86, rev. 4' (*PRU* III, p. 138):[ᵐ*mu-na-ḫi-mu*]. ᶜAmmištamru II.

RS 16.172,6' (*PRU* III, p. 147):[ᵐ*mu-na-ḫi-m*]*u*. ᶜAmmištamru II.

RS 16.201, rev. 7' (*PRU* III, p. 152): ᵐ*m*[*u-na-ḫi-mu*]. ᶜAmmištamru II.

RS 16.243,24 (*PRU* III, p. 156): [ᵐ*m*]*u-na-ḫi-mu*. ᶜAmmištamru II.

RS 16.255 D,13' (*PRU* III, p. 158):[ᵐ*mu-n*]*a-ḫi-m*[*u*]. ᶜAmmištamru II.

RS 16.255 H,2' (*PRU* III, p. 174): ᵐ*mu-n*[*a-ḫi-mu*]. ᶜAmmištamru II.

RS 16.386, rev. 19' (*PRU* III, p. 166):[ᵐ*mu-na-ḫi*]*-mu*. ᶜAmmištamru II.

RS 17.22 + 87,29 (*Ugaritica* V,5): ᵐ*mu-na-ḫi-mu*.

RS 17,149,0 (*Ugaritica* V,6): ᵐ*mu-na-ḫi-mu*.

RS 17.360,31 (*PRU* VI,40): ᵐ*mu-na-ḫi-mu*.

24) Naḫešī-šalmu.

RS 19.53,2 (*PRU* VI, 18): ᵐ*na-ḫé-ši-šal-mu*.

25) Nîr-Nabû.

RS 19.53,1 (*PRU* VI,18): ᵐ*nir*-ᵈAG. Lettre provenant vraisemblablement d'une autre ville.

26) Nuᶜmi-Rašap, fils de 'Abaya.

RS 15.111,19 (*PRU* II,9 = *KTU* 3.2): *n*ᶜ*m*[*ršp*][13]. ᶜAmmištamru II.

RS 15.131, rev. 5' (*PRU* III, p. 133): ᵐSIG_5-ᵈKAL. ᶜAmmištamru II.

RS 15.143 + 164, rev. 14 (*PRU* III, p. 117): ᵐSIG_5-ᵈKAL. ᶜAmmištamru II.

RS 15.168,20 (*PRU* III, p. 137): ᵐSIG_5-ᵈKAL. ᶜAmmištamru II.

RS 17.77, rev. 13' (*PRU* VI,43): ᵐSIG_5-ᵈMAŠ.MAŠ.

RS 18.02,17 (*PRU* IV, p. 201): ^{m}SIG$_{5}$-^{d}KAL. Probablement du temps de Niqmaddu III.

RS 18.20 + 17.371, rev. 16' (*PRU* IV, p. 203): ^{m}SIG$_{5}$-GÌR.UNUG.GAL. Niqmaddu III.

RS 18.267,3' (*PRU* VI,44): ^{m}SIG$_{5}$-^{d}MAŠ.MAŠ.

RS 18.280.8' (*PRU* VI,42): ^{m}SIG$_{5}$-^{d}MAŠ.MAŠ. 'Ibirānu.

RS 22.241,IV,5' (*Ugaritica* V,167): ^{m}SIG$_{5}$-^{d}GÌR.UNUG.GAL.

27) Nūrī-Malik, maître-scribe de Yanḫānu.

RS 20.196 A, colophon 3 (*Ugaritica* V,145): ^{m}NE-^{d}*ma-l[ik]*.

28) Rap'ānu, fils de Šumeyānu, serviteur de [Nabû] (et) de Nisaba.

Syria 12, 1931, pl. XLIV, colophon, et p. 235: ^{m}*Ra-pá-na* (gén.).

RS 21.07 A,19' (*Ugaritica* V,88): ^{m}*Rap-a-nu*.

29) Šaduya, serviteur de Nabû et de Nisaba.

RS 6.X, colophon (*Ugaritica* V,152): ^{m}*ša*$^{?}$-[*d*]*u*$^{?}$-*ia*.

RS 20.14, colophon (*Ugaritica* V,149): ^{m}*ša-du-ia*.

30) Šapaš-milku, père de 'Ili-SANGA$^{?}$

RS 15.88,12 (*PRU* III, p. 88): $^{m.d}$UTU-LUGAL. Niqmepa^{c}.

RS 15.Y,18 (*PRU* III, p. 78): $^{m.d}$UTU-LUGAL. Niqmepa^{c}.

RS 16.114, rev. 14' (*PRU* III, p. 34): ^{d}UTU-LUGAL.

RS 16.133, rev. 18 (*PRU* III, p. 60): $^{m.d}$UTU[-LUGAL]. Niqmaddu II.

RS 16.142,16 (*PRU* III, p. 77): $^{m.d}$UTU-LUGAL. Ar-Ḫalba.

RS 16.143,30 (*PRU* III, p. 83): $^{m.d}$UTU-LUGAL. Niqmepa^{c}.

RS 16.147,19 (*PRU* III, p. 90): [$^{m.d}$UT]U-LUGAL. Ar-Ḫalba ou Niqmepa^{c}.

RS 16.156,22 (*PRU* III, p. 62): $^{m.d}$UTU-LUGAL. Niqmaddu II.

RS 16.157,29 (*PRU* III, p. 84): $^{m.d}$UTU-LUGAL. Niqmepa^{c}.

RS 16.191 A,7' (*PRU* III, p. 172): [$^{m.}$]^{d}UTU$^{?}$-[LUG]AL$^{?}$

RS 16.208, rev. 6' (*PRU* III, p. 93): $^{m.d}$UTU-LUGAL. Ar-Ḫalba ou Niqmepa^{c}.

RS 16.245, rev. 13' (*PRU* III, p. 95): $^{m.d}$UTU-LUGAL. Niqmepa^{c}.

RS 16.250,25 (*PRU* III, p. 86): $^{m.d}$UTU-LUGAL. Niqmepa^{c}.

RS 16.251,16 (*PRU* III, p. 109): $^{m.d}$UTU-LUGAL. Niqmepa^{c}.

RS 16.254 D,13' (*PRU* III, p. 79): [$^{m.d}$U]TU-LUGAL.

RS 16.263,26 (*PRU* III, p. 49): ^{m}UTU-LUGAL. Niqmaddu II.

RS 16.283,17 (*PRU* III, p. 74): $^{m.d}$UTU-LUGAL.

RS 17.127, rev. (*PRU* VI,26): $^{m.d}$UT[U-LUGAL].

PT. 383 G,3' (*PRU* III, p. 176): $^{m.d}$UTU-LUGAL.

Voir aussi sous 'Ilu-milku.

31) Šipti-A.UM, fils de ^{c}Abdu, disciple de ALIM$_{x}$-SAG[?], serviteur de Nabû et de Nisaba, serviteur de Marduk et de Ṣarpanitum.

RS 22.439,IV,13' (*Ugaritica* V,163): ^{m}*šip-ṭi*-A.UM.

32) Šuna'ili.

RS 17.319,24 (*PRU* IV, p. 184): ^{m}*šu-na*-DINGIR. Probablement du temps de ^{c}Ammištamru II[14].

Scribe provenant vraisemblablement d'Ura.

33) Tamartenu.

RS 11.856,18 (*RA* 38, 1941, p. 4): ^{m}[*ta-ma*]*r-te-nu*.

RS 17.426, rev. 13' (*PRU* VI,51): ^{m}*ta-mar-te-nu*.

34) Ya^{c}didu.

RS 15.136,22 (*PRU* III, p. 122): [^{m}*i*]*a-a'-di-du*. ^{c}Ammištamru II.

RS 16.138,39 (*PRU* III, p. 145): ^{m}*ia-a'-di-du*. ^{c}Ammištamru II.

RS 16.204, rev. 15' (*PRU* III, p. 120): ^{m}*ia-a'-di-du*. ^{c}Ammištamru II.

RS 16.261 + 339 + 241,29 (*PRU* III, p. 160): ^{m}*ia-a'-di-du*. ^{c}Ammištamru II.

RS 19.98,27 (*PRU* VI,31):[^{m}]*ia-a'-di-d*[*u*]. ^{c}Ammištamru II.

35) Yadlinu.

RS 18.264, tr. 4 (*PRU* VI,65): [^{m}*ia*]*-ad-li-nu*.

36) Yanḫānu, disciple de Nūrī-Malik, serviteur de Nabû et de Nisaba.

RS 20.196 A, colophon (*Ugaritica* V,145): ^{m}*ia-an-ḫa-na* (gén.).

37) Yarīmu, père de Munaḫḫimu.

RS 15.145,22 (*PRU* III, p. 123): *ia-ri-im-mì* (gén.). ^{c}Ammištamru II.

RS 15.147, rev. 20' (*PRU* III, p. 125): [*i*]*a-ri-im-mì* (gén.). ^{c}Ammištamru II.

RS 15.190,9' (*PRU* III, p. 137): *ia-ri-mi* (gén.). ^{c}Ammištamru II.

RS 16.86, rev. 4' (*PRU* III, p. 138): [*ia-r*]*i-im-mì* (gén.). ^{c}Ammištamru II.

RS 16.156,21 (*PRU* III, p. 62): ^{m}*ia-ri-im-mu*. Niqmaddu II.

RS 16.172,6' (*PRU* III, p. 147): *ia-r*[*i-*] (gén.). ^{c}Ammištamru II.

RS 16.201, rev. 7' (*PRU* III, p. 152): [*ia-r*]*i-mì* (gén.). ^{c}Ammištamru II.

RS 16.240 (*PRU* III, p. 173): [*i*]*a*-[*r*] *i-im-mi* (gén.).
RS 16.243,24 (*PRU* III, p. 156): *ia-ri-im-mi* (gén.).
^{c}Ammištamru II.
RS 16.255 H,2' (*PRU* III, p. 174): [*ȳarīmi*] (gén.).
^{c}Ammištamru II.
RS 16.384,22 (*PRU* III, p. 165): [^{m}]*ia-ri-mu*.
^{c}Ammištamru II.
RS 16.386, rev. 19' (*PRU* III, p. 166): *ia-ri-mi* (gén.). ^{c}Ammištamru II.

38) Yaṣirānu, fils de Hūṣānu.
RS 15.118,16 (*PRU* III. p. 131): ^{m}*ia-ši-ra*[15].
^{c}Ammištamru II.
RS 16.153,6.13.16 (*PRU* III, p. 146-147): ^{m}*ia-ṣí-ra-na*, ^{m}*ia-ṣí-ra-ma* (gén.). ^{c}Ammištamru II.
RS 16.205 + 192,26 (*PRU* III, p. 154): ^{m}*ia-ṣí-ra*.
^{c}Ammištamru II.
RS 16.206,9 (*PRU* III, p. 106): ^{m}*ia-ṣí-ra-na* (gén.).
Niqmepa^{c}.
RS 16.239,4 (*PRU* III,79): ^{m}*ia-ṣí-ra-na* (gén.).
Ar-Ḫalba.
RS 16.282,16 (*PRU* III, p. 161): ^{m}*ia-ṣí-ra-nu*.
^{c}Ammištamru II.

39) Yašmu^{c}u.
RS 21.230,45 (*Ugaritica* V,81): ^{m}*ia-aš-mu-u*.

40) Yatarmu.
RS 16.269,7 (*PRU* III, p. 68): ^{m}*ia-tar-mu*. Probablement Niqmaddu III[16].

Il convient de compléter cette liste des mentions d'un *sukkallu ṭupšarru*, "chambellan-scribe", dont le nom est perdu. Deux scribes connus, Nu^{c}mi-Rašap et Ehli-Tešub, ont porté ce titre. Le premier est qualifié de *ṭupšarru sukkallu* vers la fin de sa carrière, sous le règne de 'Ibirānu (RS 17.77, rev. 13': *PRU* VI,43)[17]. Le second est appelé *sukkallu ṭupšarru* au temps de Niqmaddu IV, fils de 'Ibirānu (RS 18.21,34 = *PRU* VI,45). Il n'est donc pas facile de décider de l'identité du "chambellan-scribe" dont le nom a disparu dans les documents suivants:

RS 8.098 (*PRU* III, p. 129). ^{c}Ammištamru II.
RS 8.207, rev. 11' (*PRU* III, p. 34).
RS 15.113, rev. (*PRU* III, p. 168). Niqmaddu IV.
RS 16.148 + 254 B, rev. 15' (*PRU* III, p. 116). ^{c}Ammištamru II.

Il est étonnant qu'aucun des scribes connus d'Ugarit ne porte un nom comportant l'élément théophore "Ba^{c}al" au "Dagan", les deux dieux auxquels étaient dédiés les grands temples de l'acropole d'Ugarit. Lāṭ-Dagan est en effet un scribe étranger et l'idéogramme ^{d}IM n'apparaît que dans les noms hourrites d'Ana-^{d}IM et d'Eḫli-^{d}IM où il doit désigner le dieu Tešub. On trouve, en revanche, les théonymes ^{c}Anat, Ḫamān, Malik, Nabû, NINURTA, Rašap, Šapaš (2 noms), Yaraḫ (2 noms) et 'Ilu. Ce dernier apparaîtrait dans deux noms, à moins qu'il ne faille lire *'Ili-milku* et comprendre "le roi est mon dieu", tout comme *'Abi-milku* signifie probablement "le roi est mon père". Ce seraient deux "noms de courtisans", employant le titre royal à l'instar d'un élément théophore.

Les autres noms sémitiques des scribes d'Ugarit sont réduits à l'élément verbal, augmenté éventuellement d'une désinence hypocoristique, ou se présentent comme des noms profanes. Certains sont d'interprétation incertaine, notamment à cause de l'orthographe cryptique utilisée par les intéressés eux-mêmes. Il n'est pas possible d'entreprendre ici une étude de ces anthroponymes.

II. - Scribes de Jérusalem

Le nombre de scribes hiérosolymitains, nommément connus, est fort réduit si on le compare à celui des scribes d'Ugarit, attestés pourtant pour une période inférieure à deux siècles, alors que les scribes de Jérusalem s'échelonnent sur plus d'un demi-millénaire. La différence tient surtout à la nature de nos sources. Il convient de noter aussi que le scribe hiérosolymitain de la correspondance amarnienne ne nous est pas connu nommément, mais qu'il semble provenir de la Syrie du Nord, comme l'a montré une étude pénétrante de W.L. Moran[18]. C'est une origine semblable que suggèrent le nom du scribe de David, Šay-Ši', et celui de son fils 'Eliḥarep, qui fut actif sous Salomon. Si le premier paraît contenir l'élément théophore Ši', désignant le grand dieu lunaire de Ḫarran dans l'anthroponymie araméenne[19], le second doit probablement être rapproché du nom de 'Ili-ḥerb, gravé selon les inscriptions de Salmanasar III sur un monument de la montagne d'Atalur, dans le massif de l'Amanus[20] où le royaume araméen de Sam'al s'était constitué au début du Ier millénaire av.n.è. Bien que ces scribes d'origine vraisemblablement araméenne soient le plus anciens parmi ceux dont le nom nous a été conservé dans la documentation en provenance de Jérusalem, c'est l'ordre alphabétique que nous suivrons ici, tout comme nous l'avons fait dans le cas d'Ugarit.

1) 'Aḥiyyāh, fils de Šay-Ši' et frère de 'Eliḥarep.

I Rois 4,3: *'ḥyh*, LXX *Akhia*. Salomon. Il n'est pas impossible que *'ḥyh* ait signifié à l'origine "son frère", c'est-à-dire celui de 'Eli-ḥarep, et ait tenu lieu d'un nom devenu illisible.

2) Bārūk(yāhū), fils de Nēriyyāhū.

Jér 32,12-13.16; 36,4-32; 43,3.6; 45,1-2; Livre de Baruch: *brwk*, LXX *Baroukh*. Bulle de l'IM (*IEJ* 28, 1978, pl. 15B): *brkyhw*. Contemporain du prophète Jérémie[21].

3) 'Eliḥarep fils de Šay-Ši' et frère de 'Aḥiyyah.

I Rois 4,3: *'lyḥrp*, LXX *Eliareph*, *Eliab*, *Eliaph*. Salomon.

4) 'Elišama^{c}.

Jér 36,12.20-21: *'lyšm^{c}*, LXX *Elisama*. Joiaqim.

5) ^{c}Ezra', fils de Śerāyāh.

Esd 7-10; Néh 8; 12,26.36: *^{c}zr'*, LXX *Esdras*. Artaxerxès Ier ou Artaxerxès II.

6) Gamaryāhū, fils de Šāpān.

Jér 36,10-12.25; bulle de l'IM (*Qedem* 19, Jérusalem 1984, pl. 35:3): *gmryhw*. Joiaqim, Joiakîn et Sédécias.

7) Me'īš, fils de Manōḥ.

Sceau de la Bibliothèque Nationale, Paris, 1970. 428 (*Syria* 52, 1975, p. 108, fig. 1). Vers 700 av.n.è.[22].

8) Ṣādōq.

Néh 13,13: *ṣdwq*, LXX *Saddouk*. Artaxerxès Ier ou Artaxerxès II.

9) Šāpān, père de Gamaryāhū.

II Rois 22,3-14; II Chron 34,8-20: *špn*. Josias. Jér 36,10-12; Ez 8,11; bulle de l'IM (*Qedem* 19, Jérusalem 1984, pl. 35:3): *špn*. Joiaqim, Joiakîn et Sédécias.

10) Šay-Ši', père de 'Aḥiyyah et de 'Elḥarep.

II Sam 8,17 = I Chron 8,16: *śryh*, *šwš'*, *šyš'*, LXX *Asa*, *Sousa*. II Sam 20,25: *šy'*, *šw'*, *šyš'*, *šwš'*, LXX *Sousa*. I Rois 4,3: *šyš'*, LXX *Saba*, *Sisa*. David et Salomon.

11) Šebnā'

II Rois 18,18.26.37; 19,2; Is 22,15; 36,3.11.22; 37,2: *šbn'*, *šbnh*, LXX *Somnas*. Ezéchias.

12) Šema^{c}yāh, fils de Natan'el.

I Chron 24,6: *šm^{c}yh*, LXX *Samaias*. David (?).

13) Yehônātan.

Jér 37,15.20; 38,26: *yhwntn*, LXX *Iōnathan*. Sédécias.

14) Ye^{c}ī'el.

II Chron 26,11: *y^{c}w'l*, *y^{c}y'l*, LXX *Iièl*. Ozias/Azarias.

15) Yerēmay.

Dix bulles de l'IM (*Qedem* 4, Jérusalem 1976, p. 7-8 et pl. 6): *yrmy*. Vers 500 av.n.è.

Les scribes de Jérusalem sont, pour la plupart, des ministres ou "scribes royaux", *spr hmlk*, titre qui leur est attribué dans II Rois 12,11; II Chron 24,11 et Esther 3,12; 8,9. Il existait cependant une autre fonction scribale de haut rang, celle de "scribe-chef d'armee", *hspr śr hṣb'*, qui est mentionné dans II Rois 25,19 et Jér. 52,25[23], et dont l'office est exercé par Ye^{c}î'el (II Chron 26,11). Il y avait, par ailleurs, de simples scribes, mais ils ne sont jamais nommés dans la Bible, à l'exception de Baruch, que l'on a cependant considéré aussi comme un fonctionnaire royal[24].

Gamaryāhū, Šema^{c}yāh et Yehônātan sont les seuls à porter un nom yahwiste. Les autres éléments théophores attestés dans les noms des scribes sont 'El (Ye^{c}î'el) et Ši' (Šay-Ši'), tandis que 'mon dieu" est le sujet des propositions formées par les noms de 'Elišama^{c} et de 'Eliḥarep. Cette appellation "neutre" de la divinité est bien dans la ligne des écrits sapientiaux qui se servent volontiers du terme générique *'^{è}lōhīm*, "divinité", mais ne mentionnent jamais les scribes. De toute manière, les données dont nous disposons sont trop maigres pour se lancer dans la reconstitution d'une "spiritualité" des scribes. On se contentera donc de constater que l'habileté du scribe était une des qualités le plus appréciées de son entourage. Si Šapaš-milku d'Ugarit signait un de ses documents en faisant suivre son nom du titre de *ṭupšarru emqu*, "scribe expert" (RS 16.142,16 : *PRU* III, p. 77), l'auteur du Ps 45 ne trouvait rien de mieux pour souligner l'excellence de l'épithalame royal qu'il entonnait que de se comparer à un tel scribe: "ma langue est le calame d'un scribe habile".

Notes

1) A.L. Oppenheim, "A Note on the Scribes in Mesopotamia" dans *Studies in Honor of Benno Landsberger* (*AS*, vol. 16), Chicago 1965, pp. 253-256 (voir p. 253), cité par M. Dandamayev, *Vavilonskie Piscy*, Moscou 1983, p. 3.
2) S. Smith, *The Statue of Idri-mi*, London 1949, pl. 13, ll. 99-101. Sur ce scribe, voir aussi N. Na^{c}aman, "A Royal Scribe and His Scribal Products in the Alalakh IV Court" dans *OA* vol. 19, 1980, pp. 107-116.
3) A.F. Rainey, "The Scribe in Ugarit" dans *Proceedings of the Israel Academy of Sciences and Humanities*, vol. 3/4, 1968, pp. 139-146; W.J. Horwitz, "The Ugaritic Scribe" dans *UF* vol. 11, 1979, pp. 389-394; M. Heltzer, *The Internal Organization of the Kingdom of Ugarit*, Wiesbaden 1982, pp. 157-161.
4) T.N.D. Mettinger, *Solomonic State Officials*, Lund 1971, pp. 25-51.
5) Selon J. Nougayrol, dans *Ugaritica*, vol. 5, Paris 1968, p. 262, n. 2, la graphologie s'oppose à l'identification de ce ^{c}Abdi-^{d}[ ] avec le scribe ^{c}Abdi-Yaraḫ.
6) L'idéogramme du dieu Ninurta peut désigner, dans la Syro-Palestine de cette époque, une divinité similaire, ouest-sémitique. On trouvera une suggestion dans E. Lipiński, "Juda et 'tout Israël': analogies et contrastes" dans *The Land of Israel: Cross-Roads of Civilizations* (*Orientalia Lovaniensia Analecta*, vol. 19), éd. E. Lipiński, Leuven 1985, pp. 93-112 (voir p. 101 et n. 28).
7) Sur la reine mère Šarelli et son identité avec 'Aḫat-milki, on peut voir E. Lipiński, "Aḫat-milki, reine d'Ugarit, et la guerre du Mukiš" dans *OLP* vol. 12, 1981, pp. 79-115 (voir pp. 79-87). Les années du tableau chronologique présenté *ibid.*, pp. 82-83, doivent être abaissées en tenant compte des études de E. Wente - Ch.C. Van Siclen III, "A Chronology of the New Kingdom" dans *Studies in Honor of George R. Hughes* (*SAOC*, vol. 39), Chicago 1976, pp. 217-261, et de J. Boese - G. Wilhelm, "Aššur-dan I., Ninurta-apil-Ekur und die mittelassyrische Chronologie" dans *WZKM* vol. 71, 1979, pp. 19-38. Voir aussi K.R. Veenhof, "Chronologie van het Oude Nabije Oosten" dans *Phoenix*, vol. 27, 1981, pp. 15-34, en particulier pp. 32-34.
8) Le même nom se trouve probablement dans RS 15.145,7 (*PRU* III, p. 123): *Bu-úṣ-ma-na* (gén.). Si on veut maintenir la lecture *Bu-uš-ma-na*, on peut se référer à M. Held, "*mḫṣ/ mḫš* in Ugaritic and Other Semitic Languages" dans *JAOS* vol. 79, 1959, pp. 169-176, selon lequel "the emphatic *ṣ* becomes *š* through partial assimilation to the following *-t*" (p. 173). Ce changement pourrait n'être pas limité à ce seul cas, comme semble l'indiquer la graphie ^{m}*Ia-ši-ra* du nom du scribe Yaṣirānu dans RS 15.118,16 (*PRU* III, p. 131). Le nom *Buṣmānu* pourrait dériver du mot *būṣu*, "byssus", augmenté du suffixe *-mānu*.
9) Reconstitution hypothétique basée sur un nom hourrite attesté dans RS 15.77,19 (*PRU* III, p. 6); RS 17.78,1 (*PRU* IV, p. 196); RS 17.292,16 (*PRU* IV, p. 188).
10) Pour la distinction de Niqmaddu III et de Niqmaddu IV, fils de 'Ibirānu, on peut voir E. Lipiński, *op. cit.* (n. 7), pp. 81 et 84.
11) Nous traduisons par "déchiffreur" le mot *ṯ^{c}y*, en nous basant sur l'emploi poétique du verbe akkadien *še'û* dans *Enūma eliš* I,60; II,81; IV,66, où l'expression *šibqī še'û* signifie "pénétrer les intentions de qqn." Cette interprétation confirmerait l'identité du scribe 'Ilu-milku des tablettes mythologiques avec le 'Ilu-milku auquel le dignitaire assyrien Bēl-libur avait demandé de lire ses lettres akkadiennes à la reine 'Aḫat-milki, veuve de Niqmaddu II. Cf. E. Lipiński, *op. cit.* (n. 7), pp. 87-88. Le titre de "déchiffreur" désignerait ainsi le lecteur de documents en cunéiformes akkadiens.
12) L'idéogramme ^{d}KUR est employé dans les documents d'Emar pour dé-

signer le dieu Dagan. Le nom Lāṭ-Dagan signifie probablement "Protégé de Dagan".

13) Cf. E. Lipiński, *op. cit.* (n. 7), pp. 112-113.

14) La datation du texte repose sur le nom et la filiation d'un des témoins de l'acte (ligne 20) que l'on retrouve dans RS 17.356,20 (*PRU* VI, 38), acte rédigé par le scribe 'Iltaḥmu qui était actif au temps de ᶜAmmištamru II.

15) Pour l'emploi du signe SI, voir ci-dessus, n. 8.

16) Les documents RS 16.158 (*PRU* III, p. 62), RS 16.269 (*PRU* III, pp. 68-69) et RS 16.279 (*PRU* III, p. 70), où manque la filiation du roi Niqmaddu, sont vraisemblablement à ranger dans le règne de Niqmaddu III, frère de Niqmepaᶜ. Voir aussi E. Lipiński, *op. cit.* (n. 7), p. 81.

17) Voir *ibid.*, p. 81, n. 12.

18) W.L. Moran, " The Syrian Scribe of the Jerusalem Amarna Letters" dans *Unity and Diversity*, ed. H. Goedicke - J.J.M. Roberts, Baltimore 1975, pp. 146-166.

19) Pour l'explication du nom, cf.E. Lipiński, "Aram et Israël du Xe au VIIIe siècle av.n.è." dans *AcAn* vol. 27, 1979, pp. 49-102 (voir p. 59).

20) E. Michel, dans *WO* vol. 2, 1954-59, pp. 408-409. Le nom de 'Ili-herb est écrit respectivement [m]DINGIR-*ḫe-er-be* (Balawat 11,3), DINGIR-*ḫe-er-bi* (Monolithe II, 10), DINGIR-*ḫer-be* (Texte B de Balawat). Le rapprochement entre les noms de 'Eli-ḥarep et de 'Ili-ḥerb est favorisé par la disparition d'une distinction phonémique entre *b* et *p* en néo-assyrien; cf. W. von Soden, *Ergänzungsheft zum Grundriss der akkadischen Grammatik* (*AnOr*, vol. 47), Rom 1969, p. 4**, par. 27*b*. La montagne d'Atalur est selon toute vraisemblance identique à la montagne de Lallar, dans l'Amanus; cf. W. Röllig, "Lallar" dans *Reallexikon des Assyriologie*, vol. 6, Berlin - New York 1980-83, p. 438.

21) Voir, notamment, J. Muilenburg, "Baruch the Scribe" dans *Proclamation and Presence. Old Testament Essays in Honour of G.H. Davies*, ed. J.I. Durham - J.R. Porter, London 1970, pp. 215-238; N. Avigad, "Baruch the Scribe and Jerahmeel the King's Son" dans *IEJ* vol. 28, 1978, pp. 52-56 et pl. 15 B-D, et dans *BiAr* vol. 42, 1979, pp. 114-118.

22) P. Bordreuil, "Inscriptions sigillaires ouest-sémitique II. Un cachet hébreu récemment acquis par le Cabinet de Médailles de la Bibliothèque Nationale" dans *Syria* vol. 52, 1975, pp. 107-118. Les lettres présentent une grande ressemblance avec celles de l'inscription de Siloé. Contrairement à l'opinion de l'éditeur du cachet, le nom du propriétaire est très bien attesté au VIIe siècle. Aux témoignages recueillis par K.L. Tallqvist, *Assyrian Personal Names*, Helsingfors 1914, p. 137a, et analysés par R. Zadok, *On West Semites in Babylonia during the Chaldean and Achaemenian Periods*, Jerusalem 1978[2], p. 145, on ajoutera le nom [m]*Me-'i-su* des textes publiés par St. Dalley - J.N. Postgate, *The Tablets from Fort Shalmaneser*, Oxford 1984, n°s 10,11 et 66,20. Il convient de rappeler que le *s* néo-assyrien correspond au *š* de l'hébreu. Le nom Me'īš représente une forme *miqtal* de *'yš*, variante de *'wš*, et signifie "don".

23) Il s'agit manifestement d'un dignitaire et non d'un "secrétaire du chef de l'armée". C'est pourquoi la leçon *hspr* de 2 Rois 25:19 est préférable au *spr* de Jér 52:25, où le Targum et la Peshiṭta lisent aussi *hspr*: *spr' rb ḥyl'*.

24) J. Muilenburg, *op. cit.* (n. 21), p. 231.

Habakkuk's Dinner

An Apocryphal Story and its Aftermath

C. Molenberg, Groningen

> "How could it be written, when all Israelites completely had been captured and taken away and all those remaining people of the tribe of Judah had gone to Egypt after the murder of Gedaliah and Jeremiah with them, and when no one at all remained in the promised land, that "Habakkuk the prophet was in Judah", and that "He brought his dinner that (had been) for the mowers, to Daniel who had been thrown into the lions' den".

This question put by the East-Syrian author Išoᶜ bar Nun in his *Book of Questions and Answers*[1] draws attention to a remarkable contradiction in biblical history. In the book of 2 Kings[2] and Jeremiah[3] we are told how the people of Judah went to Egypt after the murder of Gedaliah. The apocryphal story of Habakkuk bringing dinner to Daniel, as it is told in Bel and the Dragon[4], says that Habakkuk was still in Judah. Išoᶜ bar Nun's answer demonstrates his critical attitude towards this part of the Old Testament in the version of the Seventy. According to him the story was written by someone lacking in accuracy[5].

Išoᶜ bar Nun who cites "some *theophoroi*" supports his assertion using two arguments. The first is that Daniel was thrown into the lions' den only once "as it is in his book" and not twice. The second reason is the fact that according to him, Cyrus, the Persian king, did not take over the kingdom of Astyages, king of the Medes, but that of Darius[6], king of the Medes. As an additional argument Išoᶜ bar Nun mentions the fact that there was no Holophernes in Nebuchadnezzar's army and therefore the story of Judith was an addition, just like the story of the Dragon.
The way in which Išoᶜ bar Nun deals with the story of Habakkuk bringing dinner to Daniel makes it highly probable that he considered the stories of Bel and the Dragon of secondary importance. The same applies to the story of Judith[7]. His reference to the viewpoint of the *theophoroi* also indicates his own doubts as to their credibility. The additions to Daniel were already part of the current text of the Pešitta in the fifth century AD[8]. They were translated from the Greek

version which Origenes ascribed to Theodotion[9]. Origenes seems to have considered this version of the story the better one when compared to that of the Septuagint[10].

It is clear from his first argument that Išoᶜ bar Nun used the Pešiṭta text since the Septuagint does not mention Astyages[11]. A rough survey of the impact of the story of Habakkuk on Syriac literature leads us first to Ephrem Syrus. In 1882 Lamy published the *Sermo ad Nocturnum Dominicae Resurrectionis* which is ascribed to Ephrem. In this *sermo* the way in which the angels entered the sealed grave of Jesus is compared to Habakkuk's entry into the sealed lions' den[12]. In his *Commentary on the Diatessaron* (XXI,22)[13], however, Ephrem refers to the sealed lions' den and the grave of Lazarus. The editor of this *Commentary*, L. Leloir, refers in a note to the above-mentioned *sermo*[14]. Ephrem's reference in the *Commentary on the Diatessaron* is to Dan 6:18 where the lions' den is said to be sealed. The apocryphal story at issue does not mention this fact. Elsewhere in one of his hymns *De Ieiunio*[15] Ephrem praises Daniel for fasting in the lions' den. Thus, setting aside other reasons for considering the *sermo* published by Lamy as spurious[16], we may doubt if Ephrem himself ever used the story.

One of the oldest surviving Syriac works which show traces of the history of Habakkuk's dinner is the *Lives of the Prophets*[17]. This work ascribed to Epiphanius is likely to have been Semitic in origin[18]. Its later recensions show Christian influence. These recensions contain traces of the story[19]. At the end of the book of the prophet Habakkuk in the Codex Ambrosianus Syro Hexaplaris (ninth century)[20] we find a fragment concerning the life of this prophet. According to Schermann this fragment is very similar to one of the Greek recensions, of which it might even be a translation[21]. Actually it is identical to the same fragment of the *Lives* in Syriac published by Nestlé[22]. The use of this *Life* of Habakkuk in the Ambrosian Codex of the Syro-Hexapla is surprising. This *Life* tells us that Habakkuk was of the tribe of Simeon, whereas the heading of the story of Bel and the Dragon in the Syro-Hexapla says that he was of the tribe of Levi[23].

A seventh-century reference to the *Lives of the Prophets* may be found in one of the letters of Jacob of Edessa to John the Stylite[24]. Jacob rejects the claim that Jonah, the prophet, was the son of the widow of Zarephath. This claim depended on "the superfluous stories" ascribed to Epiphanius, which were not considered trustworthy by Jacob. He argues that there is a discrepancy between the lifetime of Elijah, and of the widow of Zarephath and her son, i.e. the beginning of the reign of Ahab, on the one hand, and the time at which Jonah went to

Nineveh, i.e. the time of Pekah, the son of Remaliah, the king of Israel, and of Jotham, king of Judah, on the other hand, altogether being a period of 170 years[25]. Since the widow and her son as well as Elijah are mentioned in the surviving Syriac *Lives*, Jacob's rejection may in fact apply to this recension of the *Lives of the Prophets*[26].

Although the eight century East-Syrian author Theodore bar Koni[27] leaves out the story of Habakkuk in his description of the death of the Prophets, he or his source may have got his information from the *Lives of the Prophets* too. The same holds good for Išo^{c}dad of Merv (ninth century), who in his commentary on Dan. 14:3 explicitly says that the Habakkuk mentioned in the story of Bel and the Dragon is the same Habakkuk who wrote the prophecy[28]. In this commentary the fragment that depends on the *Lives* is part of a longer section on the story of Bel and the Dragon, to which we will return later. Some works that were written in the following ages also show traces of the *Vitae Prophetarum*. The East-Syrian author Solomon of Basra[29] as well as the West-Syrian writers Michael Syrus and Bar Hebraeus are familiar with the story of Habakkuk bringing the dinner for the mowers to Daniel as told in his *Life*. Michael Syrus quoted in the name of Epiphanius fragments of the *Lives*, including that of Habakkuk[30]. Bar Hebraeus rendered a shortened version of the *Life* of Habakkuk in his *Scholia on the minor Prophets*[31]. Since Bar Hebraeus lived in the thirteenth century[32] we may conclude that the story of Habakkuk's dinner left its traces in Syriac Literature from the seventh up to the thirteenth century mainly through the *Lives of the Prophets*.

A more critical attitude towards the stories of Bel and the Dragon was common in East-Syrian circles in about the second half of the eighth and the first half of the ninth century. Apart from Išo^{c} bar Nun, whose question we have already quoted, Theodore bar Koni[33] and Išo^{c}dad[34] were interested in these additions to the book of Daniel. For these authors these stories were not automatically considered to be reports of historical facts. Theodore bar Koni, who does not explicitly mention Habakkuk bringing dinner to Daniel, clearly expresses his opinion. When he is discussing the time at which Daniel lived, he mentions the five kings who reigned over Babylon during thirty-three years. He continues, saying:

> "As for Astyages whose story that has been written in Daniel (describes him) as (being) from the line of the Medes, we cannot know who he is. In the succession of the kings of the Medes, however, he is the eighth (king). And he is likely to be Darius. For there is no Darius in the succession of

the names of the Median kings. And Cyrus is said to have killed Astyages"[35].

By means of the identification of Darius and Astyages[36] Theodore bar Koni tries to solve the problem of Cyrus killing Astyages, who is not mentioned elsewhere in the Bible. Only in this way can he accept the story as an authentic part of the Scriptures. In this way he meets the objections of those exegetes who have noticed the differences in the names and in order of the story. For if the story were to be false the saints of old and especially Gregory of Nazianze would not have mentioned the stories of Bel and the Dragon. Unlike his contemporary Išoᶜ bar Nun, who seems to deny the authenticity of the story of Habakkuk, Theodore bar Koni accepted the stories of Bel and the Dragon, including the tale of Habakkuk's dinner as a genuine part of the Bible.

About half a century later Išoᶜdad of Merv presents the two opinions side by side, though in a somewhat different way. The bishop of Ḥedatta gives no more attention than Theodore to Habakkuk's dinner. He is interested in the stories of Bel and the Dragon as a whole. He starts with the opinion of many of the doctors[37] who considered these stories to be additions. At the end of this fragment Išoᶜdad mentions the story of Judith as well. The arguments which he uses are nearly identical to those that Išoᶜ bar Nun used in his answer. In addition to the argument that Cyrus did not take over the kingdom of Astyages but that of Darius, there is a description of the way in which Darius was deceived.

The next fragment of Išoᶜdad's work[38] contains arguments in favour of the authenticity of Bel and the Dragon. Just like Theodore bar Koni, Išoᶜdad attaches importance to the opinion of the "saints". He mentions Theodorete in addition to Gregory of Nazianze. Išoᶜdad ascribes to the bishop of Cyrus the view that Cyrus was a relative of Astyages and that the Persian king took his grandfather's kingdom[39]. He explicitly denies that Astyages and Darius were the same person. When at the end of his commentary on Daniel Išoᶜdad gives his opinion on the story of Habakkuk bringing the dinner for the mowers to Daniel in the lions' den, his explanation is for the greater part dependent on the *Lives of the Prophets*[40]. His version is, however, rather different from the relevant passage in Theodore bar Koni's work, which was also dependent on these *Lives*[41]. So we must exclude the *Scholion* as a source for Išoᶜdad. The same applies to the fragment that contains the arguments in favour of the authenticity of Bel the Dragon. Here a common source may have passed on the material to Theodore and Išoᶜdad.

But how do we interpret the discussion of the story of Habakkuk's dinner in Išoᶜ bar Nun's *Book of Questions and Answers*? Išoᶜdad's exegesis might be derived from Išo^{c} bar Nun's, just as it often is. A thorough comparison of the parallel fragments [42] in both authors shows, however, that a direct line from Išo^{c} bar Nun to Išo^{c}dad has to be rejected. Although Išo^{c} bar Nun wants to discuss only a part of the story of the Dragon, his arguments concern the stories of Bel and the Dragon *in toto*. Išo^{c}dad, who investigates the whole of these additions to Daniel, uses the very same arguments. Only one of these arguments, the one concerning Daniel's second stay in the lions' den, can actually be derived from the part of the story related to Habakkuk. So Išo^{c} bar Nun as well as Išo^{c}dad must have used a source that contained these arguments. Išo^{c}dad discusses them in their original context, whereas Išo^{c} bar Nun connects them with his own question. He must have considered the arguments which were suitable for verifying the whole story, to be relevant for part of that story as well.

But why did Išo^{c} bar Nun not formulate a question on Bel and the Dragon as such? He must have had reasons for posing the question concerning Habakkuk, but we shall never exactly know what reasons. Although it is speculation, we may think of a reason that Išo^{c} bar Nun found in the common source. The fragment on Habakkuk's life which depends on the *Lives of the Prophets* in the commentary of Išo^{c}dad might have been taken from the same source. This fragment contains the history of the occupation of Jerusalem and its surroundings and the flight of its inhabitants, guided by Yoḥanan bar Qoraḥ, to Egypt (Jer 43: 5-7)[43]. Išo^{c} bar Nun, who was a rather sceptical man, may have compared the fragments in his source with 2 Kings 25 and Jeremiah 43 and with the story of Habakkuk in Daniel. He must have noticed the contradictions and hence have formulated his question. The problems he had to deal with could only be resolved if the story of Habakkuk was of minor importance, and the material to prove the inferiority of the story of Habakkuk's dinner was available in the very same source.

So Išo^{c} bar Nun may have decided to use the arguments which his source used,to demonstrate the inferiority of the story of Bel and the Dragon as a whole for that part of the text of Daniel which gave him problems. But if he did so, his question is nothing but another proof of the great influence of the *Lives of the Prophets* - in which Habakkuk's dinner played a minor part - in Syriac literature.

Notes

1) MS. *Cambr. Add. 2017*, fol. 44v^{o}:4-11.
2) 2 Kings 25:1-26.
3) Jeremiah 39:1-43:7.
4) Cf. *The Old Testament in Syriac according to the Peshiṭta version*, part III, fasc. 4, *Dodekapropheton-Daniel-Bel Draco*, Leiden 1980, p. 48, Bel Dr. 33 and cf. 34.
5) MS. *Cambr. Add. 2017*, fol. 44v^{o}: 12f.
6) MS. *Cambr. Add. 2017*, fol. 44v^{o}:15-45r^{o}:2. A translation of Iso^{c} bar Nun's answer is given in note 42.
7) MS. *Cambr. Add. 2017*, fol.45r^{o}:2f.
8) Cf. R. Duval, *La littérature syriaque des origines jusqu'à la fin de cette littérature après la conquête des Arabes au XIIIe siècle*, Amsterdam 1970 (repr. of Paris 1907), pp. 31-34, and A. Baumstark, *Geschichte der Syrischen Literatur*, Berlin 1968 (repr. of Bonn 1922), pp. 18-19 and n. 1.
9) Cf. A. Vööbus, *The Hexapla and the Syro-Hexapla*, Stockholm 1971, pp. 53f.
10) Cf. Hieronymus, *Commentariorum in Danielem libri III(IV)*, (*Corpus Christianorum 75 A*), ed. F. Glorie, Turnholti 1964, p. 811 and Vööbus, *op. cit.*, p. 54 n. 4.
11) Cf. *Septuaginta. Vetus Testamentum Graece, Suzanna-Daniel-Bel et Draco*, ed. J. Ziegler, Göttingen 1954, *Bel et Draco*, o'.
12) T.J. Lamy, *S. Ephraem Syri Hymni et Sermones*, vol. I, Mechliae 1882, col. 529. See for a recent edition of this *memra*: Ephraem Syrus, *Sermones in Hebdomadam Sanctam*, (*Corpus Scriptorum Christianorum Orientalium* (= *CSCO*) vol. 412 (t.), vol. 413 (v.)), ed. E. Beck, Louvain 1979, *Sermo* VII, 11. 114ff.
13) Saint Ephrem, *Commentaire de l'Evangile concordant*, (*Chester Beatty Monographs*, vol. 8), ed. L. Leloir, Dublin 1963, p. 223.
14) Saint Ephrem, *ibid.*, XXI, 21, p. 223, n. 2.
15) *Des heiligen Ephraem des Syrers Hymnen de Ieiunio*, (*CSCO*, vol. 246 (t.), vol. 247 (v.), ed. E. Beck, Louvain 1964, *Hymne* III, 6. Cf. Lamy, *op. cit.*, vol. 2, p. 662.
16) Cf. Baumstark, *op. cit.*, p. 49 and n. 5; see E. Beck, Introduction to *Ephraem Syrus*, *op. cit.* (*CSCO*, vol. 413), Louvain 1979.
17) The text has been edited by E. Nestlé in *Syrische Grammatik*, Berlin 1888^{2}. For the variants in the MSS. *Br. Lib. Add. 12.178*, *Add. 14.536* and *Add. 17.193* see his *Marginalien und Materialien*, Tübingen 1893.
18) See Th. Schermann, *Propheten- und Apostellegenden* (*TU*, vol. 31,3) Leipzig 1907, pp. 132f.
19) Cf. Schermann, *op. cit.*, pp. 127f.
20) *Codex Syro-Hexaplaris Ambrosianus photolitographice editus curante et adnotante* (*Monumenta Sacra et Profana*, fasc. 7), ed. A.M. Ceriani, Mediolani 1874.
21) Schermann, *op. cit.*, p. 38, cites Nestlé's opinion given in his *Materialien*, p. 49, that the text of the Ambrosianus is in any case a translation from the Greek. Schermann, however, suggests a common source for the Syriac recension in the Ambrosian codex and *Vat. Gr. 2125* as another possibility.
22) Nestlé, *Syrische Grammatik*, pp. 99-100, vv. 270-295.
23) Apart from the Syro-Hexapla we have only found this view on the descent of Habakkuk at the end of Išo^{c}dad of Merv's commentary on Habakkuk. Cf. *Commentaire d'Išo^{c}dad de Merv sur l'Ancien Testament, IV. Isaîe et les Douze* (*CSCO*, vol. 303 (t.), vol. 304 (v.)), ed. C. van den Eynde, Louvain 1969, p. 114 (t.), p. 145 (v.).
24) MS. *Br. Lib. Add. 12.172* fol. 111v^{o}ff. Cf. Schermann, *op. cit.*, p. 4, Nestlé, *Materialien*, p. 56.
25) MS. *Br. Lib. Add. 12.172* fol. 118v^{o}, 11. 6ff.
26) Schermann, *op. cit.*, p. 4.
27) Theodorus Bar Koni, *Liber Scholiorum* (*CSCO*, vol. 55 (t.)), ed.

A. Scher, Paris 1910, p. 351, and Théodore Bar Koni, *Livre des Scholies, I (CSCO*, vol. 431 (v.)), ed. R. Hespel - R. Draguet, Louvain 1981, p. 293.

28) *Commentaire d'Išo^{c}dad de Merv sur l'Ancien Testament, V. Jérémie, Ezéchiel, Daniel (CSCO*, vol. 328 (t.), vol. 329 (v.)), ed. C. van den Eynde, Louvain 1972, p. 135, l. 3 (t.), p. 155, ll. 10f. (v.).

29) *The Book of the Bee (Anecdota Oxoniensia, Semitic Series*, vol. 1, part 2), ed. E.A.W. Budge, Oxford 1886, p. 77 (t.), p. 71 (v.).

30) *Chronique de Michel le Syrien*, ed. J.C. Chabot, vol. 4, Bruxelles 1963 (repr. of Paris 1910),p. 60 (t.); vol. 1 Bruxelles 1963 (repr. of Paris 1899), p.97 (v.).

31) Gregorii Barhabraei, *In duodecim prophetas minores scholia*, ed. B. Moritz, Lipsiae 1882, p. 17.

32) 1225/1226 - 1282; cf. Baumstark, *op. cit.*, p. 313.

33) Theodorus Bar Koni, *Liber Scholiorum*, p. 338; *Livre des Scolies*, p. 285.

34) *Commentaire d'Išo^{c}dad de Merv sur l'Ancien Testament, V*,ed. . van den Eynde, pp. 133-135 (t.), pp. 153-156.

35) *Liber Scholiorum*, ed. Scher, p. 338, ll. 15-18.

36) Theodore accepts the historicity of the Median kings mentioned by him immediately after the remarks on Astyages. This list depends on that given by Eusebius in his chronicle. Cf. Eusebius, *Die Chronik, aus dem Armenischen übersetzt (Die griechischen christlichen Schriftsteller*, vol. 20, Eusebius' Werke V), ed. J. Karst, Leipzig 1911, p. 152. The historical king Astyages is known to us from two cuneiform sources, *viz.* an inscription; see S. Langdon, *Die Neubabylonischen Königsinschriften*((VAB, vol. 4), Leipzig 1912, p. 221, ll. 28ff.; and a chronicle, see the Nabonidus Chronicle in A.K. Grayson, *Assyrian and Babylonian Chronicles* (Texts from Cuneiform Sources, vol. 5), New York 1975, pp. 104ff.; chron. 7.

37) *Commentaire d'Išo^{c}dad, V*, ed. Van den Eynde, pp. 133-134, l. 23 - l. 8 (t.).

38) *ibid.*, p. 134, ll. 9-20.

39) *ibid.*, p. 134, ll. 12-20. Cf. Gregorius of Nazianus, *Patrologia graeca*, vol. 37, cols. 472-474 and col. 592(?) and Theodorete, *Patrologia graeca*, vol 81, col. 1549.

40) Cf. *Commentaire d'Išo^{c}dad, V*, ed. Van den Eynde, p. 156, n. 1 (v.). Van den Eynde remarks: " Le paragraphe consacré à Habaquq est tiré des Vies des Prophètes (cf. Schermann, *op. cit.*, p. 20, 1.13 - p. 21,1.9; Nestlé, *op. cit.*, p. 99,1.270; 273 -p. 100, 1.284)". Although the tradition used by Išo^{c} dad is the very same as that in the *Lives*, its wording and order as well as the reference to 2 Kings 25 and Jeremiah 43, demonstrate that a direct relation between the two works is less probable. Išo^{c} dad would have found the material in one of his sources.

41) Theodorus Bar Koni, *Liber Scholiorum, I*, ed. Scher, p. 351,11.17-23. Unlike Išo^{c}dad Theodore refers to the Messianic prophecy of Habakkuk. The main subject of the fragment is the place where Habakkuk died and was buried. It reflects a part of the *Life* of Habakkuk other than the fragment in Išo^{c} dad's work.

42) Išo^{c} bar Nun, *The Selected Questions*, Ms. *Cambr. Add. 2017*, fol. 44v^{o}, l. 11 - 45r^{o}, l.6, says: "*Answer:* Some *theophoroi* ('nš' lbyšy 'lh') considered this story to be superfluous, since it was written by someone who did not give special attention to accuracy, because of the fact that Daniel was thrown into the lions' den only once, as it is in his book, and not twice, as it is in the story. For, they say, neither it is Astyages from whom Cyrus, the Persian, received the kingdom. Cyrus took over the kingdom from Darius, the Mede. In the same way they also looked at the story of the Dragon. An addition is that of Judith too, because of the fact that Holophernes, a commander of king Nebuchadnezzar, who came to Judah and was killed, never existed". (See the question at the beginning of the article). In *Commentaire*

d'Išo^{c}dad, V, ed. Van den Eynde, pp. 133-134, l. 23 - l. 8 (t.), we read: "Many of the doctors considered these two stories Bel and the Dragon to be superfluous since they were written by someone who did not give special attention to accuracy, because of the fact that Daniel was thrown into the lions' den only once, as it is in his book, and not twice as it is in his story. For, they say, neither it is king Astyages from whom Cyrus, the Persian, received the (kingdom), because of the fact that Cyrus took over the kingdom from Darius, the Mede , by means of treachery of Bosporius, his commander who cut off the top of his own ears and his nostrils and went to Darius and he (Darius) trusted him, etc. Even if others do pretend that Darius has been designated by two names, i.e. Darius and Astyages, yet notice that Astyages was the king of the Medes, and Cyrus took over the kingdom of the two of them. In the same way they also considered that story of Judith to be spurious, because of the fact that Holophernes, a commander of king Nebuchadnezzar, who came to Judah and was killed, never existed."

43) *Commentaire d'Išo^{c}dad, V*, ed. Van den Eynde, p. 135, ll. 3-15 (t.).

Tyrannen und Muslime

Die Gestaltung einer symbolischen Metapher bei Pseudo-Methodios

G.J. Reinink, Groningen

Dass auch die literarischen Zeugen einer Zeit und Kultur als *scripta signa vocis* gekennzeichnet werden können, geht besonders deutlich aus den Schriften hervor, die sich in einer ganz konkreten geschichtlichen Situation umittelbar an ein bestimmtes Lesepublikum wenden mit dem Zweck, dieses für einen bestimmten politischen, religiösen oder irgendeinen anderen Standpunkt zu gewinnen.

Zu dieser Art von propagandistischen und stark zeitbedingten Schriften gehört eine auf den Kirchenvater Methodios zurückgeführte Homilie (*mēmrā*), die in dem ausgehenden 7. Jhdt in der Syrisch sprechenden Kirche Mesopotamiens entstand[1]. Der Verfasser dieses *mēmrā* wollte seine "Zuhörer" durch eine kurzgefasste Darstellung der Abfolge der Königreiche vom Anfang bis zum Ende der Weltgeschichte davon überzeugen, dass sich die gegenwärtige Lage, in der die Muslime fast die ganze Welt beherrschen, in kurzem drastisch ändern werde. Er prophezeite, dass der Kaiser von Byzanz in kurzem mit einer Kriegsflotte gegen die Muslime ausfahren und sie in der Wüste von Yatreb angreifen werde. Dieser Angriff werde zum endgültigen Zusammenbruch der muslimischen Herrschaft führen, wonach eine Epoche von Wohlstand, Glück und Frieden auf der ganzen Erde entstehen werde unter byzantinischer Herrschaft. Diese herrliche Zeit werde bis zu den dramatischen Ereignissen der Endzeit fortwähren, weil die bevorstehende endgültige Besiegung der Muslime durch das christlich-byzantinische Reich den Anfang der bis zur Erscheinung des Antichrist dauernden Epoche byzantinischer Herrschaft über die ganze Welt bilde[2]. Die Prophezeiung des Pseudo-Methodios ist in einer Krisenzeit für die christliche Bevölkerung Mesopotamiens entstanden. Rezente politische und gesellschaftliche Entwicklungen hatten einen Zustand grosser Ungewissheit und Verwirrung hervorgebracht, der zu einem massenhaften Abfall vom christlichen Glauben und übertritt zum Islam zu führen drohte[3]. Derartige Verhältnisse bildeten einen guten Nährboden für den Gedanken, dass sich in der gegenwärtigen Krise die Zeichen der Endzeit offenbarten und die folgende Szene im Drehbuch des Endzeitdramas im Zusammenbruch der muslimischen Herrschaft bestehen werde, wonach - gemäss den Vorhersagungen in den heiligen Schriften - die schrecklichen eschatologischen Völker des Nordens die Kutlturwelt überfluten werden und schliesslich kurz vor dem Weltende sich der Antichrist offenbaren werde[4].

Auch Pseudo-Methodios erklärt die gegenwärtige Krise als "Zeichen der Endzeit"[5]. Er will seine "Zuhörer" davon überzeugen, dass die Entartung des moralischen und religiösen Lebens in den Kirchen und der zwanglose Abfall vom christlichen Glauben zu den in den heiligen Schriften vorhergesagten endzeitlichen Ereignissen gehören. Die Muslime sind nichts anderes als Instrumente in den Händen Gottes, deren Aufgabe es ist, die Spreu vom Weizen zu trennen und die wahrhaften Christusgläubigen herauszustellen[6]. Es sei ein Missverständnis, zu glauben, dass die Muslime eine dauerhafte weltpolitische Rolle spielen[7]. Pseudo-Methodios warnt seine "Zuhörer" vor dem Trugschluss, dass die politischen Erfolge der Muslime ein Zeichen dafür sind, dass sie unter dem besonderen Schutz Gottes stehen[8]. Gott liebt diese "Söhne Ismaels" nicht, benutzt sie aber lediglich, um die Sünden der Christen zu bestrafen und eine Katharsis innerhalb der Kirchen durchzuführen[9]. Wenn der Mass der Kasteiung der Christen voll ist und die Ueberheblichkeit der Muslime ihren Gipfel erreicht hat, wird der christliche Kaiser von Byzanz ihrer Macht ein Ende setzen und darauf Rache üben an all denjenigen, die den wahrhaften Glauben, das heilige Kreuz und die Ehrfurcht einflössenden Sakramente leugneten[10]. Im Zentrum der Polemik des Pseudo-Methodios gegen die Muslime und die Abtrünnigen steht der Gedanke, dass nicht ein muslimisches, sondern ein christlich-byzantinisches Reich die letzte Weltmacht auf Erden sein wird[11]. Weitaus der grösste Teil der pseudomethodiosschen "Weltgeschichte" befasst sich mit der Darlegung und Begründung dieser Anschauung mit Hilfe von aus Bibel, exegetischer Literatur und anderen Quellen entnommenen Argumenten. Um zu begreifen, weshalb Pseudo-Methodios sosehr für diese Idee Propaganda treiben muss, muss man die lange Vorgeschichte der stetig verschlechternden Beziehungen zwischen der byzantinischen Behörde und Reichskirche und den monophysitischen Bevölkerungen der ehemaligen östlichen Provinzen von Byzanz berücksichtigen. Als der Sturm der arabisch-islamischen Eroberungen über den östlichen Teilen des byzantinischen Reiches losbrach, gab es nicht wenige monophysitische Christen, die die Muslime als Erlöser von der oppressiven Politik der Byzantiner begrüssten. Infolge der Erfahrungen der Vergangenheit hegten unter den syrisch-monophysitischen Christen Mesopotamiens nur wenige ein grosses Vertrauen zu der Erwartung, dass die Ablösung der muslimischen durch eine byzantinische Obergewalt eine "Erlösung" bedeuten würde[12].

Pseudo-Methodios' *memrā* enthielt für viele seiner "Zuhörer" gewiss eine schwierige Botschaft und er war aus diesem Grunde dazu gezwungen, alle erdenklichen und ihm zur Verfügung stehenden Mittel anzuwenden, um dieser Botschaft Eingang zu verschaffen. Auf eines dieser Mittel, in dem sich das *signum vocis praedicatoris* besonders deutlich offenbart, möchte ich jetzt näher eingehen. Es handelt sich um die Art und Weise, wie unser *praedicator* die Muslime bezeichnet, um so seine *auditores* für seinen "Araberfeindlichen" und "Byzantinerfreundlichen" Standpunkt zu gewinnen.
Nur einmal benutzt Pseudo-Methodios die in den syrischen Quellen übliche Bezeichnung für Araber: *Ṭayy*[13]. Er nennt die Muslime gewöhnlich (7x) *bnay 'išmaᶜīl*, "Söhne Ismaels", entsprechend der bereits auf Eusebios zurückgehenden Tradition, die die Araber als Nachkommen Ismaels und Hagars einordnet. Dieser Name, der bei den syrischen Autoren im allgemeinen eine ziemlich neutrale Bedeutung zu haben scheint[14], wird von Pseudo-Methodios in sehr abwertendem Sinne benutzt. Für ihn kommt darin nicht nur die subalterne und minderwertige Herkunft der Muslime zum Ausdruck, indem ihr Stammvater der Sohn einer ägyptischen Sklavin war[15], sondern auch die vom Engel in Gen 16:12 ausgesprochene negative Charakterisierung Ismaels und somit seiner ganzen Nachkommenschaft. Denn Pseudo-Methodios erklärt die Bezeichnung Ismaels als *ᶜrādā*, "Wildesel" (Gen 16:12) als eine Metapher, wodurch die destruktive und kulturfeindliche Gewalt eines barbarischen Wüstenvolkes zum Ausdruck gebracht wird[16].
In religiöser Hinsicht stellt Pseudo-Methodios die Muslime als *ḥanpē*, "Heiden", dar, im Gegensatz zu den *mhaymnē*, "Gläubigen", d.h. Christen. Man darf aus der Tatsache, dass Pseudo-Methodios die "Söhne Ismaels" als *ḥanpē* bezeichnet, nicht die Schlussfolgerung ziehen, dass er gar nicht oder nur einen geringen Begriff hatte von ihren religiösen Hintergrunden. Er stellt die Muslime als *ḥanpē* dar, um zu betonen, dass jeder, der sich den Muslimen anschliesst, zu den *kāpūrē* gehört, d.h. zu denjenigen, die das Wesen des christlichen Glaubens (Christus, Kreuz und Sakramente) leugnen und aus diesem Grunde *de facto* zum reinen Paganismus abgleiten[17].

Auffallend häufig (5x) überträgt Pseudo-Methodios den Namen *ṭrūnē*, "Tyrannen", auf die Muslime[18]. Er benutzt das traditionelle Bild des Tyrannen, um die Unmenschlichkeit und Grausamkeit der Muslime hervorzuheben. Sie sind *ṭrūnē barbarāyē*, "barbarische Tyrannen", oder *ṭrūnē baᶜrīrāyē*, "wilde Tyrannen", weil sie eine rücksichtslose Gewaltherrschaft üben[19]. Die Verwendung der Bezeichnung *ṭrūnē* für die Muslime steigt jedoch über eine mehr oder weniger traditionelle metaphorische Funktion hinaus. Sie ist prägnant und steht stets in Verbindung mit dem Begriff der *mardūtā*. Unter *mardūtā* versteht Pseudo-

Methodios die Kasteiung der Christusgläubigen durch Bedrückung, Räuberei, Gesetzlosigkeit, Härte und Entweihung, die zum Zweck hat, die Spreu vom Weizen zu trennen innhalb der christlichen Gemeinden. Bei dieser *mardūtā* handelt es sich um ein im Heilsplan Gottes vorhergesehenes und in den heiligen Schriften vorhergesagtes Ereignis, das dazu dient, in den letzten Zeiten der Weltgeschichte eine Katharsis durchzuführen innerhalb der christlichen Kirchen. Die *ṭrūnē* symbolisieren jene unheiligen und widerchristlichen Mächte, denen es zeitweilig von Gott erlaubt ist, durch ihre Heimsuchungen die Schwachen im Glauben dazu zu verführen, sich aus freiem Willen vom rechten Glauben abzuwenden und ihrer unheiligen, dämonischen Lebensweise anzuschliessen[20].

Woher hat Pseudo-Methodios nun diese Idee der *ṭrūnē* als widerchristliche Mächte bekommen? Ich glaube, dass der Schlüssel für das Antwort auf diese Frage in dem folgenden Passus seines *mēmrā* gefunden werden kann:

Vat.syr.58, fol.126^r, 12-126^v,5:

lyt gyr ʿm' 'w mlkwt' dtḥyt
šmy' dmšḳḥ' dtḥsny lmlkwt'
dkrysṭyn' km' d'ḥd' gws'
bṣlyb' ḥy' hw d'qbʿ[21]
bmṣʿth d'rʿ'w'ḥyd hylh[22]
lrwm' wlʿwmq'. 'p mwkl'
dšywl hlyn d'ytyhwn ṭrwn'
dḥnpwt' l' mšḳhn[23]
dnḥswn[24] *lhd' mlkwt'*
dkrysṭyn' 'yk brt qlh
šryrt' dprwqn d'mr lwt
šmʿwn. d'ynw ḥyl' 'w mlkwt'
'w ʿm' d'yt tḥyt šmy'
dḥyltn wtqyp ḥylh dmšḳḥ
dnḥsn lḥylh rb' dṣlyb'
qdyš' hw dbh 'ḥyd' gws'
mlkwt' dywny' d'ytyh
drwmy'.

"Denn nicht gibt es ein Volk oder Königreich unter dem Himmel, das das Königreich der Christen *überwältigen* kann, solange dieses seine Zuflucht nimmt zum lebenspendenden Kreuz, das in der Mitte der Erde gepflanzt wurde und Macht hat in Höhe und Tiefe. Sogar die *Riegel der Unterwelt*, welche die *Tyrannen des Heidentums* sind, werden dieses Königreich der Christen *nicht überwältigen* können dem wahren Wort unseres Erlösers zufolge, das er zu Simon sprach (Matth 16:18b). Denn welche Macht oder welches Königreich oder Volk unter dem Himmel hat eine so grosse und stärke Kraft, dass es die grosse Kraft des heiligen Kreuzes, zu dem das Königreich der Griechen, d.h. das der Römer, seine Zuflucht nimmt, *überwältigen* kann?"

Dieser Passus nimmt buchstäblich und figürlich eine zentrale Stellung in dem *mēmrā* ein. Er befindet sich auf der Grenzlinie zwischen dem historischen (rückblickenden) und dem prophetischen Teil der Homilie und steht im Zentrum der Auseinandersetzung, dass das von Kušat, der Mutter Alexanders des Grossen, abstammende christlich-byzantinische Reich in den letzten Zeiten der Weltgeschichte die ganze Welt erobern und kurz vor dem Weltende das irdische Königtum Gott, dem Vater, übertragen wird[25]. Pseudo-Methodios stützt sich hier auf die Verheissung Jesu an Petrus (Matth 16:18), deren Wortlaut in der Pešiṭta wie folgt ist:

> *'p 'n' 'mr lk d'nt hw k'p'. w^c^l hd' k'p' 'bnyh l^c^dty. wtr^c^' dšywl l' nḥsnwnh* "Auch sage ich dir: Du bist Petrus, und auf diesen Felsen werde ich meine Kirche bauen, und die Pforten der Unterwelt werden sie nicht überwältigen".

Wichtig ist, dass Pseudo-Methodios anstelle des Pešiṭta-Textes *tar^c^ē da-šyōl*, "die Pforten der Unterwelt", die letzten Endes auf das syrische Diatessaron zurückgehende Lesart *mūklē da-šyōl*, "die Riegel der Unterwelt", bietet[26]. Wie wir sehen werden, hängt das höchstwahrscheinlich damit zusammen, dass Pseudo-Methodios auf exegetische Traditionen zurückgreift, in deren Rahmen der Diatessaron-Text von Matth 16:18b überliefert wurde.
Pseudo-Methodios deutet also die *mūklē da-šyōl*, "Riegel der Unterwelt", auf die *ṭrūnē d-ḥanpūtā* "Tyrannen des Heidentums", und introduziert als Objekt des Verbums *ḥsn* "überwältigen"[27], das sich in Matth 16:18 auf die Kirche (eventuell auf den Felsen) bezieht, die *malkūtā da-krīsṭyānē* "das Königreich der Christen", d.h. Byzanz. Mit den heidnischen Tyrannen können im Rahmen des *mēmrā* nur die Muslime gemeint sein, so dass Pseudo-Methodios seine "Zuhörer" durch den Hinweis auf diese Prophezeiung Jesu davon zu überzeugen versucht, dass die Muslime das byzantinische Reich nie besiegen können. Die Unbesiegbarkeit des byzantinischen Reiches ist jedoch eine abgeleitete. Denn tatsächlich ist nur das Kreuz Christi unbesiegbar und vermittelt dem christlichen Reich unbesiegbare Kraft, solange es seine Zuflucht nimmt (*'aḥīdā gawsā*) zum lebenspendenden Kreuz.
Wie kam Pseudo-Methodios nun zu dieser sonderbaren Exegese von Matth 16:18b? Es darf vorausgesetzt werden, dass Pseudo-Methodios' Ueberredungskraft gering wäre, wenn seine "aktualisierende" Deutung dieses Verses nicht irgendwie auf bereits vorhandene Muster zurückgreifen würde.

Die späteren syrischen Exegeten sind einstimmig der Meinung, dass es sich bei dem "Felsen", worauf Christus seine Kirche bauen wird, um das von Petrus in V.16 ausgesprochene Christusbekenntnis handelt[28]. Die auf diesen Glauben und dieses Bekenntnis gegründete Kirche wird nicht überwältigt werden durch die "Pforten der Unterwelt". Diese "Pforten der Unterwelt" werden durch syrisch-nestorianische Exegeten wie *Theodor bar Koni* und *Išo^c^dad von Merw* ausgelegt als "die Bedrängnisse, die zum Tode führen"[29]. Im sogenannten *Anonymen Kommentar* werden die *rādūpē*, "Verfolger", als Urheber dieser "Bedrängnisse" genannt[30], eine Tradition, die wir auch bei dem Monophysiten *Dionysios bar Ṣalibi* begegnen[31]. Andere syrisch-monophysitische Exegeten wie *Georgios von Be^{c}eltan*, *Severus* und *Bar Hebräus* fassen die "Pforten der Unterwelt" als eine Metonymie für "Tod" auf[32]. *Severus*, der gleichwie *Georgios von Be^{c}eltan* der Exegese des *Johannes Chrysostomos* folgt[33], fügt dieser die folgende Bemerkung hinzu (Vat. syr.103,fol.322^{v}-323^{r}):

> *šryr'yt dkd mlk' ṭrwn' qmw w'tktšw wsdrw šnd' dkl znyn. wl' šk 'škḥw lmbṭlw lšrrh dhymnwt' dbmšyḥ'. hy db^{c}dt' mtkrz' wmwdy' dbrh d' lh' 'ytwhy mšyḥ'*, "(Das ist) wirklich (so), denn, als grausame Könige (*malkē ṭrūnē/ṭarūnē*)[34] sich erhoben und sich bemühten, Folter aller Art durchzuführen, konnten sie ganz und gar nicht die Wahrheit des Glaubens in Christus vernichten, die in der Kirche verkündet und bekannt wird, (nämlich) dass Christus der Sohn Gottes ist".

Die Idee, dass die in Matth 16:18b erwähnten"Pforten der Unterwelt" jene heidnischen Mächte symbolisieren, die (umsonst) Glaubensverfolgungen entfesseln werden, um die Kirche Christi zu vernichten, begegnet also bei syrischen Kommentatoren beider Konfessionen und wurde der syrischen Tradition wohl durch die griechische Exegese vermittelt[35]. Die Uebereinstimmung zwischen dieser Exegese und Pseudo-Methodios beschränkt sich jedoch auf den Punkt, dass die "Pforten bzw. Riegel der Unterwelt" mit heidnischen, christenfeindlichen Mächten verbunden werden. Die "heidnischen Tyrannen" sind bei Pseudo-Methodios keine Glaubensverfolger *stricto sensu*, sondern Vollzieher der von Gott erlaubten *mardūtā* der Christen. Pseudo-Methodios' Exegese liegt im übrigen nicht der Gedanke zugrunde, dass zukünftige Christenverfolgungen die auf das wahrhafte Christusbekenntnis gegründete Kirche nie überwältigen können, sondern der Gegensatz: "Riegel der Unterwelt" - "die grosse Kraft des heiligen Kreuzes". Dieser Gegensatz hängt mit einem ganz anderen Ideenkreis zusammen, dessen Anfänge bei den altsyrischen Autoren zu suchen sind. Dieser tritt besonders deutlich hervor in *Jakob von Sarugs mēmrā* "über die Frage unseres Herrn und über die Offenbarung, die Simon vom Vater empfing" (Matth 16:15-19)[36].

Jakob deutet die *mūklē da-šyōl*, "Riegel der Unterwelt" (Diat.Matth 16:18) als "Tod" und "Satan", die Adam in der Unterwelt eingesperrt und den Weg zu Gott abgesperrt haben[37]. Diese *mūklē da-šyōl*, "Tod und Satan", sind die *ṭrūnē da-šyōl*,"die Tyrannen der Unterwelt", die die Kirche, die Braut Christi, hassen und sie in ihrem Gebiet zertreten wollen[38]. Der Bräutigam/Christus hat jedoch seiner Braut/Kirche versprochen, dass "Tod und Satan" sie nicht besiegen werden[39]. Er hat diese "Tyrannen der Unterwelt" in Fesseln gelegt und die Füsse der Braut auf ihren Nacken gesetzt[40]. Jakob verbindet in diesem *mēmrā* die Fesselung der "Tyrannen der Unterwelt" direkt mit dem Kreuz und dem Leiden Christi:

> "Er bändigte den Tod und überwand den Satan
> durch sein Leiden,
> und die Braut jubelte über den Segen des
> Bräutigams und über seine Verheissungen"[41].

Im folgenden *mēmrā* "über Simon Petrus, als unser Herr zu ihm sprach: *Weiche, hinter mich, Satan!*" (Matth 16:23) verbindet Jakob die *mūklē da-šyōl* deutlich mit dem Motiv des *descensus ad inferos* Christi. Hier lässt Jakob Christus sagen, dass er durch seinen *descensus* seinen "Besitz" (d.h. Adam), den die *ṭrūnē da-šyōl*, "Tyrannen der Unterwelt", raubten[42], aus der Unterwelt befreien werde:

> "... und ich werde die Pforten des Todes, die ihn
> (d.h. Adam) einschlossen zerbrechen.
> Und ich werde die hohen Riegel (*mūklē*) der Tochter
> der Finsternis zerschmettern,
> ....
> und ich werde alle Mauern (der Unterwelt) nieder-
> reissen durch das Zeichen meines Kreuzes"[43].

Etwas später lässt Jakob Christus in klarer Anlehnung an Matth 16:18 sagen:

> "Wenn ich sterbe, werden die Riegel der Unterwelt
> (*mūklē da-šyōl*) mich nicht überwältigen (*ḥāsnīn*)[44],
> und nicht kann der Tod mir widerstehen[45],
> wenn ich hinausgehe (d.h. aus der Unterwelt)"[46].

So wie bei Jakob die *mūklē da-šyōl*, d.h. die *ṭrūnē da-šyōl* (Tod und Satan) durch den *descensus ad inferos* Christi (Kreuz/Leiden/Tod) besiegt werden, worauf die Verheissung beruht, dass die "Tyrannen der Unterwelt" nie die Kirche Christi werden besiegen können, so werden Pseudo-Methodios' *mūklē da-šyōl*, d.h. die *ṭrūnē d-ḥanpūtā* (Muslime) nie das christliche Reich besiegen können, solange dieses seine Zuflucht nimmt zu dem unbesiegbaren Kreuz Christi, das die grössten und gefährlichsten Feinde der Menschheit, die *ṭrūnē da-šyōl* (Tod und Satan) besiegt hat. Pseudo-Methodios hat lediglich die "theologischen" Begriffe (Tod und Satan/Kirche) auf "politische" Grössen (Muslime/Byzanz) übertragen. Diese Annahme kann durch ein weiteres dem gleichen Abschnitt des *mēmrā* zu entnehmendes Argument erhärtet werden. Pseudo-Methodios redet im Zusammenhang mit der Exegese von Matth 16:18 über "das lebenspendende Kreuz", das "in der Mitte der Erde" gepflanzt wurde und "Macht hat in Höhe und Tiefe". Es handelt sich hier um Motive, die Pseudo-Methodios der *syrischen Schatzhöhle* entnahm. Dort ist die Vorstellung der "Mitte der Erde" mit der "Pforte der Erde",

Golgotha, dem Grab Adams und dem Kreuz Christi verbunden. Als das Kreuz oberhalb von dem Grab Adams errichtet wurde, öffnete sich die "Pforte der Erde" und das Kreuz stieg hinab und wurde über Adams Mund gesetzt. Als Christus durch den Speer verwundet wurde, da lief von seiner Seite Blut und Wasser und floss hernieder in den Mund Adams, wodurch Adam getauft wurde[47]. Es kann nicht bezweifelt werden, dass Pseudo-Methodios, wenn er im Zusammenhang mit Matth 16:18 von der "Macht" des "lebenspendenden Kreuzes" in der "Mitte der Erde" redet, auf den Sieg des Kreuzes über Tod und Satan auf Golgotha anspielt.

Wenn Pseudo-Methodios die Bezeichnung *ṭrūnē*, "Tyrannen", für die Muslime verwendet, so hat sie nicht nur die übliche metaphorische Funktion (Gewaltherrschaft, Barbarei usw.), sondern auch symbolische Bedeutung (widerchristliche Mächte der Hölle). Das Wort soll suggerieren, dass es sich bei dem bevorstehenden Kampf zwischen Byzanz und den Muslimen nicht um einen "profanen", sondern um einen "heiligen" Krieg handelt; nicht um einen Krieg zwischen Menschen und Menschen, sondern zwischen dem Kreuz und den Feinden des Kreuzes. Jedoch sei der Ausgang dieses Krieges sicher. Denn gleichwie das Kreuz die "Tyrannen" der Unterwelt besiegte, so werde es jetzt auch die muslimischen "Tyrannen" besiegen. Lediglich Byzanz besitzt diese "unbesigbare Waffe, die alles besiegt"[48].
Die enge Verbindung zwischen der *ṭrūnē*-Bezeichnung und der endzeitlichen *mardūtā* steht in direkter Beziehung zu der engen Verbindung, die Pseudo-Methodios zwischen Matth 16:18 und 2 Thess 2:1-10 hergestellt hat. Pseudo-Methodios hat die Idee der endzeitlichen *mardūtā* aus 2 Thess 2:3 entnommen, wo er das Wort *mārūdūtā* bzw. *mardūtā* (Wurzel:*mrd*), "Abfall","Rebellion" (*apostasia*) als *mardūtā* (Wurzel: *rd'*), "Kasteiung", erklärt[49]. Die *mardūtā* geht in 2 Thess 2:3 der Ankunft des Antichrist voraus. Aber auch geht in 2 Thess 2:7 *hw m' dhš' 'ḥyd*, "das, was jetzt aufhält" (*ho katechōn*) der Ankunft des Antichrist voraus. Bei diesem *hw m' dhš' 'ḥyd* handelt es sich um Byzanz, aber wieder im abgeleiteten Sinne, nämlich um das Byzanz, das "seine Zuflucht nimmt" (*'aḥīdā gawsā*)[50] zum Kreuz[51]. Denn das, was "aus der Mitte weggenommen werden muss" (2 Thess 2:7), bevor der Antichrist kommt, ist *de facto* das, was "in der Mitte der Erde aufgerichtet wurde", d.h. das Kreuz[52]. Der Gegensatz zwischen der endzeitlichen *mardūtā* und *hw m' dhš' 'ḥyd* in 2 Thess 2:3.7 setzt Pseudo-Methodios in Parallele zu dem Gegensatz zwischen *mūklē da-šyōl* und "Kirche" in Matth 16:18. Bei der *mardūtā* handelt es gleichwie bei den *mūklē da-šyōl* um die arabisch-islamische Herrschaft. Bei dem *hw m' dhš' 'ḥyd* handelt es sich gleichwie bei der "Kirche" um Byzanz. In beiden Fällen wird die Unbesiegbarkeit von Byzanz bzw. der bevor-

stehende Sieg von Byzanz über die Muslime, wodurch das Ende der *mardūtā* und der Anfang der bis zur Erscheinung des Antichrist dauernden Epoche byzantinischer Herrschaft über die ganze Welt herbeigeführt werden, auf das Kreuz zurückgeführt: das Kreuz Christi, das über die Unterwelt triumphierte.

1) Cf. S.P. Brock, "Syriac Sources for Seventh-Century History" in *Byzantine and Modern Greek Studies* vol. 2, 1976, p. 34; *id.*, "Syriac Views of Emergent Islam" (= "Views") in *Studies in the First Century of Islamic Society*, ed. G. Juynboll, S. Illinois Univ. Press 1982, pp. 17-19; G.J. Reinink, "Ismael, der Wildesel in der Wüste. Zur Typologie der Apokalypse des Pseudo-Methodios" (= "Ismael") in *ByZ* vol. 75, 1982, p. 339, n. 19; *id.*, "Die syrischen Wurzeln der mittelalterlichen Legende vom römischen Endkaiser" (= "Wurzeln") in *Non nova, sed nove. Mélanges de civilisation médiévale dédiés à Willem Noomen*, (*Mediaevalia Groningana*, vol. 5), ed. M. Gosman-J. van Os, Groningen 1984, p. 206, n. 9. Der syrische Text des MS *Vat. syr. 58* ist seit kurzem zugänglich in der Dissertation von H. Suermann, *Die geschichtstheologische Reaktion auf die einfallenden Muslime in der edessenischen Apokalyptik des 7. Jahrhunderts* (*Europäische Hochschulschriften*: XXIII (*Theologie*), vol. 256) (= *Reaktion*), Frankfurt am Main-Bern-New York 1985, pp. 34-85 (mit deutscher Uebersetzung). Weitere syr. MSS befinden sich in Mardin in der Osttürkei, cf. A. Vööbus, "Discovery of an Unknown Syrian Author, Methodios of Peṭrā" in *AbN*, vol. 17, 1976-1977, pp. 1-4.
Eine kritische und synoptische Ausgabe des syrischen Textes, der für die Verbreitung des Pseudo-Methodios nach Westen am meisten relevanten griechischen Version und der ältesten, merovingischen lateinischen Textzeugen wird inzwischen durch eine Löwener-Groninger-Arbeitsgruppe vorbereitet. Ich zitiere im folgenden den syrischen Text des MS *Vat. syr. 58*.
2) *Vat. syr. 58*, fol. 133^r, 13-134^v, 1.
3) Vgl. W.E. Kaegi, "Initial Byzantine Reactions to the Arab Conquest" in *Church History* vol. 38, 1969, p. 145.
4) Wenige Jahre bevor Pseudo-Methodios seine Prophezeiung aufschrieb, vollendete Joḥannan bar Penkaye - nicht weit von dem Entstehungsort unseres *mēmrā* entfernt - seinen *ktābā d-rēs mellē*. Das letzte 15. Buch (cf. A. Mingana, *Sources syriaques*, vol. 1, Leipzig 1907, pp. 143 -171 (t.), pp. 172 -197 (v.)), bildet eine der wichtigsten Quellen für das Verständnis der geschichtlichen Hintergründe des *mēmrā*. Auch Johannan erwartet den bevorstehenden Zusammenbruch arabisch-islamischer Herrschaft, der das Ende der Zeiten einleitet; cf. dazu weiter G.J. Reinink, "Pseudo-Methodius und die Legende vom römischen Endkaiser" (= "Pseudo-Methodios und die Legende") in *Proceedings, XIIIde Internationaal Colloquium, Eschatologie in de Middeleeuwen, Leuven, 14-16 mei 1984*, Leuven 1986 (im Druck).
5) *Vat. syr. 58*, fol. 131^v, 3-8.
6) *Vat. syr. 58*, fol. 132^v, 6-10.
7) Cf. Reinink, "Ismael", p. 341.
8) Cf. Kaegi, *op. cit.*, p. 144; Reinink, "Wurzeln", p. 198.
9) *Vat. syr. 58*, fol. 128^r, 16-128^v, 3.
10) *Vat. syr. 58*, fol. 133^r, 1-134^r, 6.
11) Cf. dazu G. Podskalsky, *Byzantinische Reichseschatologie* (*Münchener Universitäts-Schriften*, vol. 9) (= "*Reichseschatologie*"), München 1972, p. 55; Suermann, *Reaktion*, pp. 197-200. In der Entwicklung dieser Idee zeigt Pseudo-Methodios sich vor allem von der *syrischen Alexanderlegende* abhängig; siehe Reinink, "Wurzeln", pp. 204-205, und cf. zur pro-byzantinischen Propaganda der *Alexanderlegende* G.J. Reinink, "Die Entstehung der syrischen Alexanderlegende als politisch-religiöse Propagandaschrift für Herakleios' Kirchenpolitik, (= "Alexanderlegende") in *After Chalcedon, Studies in Theology and Church History offered to Professor Albert van Roey for his seventieth birthday* (*Orientalia Lovaniensia Analecta*, vol. 18), ed. C. Laga-J.A. Munitiz-L. van Rompay, Leuven 1985, pp. 263-281.

12) Cf. W.H.C. Frend, *The Rise of the Monophysite Movement*, Cambridge-London-New York-Melbourne 1979, p. 317; Reinink, "Alexanderlegende", pp. 263-264.

13) *Vat. syr. 58*, fol. 122^r, 9; im Zusammenhang mit der "arabischen" (*ṭyyt'*) Mutter der 4 in Richt 7:25, 8:3,5-21 genannten midianitischen Fürsten bzw. Könige. Pseudo-Methodios stellt die Gideongeschichten Richt 6-8 in typologischer Beziehung zu den arabisch-islamischen Eroberungen (cf. Reinink, "Ismael", pp. 339-342).

14) Cf. Brock, "Views", p. 15.

15) *Vat. Syr. 58*, fol. 121^v, 5-6.

16) Cf. Reinink, "Ismael", pp. 342-344.

17) *Vat. syr. 58*, fol. 131^r, 16-132^r, 2, fol. 132^v, 4-7; cf. zur Beziehung zwischen dem islamischen *ḥanīf* und dem syrischen Wort *ḥanpā*: *EI*^{2}, vol. 3, pp. 165-166; P. Crone-M. Cook, *Hagarism. The Making of the Islamic World*, Cambridge-London etc. 1977, pp. 13-14.

18) *Vat. syr. 58*, fol. 122^r, 9, fol. 126^r, 17, fol. 130^v, 10-11, fol. 131^r, 11-12, fol. 133^r, 6-7.

19) Cf. u.a. H. Berve, *Die Tyrannis bei den Griechen*, vol. 1, München 1967, pp. 476-498.

20) *Vat. syr. 58*, fol. 129^r, 2, fol. 130^r, 12-15, fol. 131^r, 11-13, fol. 131^r, 16-131^v, 11, fol. 132^r, 7, fol. 133^r, 2-7.

21) *lege*: *d'tqb*^{c}.

22) *haylāh* (fem.) *lege*: *haylēh* (masc.).

23) *lege*: *mškḥyn*.

24) *lege*: *dnḥsnwn*.

25) Cf. zu dieser Genealogie Reinink, "Wurzeln", p. 201, n. 14, p. 205; und besonders *id.*, "Pseudo-Methodius und die Legende".

26) Cf. R. Murray, "The Rock and the House on the Rock", in *OrChrP*, vol. 30, 1964, p. 341; S. Brock, "Some Aspects of Greek Words in Syriac" (= "Aspects") in *Synkretismus im syrisch-persischen Kulturgebiet*, ed. A. Dietrich, Göttingen 1975, p. 95.

27) R. Köbert, "Zwei Fassungen von Mt. 16,18 bei den Syrern" in *Bibl.* vol. 40, 1959, pp. 1018-1020, hat darauf hingewiesen, dass das Verbum *ḥsn* auch "widerstehen" bedeuten kann und hält diese Bedeutung von *ḥsn* für die richtige in Matth 16:18 nach dem Gedanken dass die "Pforten" bzw. "Riegel" vielmehr eine passive als eine aktive Rolle spielen und vielleicht der Gedanke, dass Christus bei seiner Hadesfahrt als Sieger in die Unterwelt vordrang, im Hintergrund steht. Brock, "Aspects", pp. 96-97, hält es für wahrscheinlich, dass Tatian in seinem Diatessaron die "Pforten der Unterwelt" durch die "Riegel der Unterwelt" ersetzte, weil er auf Ps 107:16, den er im Sinne des *descensus ad inferos* Christi auslegte, anspielen wollte. Brock meint, dass auch eine andere Uebersetzung des Verbums *ḥsn* in Matth 16:18 möglich sei: nicht "to be unable to withstand", "to be powerless against", sondern "to hold in", nach dem Gedanken, dass "Christ is breaking out of Sheol, not into it, as we find in the western harrowing of hell traditions ...." Ich übersetze jedoch das Verbum *ḥsn* stets mit "überwältigen", einerseits weil Pseudo-Methodios diese Bedeutung vorauszusetzen scheint (vgl. besonders *Vat. syr. 58*, fol. 122^v, 9-14, wo gesagt wird, dass das byzantinische Reich alle Königreiche der Welt "überwältigt hat" (*ḥsnt*) und nicht von einem der Königreiche "überwaltigt wird" (*mtḥsn'*), andererseits weil ich der Meinung bin, dass eine Uebersetzung mit "überwältigen" sehr gut möglich ist bei den syrischen Autoren, die die "Riegel der Unterwelt" bildlich auffassen als z.B. "Tod und Satan", so dass den *mūklē da-šyōl* in dieser Erklärung sowohl eine aktive wie auch eine passive Rolle beigemessen werden kann.

28) Sie stimmen in dieser Hinsicht insbesondere mit der antiochenischen Exegese überein; cf. dazu J. Ludwig, *Die Primatworte Mt 16,18,19 in der altkirchlichen Exegese* (*Neutestamentliche Abhandlungen*, vol. 19, fasc. 4), Münster 1952, pp. 53-57, 97-104.

29) Theodorus bar Koni, *Liber scholiorum* II (*Corpus scriptorum Christianorum Orientalium*) (=*CSCO*, vol. 69), ed. A. Scher, Louvain

1960, p. 113, ll. 11-12; *The Commentaries of Isho^{c}dad of Merv*, II, (*Horae Semiticae*, vol. 6), ed. M.D. Gibson, Cambridge 1911, p. 112, ll. 13-14.

30) MS *Diy. 22*, pp. 506,31-507,2; zu diesem Kommentar siehe G.J. Reinink, *Studien zur Quellen- und Traditionsgeschichte des Evangelienkommentars der Gannat Bussame* (*CSCO*, vol. 414) Louvain 1979, pp. 165-166.

31) Dionysii bar Salibi, *Commentarii in evangelia* I,2, (*CSCO*, vol.77), ed. I. Sedlaček-I.-B. Chabot, Louvain 1915, p. 382, ll. 2-3.

32) Georgios von Be^{c}eltan, *Matthäuskommentar*, im MS *Vat. syr. 154*, fol. 155^{v}; Severus, *Katene*, im MS *Vat. syr. 103*, fol. 322^{v},34-323^{r} 323^{r},4; *Gregory Abu'l Faraj commonly called Bar-Hebraeus Commentary on the Gospels from the Horreum Mysteriorum*, ed. W.E.W. Carr, London 1925, p. 50.

33) *Patrologia graeca*, vol. 57, col. 534.

34) Das Adj. *trūnā* , *tarūnā*, "hart", "grausam", hängt mit dem Subst. *ṭarānā*, "Felsen", "Stein", zusammen, wurde aber auch mit dem griech. Lehnwort *ṭrūnā*, *tyrannos*, verbunden.

35) Cf. z.B. Cyrill in *Matthäus-Kommentare aus der griechischen Kirche* (*TU*, vol. 16) ed. J. Reuss, Berlin 1957, p. 215 Fragm. 191, und Theodor von Mopsuestia in *Les homélies catéchétiques de Théodore de Mopsueste* (*Studi e Testi*, vol. 145) ed. R. Tonneau, Città del Vaticano 1949, pp. 270-271, *Hom.* X, 16.

36) *Homiliae selectae Mar-Jacobi Sarugensis*, I ed. P. Bedjan, Parisiis 1905, pp. 460-482.

37) *ibid.*, p. 476, ll. 13-20.

38) *ibid.*, p. 478, ll. 12-14.

39) *ibid.*, p. 477, l. 7, p. 478, l. 13.

40) *ibid.*, p. 478, l. 15.

41) *ibid.*, p. 479, ll. 10-11.

42) *ibid.*, p. 498, l. 13. Cf. zum Thema des *descensus* bei den älteren syrischen Autoren D. Plooij, "Der Descensus ad inferos in Aphrahat und den Oden Salomos", in *ZNW* vol. 14, 1913, pp. 222-231; J. Teixidor, "Le thème de la descente aux enfers chez Saint Ephrem" in *OS* vol. 6, 1961, pp. 25-40; R. Murray, *Symbols of Church and Kingdom*, Cambridge 1975, pp. 324-329. Vgl. zu dem Namen "Tyrann" für Tod und/oder Satan u.a. J. Kroll, *Gott und Hölle* (*Studien der Bibliothek Warburg*, vol. 20), Leipzig-Berlin 1932, p. 103; Theodor von Mopsuestia, *Hom.* V,18 (ed. Tonneau, pp. 124-127), *Hom.* XII,8 (ed. Tonneau, pp. 334-335), *Hom.* XII, 19-20 (ed. Tonneau, pp. 352-355) u.a.; Narsai, *Hom.* IV,23, 147 in *Narsai's Metrical Homilies* (*Patrologia orientalis*, vol. 40, fasc. 1, no. 182), ed. G. McLeod, Turnhout 1979, pp. 138-139, 146-147; Romanos, *Hymn.* XXXVIII, 17 in *Romanos le Melode, Hymnes* IV, (*Sources chrétiennes*, vol. 128), ed. J. Grosdidier de Matons, Paris 1967, p. 308.

43) Jakob von Sarug, *op. cit.*, ed. Bedjan, pp. 498, l. 20-499, l. 4. Jakob spielt hier auf Ps 107:16 an, mit dem in frühchristlicher Tradition des *descensus*-Motiv verknüpft ist (cf. Brock, "Aspects", pp. 95-97).

44) Siehe oben Anm. 27.

45) *nḥwr b'py* eigentlich: :in meinen Antlitz schauen".

46) Jakob von Sarug, *op. cit.*, ed. Bedjan, p. 502, ll. 16-17. Auch in der pseudoephraemischen Hymne "über Simon Petrus" liegt eine klare Verbindung zwischen Matth 16:18 und dem Kreuz, das durch seine unbesiegbare Macht die *šyōl* vernichtet, vor in *Sancti Ephraem Syri Hymni et Sermones*, IV, ed. Th.J. Lamy, Mechliniae 1902, p. 688.

47) *Die Schatzhöhle*, ed. C. Bezold, Amsterdam 1981, pp. 22, 254-256, 260; cf. dazu auch J. Jeremias, "Golgotha und der heilige Felsen", in *Angelos*, vol. 2, 1926, p. 81. Zum Einfluss der *Schatzhöhle* auf Pseudo-Methodios vgl. Reinink, "Wurzeln", p. 201; *id.*, "Der Verfassername 'Modios' der syrischen Schatzhöhle und die Apokalypse des Pseudo-Methodios" in *OrChr* vol. 67, 1983, pp. 46-64.

48) *Vat. syr. 58*, fol. 122^{v}, 13-14.

49) Cf. dazu bereits M. Kmosko, "Das Rätsel des Pseudomethodius" in *Byzantion*, vol. 6, 1931, p. 276.

50) Siehe oben. Pseudo-Methodios spielt mit den verschiedenen Anwendungsmöglichkeiten des Wortes *'ḥyd*. Das *'ḥyd* (2 Thess 2:7) wird zu *'ḥyd' gwsʾ* (das byzantinische Reich, das seine *Zuflucht nimmt* zum heiligen Kreuz) und zu *'ḥyd ḥylh* (das Kreuz, das *Macht hat* und unbesiegbar ist). Es drängt sich die Frage auf, ob Pseudo-Methodios hier auch vom *Diatessaronkommentar* des Ephraem Syrus beeinflusst wurde (*Diat.* XIV,2 zu Matth 16:15-18), wo Ephraem "den Turm, der in die Höhe führt") (d.h. die Kirche; aber auch die Verbindung mit dem Kreuz lag auf der Hand) mit dem "irdischen Turm" von Babel (Gen 11:1-9), dem vergänglichen *byt gwsʾ*, "Zufluchtsort", vergleicht. *Saint Ephrem, Commentaire de l'évangile concordant* (*Chester Beatty Monographs*, vol. 8), ed. L. Leloir, Dublin 1963, pp. 114-115.

51) Pseudo-Methodios setzt die traditionelle Exegese von 2 Thess 2:7 voraus, die dem römischen bzw. byzantinischen Reich die Herrschft bis zum Augenblick des Weltendes sichert; cf. dazu Podskalsky, "Reichseschatologie", p. 55, n. 332. Er führt sie jedoch weiter, indem er *hw m' dḥšʾ 'ḥyd* zu *hw m' dḥšʾ 'ḥyd gwsʾ* macht, wodurch die Unbesiegbarkeit von Byzanz wieder auf die Unbesiegbarkeit des Kreuzes zurückgeführt wird.

52) *Vat. syr. 58*, fol. 126^{v}, 5-11. Das Kreuz wird aus "der Mitte" weggenommen bei der Ankunft des Antichrist, wenn sich in der Abdikationsszene auf Golgatha die kaiserliche Krone zusammen mit dem Kreuz den Himmel erheben wird (*Vat. syr. 58*, fol. 135^{r}, 12-135^{v}, 3).

Aus dem Sozialleben der Jeziden (Teufelsanbeter) im nördlichen ᶜIrāq

W.H.Ph. Römer, Nijmegen

Die Religionsgemeinschaft der Jeziden ist in breiten Kreisen des Abendlandes erst im vergangenen Jahrhundert durch Karl May's vielgelesene Reiseromane *Durch die Wüste* und *Durchs wilde Kurdistan* näher bekannt geworden, nachdem der englische Ausgräber Sir A.H. Layard in seinem Bericht über eine Reise in Kurdistan viele Besonderheiten über u.a. die Jeziden mitgeteilt hatte[1].

Jeziden wohnen zum grössten Teile in N.-ᶜIrāq, westlich und nordlich von Môṣul im Bereich des Singǎr-Gebirges, in geringerem Ausmass etwa noch in der S.O.-Türkei (Gegend um Diyarbakır), in der īrānischen Provinz Aḏarbāīǧān, sowie in Armenien.Ihr Nahme "Teufelsanbeter" die ihnen die sie umgebenden Nichtjeziden beilegen, erklärt sich daraus, dass die Jeziden selber in ihrem Katechismus lehren, das Wort *Šaiṭán* dürfe deswegen nicht ausgesprochen werden, weil es der Name ihres Gottes sei[2]. Selbst nennen sich die Jeziden Dawāsin (Pl. von Dāsin). Für diesen Šaiṭān haben die Jeziden die Bezeichnung Melek Tā'ūs "Engel Pfauhahn". Er soll sich einmal gegen den Hochgott (A)jezd empört haben, dann aber nach verbüsster Höllenstrafe von diesem begnadigt worden und später zum tätigen Organ des göttlichen Willens geworden sein. So gilt der Melek Tā'ūs bei den Jeziden, ebensowie der nur noch als eine Art *deus otiosus* betrachtete Hochgott, als ein guter Gott, nicht als das Prinzip des Bösen[3]. Der Melek Tā'ūs wird in Bronze oder Eisen als Pfauhahnenfigur nachgebildet und als *sanǧaq* (Standarte) in Prozessionen in den verschiedenen Ortschaften herumgeführt. Neben diesem Hauptgötterpaar kennen die Jeziden noch weitere fünf aktive, halbgöttliche Engelwesen, die ebensowie der Melek Tā'ūs jedes sein *sanǧaq* haben. Der Hauptheilige der Jeziden ist Šêḫ ᶜAdī[4], der, ursprünglich ein berühmter islamischen Mystiker aus dem 12. Jahrhundert namens ᶜAdī ibn Musāfir, gegen Ende seines Lebens sich zu den Jeziden gestellt hat und in seiner Einsiedelei nördlich von Môṣul gestorben ist. Er scheint als Reformator unter den Jeziden gewirkt zu haben und noch heute ist für die Mitglieder dieser Glaubensgemeinschaft die alljährliche Wallfahrt zu seinem Mausoleum in der Nähe von Bāᶜaḏrī (± 65 km. nördlich von Môṣul) strenge religiöse

Pflicht[5]. Ueber die sicher als überaus synkretistisch zu betrachtenden Glaubensvorstellungen der Jeziden verfügen wir noch immer über nicht mehr als globale Kenntnisse, sind doch die Bekenner dieser Religion Andersgläubigen gegenüber i.b.a. den Inhalt ihres Glaubens wenig mitteilsam. Auch sind aus der religiösen Literatur der Jeziden bislang nur zwei Bücher, nl. das "Buch der Offenbarung" (12. Jhdt.; Autor: Šêḫ ᶜAdī?) und die "Schwarze Schrift" (14. Jhdt.), beide in arabischer Sprache, zu unserer Kenntnis gelangt. Das relativ wenige, was wir über die Jeziden und ihre religiösen und sozialen Vorstellungen und Gewohnheiten wissen, verdanken wir im allgemeinen abendländischen Gelehrten und Reisenden[6]. Da dürfte es vielleicht von einigem Interesse sein, hier auch einmal einen Orientalen zu Worte kommen zu lassen, der offenbar selber zur Religionsgemeinschaft der Jeziden gehört. Wir übersetzen dazu den Aufsatz *As-sunanu l-iǧtimāᶜījatu ᶜinda l-Jazīdījati* ("Die sozialen Gewohnheiten bei den Jeziden") von Mumtāz Ḥuṣên Ḫallu in der im Westen sicher wenig bekannten ᶜirāqischen folkloristischen Zeitschrift *'At-turāṯ aš-šaᶜbī* (*Monthly Magazine Issued by the Folklore Centre, Ministry of Information*) 4/IV[7], Baghdād 1973, S. 167-170 aus dem Arabischen. Die Muttersprache des Autors wird, ebensowie die der meisten Jeziden, wohl das Kurdische sein.

Die Eheschliessung.

Die Eheschliessung bei den Jeziden wird von zwei Gesichtspunkten her untersucht: Vom Gesichtspunkt der praktischen Gewohnheiten und vom Gesichtspunkt der gesetzlichen Regeln her.

Vom Gesichtspunkt der praktischen Gewohnheiten her.

Es kommt in den meisten Fällen eine vollständige Uebereinstimmung zwischen den beiden Personen zustande, die die Heirat wünschen. Dies geht aber nicht über eine persönliche Uebereinstimmung hinaus. Nach dieser Uebereinstimmung geht der Vater daran, um die Hand der jungen Frau anzuhalten, die sein Sohn heiraten will. Nachdem dann der Vater und die Mutter der jungen Frau (mit ihm) zu Uebereinstimmung gelangt sind, geht der Vater des jungen Mannes mit den Einflussreichsten der Männer des Dorfes zum Hause der jungen Frau und hinter ihm gehen gleich seine Verwandten und Freunde; es begleiten sie Trommel und Flöte. Man führt im Hause der jungen Frau *dabka*- und (andere) Tänze aus. Dann kehren sie zum Hause des jungen Mannes zurück und man führt ebenfalls *dabka*- und (andere) Tänze aus. Aber wenn der Vater oder die Mutter der jungen Frau sich weigert und mit der Verlobung nicht einverstanden ist, so ist der junge Mann dazu gezwungen, die junge Frau zu entführen und sie (dann) zu heiraten und diese Ehe ist legitim. Dann bezahlt er nachher die Brautgabe. Die Brautgabe ist festgesetzt bei den Jeziden. So ist es in der Gegend vom Sinǧār nicht erlaubt, dass sie (die Summe von) 150 Dināren übersteigt, zusammen mit einigen Geschenken, die der jungen Frau übereignet werden. Ebenso ist der Fall im Distrikt von eš-Šêḫān, aber in Ba^c^ašīqa und Beḥzānī ist sie ebenfalls festgesetzt, übersteigt aber auf keinen Fall (die Summe von) 110 Dināren. Es ist dem jungen Manne als Bedingung auferlegt, der jungen Frau auch ein Geschenk zu übereignen und dies ist gewöhnlich aus Gold. Nachdem er die Brautgabe bezahlt hat, steht es dem jungen Manne rechtlich zu, seine Braut zu heiraten und ist er dafür fertig. Es werden die Feierlichketien veranstaltet, gewöhnlich entweder mit (gewöhnlichen) oder mit *dabka*-Tänzen mit Trommel und Flöte. Veranstaltet werden diese Feierlichkeiten manchmal zwei oder drei Tage vor der Eheschliessung. Am Tage der Eheschliessung gehen die Teilnehmer an der Feier zum Hause der jungen Frau unter Begleitung von Trommel und Flöte und Tanz und kehren von dort zum Hause des jungen Mannes (des Bräutigams) zurück, indem die Braut bei ihnen ist. Die Feier dauert mehrere Tage und es werden währenddessen ^c^Araq und andere Getränke gereicht.

Vom Gesichtspunkt der gesetzlichen Regeln her.

Es steht dem Jeziden rechtlich zu, falls es ihm beliebt, von den Frauen zwei gleichzeitig zu heiraten und drei gleichzeitig und vier gleichzeitig, aber trotzdem heiratet er selten mehr als eine. Verboten ist die Ehe mit der Ehefrau seines Bruders oder der Ehefrau seines Onkels väterlicherseits, oder der Ehefrau des Sohnes seines Onkels väterlicherseits nach deren Tode. Ebenso ist die Ehe mit der Schwester seiner Ehefrau nach der Scheidung von ihr oder (nach) ihrem Tode verboten.

Die Heirat findet meistens vom fünfzehnten Lebensjahr an und darüber statt. Vorher ist die junge Frau nämlich minderjährig und die junge Frau heiratet selten vor diesem Alter. Die junge Frau beerbt nach ihrer Heirat ihren Vater nicht. Es steht der jungen Frau rechtlich zu, ledig und zeitlebens im Dienste ihres Vaters zu bleiben. Wenn ihr Ehemann stirbt, kehrt sie, falls sie ihm keine Kinder geboren hat, nach einiger Zeit zum Hause ihres Vaters zurück. Manchmal bleibt sie bei ihren Kindern leben und bisweilen verlässt sie ihre Kinder nach dem Tode ihres Ehemannes und geht zum Hause ihres Vaters. Es steht ihr die Heirat noch einmal rechtlich zu. Sie beerbt dann ihren verstorbenen Ehemann nicht. Die Jeziden haben bei der Heirat Klassen, durch die sie sich voneinander unterscheiden. So ist es den Söhnen der Šêḫe unter ihnen nicht erlaubt, andere als die Töchter der Šêḫe zu heiraten, so wie es auch so ist, dass es dem gewöhnlichen Volke nicht gestattet ist, um die Hand der Töchter der Šêḫe anzuhalten oder (um die Hand) eine(r) jungen Frau aus der Klasse der Pīre[8]. Was die Ehescheidung anbelangt, so wird darüber selten bei den Jeziden berichtet. Es steht dem Jeziden rechtlich zu, sich von seiner Ehefrau zu scheiden, wenn er erfährt, dass sie sich auf andere als ehrbare Handlungen einlässt, oder wegen anderer Handlungen, die zwischen ihnen beiden passieren.

Die Beschneidung.

Zu den bei den Jeziden praktizierten Gewohnheiten (gehört) die Beschneidung. Sie beschneiden nämlich ihre jungen Kinder wie die Muslime. Die Beschneidung findet meistens zwischen dem dritten und dem zehnten Lebensjahr des Jungen statt. Es kauft ein Verwandter des Kindes die Luxusgewänder, die Schuhe und andere Arten von Geschenken als diese und verteilt sie an seine Bekannten und seine Freunde, damit sie als Zeugen der Durchführung der Beschneidung auftreten. Manchmal geht mit der Eheschliessung von einer der Personen der Familie die Beschneidung der Jungen dieser Familie zusammen. Die Beschneidung findet (dann) nicht am Tage der Eheschliessung, sondern vielmehr nach der Eheschliessung um fünf oder sieben Tage (später) statt. Es werden die Feierlichkeiten und die *dabka*-Tänze auch bei beiden Gelegenheiten veranstaltet und es werden den Gästen ᶜAraq und andere Getränke gereicht und (zwar) besonders nach Beendung der Beschneidung. Ein Teil der Jeziden beschneidet ihre Söhne in einem der Krankenhäuser ohne Feierlichkeiten oder was es sonst an Bräuchen gibt. Während der Beschneidung wird bisweilen für den Jungen ein Karīf[9] genommen und dies gehört zu den edelsten Bräuchen der Jeziden. Der Jezide nimmt aus seinen Bekannten oder Freunden einen Karīf. Dadurch, dass er sein junges Kind auf seinen Schoss (d.h. den Schoss des Karīf) legt, während seiner Beschneidung, wird es mit ihm verbrüdert und es tritt der Karīf oder der Vater des jungen Mannes in dessen Leben für den anderen ein und er ist seine rechte Hand in Zeiten von Unglück und Traurigkeit. Meistens ist der Karīf ein (Muslime), d.h. einer aus den Muslimen[10] und manchmal ist er ein Jezide und wenn das Karīfen-Verhältnis zwischen Jeziden existiert, geht manchmal der eine in ein Tabu-Verhältnis zum anderen ein: Es ist dem einen der beiden (dann) nicht erlaubt, (eine) aus der Familie des anderen zu heiraten und sie sind beide wie zwei Brüder.

Die verbotenen Dinge bei den Jeziden.

Für die Jeziden gibt es verbotene Dinge wie für den Rest der Religionen. So ist das Essen von Salat[11] und Kohl[12] verboten, weil diese Gemüse die Fruchtbarkeit fördern bei Jungfräulichkeit der Menschen. Einem Jeziden ist es auch verboten, das Gesicht einer anderen als einer jezidischen Frau anzuschauen. Weiter ein Flirt mit der Frau, die das Gesetz für ihn verboten erklärt hat aus seinem Geschlecht. Auch ist für den Jeziden der Besuch von Geselligkeits- und Vergnügungsstätten verboten. Was aber dasjenige anbelangt, was ein Teil der Forscher über die Glaubenssätze der Jeziden und über ihre Gewohnheiten i.b.a. verbotene Dinge sagt, steht im Gegensatz zur Wirklichkeit. Sie leisten i.b. hierauf ihr möglichstes und unter ihnen (ist) Herr ᶜAbd er-Razzāq el-Ḥasanī. In seinem Buche *Die Jeziden in ihrer heutigen Zeit und in ihrer Vergangenheit* spricht er unter der Aufschrift *Die verbotenen Dinge* auf Seite 108 darüber, dass es dem Jeziden verboten sei, von seiner Stadt länger als ein Jahr fernzubleiben. Wenn er dazu gezwungen ist, sei seine Ehefrau (nachher) für ihn verboten. Trotzdem ist dies in Wirklichkeit anders als die Realität: Es bleiben nl. viele von den Jeziden ihrer Stadt jahrelang fern; dann kehren sie zurück, ohne dass ihre Ehefrau für sie verboten ist. Er sagt auch, dass es dem Jeziden nicht erlaubt ist, die Moscheen der Muslime und ihre religiösen Schulen zu betreten und einem Muslimen, wenn er sein Gebet verrichtet, zuzuschauen, weder in diesen Moscheen noch an anderen Orten der Verehrung als sie. Dieser Gedanke ist auch falsch. Ich habe nl. selber Hunderte von Malen die Moscheen betreten und sehe täglich, wie meine Brüder oder Freunde in meiner Gegenwart ihr Gebet verrichten, wie ja wir mit uns befreundeten Muslimen erlauben, ihr Gebet in unseren Privathäusern zu verrichten. Danach sagt er, dass es dem Jeziden nicht erlaubt sei, bei einem anderen als einem Jeziden rasiert zu werden und seinen Besitz einem anderen als einem Jeziden zu verkaufen, usw. Alle diesen Sachen kann man absolut nicht glauben und es sind (alles) andere als reelle Gedanken.

Es ist dem Jeziden auch das Schweinefleisch verboten; was den Rest der Fleisch(sort)en wie das Fleisch von Fisch und Geflügel und das Fleisch der Gazelle anbelangt, so sind diese für erlaubt erklärt, wie es in der Leitnummer, 10. Lieferung, der Zeitschrift *'At-turāṯ aš-šaᶜbī* vom Jahre 1972 erwähnt wird und wie ᶜAbd er-Razzāq auch in seinem obengenannten Buche auf der 108. Seite sagt.

Der Tod und die Bestattungsriten.

Die Jeziden legen besonderen Wert auf die Feiern der Bestattungsriten. Die Zeremonien der Bestattungsriten fangen beim Tode an. Wenn nl. ein Jezide stirbt, bereitet ihn sein Šêḫ vor. Es löst der Šêḫ dann ein wenig Staub vom Mausoleum des Šêḫ ᶜAdī in ein wenig Wasser auf. Er beginnt damit, Tröpfe von diesem Wasser auf den Mund des Sterbenden zu giessen und er spritzt andere Tröpfe auf sein Gesicht in der Weise wie es die Muslime machen während des Sterbens ihrer Toten. Wenn dann der Sterbende gestorben ist, giesst der Sêh das Wasser auf seinen Körper aus und nimmt bei ihm die religiöse Waschung vor. Dann streut er etwas vom besagten Staube auf seine voerderen Körperteile aus, so wie die Muslime Kampfer auf die vorderen (Körper)teile ihrer Toten ausstreuen. Dann bindet er seinen Kopf in ein weisses Taschentuch ein, dann bedeckt er ihn mit einem weissen Tuche. Es wird das Leichentuch über ihm zugenäht und bei seinem Nacken befestigt. Danach wird er auf zwei Hölzer gehoben, die ins Wasser des Zamzam[13)] getaucht sind und man führt ihn zu seiner letzten Ruhestätte. Voran gehen ihm zwei Qawwāle[14)]. Der eine von ihnen beiden schlägt auf sein Tamburin unter Trauertönen und der andere begleitet ihn auf seiner Rohrflöte[15)] (ein Instrument besonderer Art zum religiösen Musizieren; sie ist das, was gewöhnlich als die Nāj bezeichnet wird) mit ihren eigenen Tönen. Die Begleiter von den Männern (gehen) hinter ihm und hinter ihnen die Frauen. Nach der Ankunft auf dem Friedhof wird der Tote in sein Grab hinuntergelassen. Die Begleiter gehen weg zum Hause des Toten um seiner Familie und seinen Verwandten das Beileid zu bekunden. Es ist nicht erlaubt, den Toten von seinem Hause zu seiner letzten Ruhestätte zu tragen nach Sonnenuntergang und vor ihrem Aufgang. Die Gräber der Toten liegen in der Nähe der heiligen Pilgerorte und die äussere Form dieser Gräber unterscheidet sich nicht von jener bei den Muslimen. Die Zeremonien der Bestattungsriten werden nicht bei der Beerdigung des Toten beendet. Vielmehr ist es (so), dass die Trauer sieben Tage nacheinander dauert. Die Frauen gehen zweimal am Tage zum Grabe des Verstorbenen; es gehen ihnen das Tamburin und die Rohrflöte voran.

Die religiösen Feste.

Das Fest von Jezīd[16)].

Das ist das Fest, das unmittelbar nach dem Fasten gefeiert wird und es wird auch "Fest des Fastens" genannt, der Tatsache wegen, dass die Jeziden drei Tagen fasten. Diese Tage fallen auf den Dienstag, den Mittwoch und den Donnerstag, die dem ersten

Freitag des östlichen Monates I. Kānūn vorangehen, am Kürzesten der Tage des Jahres. Der vierte Tag (der Freitag) ist ein öffentliches Fest und es werden die Festmahlzeiten und die Feiern an diesem Tage veranstaltet. Man tauscht die besten Glück- und Segenswünsche aus und trinkt auch Wein in Fülle.

Das Fest der Gemeinschaft.

Dieses Fest beginnt am dreiundzwanzigsten Tage vom östlichen Monat Êlūl (am 6. des westlichen I. Tašrīn) und endet auf dessen dreissigstem (am 13. des westlichen I. Tašrīn). Die Jezīden gehen aus verschiedenen Gegendem zum Mausoleum des Šêḫ ᶜAdī und finden religiöse Zeremonien (die Beschreibung davon würde hier zu lange dauern) während dieser Tage statt. Dann gehen die Rückkehrer (in) zwei (Strömen) auseinander nach den Ortschaften die sie beide bewohnen.

Das Opferfest (das Pilgerfest).

Es fällt auf den ersten Tag vom Anfang des Opferfestes bei den Muslimen[17]. Es gehen die Männer der Religion zum Mausoleum des Šêḫ ᶜAdī und dort finden die praktizierten religiösen Zeremonien statt. Danach gehen sie weg nach Ihren Häusern.

Das Neujahrsfest.

Es fängt des jezidische Jahr am ersten des östlichen Monates Nīsān (am 14. des westlichen Nīsān) an und das Fest des Ser-ī Ṣāl[18] (das Neujahrsfest) fällt auf den ersten Mittwoch vom besagten Monat. Es werden die religiösen Feierlichkeiten und die Zeremonien an diesem Tage veranstaltet und die Frauen gehen auch zu den Gräbern der Toten.

Soweit der Autor. Der Zuverlässigkeitsgrad seiner Informationen lässt sich natürlich in Einzelheiten beschwerlich nachprüfen. Das Verhältnis der Jeziden zu den Muslimen müsste sich gegenüber früher[19] wesentlich gebessert haben. Auch von diesem Gewährsmann erfahren wir hinsichtlich der den religiösen Bräuchen der Jeziden zugrunde liegenden religiösen Auffassungen der Religionsgemeinde leider nur wenig Neues.

Anmerkungen

1) Cf. A.H. Layard, *Niniveh and its Remains, with an Account of a Visit ot the Chaldean Christians of Kurdistan, and Yezidis or Devil-Worshippers*, London 1970, p. 192ff.
2) Cf. M. Dietrich, *Jahrbuch für Anthropologie und Religionsgeschichte*, vol. 2, Saarbrücken 1974, p. 140.
3) Cf. Dietrich, *ad. loc.*, p. 149ff.
4) Cf. R. Frank, *Scheich ^{c}Adî, der grosse Heilige der Yezidis*, Berlin 1911.
5) E. Dammann, *Grundriss der Religionsgeschichte*, Stuttgart 1978, p. 92.
6) Ausser der oben angeführten Literatur, siehe etwa noch Th. Menzel, Art. *Yazīdī*, in *Handwörterbuch des Islam*, ed. A.J. Wensinck - J.H. Kramers, Leiden 1941, p. 806ff., sowie weitere von M. Dietrich, *ad. loc.*, p. 140, n. 1; 141, n. 2; 142, n. 3 genannte Titel. Verwiesen sei schliesslich auf die Mitteilungen der Frau G.L. Bell in ihrem Buche *Amurath to Amurath. Five Months in the Garden of Eden*, London 1911, p. 269ff. (frdl. Mitt. von J.P.M. van der Ploeg).
7) Diese Lieferung der genannten Zeitschrift schenkte mir 1973 ein Baghdader Händler namens Ǧa^{c}far al-Hurrīnī.
8) Der 2. Rang in der Hierarchie der jezidischen Geistlichen, vgl. Th. Menzel, *op. cit.*, p. 809.
9) Trotz des Nachschlagens in einigen arabischen,türkischen und kurdischen Wörterbüchern und Nachfrage bei mehreren Kollegen finde ich für diesen Terminus keine richtige Wiedergabe, obwohl die Funktion des mit ihm angedeuteten Mannes klar ist. Ich lasse darum die Vokalen unübersetzt.
10) Möglicherweise ist diese Erklärung deswegen beigefügt, weil unvokalisiertes *mslm* an sich mehrdeutig ist und die Mitteilung zunächst befremdet.
11) Cf. A. Falkenstein, in *ZA* vol. 47, 1942, p. 200.
12) Cf. D.R. Woodhead - W. Been, *A Dictionary of Iraqi-Arabic: Arabic-English*, Georgetown 1967, p. 428.
13) Es wird nicht der heilige Brunnen in Mekka, sondern ein Brunnen in einem dunklen Gewölbe des Heiligtums (Šēḫ ^{c}Adī-Mausoleum?) gemeint sein, vgl. Th. Menzel, *op. cit.*, p. 809.
14) Der 4. Rang der jezidischen Geistlichen, vgl. Th. Menzel, *op. cit.*, p. 809.
15) Cf. schon das im Sumerischen *gi-ér-ra*, akkadisch *qān bikīti* genannte Instrument für Trauermusik, cf. CAD, Q, p. 85 *qanû* lex.; B, p. 225 *bikītu* 3c2'; A. Falkenstein in *ZA* vol. 47, 1942, p. 207; Th. Jacobsen, *The Treasures of Darkness. A History of Mesopotamian Religion*, New Haven-London 1976, p. 54f.
16) Der Name des Festes hängt vielleicht mit dem Namen des 2. omajjādischen Ḫalīfen Jazīd ibn-Mu^{c}āwija zusammen, mit dem auch der Name Jezide verbunden sein könnte, cf. M. Dietrich, *op. cit.*, p. 141 mit Anm. 2.
17) Bei den Muslimen am 10. des Monats Ḏū l-Hiǧǧa gefeiert.
18) Cf. T. Wahby - C.J. Edmonds, *A Kurdisch-English Dictionary*, Oxford 1966, p. 127, s.v. *ser*.
19) Cf. etwa H. Hauser, *Kurdistan. Schicksal eines Volkes*, Diessen 1975, pp. 42f.; 93; 146; 250.

Une écriture minuscule sud-arabe antique récemment découverte

J. Ryckmans, Louvain-la-neuve

Dans une communication intitulée: "Mahmud Ali al-Ghul and the Sabaean Cursive Script" (texte à paraître), présentée au "Symposium in Memory of the Late Prof. Mahmud Ghul", tenu à l'Université du Yarmouk (Jordanie) en décembre 1984, A.F.L. Beeston a présenté le déchiffrement réalisé dès 1972 par Mahmud Ghul, mais resté inédit, du texte sabéen gravé en une écriture jusque là inconnue sur deux bâtonnets de bois exhumés en 1970 au Yémen du Nord. Cette découverte importante nous annonce la préservation d'un genre inédit de documents privés, appelés à modifier profondément notre conception de la société et de la culture sud-arabes, fondée jusqu'ici sur des écrits constitués d'inscriptions monumentales rédigées à la troisième personne, ou de graffites rupestres assez insignifiants. Elle nous révèle aussi - ce que nous ignorions absolument[1)] - la nature du support sur lequel ces documents de la vie de tous les jours étaient consignés, et le genre d'écriture réservé à ce type de message. D'autres bâtonnets semblables ont été mis au jour ces dernières années au Yémen du Nord. Nous avons participé, en juillet 1985 à l'Université de Marburg, avec les Prs W.W. Müller et Yusuf Abdallah (Ṣan^{c}ā'), ainsi que le Dr. N. Nebes, au déchiffrement de certains de ces nouveaux documents, alors en dépôt au Seminar für Semitistik de W.W. Müller. Notre recherche n'aurait pu prendre forme sans le stimulant de ce travail d'équipe passionnant.

La présente contribution se limite à la description de la nouvelle écriture, à l'exclusion du contenu des textes. Elle prend tout naturellement pour point de départ la graphie des deux bâtonnets déchiffrés par M. Ghul (désignés sous les sigles "A" et "B"), puisque ce sont les seuls pour lesquels nous avons pu utiliser des photographies, mises à notre disposition dès 1977 par M. Ghul, et avons pu en tirer par décalque des fac-similés fiables. Sur cette base solide une comparaison valable peut s'instaurer, d'une part avec la graphie des sept autres bâtonnents examinés, d'après notre copie d'ensemble assez rapide, doublée sur place d'une tracé plus soigné de lettres caractéristiques; et d'autre part, avec la graphie de quelques rares graffites, hybrides ou non, qui reproduisent des lettres de la même écriture. Le nombre des bâtonnets dont on connaît l'existence, et l'évolution graphique attestée dans ceux que nous avons examinés, indiquent qu'il s'agit d'une écriture bien fixée, et d'un type de support largement utilisé. La tradition arabe[2)] signale l'usage ancien d'écrire sur des tablettes de bois, mais aussi sur des nervures de palmes - support présent parmi les bâtonnets examinés. Nous n'avons pas connaissance, en dehors de l'Arabie et des Bataks de Sumatra, d'autres exemples de l'emploi de bâtonnets de bois comme support usuel de textes étrits.

La référence de comparaison de l'écriture sera l'écriture des inscriptions monumentales, qui témoigne d'une stabilité remarquable durant toute sa longue existence. D'autant plus que, comme on le verra ci-dessous, la plupart des lettres de l'écriture des bâtonnets se ramènent sans difficulté aux signes correspondants de l'écriture monumentale. C'est que notamment - contrairement aux alphabets des graffites rupestres, qui présentent de nombreuses lettres aberrantes ou dont l'axe est pivoté par rapport à celui de l'écriture monumentale - les lettres de cette écriture révèlent un prototype scrupuleusement aligné (la lettre *m* constitue une exception remarquable) sur l'axe vertical qui régit les caractères de l'écriture monumentale. Autre trait commun des deux écritures: l'emploi obligé de la barre de séparation entre les mots, alors que celle-ci manque le plus souvent dans les graffites rupestres. Les rares graffites sur pierre ou bronze qui ont des affinités avec l'écriture manuscrite sont d'ailleurs associés à un contexte monumental et non rupestre. Ajoutons que certains bâtonnets utilisent le système sabéen moyen de datation par l'éponyme en fonction, utilisé dans les inscriptions monumentales, alors qu'il s'agit de lettres et autres documents privés.

L'écriture proposée à notre étude est une écriture cursive, qui a la souplesse d'une écriture tracée à la main courante sur un support offrant peu de résistance. On évitera l'appellation de "cursive" qui, en épigraphie sud-sémitique, est associée à l'écriture des graffites rupestres, dans la mesure où ils présentent des irrégularités de module et des différences de formes individuelles, par rapport à l'écriture "monumentale" strictement normalisée des inscriptions. Mais alors que cette dernière est une écriture *capitale*, s'inscrivant entre deux lignes de portée, l'écriture à étudier est une *minuscule*. Certains caractères n'occupent qu'une fraction de la portée au-dessus de la ligne d'écriture: le *corps* de la lettre; la plupart comportent au moins un élément - hampe, oeillet... - qui s'écrit au-dessus de la ligne, à un niveau respectif distinct, mais sensiblement constant pour les diverses occurences d'un signe donné, même dans des graphies émanant de mains différentes. Cette écriture s'organise donc, comme toute minuscule, sur une portée de plusieurs lignes, et ce canon, d'abord implicite, s'est cristallisé. L'écriture est généralement inclinée du haut à droite vers le bas à gauche dans la graphie du document A qui nous sert de référence (*Fig. 1* et *2*, no 2) - sauf les lettres *ṯ*, *š* et *q* - suivant un mouvement général incurvé, le creux à gauche. Elle est posée sur une horizontale imaginaire avec laquelle tend à coïncider l'extrémité des appendices (particulièrement développés dans A) qui prolongent vers la gauche la plupart des lettres (sauf *m*, *z*, *ś* et *q*, ainsi que les lettres à hampe: *h*, *ġ*, *f*, *t* et *ḍ*). On ne peut cependant parler d'une écriture liée, car les caractères, quand ils se touchent, ne sont que juxtaposés: le tracé de chaque lettre est engagé à son niveau propre, toujours nettement au-dessus de la ligne, sans jamais se rattacher organiquement, par une ligature, à la fin du caractère précédent.

En constatant, d'après ce qu'on a vu plus haut, que l'écriture minuscule se présente dans le même contexte culturel que les inscriptions monumentales, on peut la qualifier de *forme manuscrite de l'écriture monumentale*, utilisée pour les besoins de la vie courante et adaptée à un support relativement "rapide". Elle se trouve donc, par rapport à l'alphabet monumental, dans la même relation que notre écriture manuscrite à l'égard du caractère imprimé avant l'invention de la machine à écrire. Le texte des inscriptions à graver devait être confié aux lapicides spécialisés sous la forme d'originaux manuscrits en minuscule. Les rois de Qatabān signaient de leur main leurs décrets "gravés dans le bois et dans la pierre"[3]; comme le texte sur pierre ne porte pas de signature, c'est le texte sur bois qui était signé, et apparemment conservé dans des archives rédigées sur bois (bâtonnets et/ou tablettes de bois).

Ici se pose la question: le bois, et plus spécialement les bâtonnets, était-il le support original et normal de l'écriture manuscrite? Les bâtonnets sont longs d'une douzaine à une vingtaine de cm. Ce sont des segments, d'environ 3 cm de diamètre, de branches de bois divers: durs et denses, ou tendres et même provenant d'arbustes ou de roseaux à moëlle; ils sont parfois vermoulus. Une marge de quelques cm peut être laissée libre à gauche, pour permettre la préhension du scribe. Le texte débute immédiatement en-dessous d'une longue ligne gravée horizontalement. Des essais suggèrent que les bois - toujours inscrits longitudinalement, en suivant le fil des fibres - étaient gravés fraîchement écorcés, pour présenter une surface plus tendre, et éviter la formation de barbes dans le tracé. L'instrument n'était pas un poinçon, mais plutôt une lame à deux tranchants, taillée en triangle à la pointe très effilée, et qui pouvait aisément entailler le bois à contre-fil. Mais même dans ces conditions, la gravure du bois reste relativement ardue, tributaire du sens des fibres, ce qui devrait provoquer une certaine raideur, ainsi que des dérapages dans le tracé des courbes. Les originaux montrent au contraire en général une grande souplesse de formes (même si dans certaines graphies les oeillets circulaires sont évités), et des pleins et déliés (que nos copies ne rendent pas adéquatement) dont la finesse approche parfois celle d'un tracé à la plume. Sans doute les scribes, peut-être surtout professionnels, étaient-ils habiles, et des procédés encore inconnus permettaient-ils d'amollir encore la surface du bois frais. Plus probablement, l'écriture sur bois conservait la souplesse de ses formes en partie aussi parce qu'elle se calquait sur l'écriture utilisée sur des supports plus "rapides", comme la tablette à cire ou le parchemin, dont l'usage est indirectement attesté[4)].

Le statut, défini plus haut, de l'écriture manuscrite, n'exclut pas que celle-ci ait pu servir, mais exceptionnellement, pour des graffites gravé dans la pierre ou le bronze[5)]. De fait, on n'en trouve la trace que dans moins d'une demi-douzaine de petits textes, parmi les milliers d'autres attestés sur ces supports en Arabie du Sud. Lorsque nous avons établi ce rapprochement[6)], notamment à propos du graffite HI 2, B (reproduit *Fig. 2*, no 15), A. Jamme nous a objecté que ce texte, écrit en une *cursive* presque liée, et *gravé dans la pierre*, infirmait la distinction que nous maintenions entre l'écriture des bâtonnets (à notre avis essentiellement réservée aux usages de la vie courante sur des matériaux légers) et les écritures dites "cursives" de nombreux graffites rupestres en alphabets de type "thamoudéen", répandus dans toute l'Arabie méridionale. Il s'agissait à son avis, dans tous ces cas, de témoins de même statut de "l'écriture cursive", utilisée (quel qu'en soit le support ou la destination) dans tous les usages autres que ceux de l'écriture "monumentale", réservée à des tailleurs de pierre spécialisés. On a répondu plus haut à cette objection. L'énorme diversité et le caractère hybride des alphabets des graffites rupestres[7)], n'ont rien de comparable à la graphie exclusive (la rareté des exceptions confirme la règle!) et la nature foncièrement homogène de la minuscule des bâtonnets.

<u>Traces de l'écriture manuscrite dans des graffites sur pierre ou sur bronze</u>.

1. Jamme 768[8)] (*Fig. 2*, no 14). - Gravé sur un bloc taillé provenant du temple de Mārib. Les deux lignes - la seconde (un mot mutilé) fortement décalée vers la droite par rapport au début de la première) - nous paraissent former deux textes distincts, désignés par (a) et (b).

Le texte (a) (*Fig. 1-2*, no 3; ligne 1 de Jamme), comprend trois mots isolés par des barres de séparation. La lecture des deux premiers, *'bkrb bn*, est claire. Jamme lit le troisième *brtn*, mais il ne reste du "*n*" mutilé qu'un petit fragment (qui peut appartenir à une barre de séparation), mais si près du "*t*" qui le précède, qu'on ne voit pas où se logerait la large courbe vers la droite qu'on attend de la partie inférieure d'un *n*. La lettre lue "*t*", avec ses sortes d'empattements en sens contraire, ne rappelle nullement la simple croix du "*t*" des graffites "cursifs". Il s'agit à notre avis d'un *ṯ* de l'écriture minuscule (à comparer aux autres graphies de cette lettre, *Fig. 2*, nos 2-13 : nous lisons un nom propre) *brṯ*[.]. Les lettres sont régulières, et leur corps s'inscrit dans une rectangle presque carré. A un peu plus du double de la hauteur du *corps* culminent les barres de séparation, les antennes de *'* et *k*, ainsi que ce qui correspond à l'oeillet supérieur du *ṯ*: ce sont les proportions de l'écriture minuscule; mais il s'agit d'une forme ancienne, notamment parce que les jambages des lettres, déjà uniformément incurvés contrairement à l'écriture monumentale, ne sont pas encore recourbés vers la gauche comme dans l'écriture minuscule habituelle.

Le texte (b) (*Fig. 1*, no 4; ligne 2 de Jamme) est plus récent que le précédent. Nous y voyons le premier élément d'un nom théophore *lḥy*[..] (Jamme: *bqyn*). Les lettres ont déjà leur forme particulière dans l'écriture minuscule (battant du *l* attaché à droite *ḥ* ouvert vers le bas...) mais le tracé n'a pas encore la souplesse et l'effet de traînée vers la gauche des autres graphies minuscules.

2. HI 2, B[9]) (*Fig. 1*, no 13; *Fig. 2*, no 15) - Graffite hybride, finement gravé sur la tranche d'un bloc portant un texte monumental. La lecture que Jamme propose de ce texte énigmatique est peu convaincante, car le texte a été lu tête en bas! La remise à l'endroit (appliquée *Fig. 2*, no 15) fait apparaître - outre des caractères indéchiffrables ou repris à l'écriture monumentale - trois caractères typiques de l'écriture manuscrite: *'*, *b*, et *w*. Les formes sont anciennes, mais montrent déjà un effet terminal de traînée vers la gauche.

3. Graffites sur bronze (*Fig. 1*, no 12 et 13; *Fig. 2*, no 12). - Révélés par une restauration, sur la statue d'homme en bronze, provenant de Naḫlat al-Ḥamrā', conservée au Musée de Ṣanᶜā'. Cette statue porte une inscription sabéenne bien connue, qui mentionne un souverain datant au plus tôt de la fin du IIIe s. après J.-C.[10]). Les deux graffites qui nous intéressent figurent sur une photo retouchée que W.W. Müller nous a aimablement prêtée. Le premier graffite, que nous appelons Bronze (a) (*Fig. 1* et *2*, no 12), comprend deux mots en pure écriture minuscule, qui fournissent les lettres *s*, *r*, *t* et *ṯ*.

Le *s* a la forme "récente" (voir ci-dessous), compatible avec la date tardive de la statue qui porte le texte- ou du moins du souverain qui y est nommé.

Des lettres en écriture manuscrite figurent parmi des caractères indéchiffrables ou empruntés à l'écriture monumentale, dans un second graffite, Bronze (b) (*Fig. 1*, no. 13) de quatre lignes, gravé un peu en dessous du précédent, sur le dessin d'un animal. On y distingue des formes relativement anciennes des lettres *'*, *s*, *l*, *r* et *ḥ*.

Analyse comparative des graphies minuscules.

Les *Fig. 1* et *2* donnent successivement: l'alphabet monumental (représenté par une forme ancienne attestée) et sa translittération (no 1), puis une forme typique de chaque lettre de A (no 2). Les lettres sont regroupées d'après l'affinité graphique de leur forme dans A. L'écriture de B est presque identique à celle de A: on peut en juger d'après un extrait de ce texte (*Fig. 2*, no 17). Le *ẓ* n'est pas encore attesté. Pour les autres bâtonnets (nos 5 à 11) est retenu un spécimen typique (parfois deux) de chaque lettre de l'alphabet se présentant clairement dans notre copie. Un astérisque marque les lettres dont l'identification n'est pas définitive. Les bâtonnets sont désignés par deux chiffres reliés par x: la longueur de l'objet en mm, et le nombre de lignes. La notation "± 180x12" (no 6), exprime l'incertitude sur les dimensions et le nombre de lignes: nous n'avons déchiffré que les cinq premières lignes de ce texte qui en compte une douzaine. Pour les textes sur pierre, nous avons reproduit tels quels les fac-similés de Jamme (*Fig. 1-2*, nos 3, 4, 12 et 13, et *Fig. 2*, nos 14 et 15). Les lettres des textes sur bronze sont reproduits par décalque d'un agrandissement photographique (*Fig. 1-2*, nos. 12 et 13). Les graphies sont présentées dans l'ordre chronologique - très provisoire, vu les lacunes de la documentation - que nous leur assignons, sauf le texte de référence A (no 2), donné en premier lieu (il ferait normalement suite au no 8). Les deux graphies hybrides (no 13) ne sont pas classées. A l'exception des quatre premiers, apparemment plus anciens, les textes devraier s'échelonner entre la fin du IId siècle et la fin du IVe.

Anticipons ici sur les résultats de notre analyse, pour justifier notre classement. Le *d* du texte no 5 est l'intermédiaire entre le *d* monumental et celui de toutes les autres graphies qui attestent cette lettre. Ce serait le plus ancien des bâtonnets examinés. Les hampes de ce *d* sont croisées, et suivies d'un petit trait vertical (qui figure le côté du triangle du *d* monumental). A cette forme se rattachent les graphies où les hampes, devenues parallèles, conservent encore le trait vertical (nos 6 et 7), ainsi que le no 8, où l'on trouve à la fois la forme précédente, et une autre, où le trait vertical est remplacé par un petit *b*, forme attestée dans A (no 2), et dans les nos 9, 10 et 11.

Le *s* présente une forme encore proche de la lettre monumentale, mais où le jambage de droite se recourbe vers celui de gauche au niveau de la ligne d'écriture (nos 6, 7, 8, 2 et 13). Sauf le dernier, ces textes fournissent chacun des exemples de *d*. Dans 6 et 7, c'est la forme à trait vertical; dans le no 2, il a la forme plus récente, et le texte no 8 contient les deux formes. Un autre type de *s* apparaît dans les nos 9, 11 et 12. A la place des jambages reliés par une boucle fermée, la lettre présente, sous l'antenne, un demi-cercle ouvert vers la gauche, et se prolongeant vers le bas à gauche par un appendice en dessous de la ligne d'écriture. Certaines variantes non recensées (voir le même phénomène, mais pour la lettre *k*, au no 8) montrent que la forme est issue de la première: la boucle ne remonte pas jusqu'à la base de l'antenne, laissant un hiatus à gauche. Dans les deux premières des graphies citées, les nos 9 et 11, un *d*, sous sa forme récente, est attesté également. En d'autres termes, la forme récente du *s* s'est implantée après la forme récente du *d*.

Une forme récente du *'* s'est développée parallèlement à celle du *s*: elle apparaît dans deux graphies où figure le *s* récent: les nos 9 et 11. Par contre, *k* s'est développé dans deux directions parallèles: l'une suivant la ligne du *s* ancien à boucle fermée (mais ici triangulaire): nos 7, 8, et 2 - textes moyens - mais aussi no 11 (où la lettre subit une stylisation comparable à celle de certains alphabets coufiques): texte à *s* récent. L'autre forme est schématisée (elle rappelle un *aleph* hébraïque): elle est déjà présente (en gestation) dans Ja 768 (a) (no 3), et au no 5 - deux textes anciens, ainsi que dans le no 9, alors que les deux formes voisinent dans le no 10, assez récent à en juger par la forme évoluée du *m* qui y figure ...

Lettres *'*, *k*, et *s* (*Fig. 1*). - Leur ductus [11] est similaire et comporte deux traits: l'un part du sommet de l'antenne, forme le jambage de droite, et s'incurve ensuite vers la gauche pour rejoindre éventuellement le second trait. Celui-ci part de l'angle formé par l'antenne et le jambage, s'abaisse verticalement, puis s'incurve vers la gauche et se termine en appendice terminal plus ou moins horizontal. Ces trois lettres sont très proches de l'alphabet monumental, si on les compare aux formes habituelles qu'elles présentent dans les graffites rupestres. - Les formes particulières des autres graphies que A ont été analysées ci-dessus.

Lettres *b*, *ᶜ*, *l* et *y* (*Fig. 1*). - Malgré leurs caractéristiques propres, elles se confondent souvent. Le *b* a gardé de sa forme originelle une tendance à se présenter comme un rectangle ouvert en bas; il est plus grand que les trois autres, et il peut, comme elles, se refermer en triangle. Le *c* est d'ordinaire petit, et son appendice horizontal s'attache directement à l'extrémité gauche du triangle. Le triangle du *l* se place en principe plus haut sur la ligne que les trois autres lettres. Quant au *y*, il se distingue souvent par un coude à la hauteur du triangle, et l'appendice terminal forme un angle assez net avec le trait vertical. Le ductus des quatre lettres est similaire: un premier trait part du sommet de la lettre vers la droite pour former un angle aigu: deux côtés du triangle (dans les graphies plus anciennes on doit plutôt parler d'une boucle arrondie). Le second trait s'abaisse verticalement du même point de départ, puis après un trajet variable suivant la hauteur de la lettre, s'incurve vers la gauche pour former l'appendice terminal. Le *y* peut donner l'impression d'être écrit d'un seul trait partant du bas du triangle, et décrivant celui-ci dans le sens contraire des aiguilles d'une montre. Graphiquement parlant, le coude qu'on a signalé répondrait au mouvement de la main effectuant ce tracé dans ce sens. Il semble attesté dans le texte Ja 768 (*Fig. 1*, no 4). Des raisons techniques (début du tracé coïncidant avec l'angle de l'écriture[12)], et à contre-fil du bois) l'auraient fait abandonner dans l'écriture sur bois, car tous les bâtonnets examinés attestent le ductus en deux traits pour les quatre lettres en discussion.

Le trait oblique du *l*, dirigé vers la gauche dans l'écriture monumentale, est figuré dans toutes les graphies (sauf celle du no 5, voir ci-dessous) par un triangle à *droite* de l'axe de la lettre, donc du côté *d'où vient* l'écriture. La raison est calligraphique: amorcer le trait depuis la direction d'où vient l'écriture, pour éviter des retours en arrière dans le tracé. Exemple comparable: en capitale romaine, le F porte ses deux horizontales à droite, dans le sens *vers où* va l'écriture. Transcrit en écriture manuscrite "anglaise" le F majuscule porte ses principales fioritures à gauche (*Fig. 2*, no 16), donc du côté *d'où vient* l'écriture! - Dans le no 5, le contexte impose d'identifier à *l* un caractère particulier formé de deux hampes rapprochées, réunies par une ligne sinueuse.

Lettre *m* (*Fig. 1*). - Ductus en deux traits: un angle aigu tracé comme dans les lettres précédentes, puis une courbe tracée du haut vers le bas à droite. On observe une fin de lettre analogue, tracée dans le sens contraire des aiguilles d'une montre, pour le *ś* et le *q*. L'origine de cette forme, sans lien apparent avec le *m* monumental, demeure obscure, car la seule forme divergente attestée (au no 5) (deux obliques parallèles tracées d'un seul jet, et réunies par une ligature oblique), n'est qu'une abréviation des deux traits du ductus normal. On pourrait songer à une forme primitive qui serait similaire à celle du *m* dans certains graffites repustres et en lihyanite: ovale déformé évoquant le contour d'un boomerang.

Lettres *r* et *g* (*Fig. 1*).- Se confondent souvent. Dans A (no 2) le *r* est angulaire, comme le *g*, mais plus petit. Dans d'autres graphies, les deux lettres ont la même forme d'un demi-cercle de petite dimension.

Lettres *w*, *ḥ* et *ṭ* (*Fig. 1*).- Elles se ressemblent. Le tracé du *w* comporte trois traits: le premier, oblique, s'abaisse vers la droite, puis se recourbe vers le bas à gauche; le second part du milieu du trait oblique, s'incline à gauche vers la ligne d'écriture, et se termine en appendice horizontal. Un troisième trait assez bref, abaissé verticalement depuis le point de départ du premier trait, complète la lettre à gauche. La forme primitive paraît être en deux traits: un ovale, tracé dans le sens des aiguilles d'une montre, à partir du bas à gauche, par le haut, vers le bas à droite, et au creux duquel es ajouté le trait vertical que l'on trouve dans la forme monumentale. Un tel ductus apparaît tel quel dans le texte hybride HI B, 2 (*Fig. 1*, no 13; *Fig. 2*, no 15). Le ductus en trois traits, où la partie initiale du premier trait primitif est remplacée par un troisième trait de haut en bas, s'est peut-être développé dans l'écriture sur bois, pour éviter un tracé dirigé à la fois à rebours de l'angle de l'écriture et à contre-fil des fibres du support.

Cette dernière remarque s'applique aussi au *ḥ* qui présente un ductus en deux traits seulement dans Ja 768 (b) (*Fig. 1*, no 4) et Bronze (a) (*Fig. 1*, no 12). Le *ḥ* ressemble au *w*: son ductus se décompose de la même façon, mais le dessin des traits 1 et 3 est plus petit, et plus tassé dans le sens vertical. Le sommet de la lettre s'établit aussi plus haut sur la portée.

Le *ṭ* est formé d'une hampe partant du sommet de la portée, et s'infléchissant vers la gauche; à mi-hauteur, cette hampe est barrée par une structure horizontale qui, selon les graphies observées, se presente tantôt comme une barre cantonnée à chaque extrémité d'un petit trait vertical, tantôt comme l'addition des traits 1 et 3 des lettres *w* ou *ḥ*.

Lettres *d* et *ḏ* (*Fig. 1*). - Elles ont en commun deux hampes verticales jumelées. Celle de gauche du *d* se présente dans A (*Fig. 1*, no 2), suivie d'un petit signe *b* placé un peu au-dessus de la ligne d'écriture. L'origine et les variantes de cette forme ont été exposées ci-dessus.

Dans le signe *ḏ*, la hampe de gauche s'infléchit à mi-hauteur vers la gauche puis se redresse légèrement vers la droite à hauteur de la ligne d'écriture. Entre les deux hampes, un troisième trait s'insère face à cette courbe; il s'incurve dans le sens contraire, et passe sous la hampe de gauche pour s'achever en un appendice horizontal. Ces deux courbes se combinent (dans le sens inverse de celles de la lettre *q*) pour former un ovale, qui correspond à l'espace délimité par les deux transversales dans le caractère monumental. Dans les autres graphies, le tracé est plus schématique. Une forme pariculière de *d̲* (?), apparemment fort évoluée, apparaît dans le texte no 10, qui atteste d'autre part la forme dérivée du *m* évoquée plus haut.

Lettres *t̲* et *ṣ* (*Fig. 2*). - Le ductus et l'aspect général des deux lettres est assez similaire. Alors que les deux oeillets du *t̲* monumental sont superposés dans l'axe vertical, l'axe est ici oblique, et les oeillets rendus par des triangles. Ductus en trois traits: l'angle supérieur; un trait sinueux partant du sommet (formant la partie gauche de l'oeillet primitif) vers la droite, puis se courbant vers le bas au-dessus de la ligne d'écriture; et enfin le trait final, abaissé verticalement depuis le milieu du second trait, et se coudant à l'horizontale vers la gauche. Un *t̲* comparable à celui de A apparaît dans le graffite ancien Jamme 768 (a) (*Fig. 2*, no 3). La lettre est placée haut sur la portée, et (d'après la copie) le ductus est en deux traits: l'un, vertical, combine les traits 1 et 3 ci-dessus; l'autre correspond au trait 2. Dans les autres graphies, le *t̲* est plus tassé que dans A, et on retrouve plus nettement l'oeillet primitif sous la forme d'un ovale, généralement tracé en deux traits (clairement visibles dans Bronze (a) (*Fig. 2*, no 12), sauf peut-être dans les textes 6 et 8 de la fig. 2, où les deux oeillets semblent tracés en un seul trait en forme de S.

Le *ṣ* s'écrit en quatre traits: les deux premiers reproduisent le tracé du *t̲*, les deux suivants, celui des 2e et 3e traits du *w*. La présence du 3e trait, médian, rappelle la forme ancienne du *ṣ* monumental, dans laquelle la lettre s'appuie sur un triple jambage.

Lettre *n* (*Fig. 2*). - Elle occupe toute la hauteur de la portée. Son aspect sinueux dans la graphie de A est graphiquement conditionné par la préparation de la grande boucle qui se termine en appendice horizontal. A connaît aussi une forme plus sobre (semblable à celle du no 6), seule attestée dans B (*Fig. 2*, no 17). Dans les nos 5 et 9, *l* est écrit en deux traits. Enfin dans 10, la hampe courbe s'abaisse jusqu'à la ligne d'écriture et s'achève en une courte oblique vers la gauche, dessinant une sorte de V aux branches inégales: forme apparemment très évoluée.

Lettres *h* et *h̲* (*Fig. 2*).- Elles dérivent sans doute d'une forme archaïque (à corolle en V) de leur équivalent monumental. Le *h* comporte une longue hampe oblique, qui peut s'abaisser jusqu'en dessous de la ligne d'écriture, et sur laquelle se greffe (parfois en laissant un hiatus assez sensible) le trait oblique de gauche formant la fourche. (Dans la graphie de B, le ductus paraît être en trois traits, car la partie inférieure de la hampe ne prolonge exactement aucune des deux branches de la fourche).

Le premier trait du *ẖ*, partant du sommet de la portée, s'abaisse en oblique vers la gauche, puis se redresse vers la droite, avant de se terminer par une ample boucle et un appendice horizontal. La boucle est analogue à celle du *n* et du *'*: elle répond, dans les trois lettres, à un angle en forme de manivelle dans le tracé monumental. Le second trait est formé d'une longue oblique rejoignant à angle aigu le milieu du premier trait, pour former la partie droite de la fourche. Les deux éléments de la fourche sont légèrement bombés vers l'extérieur. Dans d'autres graphies (nos 6, 8 et 9), c'est l'oblique de droite qui paraît appartenir au premier trait du ductus.

Lettre *ġ* (*Fig.* 2). - Attestée jusqu'ici une seule fois, dans A (no 2) simplifiée (?) à partir du *ġ* monumental, ou du *ġ* en forme de svastika de certains graffites rupestres du sud de l'Arabie centrale[13].

Lettre *z* (*Fig.* 2). - S'écrit en deux traits: l'un forme d'abord une courte ligne horizontale, tracée du sommet vers la droite, et qui s'abaisse ensuite obliquement vers la gauche, jusqu'à la ligne d'écriture ou au delà. Un second trait part du milieu de cette oblique vers la droite, et se recourbe vers le bas à gauche, pour rencontrer le premier trait sur la ligne d'écriture. L'ensemble rappelle notre *b* minuscule italique. La graphie du no 11 présente un ductus divergent, en un seul trait, semblable au tracé d'un Z majuscule écrit en imprimé dont on compléterait le tracé, sans lever la plume, d'un trait oblique partant de l'extrémité inférieure droite vers le haut à gauche.

Lettre *f* (*Fig.* 2). - Longue hampe oblique, légèrement incurvée, creusée vers la gauche, et sur le milieu de laquelle se greffe, à droite, une sorte de jambage, qui se limite souvent à un petit trait parallèle à la hampe. Ce signe peut être ramené au caractère monumental ancien: un losange aux angles latéraux émoussés, dressé sur une pointe. La forme intermédiaire devait être un haut demi-cercle, ouvert vers la droite, et portant au centre un petit croissant tourné vers l'intérieur: c'est une forme comparable à celle (en module majuscule) qui se présente dans d'anciennes inscriptions éthiopiennes[14] et qui est d'ailleurs à la base des combinaisons syllabiques de la valeur *f* dans le syllabaire éthiopien. La forme concave de la hampe, qu'on observe dans toutes les graphies, est évidemment conditionnée par l'allure générale incurvée de l'écriture minuscule.

Lettre *š* (*Fig.* 2).- Très semblable à l'original monumental ancien, mais comme pour le *ṯ*, l'axe du *š* est penché vers la gauche.

Lettre *ś* (*Fig. 2*).- Le ductus est en deux traits, tracés de haut en bas: un ">" auquel s'imbrique un "<". Le tracé se termine donc en bas et vers la droite, comme le *m* et le *q*. Dans le texte no 10, un triangle dressé sur la pointe, et surmonté de deux petits traits verticaux pourrait représenter *ś*, mais sa forme géométrique contraste avec l'allure du texte. A.F.L. Beeston[15)] a noté dans le document A une forme analogue qu'il lit "7" (VII).

Lettre *t* (*Fig. 2*).- Longue hampe oblique, barrée d'un trait horizontal plus petit, dont l'angle s'écarte de celui de l'original monumental, pour éviter une oblique tracée dans l'axe même de l'angle de l'écriture.

Lettre *q* (*Fig. 2*).- Un trait vertical se termine par un crochet ouvert à gauche, et un trait recourbé, qui s'amorce à gauche du crochet, forme avec lui la figuration de l'oeillet central du *q* monumental, et s'incurve vers la droite (comme le *m* et le *ś*).

Lettre *ḍ* (*Fig. 2*).- Les deux longues obliques (légèrement bombées) reliées par un trait horizontal rappellent la lettre monumentale, qui toutefois est fermée en haut et en bas.

Puisse cette étude préliminaire contribuer au déchiffrement des textes en minuscule, et hâter la phase d'interprétation de cette documentation d'un intérêt exceptionnel.

Notes

1) J. Ryckmans, "De quelques divinités sud-arabes" dans *ETL* vol. 39, 1963, p. 458.
2) Cf. Th. Nöldeke - F. Schwally, *Geschichte des Qorāns*, vol. 2, Leipzig 1909, p. 13; Ryckmans, "De quelques divinités", pp. 458-459; A. Grohmann, *Arabische Paläographie*, vol. 1, Wien 1967, p. 93.
3) Ryckmans, "De quelques divinités", p. 458, n. 2; cf. *Répertoire d'Epigraphie Sémitique*, vol. 6, Paris 1935, p. 318, n° 3854, l. 10, et p. 218, n° 3566, l. 21.
4) Ryckmans, *ibid.*
5) Cf. J. Ryckmans, "Alphabets, Scripts and Languages in Pre-Islamic Arabian Evidence" (Comm. au IInd International Symposium on Studies in the History of Pre-Islamic Arabia à Riyadh, 1979), dans *Studies in the History of Arabia*, vol. 2: *Pre-Islamic Arabia*, ed. A.T. Ansary, Riyadh 1984, p. 79, sur l'écriture de graffiti européens selon qu'ils sont gravés dans le support, ou simplement tracés (à l'encre, etc.) sur le support.
6) Ryckmans, "Alphabets" , p. 79 et n. 34, pp. 84-85. Nous avons utilisé l'enregistrement de la discussion qui a suivi la communication.
7) Voir notamment les tableaux de A. Jamme dans *Qataban and Sheba*, ed. Wendell Phillips, New York 1955, p. 42, et A. Jamme, *Sabaean and Hasaean Inscriptions from Saudi Arabia* (*Studi Semitici*, vol. 23), Roma 1966, fig. 19 (où plusieurs dizaines de formes de ' sont données. *Aucune* ne correspond au ' minuscule.
8) A. Jamme, *Sabaean Inscriptions*, Baltimore 1963, p. 230 et pl. P.
9) A. Jamme, "Inscriptions from Hajar bin Humeid" dans *Hajar bin Ḥumeid. Investigations at a Pre-Islamic Site in South Arabia*, ed. G.W. van Beek, Baltimore 1969, p. 337, fig. 131 face à p. 352, et pl. 46 b, p. 307.
10) W.W. Müller, "The Inscriptions on the Hellenistic Bronze Statues from Nakhlat al-Hamrā', Yemen" dans *Proceedings of the Seminar for Arabian Studies*, vol. 9, 1979, pp. 79-80.
11) Cf. J. Mallon, *Paléographie Romaine* (*Scripturae: Monumenta et Studia*, vol. 3), Madrid 1952, p. 22, 3°.
12) "La position dans laquelle s'est trouvé placé l'instrument du scribe par rapport à l'écriture" : J. Mallon, *op. cit.* p. 22, 2°.
13) Cf. A. van den Branden, *Les textes thamoudéens de Philby, I : inscriptions du Sud* (*Bibliothèque du Muséon*, vol. 39), Louvain 1956, p. 55.
14) A.J. Drewes et R. Schneider, "Origine et développement de l'écriture éthiopienne" dans *AE* vol. 10, 1976, p. 100 et fig. 1, VIII-XIII.
15) Dans la communication citée en début d'article.

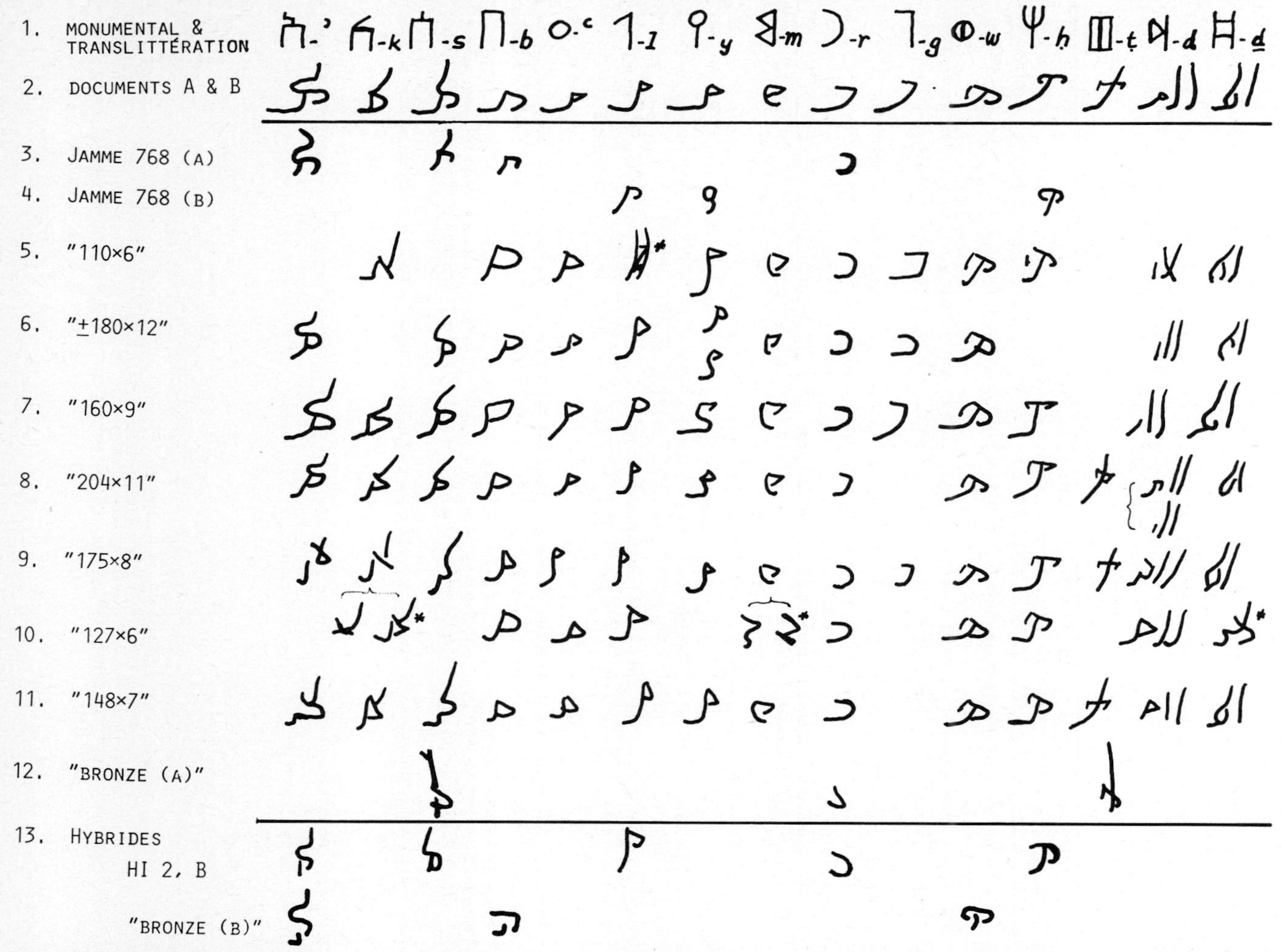
1. MONUMENTAL & TRANSLITTÉRATION
-ʾ -k -s -b -ʿ -l -y -m -r -g -w -ḥ -ṭ -d -ḏ
2. DOCUMENTS A & B
3. JAMME 768 (A)
4. JAMME 768 (B)
5. "110×6"
6. "±180×12"
7. "160×9"
8. "204×11"
9. "175×8"
10. "127×6"
11. "148×7"
12. "BRONZE (A)"
13. HYBRIDES
HI 2, B
"BRONZE (B)"

FIG. 1.

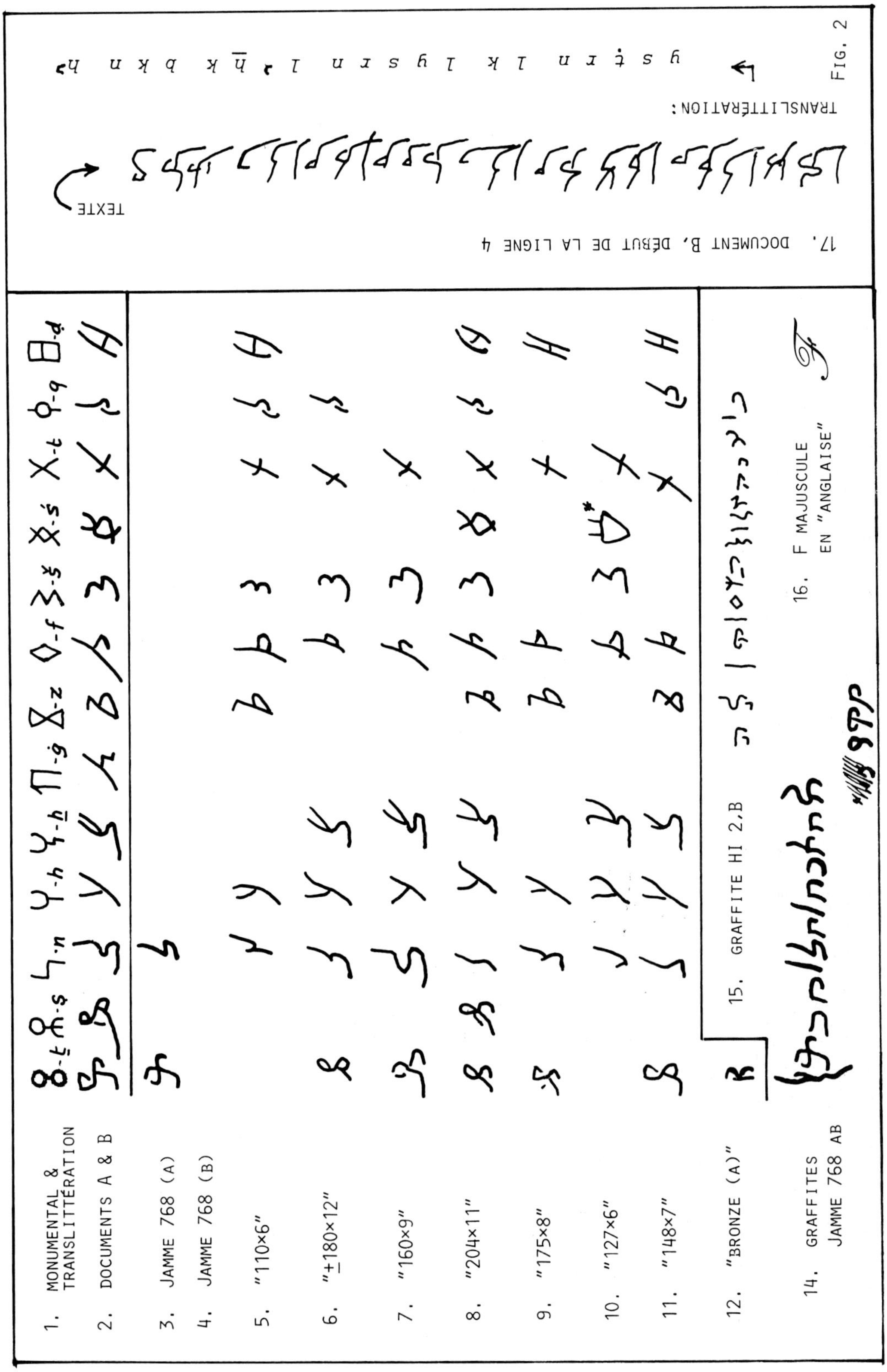
1. MONUMENTAL & TRANSLITTÉRATION
2. DOCUMENTS A & B
3. JAMME 768 (A)
4. JAMME 768 (B)
5. "110×6"
6. "±180×12"
7. "160×9"
8. "204×11"
9. "175×8"
10. "127×6"
11. "148×7"
12. "BRONZE (A)"
14. GRAFFITES JAMME 768 AB
15. GRAFFITE HI 2,B
16. F MAJUSCULE EN "ANGLAISE"
17. DOCUMENT B, DÉBUT DE LA LIGNE 4
TEXTE
TRANSLITTÉRATION:

FIG. 2

The Role of Jewish Studies in Biblical Semantics

J.F.A. Sawyer, Newcastle-upon-Tyne

The gap between Biblical Studies and Jewish Studies is evident everywhere. A specialist in *Miqra* may live in a different world from a specialist in *Yahadut*: the one is concerned with ancient Israelite history and archaeology, the other, if he is interested in the Bible at all, with how it has been interpreted in the post-biblical sources. I want to argue that, since the Bible is not merely an ancient near eastern text like the Gilgamesh Epic or the Annals of Sennacherib or the Merneptah Stele, but a living document in the religious and cultural life of many communities, Hebrew-speaking and non-Hebrew speaking, Jewish and non-Jewish, the evidence of the post-biblical Jewish sources, in particular the Mediaeval and Modern Hebrew literature, is just as important for biblical semantics as the ancient material, if not more so.
Certainly this applies to biblical exegesis, biblical theology and other branches of biblical studies as well. I have chosen to concentrate on semantics, that is to say, that branch of linguistics devoted to discussing and describing the meaning of words and phrases, first, because since James Barr made us all think seriously about the subject a quarter of a century or so ago, the Jewish sources have been neglected, and second, because it highlights some of the issues by focussing on relatively small and circumscribed pieces of language.
I shall present my argument first, then give some examples, and finally draw some practical conclusions. I want to make four basic points, none of them unexpected, but which nevertheless add up to what I hope is a convincing case for a shift of emphasis in biblical semantics.

(1) Translation is still by far the commonest method of semantic analysis, in spite of the fact that it is manifestly the crudest and most primitive. There are plenty of familiar theoretical reasons why translation is inadequate as a method of describing meaning, and I need not go over them now. But obviously if it were possible to work within Hebrew some at least of the inevitable errors

and confusion could be avoided. Of course I am not arguing that such definitions would inevitably be correct, or indeed that native Hebrew speakers always know best! But it is true that they can handle or detect associations, overtones, semantic overlap, distinctions between synonyms and so on, without some of the preconceptions, distortions and red herrings that are introduced by translation. One might almost say that Hebrew-speaking Jewish scholars have in some respects been using a better semantic method than some of us without knowing it. To put it another way, monolingual lexicons like La Rousse and the Oxford English Dictionary, not to mention Eliezer Ben Yehuda's *Thesaurus totius hebraitatis* and Even Shoshan's *Ha-millon he-ḥadash*, contain semantic material of a quite different order of subtlety from what is contained in Gesenius or BDB or KBL. It will not all be equally relevant, but it must be taken into account.

(2) The Hebrew Bible contains a relatively small and unrepresentative selection of the language actually used in ancient Israel. This will instantly be expanded when the far larger corpus of post-biblical Hebrew is added to it. This seems too obvious to mention, and yet the practical implications of it are still not fully realised. Conclusions are drawn from the absence of a term from the Hebrew Bible, such as the general term for metal, *matteḵet*, although the word is well known from Mishnaic times, and surely absent from the Bible only by accident. Rare words like *haṣnĕaʿ* or *ṣānaḥ* are discussed in isolation as if the Biblical corpus was all the evidence there was. Even in the case of comparatively frequent words like *ʿiḇrī* or *hōšīaʿ*, vital clues to their meaning that will only emerge from a larger corpus are missed because of the continuing compartmentalization of Hebrew studies.

(3) Philologists over the last hundred years or so have consistently favoured other Semitic languages, ancient and modern, to the virtual exclusion of post-biblical Hebrew. The Qumran material is the exception. A cursory look through KBL and its successor show how definitions of Arabic cognates are far more frequent than references to Mishnaic or Modern Hebrew Usage. This may be partly due to the relatively close relationship that exists between all the Semitic languages, in comparison with the far more complex Indo-European language family, and to the abundance of available material, especially from antiquity. There are still those who, when puzzled by a difficult Hebrew word, reach first for their Aistleitner or their von Soden and begin their semantics from outside Hebrew. In fact most of the Semitic languages employed in this way are historically and geographically far more distant from Biblical Hebrew than Mediaeval and Modern Hebrew, and as can be seen from the results, frequently

less helpful. The dangers involved in using post-biblical Hebrew are obvious: allowances have to be made at every stage for a long, complex and perhaps uncertain semantic history from the Biblical text to Even Shoshan. Post-biblical Hebrew may contain artificial creations based on actual misunderstandings of the Biblical text, for example. But that semantic history is seldom going to be as long, complex and uncertain as the historical link between a word in Hebrew and its cognate in Ugaritic or Assyrian. I have no intention of belittling the contribution of Ugaritic Studies to the semantics of Biblical Hebrew, or for that matter to the semantics of post-biblical Hebrew, but to stress the importance of the vast post-biblical corpus as an integral part of all Biblical semantics as well.

(4) The text of the Hebrew Bible, as we have it today, is itself a product of the post-biblical period, and therefore in a very real chronological sense closer to the Hebrew of the Mishnah, Talmud, Midrash, Piyyut and the rest than to any other linguistic evidence. The Massora is not an ancient near eastern text. To recover ancient near eastern originals, containing what the writers of ancient Israel actually wrote or how they were actually understood by their contemporaries, has been the goal of Biblical scholars for well nigh two centuries, and for that exercise relics of the ancient near eastern cultures are obviously important. But today, in the light of the recent writings of Phyllis Trible, Robert Alter, Francis Landy and many others, surely we have discovered that the plain meaning of the text - and that usually means the Massora in the first instance - is at least as important and certainly as fascinating as the hypothetical reconstructions of "originals". Recent interest in "reader-response", for example, suggests we should sometimes pay as much attention to what people thought a text meant as to what it actually, originally did mean. In the history of religion this is certainly a valuable insight.

Some scholars will continue to excavate the earliest layers of biblical tradition and take a special interest in "bed-rock" when they find it. But for those who seek to understand the text as it stands and how it has been understood down the centuries, there is still a rich fund of semantic material to be exploited in the roughly contemporary sources.
The few examples I have chosen to illustrate my point come from my own work and that of colleagues and graduate students of mine, who have put into practice the dictum: "Even Shoshan (or for more advanced hebraists, Ben-Yehuda) before Jastrow, Jastrow before BDB, and BDB before Aistleitner". Such advice will smack of heresy to many, no

doubt, perhaps especially among the teachers of Hebrew-speaking students in Israel; but it can have valuable results, and if what has been said above contains even a grain of truth, this should be no surprise to anyone.

First I shall look at a few familiar words from Gen 1. *meraḥefet* occurs only twice in the Hebrew Bible (Gen 1:2; Deut 32:11), but seems to have been a common enough word in post-Biblical Hebrew. A talmudic discussion explains it as "touching and yet not touching", while modern Hebrew dictionaries cite as examples of current usage *sakkana meraḥefet* "impending danger", and Bialik's *kĕ^c^en ^c^av yeḥida u-qĕṭanna meraḥèfèt u-tĕluyya* "like a small single cloud hovering, suspended". *merḥafa* is a "hovercraft". This is all part of the linguistic evidence, at least as important as the Ugaritic and Syriac data usually quoted, and yet frequently ignored (Middleton, 1985).

dèšè' and *^c^eśèv* (Gen 1:11f.) provide another example of how important data is neglected. HAL has nothing to say on their meaning in post-biblical Hebrew, although it carefully quotes a helpful Akkadian cognate of *dèšè'* and the definition of an Arabic cognate of *^c^eśèv*. In fact once again Even-Shoshan has some valuable examples of post-biblical usage, which distinguish the two terms: *dèšè'* is cultivated greenery, like "grass" or "lawn" in English, while *^c^eśèv* includes all vegetation except trees.

Such data would immediately assist the commentator in his search for nuances. For example, perhaps the choice of *dèšè'* suggests order and uniformity of colour and texture, and the *^c^eśèv* and *^c^eṣ* all the rich variety of vegetation that transforms "dry land" into "the Earth". Too much reliance on comparative philology and translation inhibits that kind of semantic analysis, whether or not this particular suggestion convinces.

Next, three words that happen to be hapax legomena in the Hebrew Bible, but well known in the post-biblical Hebrew literature. *'al-mawet* occurs in Proverbs 12:28. If our primary objective is to reconstruct ancient Israelite meanings, then it is possibly correct to emend this to *el-mawet* "to death", and thus remove the one specific reference to immortality from the text. But to describe the meaning of the text as it stands is also a valid objective, and if that is the case, then once again occurrences listed in Even-Shoshan, where the term is listed as an ordinary word for "immortality", are an essential part of our data. Incidentally, in this case the word also appears in Ugaritic, indicating a remarkable degree of continuity from Second

Millenium B.C. Syria to the post-biblical Jewish literature. The total absence of the word from the text of the Hebrew Bible (or almost total absence, if the text of Proverbs 12:28 is correct), whether due to chance or to theological factors, does not prove that it did not exist in the vocabulary of ancient Israel, and it is extraordinary that HAL has simply omitted it altogether.

Similar considerations apply to the word *lilit* (Isa 34:14). Post-biblical usage provides ample evidence for the meaning of the term. We are dealing in this verse with supernatural creatures coming out to haunt the ruins of Edom and the rich post-biblical Jewish traditions about Lilith are surely closer and more illuminating than the Akkadian material usually cited.

raz is Isaiah 24:16 is a third hapax legomenon whose meaning, especially in the context of a passage almost universally regarded as "apocalyptic" in some sense (Isa 24:27), is well known. The Jewish sources have no difficulty in making good sense of the verse: Targum Jonathan, for instance, has "(sc. then a divine voice went forth saying) 'My secret is mine, my secret is mine'." Yet modern commentators ignore this evidence entirely and translate instead "I pine away, I pine away" (RSV) or "villainy, villainy!" (NEB) or "Enough, enough!" (JB).

The meaning of relatively common words is discussed by reference only to Biblical occurrences and evidence from other languages, as though the vast corpus of post-biblical Hebrew did not exist. *miškan* is another example. For years the ancient translations *skene* and *tabernaculum*, together with the recurring word-pair *miškan/ ohel* , persuaded scholars that *miškan* denoted some kind of portable dwelling or tent. A quick glance at a dictionary of all periods of the Hebrew language shows that the word is a general term for any kind of dwelling where one makes one's home. The usage of the verb *šakan*, both in the Bible and outside it, confirms this (Love, 1975).

The phrase *qol demama daqqa* has recently been discussed in a very convincing article by S. Prickett. It is interesting that a look at Rashi would have assisted the author to come to the same conclusion. Rashi explains the phrase as either referring to the sound of secret prayer, or to tinnitus, a condition of the ears in which one hears a ringing sound that no-one else can hear. Both are attempts, like that of Prickett, to interpret the phenomenon as the fourth in a series of mysterious experiences, accompanying Elijah's confrontation with God, and nicely pick up the overtones which this strange Hebrew phrase obviously has.

Finally, another hapax legomenon which raises some different problems. There is little agreement about the meaning of *ḥŏggā'* in Isaiah 19:17: "in that day ... the land of Judah will become a terror to all Egypt". The question is why did the author choose this word for "terror" and not another in this context? Can we detect any special nuance or association? The dictionaries, grammars and commentaries have nothing to suggest. But occurrences cited in Even-Shoshan perhaps give us a clue. First, a play on words is quoted from the writings of Simha Ben Zion (1870-1932): *lo ḥag 'ella ḥŏggā' haya birušalayim* "it was not a feast but a terror in Jerusalem". Perhaps there is an allusion in our verse to the first passover, a time of terror for the Egyptians. But there is a second piece of evidence contained, both in Bauer-Leander and Even Shoshan. *ḥŏggā'* denotes a foreign or pagan festival. The final Aleph, as in various other nouns, gives the word clearly identifiable foreign associations. The verse then suggests to the reader (to this reader at any rate) that Egypt "in that day" will be overrun by some terrible foreign event comparable to the slaying of the firstborn on the first Passover night, and the choice of the word *ḥŏggā'* subtly encapsulates that powerful intention. Such a suggestion could never be gleaned from BDB or HAL or from Driver's *JTS* article on the subject. It may not be correct, but it nonetheless illustrates the degree of subtlety we should be aiming for, and for that the post-biblical corpus is invaluable.

I hope I have shown that there is a gap between Jewish Studies, represented here however cursorily by dictionaries of post-biblical Hebrew, on the one hand, and Biblical Studies as represented by many of the non-Jewish commentaries and dictionaries on the other, and that the gap is worth bridging. Let me conclude with some practical suggestions on how this might be done.

(1) We must encourage our students to become just as familiar with Jastrow and Even-Shoshan (or the like) as they have traditionally been with BDB , ANET, CML, etc. This will open up a whole new dimension in Biblical Studies for them. It will provide them with a different way of looking at the Bible and thinking about meaning.

(2) A wider and deeper grasp of Hebrew should come before Ugaritic, Aramaic, Syriac and the other Semitic languages. This must obviously include Mishnaic and Modern Hebrew, but now that the Penguin Book of Hebrew Verse is available, there is no reason why their range of experience should not be even wider and more adventurous. Non-Jewish Biblical scholars, and I would include New Testament specialists in particular, simply do not know what they are missing.

(3) With the greatest respect to the Biblical archaeologists

and ancient historians who have contributed so much to Biblical Studies over the last two centuries, I would repeat that the Hebrew Bible is not mearely an ancient near eastern text, but a living text, and the foundation of several world religions. So long as it is still studied in departments of religious studies and theology, and so long as the Massoretic text still holds pride of place in the study of the Bible - and I do not see any signs that this situation is changing - then the vast corpus of post-biblical Jewish literature which is roughly contemporary with it must take pride of place in Biblical Semantics.

It is with the greatest pleasure that I offer this as my contribution to the *Hospers Festschrift*. My association with Groningen was a short but happy one, and I owe that association entirely to Hans Hospers, for whose command of Semitic Linguistics I have the highest regard.

References

J. Aistleitner, *Wörterbuch der ugaritischen Sprache*, Berlin 1967[3].

R. Alter, *The Art of Biblical Narrative*, New York 1981.

E. Ben-Yehuda, *Thesaurus totius hebraitatis, veteris et recentioris*, 17 vols., Jerusalem 1959.

T. Carmi, *The Penguin Book of Hebrew Verse*, Harmondsworth 1981.

A. Even-Shoshan, *Ha-millon he-ḥadash*, 3 vols., Jerusalem 1971.

Hebräisches und Aramäisches Lexicon zum Alten Testament, 3 vols., ed. W. Baumgartner, 1967-1983 (= *HAL*).

M. Jastrow, *A Dictionary of the Targumim* etc., 2 vols., New York 1886-1903.

E.Y. Kutscher, "Mittelhebräisch und Jüdisch-Aramäisch im neuen Köhler-Baumgartner" in *Hebräische Wortforschung*, *Studia Veteris Testamenti* vol. 16, 1967, pp. 158-175.

F. Landy, *Paradoxes of Paradise. Identity and Difference in the Song of Songs*, Sheffield 1983.

V. Love, "A Semantic analysis of the word *shakan* in Biblical Hebrew" (unpublished thesis, University of Newcastle upon Tyne 1975).

D.F. Middleton, "Whence the feet?" in *JJS* vol. 36, 1985, pp. 61-71.

S. Prickett, "Towards a rediscovery of the Bible: The problem of the still small voice" in *Ways of Reading the Bible*, ed. M. Wadsworth, Sussex 1981, pp. 105-117.

J.F.A. Sawyer, "Hebrew terms for the resurrection of the dead" in *VT* vol. 23, 1973, pp. 218-234.

J.F.A. Sawyer, "A change of emphasis in the study of the prophets" in *Israel's Prophetic Tradition*, eds. R.A. Coggins *et. al.*, Cambridge 1982, pp. 233-249.

A. von Soden, *Akkadisches Handwörterbuch*, Wiesbaden 1965-1982.

P. Trible, *Texts of Terror*, Philadelphia 1984.

E. Ullendorff, "Is Biblical Hebrew a Language?" in *BSOAS* vol. 34, 1971, pp. 241-255.

Emphatic or Asseverative *kî* in Koheleth

A. Schoors, Leuven

Koheleth uses the particle *kî* frequently; in more that ten of these instances, *kî* can have an asseverative function. In the framework of a detailed study of the language of Koheleth, I have analyzed the function of this particle in the contexts where it occurs, and I am glad to present here the results as a modest contribution in homage of Professor J.H. Hospers.

According to G. Wildeboer, *kî* in Koh 2:12 means something like "ja, halt", "da fällt mir ein"[1]. This explanation is rather farfetched, and a simple explicative conjunction will do here, especially if v. 12b were a later addition[2]. The *kî* of Koh 2:26 has been considered as emphatic by F. Ellermeier[3]. This is an acceptable interpretation but an explicative conjunction is possible as well and, as a matter of fact, the meaning is practically the same in both suppositions.

In Koh 5:6, the second *kî* is emphatic; such is the opinion of E.S. Artom, R. Gordis and W.J. Fuerst, whereas A. Lauha considers the first *kî* to have that force[4]. This verse is very difficult and the ancient versions were also desperate when they had to translate it. The second *kî* is sometimes taken for an adversative, whether opposing the fear of God to the forbidden acts of v. 5 or to the many dreams and words of 6a[5]. This reading is reflected in the Vg. *vero* and Sym. *alla*. When we parse the preposition in *b^e rōb* as concessive, an emphatic force of the second *kî* is obvious: "In spite of all the dreams, follies and idle chatter, indeed fear God" (Gordis). But again, in such an interpretation, emphatic and adversative *kî* are closely related, the adversative force being a specific case of its asseverative function[6]. It seems that the best solution is to give emphatic force to the first *kî* and to consider the second as a repetition of it, be it intentional or an intrusion by dittography[7].

Also in Koh 4:14 and 5:19, A. Lauha finds an emphatic *kî*[8]. In the first instance, a number of scholars prefer an explicative function, as they consider v. 14 as an explanation of v. 13. Thus

A.H.Mc Neile regards 14a "for he managed to escape from prison to be king", as explaining why the young man is wise, whereas 14b "for even in his kingdom he was born poor", would clarify why he is *miskēn*. Reichert-Cohen, however, suppose that v. 14 gives the reason of the superiority of the poor and wise boy. A still more complicated solution is that of J.J. Serrano, according to whom v. 14a refers to the young king, whereas 14b views the older one, who, king by birth, finishes as a poor man[9]. All these explanations are rather involved and especially the last one is clearly contrary to the logic of the text. G.S. Ogden parses the verse as a double concessive clause. This is possible but hard to prove because of the very obscure meaning of the whole context[10]. An original parsing was proposed by Gregorius Thaumaturgus, who read v. 14 as an object clause depending on *lō'-yāda^c l^ehizzāhēr ^côd* in v. 13: "cui in mentem non venit fieri posse ut quispiam ex carcere ad regni gubernacula constituatur"[11]. But it is hard to accept that this is the meaning of the Hebrew text. Emphatic use of *kî* appears to be the most satisfactory way out of the problem. As to Koh 5:19, A. Lauha reads it as a continuation of v. 17: a major advantage of simple joy is that it fills man so as to forget the shortness of life. Thus v. 19 is a reinforcement of what precedes, and this is underlined by an asseverative *kî*[12]. But an alternative explanation, suggested by N. Lohfink, is acceptable as well: when God has given all these things in life, his most true gift is that such a man must not often think of how short his life is[13]. V. 19 then is a noun clause introduced with a nominalizing *kî*, in apposition with the demonstrative pronoun *zōh* in v. 18: "this is God's gift that..."[14]. Again the deeper sense of both interpretations is the same.

In Koh 6:8, A. Lauha finds another emphatic *kî*, which again is fully acceptable[15]. E. Elster regarded it as adversative, but *kî* has that meaning only after a clause which is at least implicitly negative[16]. It certainly is a solution of embarassment to move the *kî* to the beginning of the next verse, as H.L. Ginsberg does[17]. The *kî* would be secondary, since the Qumran text reads *kmh ywtr*, but LXX *hoti* renders this possibility rather doubtful.

The *kî* of Koh 7:7 is quite problematic. According to A. Lauha, the verse has no logical connection with what precedes and he is of opinion that the *kî* clause was meant to explain a proverb which is missing. On this point he follows some older scholars such as F. Delitzsch, G. Wildeboer and A.H.Mc Neile[18]. Such a supposition solves the problem but it is purely hypothetical. The only evidence for this is some space in the fragmentary manuscript discovered at Qumran[19]. E.H. Plumptre has suggested a logical connection with the preceding verse: the mirth of fools, i.e. of the godless, is vanity for it issues in oppression and bribery[20]. But this connection is rather weak. It is possible to give a causal or explicative function to *kî*, if we understand the connection thus: It is better to listen to a wise man's rebuke than to the praise of fools (v. 5), but this too is vanity (v. 6), for oppression and bribery can corrupt even the wise man (v. 7). This works even if vv. 6b-7 are a later addition. Still, the *kî* of v. 7 can also be read as an asseverative particle, as suggested already by M. Geier[21].

Also in Koh 7:20, an asseverative *kî* is possible[22]. If we take it as an explicative conjunction, it is not easy to tell to what in the context the explication refers, as may appear from the variety of opinions among the critics. Some see a connection with v. 19: despite the fact that a man fears God (v. 18), he is certain to fall and sin during his lifetime, and for that reason he requires the protective power of wisdom[23]. Others suppose a connection with the following verse: Since there are no righteous people, therefore do not give heed to all the things that men say[24].

Koh 8:6 can be understood as an explication of the preceding verse, as may appear from the terminology (*rāᶜ*, *ᶜēt ûmišpāṭ*), which is common to both verses. F. Delitzsch and G. Wildeboer regard even the fourfold *kî* in vv. 6-7 as introducing four co-ordinated arguments for v. 5[25]. But according to N. Lohfink, vv. 6-7 are quotations of former expositions, with which Koheleth rejects the proverb of v. 5. Therefore he translates *kî* not by "for" but by "surely" (allerdings)[26]. This is a most convincing exegesis. Thus we apparently have here another instance of emphatic *kî*. A similar approach is needed for Koh 8:12. The use of *kî gam* with the meaning "although" is characteristic of Koheleth, who uses it instead of classical *gam kî*[27]. F. Delitzsch and R. Gordis accept the same meaning here[28]. And this makes sense within verse 12: the sinner prolongs his life, although I know that it will be well with those who fear God. But R. Gordis himself admits that *yôdēaᶜ* introduces a restatement of a conventional idea which Koheleth does not accept. Thus we must consider v. 12 in a broader context. The whole pericope of Koh 8:10-15 deals with the problem of retribution. In the vv. 10-12a the author remarks that the sinners are not punished. He then quotes traditional wisdom, according to which it will be well with the righteous and not with the wicked. I know that traditional doctrine, he says. But then he restates that it does not work, and concludes by commending enjoyment (vv. 14-15). Thus the function of *kî* in v. 12b is similar to that in 8:6: "Surely, I know ..."[29]. We have here an emphatic *kî*, but it must be admitted that it has concessive force. The concession, however, is not only connected with the preceding sentence, but with the whole context, and, more in particular, it is preparing for the statement in v. 14: "Surely I know ... but reality is different". There is no reason then to regard 12b-13 as an orthodox gloss, *pace* A. Lauha, who parses *kî* as emphatic anyway[30]. A gloss would only be acceptable if we stick to the inferior interpretation which we find, with minor divergencies, in the Revised Standard Version and the New English Bible: "A sinner may do wrong and live to old age, yet I know that it will be well with those who fear God"[31].

A. Lauha pretends that in Koh 9:1, *kî* does not express a logical connection with the immediately preceding context, but must be regarded as an asseverative particle, which underlines that the unit which begins here is connected with Koheleth's general ideas[32]. This is a possible reading but the pericope which begins here can be connected with what precedes it, the theme of 8:19-8:2 being: "man's knowledge is limited and incompetent for the high goal of mastering fundamental or ultimate questions"[33]. However, G.S. Ogden has adduced convicing arguments to regard 8:16-17 as a conclusion and 9:1 as the beginning of another pericope: he refers to a number of rhetorical features, the most important of which is the *inclusio* of *nātattî ʾet-libbî lāḍaᶜat ḥokmâ* in v. 16, which refers to 1:13-17 and 8:9, thus spanning the whole of 1:13-8:17. In 9:1 the author opens a new section with a significantly varied example of the *nātan lēb* phrase, viz. *ʾet-kol-zeh nātatti ʾel-libbî*[34]. Thus a possible connection of 9:1 with the preceding verses would be quite loose indeed, and the emphatic meaning of *kî* at the beginning of the pericope becomes highly probable. In Koh 11:8 again *kî* can be emphatic. H.L.Ginsberg remarks that *kî ʾim* here has the value of *ʾapîlû* and E.S. Artom equals *kî* to *lākēn*. H. Witzenrath calls it a "bekräftigendes Modalwort"[35]. This is preferable to an explicative meaning, although the latter cannot be excluded[36].

The *kî* of Koh 7:18 is translated "Ja" by A. Lauha, which means that he regards it as emphatic, although he does not go into the question in his commentary[37]. According to M. Geier its force is adversative[38]. This is possible after the negative phrase in v. 18a, but the adversative is rather weak, since, on the whole, 18a is not negative. This *kî* is commonly understood as explicative: "It is good to do both, for he who fears God fulfills both". Even the emphatic meaning suggested by Lauha comes very close to a causal one.

According to Lauha again, the verses 11:1,2,6 show a parallel structure: a concessive imperative, followed by an adversative *kî*. In his parsing of *kî* he follows F. Ellermeier[39]. Lauha asserts that these *kî* - clauses cannot express the motive for the preceding clauses, but G.S. Ogden, following the common opinion, calls them motive clauses without further comment[40]. Lauha's reading of the text is possible *in se*, but it does not recommend itself. Especially in v. 6 the causal nexus between the two halves of the verse is patent: you should sow in the morning and the evening, i.e. always, because you do not know which time is the most suitable. The case of vv. 1-2 is more difficult because the exact meaning is not clear and much debated. Lauha supposes that they convey the idea that one cannot presage whether carelessness will result in damage or prudence in advantage. This interpretation has some famous defenders, such as K. Galling, H.W. Hertzberg and F. Ellermeier[41]. In the opinion of these scholars the imperatives do not really express an order or advice; they have a conditional or concessive force: "Suppose you throw your bread on the water, still you would find it back after a long time". But in general the critics consider the imperative clauses as an advice given by Koheleth, although they are divided as to what the advice exactly means: the ancient tradition, e.g. Jerome and Rashi, followed by many moderns, read here a counsel to practise charity, but in modern scholarly literature a strong tendency favours a different interpretation: take risks by investment in a trading venture, more in particular in maritime commerce (v. 1), but divide the risk, "do not put all your eggs in the same basket" (v. 2). In both interpretations *kî* introduces motive clauses.

In sum, in Koheleth emphatic *kî* occurs several times, but in most of the instances an alternative understanding, mostly causal-explicative, is possible.

Notes

1) G. Wildeboer, *Der Prediger* (*Kurzer Handkommentar zum AT*, vol. 17), Tübingen 1898, p. 128.
2) Cf. W. Vischer, *Der Prediger Salomo*, München 1926, p. 65; J.J. Serrano, *Qohélet o Eclesiastés*, in *La S. Escritura, texto y comentario, AT*, vol. 4, Madrid 1969, p. 548; W. Zimmerli, *Prediger* (*Altes Testament Deutsch*, vol. 16/1), Göttingen 1980, pp. 155-156.
3) F. Ellermeier, *Qohelet. Teil I. Abschnitt 2, Einzelfrage Nr.7*, Herzberg am Harz 1968, p. 10.
4) E.S. Artom, *Ḥāmēš m^{e}gillôt m^{e}pōrāšôt* (*Sifrê hammiqrā'*, vol. 13), Tel Aviv 1967, p. 82; R. Gordis, *Koheleth - the Man and his World*, New York 1955, pp. 239-240; W.J. Fuerst, *The Books of Ruth, Esther, Ecclesiastes, the Song of Songs, Lamentations* (*Cambr. Bible Comm. on the NEB*), London 1975, p. 122; A. Lauha, *Kohelet* (*Biblischer Kommentar AT*, vol. 19), Neukirchen 1978, p. 97.
5) H.L. Ginsberg, *Koheleth* (Heb), Tel Aviv 1961, p. 86; A.H.McNeile *Introduction to Ecclesiastes*, Cambridge 1904, p. 69; F. Delitzsch, *Hoheslied und Koheleth*, Leipzig 1875, p. 290; Lauha, *loc. cit.*
6) Cf. A. Schoors, "The particle *kî*" in *OTS* vol. 21, 1981, p. 251.
7) That the second *kî* is dittographic has been suggested by A. Strobel, *Das Buch Prediger*, Düsseldorf 1967, p. 84.
8) Lauha, *op. cit.*, pp. 92 and 107-108.
9) McNeile, *op. cit.*, p. 66; V.E. Reichert-A. Cohen, *Ecclesiastes*, in *The Five Megilloth* (*The Soncino Books of the Bible*), London 1946, p. 135; J.J. Serrano, *op. cit.*, p. 557.
10) G.S. Ogden, "Historical Allusions in Qoheleth iv 13-16" in *VT*, vol. 30, 1980, p. 313; cf. W.A. Irwin, "Eccles. 4,13-16" in *JNES* vol. 3, 1944, pp. 255-257.
11) Gregorius Thaumaturgus, *Metaphrasis in Ecclesiasten, ad loc.*
12) Lauha, *op. cit.*, p. 113; cf. A. Chouraqui, *Les cinq volumes, s.l.* 1975, p. 135.
13) N. Lohfink, *Kohelet* (*Die Neue Echter Bibel*), Würzburg 1980, p. 46.
14) Cf. Schoors, *op. cit.*, p. 261.
15) Lauha, *op. cit.*, p. 108; Chouraqui, *op. cit.*, p. 136.
16) E. Elster, *Commentar über den Prediger Salomo*, Göttingen 1855, p. 92, Cf. Schoors, *op. cit.*, pp. 251-253.
17) Ginsberg, *op. cit.*, p. 93.
18) Lauha, *op. cit.*, p. 122; Delitzsch, *op. cit.*, p. 312-313; Wildeboer, *op. cit.*, p. 145; McNeile, *op. cit.*, p. 74. Cf. *BHS*.
19) Cf. J. Muilenburg, "A Qoheleth Scroll from Qumrân" in *BASOR* vol. 135, 1954, pp. 20-28, esp. p. 26.
20) E.H. Plumptre, *Ecclesiastes* (*Cambridge Bible*), London 1890, p. 162.
21) M. Geier, *In Salomonis Regis Israel Ecclesiasten Commentarius*, Lipsiae 1668, p. 240; cf. *Revised Standard Version*; Artom, *op. cit.*, p. 87; Chouraqui, *op. cit.*, p. 137.
22) Cf. R.F. Johnson, *A Form-Critical Analysis of the Sayings in the Book of Ecclesiastes*, 1973, p. 163 (Emory University dissertation).
23) Reichert-Cohen, *op. cit.*, p. 156; Delitzsch, *op. cit.*, p. 323.
24) Wildeboer, *op. cit.*, p. 147.
25) Delitzsch, *op. cit.*, p. 336; Wildeboer, *op. cit.*, p. 150.
26) Lohfink, *op. cit.*, p. 61. Cf. already D. Castelli, *Il libro del Cohelet, volgarmente detto Ecclesiaste*, Pisa 1866, p. 274.
27) Cf. Gordis, *op. cit.*, p. 287.
28) Delitzsch, *op. cit.*, p. 341; Gordis, *op. cit.*, pp. 287-288.
29) McNeile, *op. cit.*, p. 78; Lohfink, *op. cit.*, p. 62.
30) Lauha, *op. cit*, p. 257.
31) A similar interpretation in Geier, *op. cit.*, p. 318; Elster, *op. cit.*, p. 107.
32) Lauha, *op. cit.*, p. 166; cf. Chouraqui, *op. cit.*, p. 144.
33) Fuerst, *op. cit.*, pp. 137-138.
34) G.S. Ogden, "Qoheleth ix 1-16" in *VT* vol. 32, 1982, pp. 158-160; cf. A. Schoors, "La structure littéraire de Qohéleth" in *OLP* vol. 13, 1982, pp. 109-110.

35) Ginsberg, *op. cit.*, p. 127; Artom, *op. cit.*, p. 100; H. Witzenrath, *Süss ist das Licht*, St. Ottilien 1979, p. 11; cf. already Elster, *op. cit.*, p. 126.
36) E.g. Johnson, *op. cit.*, p. 101; Delitzsch, *op. cit.*, p. 384.
37) Lauha, *op. cit.*, p. 131; cf. Chouraqui, *op. cit.*, p. 139.
38) Geier, *op. cit.*, p. 267.
39) Lauha, *op. cit.*, pp. 201-203; cf. F. Ellermeier, *Qohelet. Teil I. Abschnitt 1: Untersuchungen zum Buche Qohelet*, Herzberg am Harz 1967, p. 255. Also Chouraqui, *op. cit.*, p. 149.
40) G.S. Ogden, "Qoheleth xi 1-6" in *VT* vol. 33, 1983, pp. 224-226.
41) K. Galling, *Der Prediger* (*Handbuch zum AT*, vol. 1,18), Tübingen 1969, p. 119; H.W. Hertzberg, *Der Prediger* (*Kommentar zum AT*, vol. 17,4), Gütersloh 1963, p. 199; Ellermeier, *op. cit.*, pp. 256-259. Cf. H. Brandenburg, *Das Buch der Sprüche und das Hohelied*. Giessen 1971, p. 177.

Some Remarks on Cuneiform *écritures*

H.L.J. Vanstiphout, Groningen

Lees maar; er staat niet wat er staat.
(Martinus Nijhoff)

1.1. The comparative popularity of Assyriology in the latter half of the 19th century may be ascribed very roughly to three reasons: the splendour of the mostly Sargonid monuments; the romantic story of the decipherment of the script; and not least the stunning revelations of the literature contained therein. The ensuing scramble for tablets can only be interpreted from an interest in this literature; also, the large readership enjoyed by e.g. George Smith's *Chaldean Account* cannot be explained by the biblical link alone[1]. Thus interest in cuneiform literature has a respectable tradition, notwithstanding the fact that one still sometimes may be confronted with scathing references to "the lofty plane of literary texts". While I am well aware of the relative quantities of tablets devoted to literature and to other use[2], and I am not willing to reopen the Tammuz-Onion debate[3], and I certainly would agree that we do have great difficulties to master before we can begin to appreciate or understand this totally different literature, still it seems to me that there are three good reasons for a continued, even strengthened, occupation with these texts as literature. First there is their intrinsic value as literary artefacts; surely to define the relevance or importance of any literature in terms of its nearness to us in time or space would be anti-humanistic, and therefore anti-intellectual. Secondly, since we happen to possess the first fully-fledged literary system *on record* (or, by that token, maybe even absolutely?)[4], we are under an obligation to our colleagues in other fields of the humanities to treat this literature as literature, since only in this way can it be put to meaningful comparative use. But thirdly, and perhaps most importantly, within the narrower confines of traditional Assyriology we might be more aware of the fact that these texts were produced by Mesopotamians for Mesopotamians - who presumably knew that they were doing. It follows that these texts are as necessary for a reconstruction or understanding of Mesopotamian society as are other documents, traditionally regarded as more "relevant". In contrast to those more practical documents, literary texts do not just show the elements from which a system (of trade, or banking, or administration, etc....) underlying the fabric of society can be extrapolated; they are the only group of texts, paradoxically, intended at least partially to speak immediately about aspects of the system of society, or the interpretation of the world, or the framework of history - in short, about Mesopotamian Man himself. This of course also implies that our occupation with this material must be more than antiquarian or 'philological' in the narrow sense. Instead of gleaning interesting bits (usually 'parallels') from the fragmented materials, or the 'ostentatious humility'[5)] with which one confines oneself to closing up gaps in the documentation, we might try to represent and understand in an articulate way the material we do have in its natural environment, i.e. in its synchronic and diachronic sequences, and so hope to reconstruct the (partial) systems of literature *as they were written down*.

1.2. In order to indicate symbolically, as it were, an approach which I think is worthwhile, and not solely to show my erudition, I have opted for the somewhat modish expression *écritures*[6)]. Quite apart from the rather pedestrian observation that we only have written cuneiform literature, I think there is indeed a close link between writing and literature. Now writing may be perceived under various but complementary angles. Its first, <u>operational</u>, aspect consist of the execution of signs by means of an instrument on a carrier, whereby the signs are meant to represent language. Closely related is a second, <u>functional</u>, aspect: the operation is intended to convey by proxy a message, and consists therefore of the fixation in time and space of an otherwise ephemeral communication. Roman Jakobson's communication scheme[7)] applies here with a vengeance, since the operation itself establishes contact and presumes the code, while on the other hand the intention is precisely to get the message through in the absence of the addressee and sometimes the context. Therefore this functional aspect also covers conditions under which, or reasons for which, this message is thus twice encoded. A third, <u>material</u>, aspect is that the result of the operation, originated under the existing conditions, constitutes a concrete object[8)]. Starting from the realization of this material aspect of writing modern literary criticism has added a fourth and specifically 'literary' dimension - or even definition - of writing. While partaking of the other three in more than one way, it is not co-extensive with any of them or with their combination. This *écriture* may be paraphrased as <u>mode of writing</u>[9)], and it is thought to take up a middle or even mediating position between the horizontal dimension of language (horizontal also in the sense of being the extreme limit of common language available to and confining the 'writer) and the vertical dimension of style (i.e. personal style, which is rooted in everybody's psychological or even biological history. In Barthes' words style is "the writer's 'thing', his glory and his prison; it is his solitude")[10]. In contrast to both these dimensions, *écriture*, also but not exclusively defined by the three first mentioned aspects, may be said to consist of the (linguistic) form of litery language put to actual use, and thus having its own indication of social and historical meaning - which is not to say that it is historically determined, for:

> "Thus the choice of, and afterwards the responsibility
> "for, a mode of writing point to the presence of freedom,
> "but this freedom has not the same limits at different
> "moments of history. It is not granted to the writer to
> "choose his mode of writing from a kind of non-temporal
> "store of literary forms. It is under the pressure of
> "history and tradition that the possible modes of writing
> "for a given writer are established; there is a history
> "of writing .... Writing is precisely this compromise
> "between freedom and remembrance, it is the freedom which
> "remembers and is free only in the gesture of choice, but
> "is no longer so within duration .... Any written trace
> "precipitates, as inside a chemical at first transparent,
> "innocent and neutral, mere duration gradually reveals
> "in suspension a whole past of increasing density, like
> "a cryptogram"[11].

Heady stuff this; yet also this concept of *écriture* may have some practical value for us.

1.3. The purpose of this paper is then to sketch some ways in which one or another of these aspects of *écriture*, or perhaps even their combination, may be perceived to have shaped cuneiform, especially Mesopotamian, Literature[12].

2. The most immediate aspect of cuneiform literature is of course that it consists of lumps of clay, flattened and otherwise shaped into tablets and when still moist inscribed with the sharp end of a reed stylus. The signs are originally pictographic *and* abstract, but since rounded lines are difficult to execute, and it is generally cumbersome to keep on shifting the position of either tablet or stylus, the signs evolved quickly into assemblages of simple strokes, mainly in the directions N, NW and W[13].

2.1. Clay is of course abundant in Mesopotamia; it is also a very bulky material, and two most important effects of this bulkiness have been noticed before[14]. The weight or bulk of the carrier has seemingly prevented the conception of long compositions - understandably so, since even lugging Campbell Thompson's Gilgamesh edition[15] to classes is sometimes awkward. On the other hand, it is ironic that the very same factor which probably played a major role in the demise of cuneiform as such - the clay - has also assured its preservation, since it is virtually indestructible. In fact the matter of the influence of the material on the length of compositions is a bit more complicated. The longest *series* are lexical compilations[16], and their length is not matched by any literary composition. Furthermore the range of formats used for literary (and other) tablets has not remained stable through two and a half millennia; there were technical changes having implications for the shape of tablets, and probably themselves implying shifts in the functional aspect of the writings. To indicate only one area where such matters played a role: although there are relatively long compositions in the Old Babylonian period[17], these seldom exceed the length of *Lugal-e*[18]; some of them were executed on, among other formats, large tablets containing the complete compositions, sometimes on 'prisms'. While the status of these prisms remains debatable, it is obvious that they were not held in the hand, but mounted on pieces of wood or other material[19]. Since it would be impractical to hold the larger tablets while writing, we may also surmise that these too were mounted on (wooden?) frames while the writing was executed. This may be confirmed from the later type of big library copies, larger and much thinner than the OB big tablets. Tablets even tend to become objects of aesthetic value in their own right. They also tend to contain more and more text, and to arrange themselves in even larger series containing much longer compositions[20].

2.2. While the matters indicated above may be said to touch writing or our compound object of *écriture* only externally, there seems to be a possibility that the tablet as such has also had some influence on the shape of cuneiform literature in a specific way. The increasing length of compositions has already been remarked upon; yet more may be said since this first observation already implies that also the absolute length of compositions may depend upon the size of the material object. A purely arbitrary and eclectic survey of some Standard Sumerian compositions from OB times may illustrate this[21]:

Approximate number of lines:

1) Lipit-eshtar ode B[22]	60	15) *uru*^{ki} *na-nam*[36]	250
2) *en-e nĩg-du*$_7$*-e*[23]	105	16) *šà-ga-né ĩr im-si*[37]	260
3) *ab-ba ki-ri-a-šè*[24]	110	17) *uru*^{ki} *kug-kug-ga*[38]	280
4) *lú-kin-gi-a*[25]	115	18) *u*$_4$*-ri-a u*$_4$*-sud-rá*[39]	280
5) *é u*$_4$*-huš-an-ki*[26]	120	19) *sag-ki gĩd-da*[40]	280
6) *u*$_5$*-a a-ù-a*[27]	130	20) *sig*$_4$ *mùš-za-gĩn-ta*[41]	280
7) *ege-nun-e*[28]	130 (150)	21) *ur-sag-e*[42]	350
8) *u*$_4$*-ri-a-ta*[29]	140	22) Inanna and Enki[43]	410

9) *nin-me-šár-ra*[30]	150	23) *lugal-bàn-da kur*[44]	420
10) ^{d}*en-líl-sud-rá-šè*[31]	160	24) *tùr-ra-na mùš*[45]	440
11) *hur-sag-an-ki-bi-da*[32]	200	25) *u*$_{4}$*-ul-an-ki-ta*[46]	490
12) *e* ^{giš}*al-e*[33]	200	26) *é-u*$_{6}$*-nir an-ki-da*[47]	550
13) *an-gin*$_{7}$*-dím-ma*[34]	210	27) *lugal-e*[48]	560
14) *an-ta-è-a-ra*[35]	230	28) *ELA*[49]	640

It would of course be foolhardy to draw hard conclusions from this incomplete, erratic and random sample. Yet even allowing for the probability - which I do not doubt for a moment - that drawing up a complete list may well close up many gaps between the line totals, some points may be registered:

a) About 650 ll. seems to be the maximum length for an OB Sumerian composition. One should contrast this to *Atra-hasis*, with ab. 450 ll. for its first tablet alone, to *enūma eliš*, with ab. 1000 ll., and to the late Gilgamesh epic, for which ab. 3450 ll. may be calculated[50]. A lower limit of length is less easy for the Sumerian texts of the OB period; all one can say is that it may be presumed that the shortest composition written by itself on one tablet would be ab. 50-60 ll. long[51].

b) Items 2 to 16 show length to accrue gradually on the whole. Up to ab. 100 ll. the variation may be in the region of only 4 to 5 ll.; upwards from 120 the variation is mostly in the region of 10 to 20; that there is no item in the list having 180 ll. is amost certainly an accident.

3) Even in so arbitrary a list it immediately strikes us that there seems to be a decided preference for ab. 280 ll. as the length of medium compositions.

4) Above the 280 ll. mark the numbers jump by ab. 50 to 80 ll. in most cases.

A slight indication of what may be at hand here is the seemingly innocuous fact that items 26 and 27 contain double the amount of the popular size of items 17 to 20 and, at least within an acceptable range, four times the also rather popular size represented by items 6 to 9. It has long been known that the OB compositions in Standard Sumerian may be written on a variety of tablet sizes, a fact duly recognized in the best modern text editions[52]. Thus there are typical OB literary tablets containing ab. 25, 30, 35 or even 40 lines to a side; all these formats are used to make up serial editions of different size tablets and differently columnized large tablets. Also, in the case of compositions showing subdivision marks, the extant single column tablets usually coincide with these subdivisions[53]. This is of course already an important way of influencing

the shape of a text. It may rightly be said that this is more a matter of laying out the text: if necessary or simply if wanted the choice of the most opportune tablet size for the serial editions will have been dictated by the structure of the (unwritten?) text.
2.3. Yet there are indications that in fact the reverse may have happened: that the size of typical one column tablets may have brought about at least some formal features of the larger text, such as articulations within the structure of the text.

a) The Standard version of *The Instructions of Shuruppak*[54] has ab. 280 ll. laid out in the complete edition *OECT* vol. V 33 over four columns: 1-75, (76)-150, 151-(221), 222-(280). This means cols. of ab. 75 ll. allowing for a bit of blank space at the end of vol. IV. The division of the text on smaller formats confirm this picture: text U_2 (*UM 29-16-240*) contains the second half of the composition on a double column tablet starting with l. 158 - which happens to be the point where the third series of admonitions begins. Also at least some single col. tablets confirm this, although it does not seem possible to present a complete serial edition of the composition on connected single col. tablets of ab. 75 ll. with absolute certainty for the time being[55]. But much more important is the fact that the introductory formula breaking up and organizing the instructions into three series occurs at three points in the texts:
   - after the mythical introduction: ll. 6-12;
   - after the first series: ll. *78*-87;
   - after the second series: ll. *147*-157.

   The conclusion lays at hand that the organization of the otherwise unorganized (?) stream of admonitions is organized according to the *size* of single col. tablets appropriate for short compositions, i.e. ab. 65-75 ll.

b) Although the text material of *Ninmešarra* does not show with certainty tablets of 60+ lines (a possible exception is text W = *UM 29-13-535*)[56], an articulation with this format as its base remains very probable. A more natural division of the text seems to be a single col. tablet of ab. 50 lines - a type well attested; yet this seems to be more a matter of the *absolute* length of ab. 150 ll. The main articulations are: 1-65 ("Exordium"), 66-136 ("Argument"), and 137-153 ("Peroration"), which shows that the principle that a basic segment of text should be ab. 60-70 lines is seemingly so strong that it is even applied when the total size of the resulting text makes it somewhat awkward.

c) Other examples confirm this observation. In *Enmerkar and Ensuhkešdanna*[57] very important points in the story occur at ab. l. 70 (Enmerkar receives Aratta's challenge), l. 140-162 (the literal repetition of ll. 140-149 as 153-162 probably indicates that the caesura is at about l. 150; the sections contain the words of the minister of Aratta putting the challenge into effect); l. 222 (the beginning of the sorcery contest). In *The Curse of Agade*[58] relevant articulations may be found at ab. l. 85 (the end of Naram-Sin's dream) l. 148 (the end of the description of the destruction of the Ekur), l. 209 (the end of the description of the Gutian invasion). Lastly, compositions such as *Lugal-e* and *LU* are clearly organized into single col. sections of text[59].

The point of these preliminary investigations is that a case can be made for the hypothesis by which literary scribes at least in a significant number of cases arranged their text according to division marks dictated by tablet size instead of exclusively the other way around. The most popular single col. size seems to have been the 70 to 80 line tablet, at the same time the most frequent type and the type used for most short compositions[60].

2.4. Thus it might be stated that the basic unit, as well as the material end product, of cuneiform *écriture* is the *tablet* in a very specific way: at least in the OB period in Standard Sumerian literature tablet size has helped to define and shape the text, thus putting the tablet on a higher level than the purely material one of writing material. This ideological homology between tablet and *écriture* may be seen indirectly from the care with which many of the tablets were executed, from the cultural function to which some tablets were put, and not least from admittedly partisan texts extolling writing and all it stands for[61]. More direct in a way are the instances where tablets are an important motif in the development of a story: in *ELA* a tablet is written to help the messenger over his difficulty with the long and complicated message. Since it is stated that this was the first time the passage has caused arguments as to the question how the ruler of Aratta was able to read this first ever tablet. Although the text does not explicitly say so, it has been defended that he could, indeed, 'read' it[62]. On the other hand, some would say that he obviously could not, so that the passage is a logical mistake in the text. I would submit that the motif of the tablet caps the whole line of reasoning in the text, *viz.* that the text is about Sumer's cultural supremacy, best expressed by means of the tablet. Remark that the passage is placed immediately before Ishkur's intervention, which brings about the climax leading to the conclusion.

Perhaps one might say that this tablet epitomizes Sumer's cultural supremacy, which is also blessed by divine intervention [63]. Apparently, this is what matters. In *Enmerkar and Ensuhkeshdanna* the passage about the tablet is not quite clear. The text as it stands at least suggests that here also Enmerkar is making a tablet, not merely receiving one. In this case we do not know what was on this tablet, but we see that he reaches a portentous decision immediately afterwards. On the other hand it is not inconceivable that the lines in question intend to convey in a high-flown manner that Enmerkar pondered and studied the difficulty as one would study and examine a clay tablet[64]. A point common to both readings seems to be that a tablet is on an altogether higher and more important level than the mere recording of a message. That *écriture*, or a tablet, in this way of thinking has indeed an almost superhuman portending force is stated quite clearly in some places. In the newly discovered Sumerian Sargon legend it is quite clear that the existence of writing tablets is taken for granted; yet the point remains that the tablet intended to cause Sargon's death will cause Ur-zababa's downfall instead[65]. And certainly it is significant that what Anzu steals from Enlil is not the Fates, but the tablet-of-Fate[66].

3. It has been remarked that in many modes of writing an important feature is the fact that words are not used according to the social function of (spoken) language, *viz.* with a unitary or purely relational value. The power and relevance of this literary (or written) use of words resides in the fact that they are pregnant with all past (or for the reader, even future) specifications: their meaning is an ambiguous and global one - it is "full of gaps and full of lights"[67]. In cuneiform and especially classical Sumerian literature this is very much the case, and again for a specific reason and in a specific way. The cuneiform system of writing is a mixed system, consisting of a syllabic-phonemic part and a non-phonemic, logographic part. This system allows for several 'readings' of a single logogram, and the number of readings grows with the adaptation of the system to the Akkadian language in a straight manner but also, indirectly, from the consequences of the structural anisomorphy of Sumerian and Akkadian[58]. Thus, while the system itself already allows considerable possibilities for punning and intended ambiguity - a prime example is the *Hymn to the Hoe*[69] - this effect is appreciably enhanced by historical circumstances. The scribes who wrote down the bulk of Standard Sumerian literature, and presumably largely composed it, were educated in Sumerian as a subject as well as a medium in the Edubba[70]. A large part of their training consisted in mastering

the lexical lists, so that these were never very far removed from their mental horizon. Therefore one might say that punning and *double entendre* are not merely instances of their showing off their ingenuity or inventivity - though it is that as well, of course. But also it is their understanding of the literary language and mode of writing as present in their cultural environment - in short, it is an instance or a feature of their *écriture* as well. Obviously this conscious 'masking' of the text by integrating different *domains* as well as different *levels* of meaning is most important in texts that also otherwise are connected with erudition and ingenuity. A fine example is the couplet with which the Hoe challenges the Plough:

"Plough, you trace furrows - what is your furrow-tracing to me?"
"Plough, you cut (furrows) - what is your (furrow)cutting to me?"

which may also be read as:

"Plough, you are tall - what is your tallness to me?"
"Plough, you are weighty - what is your weightiness to me?"[71)]

But also other texts should be examined for the use of their vocabulary in this way, and, generally, it should be noted that many compositions outside the class of "school compositions" have to do with (verbally) *outwitting* an opponent[72)]. This culturally defined insistence on word or sound play has also led to a somewhat forbidding assemblage of symbolicisms in a number of texts of a perhaps more serious nature (*Hymn to the Hoe, Temple Hymns*)[73)]. There are no easy keys to crack this system of symbols, but one suspects that a close study of their symbolism along these lines could be rewarding. This matter deserves separate investigation, yet it should not be divorced from a more global formal approach to their concept of poetic language as such - of which language these symbolisms steeped in erudition and literature and current poetic convention (in short, in *écriture*) would form a major feature.

3.1. In some ways connected to this specific use of language in literary texts there is also the matter of *intertextuality*. This is no mere matter of copying or taking over from older compositions, but has to do with the almost universal fact that any literary composition 'means' within the system of literature perceived as such at the moment of composition. This may take the form of crude adaptation, as exemplified by some of the ways in which chunks of the Ninurta literary tradition were taken over in *enūma eliš*[74)]. But also, and far more subtly, it may be seen in underlying references to other parts of the literary system, even to other kinds of literature. An example is found in *Gilgamesh and Agga*: the means by which Agga and his host are defeated consist apparently in Gilgamesh' *melammû* or aura. Yet this aura is linked, rather craftily, to a "description" of

Gilgamesh in the form of some traditional formulae occurring as typologies for the ideal king in Royal Odes[75]. Again, intertextuality is involved in relation to (a part of) what medieval authors would probably call *inventio*: the awareness of existing texts may breed as it were other texts[76]. A specific instance may be found in the 'mythological' introduction to and setting of most Sumerian Debate poems, presupposing the genre of mythological narrative poems about origins. And here again there is at least one instance of a high degree of literary consciousness in that the traditional mythological introduction in the *Debate of the Hoe and the Plough* is omitted at the beginning, but recurs later on as part of the evidence adduced by the Hoe for its supremacy. Its functional place at the beginning of the composition is then taken by a hymnal introduction which looks like a counter-hymn, in that it stresses the Hoe's poverty, simplicity and smallness[77].

3.2. The last example has already shown that intertextuality, in its more explicit form of conscious reference to other works, may be used in an ironical way. This phenomenon is met with in the most unexpected places: it may suffice to point to Enlil's rather boorish remark in the *Lamentation over Sumer and Ur* which presupposes a knowledge of the system of history as presented by the *Sumerian King List*[78]. In fact, one may well surmise that irony is never very far away in most classical Sumerian literature, and also in much of Akkadian Literature. It may perhaps not exactly be omnipresent, but it reaches far. I think we may hazard a guess as to the reasons for this. On the one hand there is the fact that certainly Classical Sumerian literature, and in a lesser way also Akkadian literature, consciously use language - and words - with all its aspects, including the derived, script-bound polyvalence of signs, which widens the scope for irony appreciably. Furthermore, even the overt and blatant references to other texts are so numerous that it must be concluded that intertextuality is indeed very strong; it is not impossible, it is even probable, that quite a few scribes in the OB period carried the whole of Classical Sumerian literature if not in their heads, then at least in their broader awareness. Of course this enhances irony, since the tendency towards *double sens* inherent in the writing system and the functionally bilingual situation is tripled, as it were, by the constant presence of 'other' literary forms or environments, whether or not these are openly referred to. I think there is even a further, perhaps more socio-cultural, reason for the heavy incidence of irony. To return to our section 2., it must be remarked that although clay is abundant in Mesopotamia, writing clay tablets must have remained an occupation of relatively low frequency and small diffusion; the main reason will have been the complicated nature of the script and the ensuing high cost (in abstract terms) of training and thus indirectly of *écriture* - or tablets[79]. All these factors will also have caused a class or group consciousness, which can indeed be found often in overt or hidden references to the value of the scribe over that of other people[80]. But every scribe or composer of literary works knows that he is in a way *writing* for other scribes, that his *écritures*, in the more technical sense, will only reach his brethren in the craft, who have about the same education and erudition, but which also gives him much scope to trade on this supposed knowledge of other texts. In fact the references to *tablets* referred to above (section 2.4) also taste faintly of irony, which in this case is self-irony[81]. This is surprising, for scribes (read: intellectuals) throughout the ages have not always or in every culture excelled in this.

3.3. All the preceding remarks have concentrated on the really "written" aspects of cuneiform *écriture*. Yet one of the implications of the scarcity and expense of writing is that most people could not read, and that consequently the consumption of *écriture* was auditive, or aural[82]. This is a real difficulty for us, since we have no way of reconstructing an audience, and therefore no way of checking in how far this auditive aspect of the life of literature interfered with the autonomous existence of the written text. In any case we can but remark that, except for very few instances where probably really different stories have somehow confluenced[83], in those cases where texts differ appreciably, one version is padded out against the other. And this padding out is done with strings of text lines built upon list of items from lexical texts - another kind of writing closer to the scribes than to other people[84]. Yet the problem of *oral literature* exists. In how far is our *écriture* merely a fixation of something existing beforehand in oral form, and only written down when people (Who? The composer? The audience? Both?) were satisfied that it had reached its best form? The difficulties with the oral literature theory in this crude way are many; many of the so-called characteristics of oral literature are no longer accepted as such. Indeed, one may well ask "How oral is oral literature?"[85]. Of course, much more study of individual texts is needed, but I would provisionally suggest that at least Sumerian classical literature shows so many explicitly "written" features that a *direct* oral forerunner is very hard to point out[86]; a better opportunity seems to lie in a close comparison between OB Akkadian and later versions of 'identical' texts; but here again, this might only be a shift in mode (in this case also fashion) of writing - or *écriture*[87]. Furthermore, I feel that especially in the case of epic or other narrative texts we should bear in mind that even if somehow an oral form could be found preceding the written fixation (how would this be done?), the probabilities are that the difference would be very small: what we surely know of oral narrative poetry now shows that the *performance* in these cases where such things can be controlled, plays the same role of extracting the discourse from the *hic et nunc* and the socialized narrowing of application, and of *fixing* the discourse, thereby also creating possibilities for enriching its form and contents. Where, in those circumstances, is the difference with *écriture*?[88)]

4. Undoubtedly there are many more important specific aspects of cuneiform literature. I have selected only these few, since they seem to me to be the most immediate general characteristics of this literature viewed under its aspect of an assemblage of cuneiform tablets. I am well aware that even so these aspects ought to be studied more deeply, but this should happen either in detail on individual texts, or globally in a long and exhaustive study. Provisional as these remarks are, it gives me great pleasure to offer them to a man who has always been interested simply in writing, more so when it is bedevilled with not just one, but two or three or more possible readings and when its formal aspect is dictated by the carrier, and mostly so when its correct practice as producer and consumer depends on a deep and wide knowledge of all and sundry texts - and on irony.

Notes

1) See G. Smith, *The Chaldean Account of Genesis, containing the description of the Creation, the Fall of Man, the Deluge, the Tower of Babel, the Times of the Patriarchs, and Nimrod; Babylonian Fables, and Legends of the Gods; from the Cuneiform Inscriptions*, London 1876. The lively interest in intellectual circles in Great Britain at the time may be seen from the fact that in the London Weekly *The Athenaeum* in the sixties and seventies of the past century we see not only T.H. Huxley stoutly defending his ancestry against all comers, but we also regularly meet Rawlinson, Hincks, Bosanquet, Fox Talbot, even Oppert and Ménant. And Messrs. Gilbert and Sullivan thought that the ability to "read and write cuneiform" would make "the very model of a modern major general". The scramble for tablets has been recounted many times; one of the most enjoyable accounts is still H. Rassam, *Asshur and the Land of Nimrod*, New York 1897, if only for the amount of gossip and backbiting contained therein.
2) See A.L. Oppenheim, *Ancient Mesopotamia*, Chicago 1964, pp. 16-19.
3) See I.J. Gelb, "The Philadelphia Onion Archive" in *Studies in Honor of Benno Landsberger* (*AS*, vol. 16), ed. H.G. Güterbock-Th. Jacobsen, Chicago 1965, pp. 57-62, esp. p. 62. Gelb's attack may be justified in thrust; it is not so in direction. The tendency he was opposed to was proposed by an archaeologist, not by a literary scholar: A. Moortgat in *Compte rendu de la 3e rencontre assyriologique internationale*, Leiden 1954, pp. 18-41. His position about the immortality of Tammuz had been earlier expressed in his book *Tammuz. Der Unsterblichkeitsglaube in der altorientalischen Bildkunst*, Berlin 1949, but was completely demolished at the Leiden Rencontre precisely on literary grounds. In no sense whatsoever has there ever been a 'debate' between these two factions inside philological Assyriology, and therefore public declarations of the type "Personally, I have always sided with the onions" are not only vainglorious; they are empty. Literary texts, as well as onions, are facts from daily life. And while it may be true that we will never know what the nectar of the gods was until we discover what was the daily bread of the people, it strikes me as somewhat strange that we so often omit to ask the Mesopotamian himself: what did *he* think? Some of his thoughts he may have written down, even in non-tabulated form.
4) That is, *if* some modern theorists are right, written fixation - or *écriture* - tends to expand literature into a complete system. The most important motive force will be intertextuality, made possible by written fixation.
5) For this term, and also for the thought, see P. Zumthor, *Parler du Moyen Age* (= *Parler*), Paris 1980, p. 91.
6) R. Barthes, *Le degré zéro de l'écriture*, Paris 1953. I used the translation (by A. Lavers - C. Smith) R. Barthes, *Writing Degree Zero*, New York 1967.
7) R. Jakobson, "Linguistics and Poetics" in *Style in Language*, ed. T. Sebeok, Cambridge, MA 1960, pp. 350-377. See also L.R. Waugh, *Roman Jakobsons's Science of Language*, Lisse 1976, pp. 23-26.
8) This statement should perhaps be expanded. Of course the concrete object in our case is a prepared lump of clay with a text on it. Both aspects are necessarily present, and to the Mesopotamian - and the Assyriologist - they are a whole: a *tuppum*.
9) See Barthes, *op. cit.*, pp. 9-18; J. Culler, *Structuralist Poetics*, London 1975, pp. 133-135; J. Derrida, *L'écriture et la différence*, Paris 1967, *passim*. Derrida takes the view that a written text (an *écriture*) can only be taken as independent from writer and reader alike - which is certainly not absolutely wrong in the diachronic sense. This position has been admirably expressed by P. Mullen in the *Times Literary Supplement* of 18 October 1985 in the form of a poem:

DECONSTRUCTION

D'ya wanna know the creed'a
Jacques Derrida?
Dere ain't no reada
Dere ain't no wrider
Eider.

Somewhat less compactly, P. Zumthor gives two more complementary and concrete approaches to writing. In *Parler*, pp. 83-87, he elaborates on the material and socio-cultural circumstances accompanying the act of writing; in *id.*, *Essai de poétique médiévale*, Paris 1972, he applies *écritures* to the great generic categories empirically found in Medieval literature.

10) Barthes, *op. cit.*, p. 11.

11) Barthes, *op. cit.*, pp. 16-17. In view of the simile used by Barthes (writing is a cryptogram), it is interesting to note in passing that J. Derrida, one of the inventors of the term *écriture* with this content, also coined a term *grammatologie* (J. Derrida, *De la grammatologie*, Paris 1967) for the study of *écriture*. Cf. I.J. Gelb, *A Study of Writing*, Chicago 1969^3, who pleads for a new science of writing to be called 'grammatology' (pp. V, 23 and 249).

12) At least in this sense that the articulation, textual shape and size, polyvalence of "meaning", allegory perhaps but certainly irony, and also consumption, are (partially) to be ascribed to aspects of the act of writing and the circumstances in which this act is performed.

13) See generally M. Powell, "Three Problems in the History of Cuneiform Writing: Origin, Direction of Script, Literacy" in *Visible Language* vol. 15, no. 4, 1981, pp. 419-440; M. Civil, "The Sumerian Writing System: Some Problems" in *OrNS* vol. 42, 1973, pp. 21-34; I.M. Diakonoff, "Ancient Writing and Ancient Written Language" in *Sumerological Studies in Honor of Thorkild Jacobsen* (*AS*, vol. 20), ed. S.J. Lieberman, Chicago 1976, pp. 99-121.

14) M. Powell, *op. cit.*, p. 435.

15) R. Campbell Thompson, *The Epic of Gilgamish*, Oxford 1930, measures 38,5x26x2,5 cms.

16) See e.g. M. Powell, *op. cit.*, p. 435.

17) See below.

18) See below note 20.

19) As to their status, W.W. Hallo - J. van Dijk, *The Exaltation of Inanna*, New Haven 1968, p. 38, interpret these 'prisms' (many of them are four-sided anyway) as "models for dictation". One would then naturally expect them to be real 'models' in the sense that they give the best or at least a reliable text. This expectation is not always fulfilled: J.S. Cooper, *The Curse of Agade*, Baltimore 1983, p. 46, remarks upon the poor quality of the prisms (and one other complete edition). As to their mechanics, note that many of them still show marks of (wooden?) pins or even holes drilled right through prisms:see J.B. Nies-C.E. Keiser, *Historical, Religious and Economic Texts and Antiquities* (*Babylonian Inscriptions in the Collection of James B. Nies*, vol. 2), New Haven 1920, p. 35 and photographs pl. 62-64.

20) See below, section 2.2., remark a). There are many beautifully produced big tablets in e.g. the *K* and related collections of the British Museum. See e.g. Fr. Thureau-Dangin, *Une relation de la huitième campagne de Sargon*, Paris 1912; W.G. Lambert, "The Fifth Tablet of the Epic of Erra" in *Iraq* vol. 24, 1962, pp. 119-126, published a literary tablet shaped in such a way that it could be worn as an amulet. A remarkable series of handsomely made tablets contained the complete text of the compositions *Angimdimma* (see below n. 34) and *Lugal-e*; see H. Vanstiphout, review of J. van Dijk, *Lugal-e ud me-lám-bi nir-ĝál*, Leiden 1983, to appear in *Aula Orientalis*. These tablets are single column, and the double lines are neatly surrounded on all sides by a double ruling, producing a very nice box-like effect, or even the effect

of writing boards - which may be just coincidence. This tablet type is unique (see C.B.F. Walker *apud* J. Cooper, *op. cit.* in n. 34, p. 35, n. 1).

21) I have only chosen from among those compositions whose size is known or can be guessed with some confidence. Perhaps a complete list of known composition lengths would be interesting from a statistical point of view. Note in any case that the numbers must not be taken absolutely. Tablets do not work like this.

22) H. Vanstiphout, "Lipit-Eštar's Praise in the Edubba" in *JCS* vol. 30, 1978, pp. 33-61.

23) There is no edition, though one by G. Farber-Flügge is forthcoming. See provisionally the text from Ur in C.J. Gadd-S.N. Kramer, *Ur Excavations. Texts, VI. Literary and Religious Texts*, 1st part (= *UET* 6,1), London 1963, no. 26; with duplicates, the text can be completely reconstructed - though hardly understood.

24) S.N. Kramer, *Two Elegies on a Pushkin Museum Tablet*: *A New Sumerian Literary Genre*, Moscow 1960; A.W. Sjöberg, "The first Pushkin Museum Elegy and new Texts" in *JAOS* vol. 103, 1983, pp. 315-320.

25) W. Römer, *Das sumerische Kurzepos 'Bilgameš und Akka'*, Neukirchen 1980; the review by J. Cooper in *JCS* vol. 33, 1981, pp. 224-241 is indispensable. See also H. Vanstiphout, "Towards a Reading of 'Gilgamesh and Agga'. Part 1: The Text" to appear in *Aula Orientalis*; *id.*" --. Part 2: Construction" to appear in *OLP* vol. 17, 1986.

26) A.W. Sjöberg, "Nungal in the Ekur" in *AfO* vol. 24, 1973, pp. 19-46; see now T. Frymer-Kensky in *RA* vol. 79, 1985, pp. 93-94 who discovered a main caesura at l. 63!

27) S.N. Kramer, "U_5-a a-ù-a: A Sumerian Lullaby" in *Studi in onore di Eduardo Volterra*, vol. 6, Roma 1969, pp. 191-205.

28) G. Gragg, The Kesh Temple Hymn" in A. Sjöberg-E. Bergmann, *The Collection of Sumerian Temple Hymns*, Locust Valley, N.Y. 1969, pp. 157-188. Two totals are given since one exemplar adds a strophe - unduplicated - of 18 ll. See *ibid.*, p. 175.

29) C.A. Benito, *'Enki and Ninmah' and 'Enki and the Word Order'*, University of Pennsylvania 1969 (diss.); the text listed here is *Enki and Ninmah*.

30) Hallo-Van Dijk, *op. cit.* in note 19.

31) D.D. Reisman, *Two Neo-Sumerian Royal Hymns*, University of Pennsylvania 1969 (diss.), pp. 41-102 (The great Enlil Hymn).

32) The Dispute between *Lahar and Ashnan*. There is no edition; see provisionally *UET* 6, 1 nos. 33-35 with duplicates.

33) The dispute between *the Hoe and the Plough*. No edition; see H. Vanstiphout, "On the Sumerian Disputation between the Hoe and the Plough" in *Aula Orientalis* vol. 2, 1984, pp. 239-251 for bibliographical references and a study.

34) J.S. Cooper, *The Return of Ninurta to Nippur* (*Analecta Orientalia* vol. 52), Rome 1978.

35) The *Inanna hymn* in Reisman, *op. cit.* in note 31, pp. 147-211.

36) W. Heimpel, "The Nanshe Hymn" in *JCS* vol. 33, 1981, pp. 65-139.

37) B. Alster, *Dumuzi's Dream*, Copenhagen 1972.

38) P. Attinger, "Enki et Ninhursag̃a" in *ZA* vol. 74, 1984, pp. 1-52.

39) B. Alster, *The Instructions of Šuruppak*, Copenhagen 1974.

40) Cooper, *op. cit.* in note 19.

41) A. Berlin, *Enmerkar and Ensuhkešdanna. A Sumerian Narrative Poem*, Philadelphia 1979.

42) A.J. Ferrara, *Nanna's Journey to Nippur* (*Studia Pohl: series maior*, vol. 2), Rome 1973.

43) No *incipit* is preserved. G. Farber-Flügge, *Der Mythos 'Inanna und Enki' unter besonderer Berücksichtigung der Liste der m e* (*Studia Pohl*, vol. 10), Rome 1973.

44) C. Wilcke, *Das Lugalbandaepos*, Wiesbaden 1969.

45) The lamentation over Ur (= *LU*). A new edition is forthcoming. See S.N. Kramer, *Lamentation over the Destruction of Ur* (*AS*, vol. 12), Chicago 1940.

46) The second Lugalbanda Story, of which there is no edition. See most recently W. Hallo, "Lugalbanda excavated" in *JAOS* vol. 103, 1983, pp. 165-180.
47) Sjöberg-Bergmann, *op. cit.* in note 28.
48) Van Dijk, *op. cit.* in note 20.
49) S. Cohen, *Enmerkar and the Lord of Aratta* (= *ELA*), University of Pennsylvania 1973 (diss.).
50) W.G. Lambert-R. Millard, *Atra-hasis. The Babylonian Story of the Flood*, Oxford 1969; W.G. Lambert-S.B. Parker, *Enuma eliš. The Babylonian Epic of Creation. The Cuneiform Text*, Oxford 1966. See also Campbell Thompson, *op. cit.* in note 15. The length of the Gilgamesh epic is calculated on the basis of ab. 300 ll. per tablet (i.e. ab. 50 ll. per col.) for tablets I-XI and half length for tablet XII.
51) This is borne out by the facts, more or less. There are even shorter individual compositions (short tales etc.), but these are found only on chrestomathy tablets. Some examples of short compositions are: S.N. Kramer, "Ninurta's Pride and Punishment" in *Aula Orientalis* vol. 2 1984, pp. 231-237; *id.* in *op. cit.* in note 24, the second elegy; *id.* "The Ideal Mother: A Sumerian Portrait" in *Bell* vol. 40, 1976, pp. 403-421.
52) See e.g. Cooper, *op. cit.* in note 19, pp. 41-49; Hallo, *op. cit.* in note 46, pp. 171-172; Hallo-Van Dijk, *op. cit.* in note 19, pp. 36-39.
53) As the forthcoming new edition will show, this is the case in *LU*.
54) Alster, *op. cit.* in note 39, pp. 26-33.
55) *ibid.* pp. 28-29. From the material presented there this matter cannot be resolved, but neither can it be denied as a possibility. Only autopsy can tell.
56) Hallo-Van Dijk, *op. cit.* in note 19, p. 38.
57) Berlin, *op. cit.* in note 41.
58) Cooper, *op. cit.* in note 19.
59) *LU* (see note 45) shows three lengths for the songs: ab. 40 ll. (4 songs), ab. 45 ll. (2 songs) and 55 to 75 ll. (3 songs). *Lugal-e* (see note 20) is more regular: no tablet has less than 40 ll.; no tablet has more than 54 ll. - and the extremes may be brought more closely together by close study of the text.
60) See note 51.
61) See A.Sjöberg, "In Praise of Scribal Art" in *JCS* vol. 24, 1972, pp. 126-131; *id.*, "Der Examenstext A" in *ZA* vol. 64, 1975, pp. 137-176.
62) See the text in *ELA*, pp. 85-87 and 136-138, ll. 500-540. See G. Komoróczy, "Zur Ätiologie der Schrifterfindung im *Enmerkar*-Epos" in *Altorientalische Forschungen* vol. 3, Berlin 1975, pp. 19-24, which is an interpretation perhaps confirmed by the discoveries of M.W. Green, "Animal Husbandry at Uruk in the Archaic Period" in *JNES* vol. 39, 1980, pp. 1-35, esp. pp. 16-17. Incidentally, no satisfying interpretation of l. 540 has been given. I wonder whether - since Enmerkar has just invented writing (l. 504) - we do not have here the very first mention of the term *cuneiform* in the Sumerian: "It is a nail!" (gag-àm).
63) In order to understand this in its context, a formal study of the 'Matter of Aratta' is needed. See a first attempt in H. Vanstiphout, "Problems in the 'Matter of Aratta'" in *Iraq* vol. 45, 1983, pp. 35-42.
64) See Berlin, *op. cit.* in note 41, pp. 44-45, ll. 76-77 and the comments on p. 73. The equatives might point to a simple simile. Yet I think with Berlin that the reference is to a 'real' tablet.
65) See J.S. Cooper-W. Heimpel, "The Sumerian Sargon Legend" in *JAOS* vol. 103, 1983, pp. 67-82, esp. ll. 30, 53-56 and p. 82. It should not pass unnoticed that with this discovery the matter of the legendary tales about Akkadian heroes (see the admirable summary by J. Goodnick Westenholz, "Heroes of Akkad" in *JAOS* vol. 103, 1983, pp. 327-336) becomes really very interesting. For we see

that the well-known "Aussetzungsmotiv" (see most recently B. Lewis, *The Sargon Legend*, Cambridge, MA 1978, with plenty of references) is now combined *in the person of the hero* with the Uriah or Bellerophon motif (the Letter of Death) - as it is in many later forms of the tale; see e.g. E. Cosquin, "Le lait de la mère et le coffre flottant" in *Revue des questions historiques n.s.* vol. 39, 1908, pp. 353-425; S. Grudzinski, "Vergleichende Untersuchung und Charakteristik der Sage vom Findelkind das später Kaiser wird" in *Zeitschrift für romanische Philologie* vol. 36, 1912, pp. 546-576; V. Tille, "Das Märchen vom Schicksalskind" in *Zeitschrift des Vereins für Volkskunde* vol. 29, 1919, pp. 22-40. This is certainly one more pressing reason for a general study of this extremely interesting group of texts (see Goodnick Westenholz, *op. cit.*, p. 336), perhaps deserving of the name *gesta accadorum*.

66) See provisionally B. Hruška, *Der Mythenadler Anzu in Literatur und Vorstellung des alten Mesopotamien*, Budapest 1975. A new edition by M. Vogelzang is in preparation.

67) Barthes, *op. cit.*, pp. 43-52.

68) See now the impressive analysis by A. Cavigneaux, *Die sumerisch-akkadischen Zeichenlisten. Ueberlieferungsprobleme*, Ludwig-Maximilians-Universität zu München 1976 (diss.).

69) See note 23. The same tendency may be seen in *The Hoe and the Plough*, for which see note 33. One example may suffice: at one point the plough is boasting in terms not unlike those used in Royal Odes (nobles at the side, the country kneeling down, the foreign countries looking up awestruck ...); the hoe turns this into a gang of workmen repairing the plough with the ploughman standing by exasperated and, one imagines, cursing. This is of course a carnavalesque situation in the full socio-cultural meaning of the term. And then see the remarks of P. Zumthor in *Parler*, pp. 70-72. In this connection it is exciting to note that King Ishme-Dagan had this Debate performed for him (see M. Civil, "Išme-Dagan and Enlil's Chariot" in *JAOS* vol. 88, 1968, pp. 3-14, esp. p. 7 l. 83).

70) For the Eduba, see A.W. Sjöberg, "The Old Babylonian Eduba" in *AS*, vol. 20, pp. 159-179; see also H. Vanstiphout, "How Did They Learn Sumerian?" in *JCS* vol. 31, 1979, pp. 118-126.

71) Vanstiphout, *op. cit.* in note 33, pp. 240-241.

72) Such as *ELA*, *Enmerkar and Ensuhkešda*, a number of Enki stories and his behaviour in general (a thorough study is needed; see provisionally R. Falkowitz, "Discrimination and Condensation of Sacred Categories: The Fable in Early Mesopotamian Literature" in *Entretiens sur l'antiquité classique* vol. 30, 1984, pp. 1-32, esp. pp. 13-24).

73) See note 23 and note 28.

74) W.G. Lambert in *ZDMG* Suppl. 3, vol. 1, 1977, pp. 64-73, esp. 70-71.

75) See e.g. the Lipit-eštar odes B (see n. 22) and A (F.R. Kraus, "Das altbabylonische Königtum" in *Le palais et la royauté. Archéologie et civilisation*, ed. P. Garelli, Paris 1974, pp. 235-261, esp. pp. 250-252).

76) This might happen by straight parody: see the text edited by E. Sollberger, "The Rulers of Lagaš" in *JCS* vol. 21, 1967, pp. 279-291. It might also happen more subtly, and this might even give scope for the rise of new genres, as in the *Tale of the Fox* (See W.G. Lambert, *Babylonian Wisdom Literature*, Oxford 1960, pp. 186-209), where clever use is made of at least three other literary kinds (Fable, Dispute, Epic) in order to make an original genre: the satirical animal epic. The patchwork technique, consisting of making new works out of bits and pieces of existing works by *assemblage*, is much used in the later periods for liturgical works (See M. Cohen, *Sumerian Hymnology: The Eršemma*, Cincinnati 1981, *passim*, and R. Kutscher, *Oh Angry Sea*, New Haven 1975). Yet it never reached the high quality of e.g. the *ecbasis captivi*, Charles Jennens' libretto for Händel's Messiah or for that matter the text of the Roman Mass.

77) See Vanstiphout, *op. cit.* in note 33, pp. 248-249.
78) There is no edition of the *Lamentation*, though one by P. Michalowski is forthcoming; see S.N. Kramer in *ANET*[3] pp. 611-619. The remark is found in ll. 366-372, and refers to Th. Jacobsen, *The Sumerian King List* (*AS* vol. 11), Chicago 1939, *passim*, where these or comparable terms are used for the change of dynasties.
79) We have no idea of the real cost in micro-economic terms. It stands to reason that it must have been costly to keep up this kind of training over a longer period for even quite small groups of pupils. As far as I know calculations of the incidence of literacy based upon amounts and typological distribution of tablets have not as yet been undertaken, I presume for the very sound reason that the ratio one would have to use will depend heavily upon the political preference or the degree of optimism of the calculator.
80) See note 61.
81) See Cooper-Heimpel (*op. cit.* in note 65), p. 82.
82) See Zumthor, *Parler*, pp. 84-85.
83) E.g. the central Gilgamesh text: the Adventure of the Cedar Forest, for which see now A. Shaffer, "Gilgamesh, the Cedar Forest and Mesopotamian History" in *JAOS* vol. 103, 1983, pp. 307-313.
84) Cases in point are *The Home of the Fish*; see H. Vanstiphout, "An Essay on 'the Home of the Fish'" in *Studia Paulo Naster oblata II: Orientalia antiqua* (*Orientalia lovaniensia analecta*, vol. 13), ed. J. Quaegebeur, Leuven 1982, pp. 311-319, esp. the schemes; also Attinger, *op. cit.* in note 38: the text from Ur adds what is essentially a simple list.
85) See R. Finnegan, "How Oral is Oral Literature?" in *BSOAS* vol. 37, 1974, pp. 52-64. See also L.D. Henson, "The Literary Character of Anglo-Saxon Formulaic Poetry" in *Publications of the Modern Language Association*, vol. 81, 1966, pp. 334-341, who erodes the oral-formulaic theory by proving that the formulae in Anglo-saxon poetry belong to the lettered style, heavily influenced by the Latin example.
86) The closest we come to this might be surmised to be the proverbs and other short stories and fables, interspersed between proverb collections. Yet the proverb format is not especially oral, and the fable certainly is not. Doubts about the "popular" or "oral" character of this group of texts have been raised - quite rightly - by R. Falkowitz, *The Sumerian Rhetoric Collections*, University of Pennsylvania 1980 (diss.).
87) M. Vogelzang has shown a definite and almost quantifiable shift of *écriture* by closely comparing some "identical" passages of the OB and the later versions of the Anzu poem, in her communication to the 32nd *Rencontre assyriologique internationale* (Münster 1985).
88) In modern studies of the problem some negative conclusions seem to be: a) there is not that much difference between traditional written and traditional oral literature; b) the differences there are, are not those used as criteria by the great theorists of oral literature. See R. Finnegan, *Oral Poetry*, Cambridge 1977; P. Zumthor, *Introduction à la poésie orale*, Paris 1983; W.J. Ong, *Orality and Literacy*, London 1982; see also Zumthor, *Parler*, p. 85.

Two Akkadian Auxiliary Verbs

Le'ûm "to be able" and *mu'ā'um* "to want"

K.R. Veenhof, Leiden

Auxiliary verbs are poorly represented in the classical Semitic languages, where tense, mood, aspect and even semantic specifications of the verb are expressed by means of inflection and the use of specific verbal stems. This makes an analysis of the use of the two best known Akkadian auxiliary verbs worthwhile, in particular the way in which these frequently negated verbs are syntactically related to the verbal form which expresses the main verbal meaning of the sentence and to its direct or indirect object. Some introductory remarks on the meanings and tenses of these verbs (which implies a morphological analysis) have to be made first.

1. Auxiliary and main verb

Both verbs do not only qualify other, main verbs, but occur also independently. This is not only the case in subordinate clauses, where a main verb can logically be supplied from the main sentence, e.g. by interpreting *kīma tele'û epuš* "do as you can" as abbreviation of *kīma epēšam tele'û epuš*. *Le'ûm* (see *CAD* L 155f., 2) is well attested as "to have power (over)", "to overpower", with personal accusative object, and as "to win (against)" in connection with lawsuits (even in the stative, without object, *le'āku*, "I am the winner", OB Susa). In Ugarit a legal document can be its subject since it "prevails over" somebody. In OA we have, moreover, some occurrences of a form with *t*-infix, *la al-té-e*, used in an absolute sense, which seems to mean "I am at the end of my possibilities"[1]. In some cases where we could supply an infinitive (e.g. *epēšam*) a translation "to master" makes sense (*CAD* L, 154b-c), in particular when the object is an abstract noun (once *marûtam*, "the art of fattening"). In some OAkk names *ì-le* occurs in the meaning "(the god) has overpowered", as is clear from examples where a personal pronoun in the accusative follows (*ì-lí-ši-na-at*, *MAD* 3, 158).
Evidence for the use of *mu'ā'um* as an independent verb is less clear but still available in OA to which this always negated verb is restricted. Again we are tempted to supply a main verb from a preceding

sentence, since *lā mu'ā'um* normally refers back to an activity mentioned before. Assuming the standard construction with the main verb in the infinitive (accusative) we may be entitled to regard *ṭuppī luptā šumma lā tamu'ā* ("write my tablet, if you don't want ...", BIN 6,201:19) as abbreviation of *šumma lapātam lā tamu'ā*. But there are several occurrences without infinitive and with a nominal or pronominal object and a few *lā imu'a/imū's* in absolute use, which require a translation "he refused", "he was unwilling". Examples are CCT 4,24a: 42 (in reaction to a request of a favour[2]) and ICK 3,141:29 (object a verdict; see *CAD* M 436b,c-e). As was the case with *le'ûm* we also have a few occurrences of a form with *t*-infix in absolute use[1].

2. Morphology and tense

Both verbs occur mostly in the present tense, not surprisingly since they describe a person's ability or frame of mind. *GAG* § 78b considers *ile'i* a "prefixed stative" (actual statives are rare and late, or derived from the verb used independently as "to win"), but does not mention *imu'a* as such. *GKT* 235 note 1 observes that in conditional sentences with *šumma* only the present occurs. Still, we have a small number of occurrences of the preterite and some forms with *t*-infix. Distinguishing between present and preterite is syntactically not always easy and requires also a morphological analysis, complicated because the verbs, *l'i* and *mū'*, both are "double weak".

2.1. *le'ûm*

2.1.1. The present regularly shows "strong", uncontracted forms and the presence of the "aleph" or syllable boundary is frequently indicated. We have forms with and without "Umlaut"; those attested are (cf. also *CAD* L 152f.):

ala'e OAkk MVN 3,104:6' (*a-la-e*); OB, once AbB 6,218:28 (*i-la-a'-a*, fem. plur.); MA KAV 1 ii:76,88 (*i-la-a-'e*, *i-la-'-e*); EA 286:42,287:58 (Jerusalem, *a-la-a'e*; cf. 137:27 and 211:18); Ugarit PRU 4,136:43 (*i-la-e-šu*), *Ugaritica* 7 pl. 29 RS 34.147:2 (*i-la-a'-e*); NA

ale'e OA passim, once *a-li-i* CCT 4,7b:25

ele'i OB passim, usually *e-*<u>LI</u>*-i*, but also *e-le-'i*, AbB 10,7:27, *e-li-'i* AbB 4,137:10, *i-le-'i* AbB 4,119:8, *i-le-'ù-ú* AbB 2,147:10 (plur.)

ele'e/i passim MB (including Boğazköy and Ugarit) and NB.

The final vowel coalesces with that of a vocalic ending: *ta-le-a* (2nd pers. plur. OA), *te-le-ú* (2nd pers. sing. subjunct. OB; note *te-le-'ù-ú*, subj. AbB 6 153:17). The syllable boundary can be indicated by plene writing, with extra vowel sign: *te-le-e-a-ú* AbB 5,159:13' (*a* for aleph?), *te-le-e-i* AbB 6,103:23, *ta-le-e-a-ni* ICK 1,13:14; KTHahn 15:23 (OA). The last form cannot be parsed as **tale'eāni* in view of the spelling *ta-le-a-ni* in KTS 21b:12 and BIN 4,220:9, but it is noteworthy that in OA all forms of the sing. in the subjunctive (ca. 15 times) use the plene writings like *a-le-e-ú*. The extra *-e-* could mean *ale'e'u*, *alē'u*[3] or suggest a glide as syllable boundary. This possibility is suggested for *a-le-e* (OA) in *GAG* § 106t, but is unlikely in the absence there of even one single writing with extra *-e-* or *-i-* (as is the case in *tù-qá-i-a* // *tù-qá-a* for *tuqajjā*).

GAG § 106t assumes for OB also contracted forms of the present, *ilî* in southern Babylonia (e.g. CḪ § 54, xv:20, written *i*-<u>LI</u>-*i*). A graphic distinction between *ile'i* and *ilî* is impossible, if the syllable boundary is not clearly marked, since <u>LI</u> has the values /*le*/ and /*li*/. Von Soden's conclusion rests on comparison with a similar verb, *še'ûm*, "to look for", for which he notes the spelling *i*-<u>ŠI</u>-*i*, taken as *išî*. Such spellings are not common but limited to the Larsa area. In this group of texts (*AHw* 1223a,2), however, we also have a spelling *i*-<u>ŠI</u>-*'i-i* (YOS 8,72:9), with syllable boundary. A form **iši'i* being impossible (without contraction the second vowel should be *-e-*), we have to assume a purely graphic feature: the use of <u>ŠI</u> to write /*še*/, actually attested for southern Babylonian OB according to *Das akkadische Syllabar*, 1967[2], 50 no. 261 ($še_{20}$).

For northern Babylonia *GAG* § 106t assumes a contraction to *ilê*. The evidence consists of a limited number of spellings with final *-e* of which I can list AbB 1,50:8; 6,4:15; 7,157:11; 9,88:11; 252:12; 262:23; PBS 7,82:12 and ARM 1,91:7'; 2,127:46. Possibly also UCP 9/4 no. 21:25, with a spelling *e*-<u>LI</u>, a present tense according to the context. These references support Von Soden's conclusion, but not unanimously. In AbB 6,4 we have both *e*-<u>LI</u>-*e* and *e*-<u>LI</u>-*i* (l. 12), in AbB 1,50:8 the spelling *ti*-<u>LI</u>-*e* indicates irregular spelling of *i/e*, and PBS 7,82:15 has a spelling *i*-<u>LI</u>-*i* (Stol, AbB 11,82 reads the name [*i-l*]*i-ma-i-le-e*). Moreover, two of the references, AbB 9,252 and 262, are in typically southern texts (from the "Water for Larsa" archive). It is difficult to make a choice between the alternatives (contracted forms (*ilê*) or irregular spellings) and perhaps a third solution: *ile'e* (with vowel harmony), cannot be excluded. Note in this context ARM 10,101:17 with the accusative suffix *-inni*: *te-le-e-en-ni*, *tele'enni*.

2.1.2. The preterite is strong (*il'e*, etc.) in OAkk (*il-e*, /*jil'e*/ in names), OA (*ta-al-e-ú* VAT 9218:28, il_5*-e-ú-ni* TC 3,32:25) once in Mari (*il-ú*, 3rd pers. sing. subj., ARM 2,30:9), and perhaps in Boğazköy, *i-el-'i*, KUB 3, 14:77. In OB we have *ilē*, with contraction, according to *GAG* 106t, a form graphically indistinguishable from a putative contracted south Babylonian present *ilê*. But it is remarkable that none of its occurrences - identified from context, in a report on past action or from the *consecutio temporum* - shows a plene-writing. We always have *e/i*-LI in ARM 2,101:18; 4,23:15; 10,57:13; A 1101 (*La voix de l'opposition en Mésopotamie*, 1973, 184):10; TCL 18,150:21; 152:18; VAS 7,10:9. A rare plural form (graphically identical to the present, unless the syllable boundary is expressed in writing, as in *i*-LI-*'ù* CT 29,17:10) is *i*-LI-*ú* in ARM 1,74:12. We also have two curious spellings in one and the same text, the record Gauthier, *Dilbat* 30:12f., where the context demands a preterite ("they won (the lawsuit) against them"): *i*-LI-*ú-šu-nu-ti* (13)*i*-LI-*i-ú-šu-nu-ti*. The curious repetition, if not a simple mistake, could imply that the second spelling is the corrected, better one. It might indicate a glide, *ilijū*, or long *ī*, *ilī'ū*. The latter interpretation finds support in CT 8,42a:8, *i*-LI-*i-šu-nu-ti*, "he won against them", and would suggest a preterite form *ilī*. It is difficult to make a choice when the ancient spellings are not consistent. *CAD* may be right in preferring *ili*, even without long final vowel. The two occurrences with additional *-i-* are both before long personal suffixes and may represent secondary lengthening, perhaps due to stress[4)].

2.1.3. The perfect tense in OB is written *te-el-te-a* (AbB 8,101:12), *il-ti-'ù* (AbB 6,12:7), *el-ti-'e/i* (IḪ) (Gilg. P.I:9); cf. *il-te-'e* in Alalakh Texts 13:10. This indicates an uncontracted form *ilte'e*, supported by writings in Boğazköy, where *el-te-'e*[5)] alternates with *el-te-'-e*. Later spellings with *el-te-e* (Ugarit, Alalakh level IV, see *CAD* L 155f.) may reflect the same form but also a contraction to *eltē*.

In OA we have six occurrences of a form written *al-té-e*: RA 51,5:29 *ina ṣibtim lā al-té-e*; KTHahn 5:5 *lā al-té-e amuwat*; BIN 6,23:24 *ina pirdātim la al-té-e*; CCT3, 7a:16 (why does she say) *ulā al-té-e*; CCT 4,26b:10 *malama kaspim 5 mana gamālika ula al-té-e*; ICK 1,183:22 *šumma al-té-e*. There are no syntactic reasons to take them as perfects, as *GKT* § 98a does ("I have now become powerless"?), and in KTHahn 5 *al-té-e* is followed by a present tense. *AHw* 547a and *CAD* L 156,3 take them as I/2 or Gt stem, presumably in the present tense, which seems required by the context. The form with *t*-infix seems to lend a particular, even emotional emphasis to the declaration of inability, as the context of KTHahn 5 shows. CCT 4,26b supports this idea, when compared to the normal construction *gamālka ale'e*, "I am able to do you a favour". Both the *-ma* added after *mala* and the word order *kaspum 5 mana* (instead of *5 mana kaspim*) warrant a translation: "I am absolutely unable to do you a favour, even for an amount of only 5 minas of silver". See below on *mu'ā'um* with *t*-infix.

2.2. *mu'ā'um*

2.2.1. This verb, attested only in OA, according to *GKT* § 98b has the following forms. Present tense *amu'a* (*a-mu-a*, also written with glide *a-mu-wa*); the final *-a* coalesces with the vowel of a vocalic ending: *i-mu-ú* (3rd pers. plur., ATHE 63:3), *ta-mu-a-ni* (2nd pers. plur. subj., kt c/k 101:10), *ta-mu-ú* (2nd pers. sing. subj., KTS 17:8). Preterite: *amū*, written *a-mu-ú* (<*amū'*), certainly attested in CCT 5,17b:18 and TC 3,84:36[6]. Perfect: *amtu'a* (also written with a glide, *am-tù-wa*), plural *im-tù-u-ni m* (CCT 3,49b:8).

2.2.2. Almost all occurrences seem to be in the present tense, apparently because a rather static description of a person's will or willingness is used: "he is/was willing to ...". A punctual preterite would be needed to report a negative decision reached in the reference time of the letter: "he refused". The scarcity of preterites indicates that even in such cases the focus normally is on the result of such a decision, reported in the present tense used as a time neutral (prefixed) stative. The two certain references for a preterite we have occur when the verb is used in an absolute sense, without object, e.g. in CCT 5,17b, a testimony in the first person of an encounter which had taken place. The person speaking reports that when he was made a commercial offer "he refused". But in such contexts one also uses the present tense (examples quoted *CAD* M 436b,e). Actually, preterite forms may be less rare than it seems, because verbal forms with plural or subjunctive ending (where the final *-a* of the present tense disappears may be present as well as preterite.Of the texts quoted in *CAD* M 436b,e, CCT 4,28a could be a preterite, and this may be true of CCT 4,24a:42 and BIN 4,151:23 too. At times only context and syntax may provide a clue. The present tense is used in *šumma*-sentences, in some relative sentences (e.g. *ša la imûni* , EL 274B:12) and has to be assumed when the scribe uses other verbs in the present tense (ICK 2,141:29f. *kīma... lā imûma sikkī ukallu*; KTS 17:17f.: *ištuma lā tamû* refers back to preceding *lā imu'a*). In some cases it is impossible to decide, and only statistical arguments favour the present tense.

The fact that only two certain attestations of *imū* as preterite are known may raise the question whether a preterite really exists or is used. Could these forms, since there is no semantic or syntactic problem in taking them as such, not be in the present tense (irregular writings, perhaps contracted)? There is good reason for this question on account of the following facts: a) The only precative attested is *li-mu-a* ("if he is willing", *JCS* 15,127:21, alternative to the negative *laqā'am lā imua* in line 28), which implies a preterite *imu'a*, identical to the present tense. Were both identical or took the scribe, in the absence of a preterite, the present *imu'a* as a base for his precative? *GKT* § 98b tries to solve this problem by writing *limū'a(m)*, suggesting a short form of a ventive after *imū*, in itself uncommon. But the ventive is unusual with this verb and we have only one attestation in *lā im-tù-ú-nim* (CCT 3,49b:8), where it may be due to attraction since the main verbal action is *alākum*, "to go, to come". b) In VAT 9251:6 the form *i-mu-ni-a-tí* (preterite, without -*a*-) is used, where the closely connected text TC 2,10:rev.11' describes the same fact with *i-mu-a-ni-a-tí*. c) In Ka 1092 (courtesy V. Donbaz), *maḫāram lā i-mu-a* in line 35 alternates with *laqā'am lā a-mu-ú* in line 40. d) The plene writing *a-mu-ú* in what seems to be preterite forms in the singular is unusual in OA which does not systematically indicate final long vowels; cf. the forms of *awā'um* (*GKT* § 99a) preterite G and Gt singular in the indicative. Could *a-mu-ú* (*amū* or *amu'*) be a contracted form of *amu'a*, which would imply a preterite *amu'a* or the existence of a present tense only? I see no possibility to decide the matter. For our syntactic analysis of the constructions of the auxiliary verb, fortunately, it does not make much difference.

2.2.3. We have, finally, four occurrences of a form with *t*-infix which *GKT* § 98b interprets as perfects, *CAD* M 435b as I/2 or Gt stems, and *AHw* 665a as I/3 or Gtn stems. Who is right? The texts are syntactically not very informative. KTS 42a:1 is the first line of the "second page" of a missing letter and allows no conclusions TC 3,93:27 reads: "the god said": *awātini ulā im-tù-a* (preceded by *kala awātim .... tamtiši*); CCT 4,49b:8: "since ... they are holding back the caravans" *alākam lā im-tù-ú-nim*; BIN 4,45:35: "the 30 textiles which PN_1 brought up from GN PN_2 *lá im-tù-a-šu-nu*, saying ...". A choice, again, is difficult, since all occurrences seem to admit a translation as present tense ("he refuses", "is unwilling"), the syntax does not demand a perfect (notwithstanding *tamtiši* in TC 3,93[7]), and the use of a form with *t*-infix seems to be conditioned by semantics. An interpretation on analogy with *alte'e*, treated above, seems advisable. A perfect(ive present) is not excluded, but a lexical Gt seems preferable.

2.3. *lēmu/lemû*

We have to include this word because its meaning, "being unwilling", and its constructions are very similar to those of *mu'ā'um*. Being attested in all periods of Babylonian, but conspicuously absent in OA, it seems to be in good complementary distribution with OA *lā mu'ā'um*[8].

2.3.1. *CAD* L 125, which lists the word als "*lemû* (*lemu*, *lemmu*) adj.", observes in its discussion that only stative forms are attested in context, while some lexical lists give *lēmu* as an "adjectival form". In order to explain this feature it remarks: "Possibly there existed a defective verb **lemû* and from MB on its stative *lemi* was replaced by the predicative state *lēm(u/i)*". The use of the words "predicative state" implies an interpretation as an adjective or "adjectival form". This picture needs correction. The ending of the OB stative clearly is *-u*, as indicated by two OB references quoted in *CAD* to which we can add AbB 8,103:11': *le-mu-ú nadānam* (3rd pers. sing. masc.). The words "predicative state *lēm(u/i)*" suggest the existence of a form without final vowel, which is not correct, since the late form *le-em-ma* is not to be taken as *lēm* + enclitic particle *-ma*, but as alternative spelling of *lēm* + vowel, as the variant *le-em*!*-mu* shows. The references in the lexical lists, *le-e-mu*, also indicate the final vowel, not a nominative ending. The form *lēmu*, moreover, is not late but rather old. It has turned up recently in an Ur III text (21st century B.C.), NSATN no. 613:8: *li-i-mu nadāniš*, "he is unwilling to give" (again with *-u* as final vowel).

2.3.2. All forms attested are in the stative and there is no reason to consider the word an adjective; it is never used attributively or substantivized as a noun[9]. Since it shows personal inflection (note the forms of the 2nd pers. sing.) and a verbal rection (it governs an infinitive in the accusative), it has a clear verbal character. Together with the fact of the complementary distribution with *la mu'ā'um* this suggests an interpretation as a compound of the negative particle *lā* + a finite form (presumably *imu'a/imū*) of the verb *mu'ā'um*, which also accounts for final *-u*. The structural impossibility of a verb consisting of a particle + finite verbal form is responsible for the fact that the resulting word was treated as kind of "pseudo stative". It differs from *laššu*, also a compound (of *lā + išû*), which lacks a verbal rection and is attested not only with stative endings but also as an adjective[10].

The (original) long first vowel must go back to contraction in the compound, subsequently shortened in order to adapt the word (almost a quadriliteral stem) to the pattern of the verbs *tertiae infirmae* with final *-u*. The spellings of the 2nd pers. sing. (*le-me-a-at, le-me-a-ti, le-mi-at, le-ma-at)* indicate a proces of colouring, assimilation and contraction of vowels (*limu'at* > *lemu'at* > *leme'at* > *lemât*)[11]. *Lēmu/lemû* is normally construed with inf. in the accusative, but in a few later texts it also occurs with an impersonal object, a word, a prayer, where we have to translate "to disobey, to refuse".

3. Syntactic relations

We treat all three auxiliary verbs together, because there is a basic similarity in the way they are construed, though not all possibilities are attested with all three, probably mainly in consequence of their distribution and frequency. See for references not given *AHh*, *CAD* and, for constructions with the infinitive, J. Aro, *Die akkadischen Infinitivkonstruktionen* (Helsinki, 1961; StOr 26).

3.1. *With finite verb in a paratactic construction (only le'ûm)*

Statistically rare but attested in old and young texts. In OAkk: [5'] *be-lí mi-*su_4 [6'] *la a-la-e-ma* [7] *la a-la-kam*, "my lord why is it impossible that I come?" (MVN 3, 104 rev: 5'ff.; repeated *lā* in an interrogative sentence, cf. *MAD* 3, 157). In OA: *aššumi* [19] *PN*... [20] *merašu mēt* [21] *lá ni-*il_5*-e-ma lá ni-li-ik-šum*, "as for PN..., (since) his son is dead we could not go to him" (C 18:18ff.; unpubl., transliteration Landsberger). In OB: *kīmaman te-le-'i di'am kabta kullatiššu tašdud*, "(if not...), how could you have endured this grave *di'u* disease in its entirety" (*RB* 59, 1952, 246:51; composition about a "righteous sufferer"); note the asyndetic construction without connecting *-ma*.

Younger texts (*CAD* L 154b, c) show various constructions. In the imperative, with *-ma*: *le-'-e-ma maṣṣarta... ú-ṣur-ri*, "try to keep watch" (*YOS* 3, 144:13; NB). Without *-ma* and without tense agreement: *šumma te-le-'-e taštaṭar*, "if you are able to write" (*BSOAS* 20, 264:9; the perfect of the conditional sentence does not affect *le'ûm* which retains its customary present tense)[12].

In NA *šunu i-la-'-i ikabbusū*, "they will come when possible" (ABL 531 rev:15), the lack of number agreement indicates that *ila'i* functions as an impersonal modal particle, "possibly", comparable to *ibašši*, "certainly, really, actually" (*CAD* B, 155) and *laššu* in *laššu lā*, "absolutely not" (*CAD* L, 110a, c)[13].

3.2. *With infinitive*

3.2.1. With *infinitive in the terminative* (cf. Aro 116ff.)

An early example is *2 ma-na* <u>KÙ.BABBAR</u> [5] *ša um-ma at- ta- ma* [6] *PN* [7] *li-ti-na-ku-um* [8] *li-i-mu na-da-/ni-iš*, "as for the 2 minas of silver of which you said: 'PN must give them to you', he is unwilling to give (them)" (NSATN 613:4ff., Ur III). One may compare *PN nadāniš qabi*, "PN is under order to give" (*RA* 13, 133:10, Ur III; cf. *MAD* 2^2, 142 bottom), which may alternate with a construction with infinitive in the accusative, *nadānam iqbi*, (TMH NF I/II 7:7t.) In OA: *šumma* <u>TÚG</u> *lá i-mu-ú lá-qá-iš*, "if they refuse to take the textiles" (TC 1,

13:11ff.), where an infinitive in the terminative is the only possible solution (now supported by its occurrence with *līmu*), which refutes the hesitations of Hecker and Hirsch[14]. With pronominal suffix in OA: *mamman lá-qá-i-šu úlā i-mu-wa*, "nobody wants to take it" (TC 2, 42:13). Interpretation as infinitive in the genitive[15], accusative singular (Aro 106, 3.123), or plural (*GAG* § 150a) is very unlikely; the accusative is different, attested in *mamman lá-qá-ú'šu lá i-mu-a*, "nobody wants to take it" (OIP 27, 13:13'ff.; with vowel harmony, from *laqā'ašu*). No OB examples are attested (note a similar construction in *tabāliš ulā anandikka*, UET 5, 10:10), but the construction survives in the later 'hymnic-epic dialect', *naparšudiš lā le'e/a*, "they are unable to escape" (*Enūma Eliš* IV:110; cf. *AfO* 26, 1978/9, 26b, b).

3.2.2. With *ana* + *infinitive*.

Very common for expressing purpose and goal, but there is, in particular in OB with verbs like *qabûm*, "to order", and *šapārum*, "to order in writing", some overlap with inf. in the accusative as object of a sentence (Aro 124f.). The ambiguity may be rooted in the availability in older Akkadian of the two constructions mentioned under 3.2.1., *nadāniš nadānam qabi*[16]. The use of *ana* + inf. with our auxiliary verbs could reflect the same ambiquity, but being mainly restricted to provincial, 'peripheral', Akkadian, substrate influence seems more likely (note e.g. in Hebrew the regular use of *yākōl* + *l^e* + inf.)[17].

Boğazköy: *parzilla ana epēši le-mi-e-nu*, "we are not willing to make iron" (KBo 1, 14:21); *ana šullumišu lā i-le-ú*, "if they are unable to pay back" (PRU 4, RS 17.130:27; edict of Hattusili III discovered at Ugarit[18]). Ugarit: the ships are very old *lā i-la-a'-e ana alāki ajjakamma*, "they are no longer able to go anywhere" (RS 34.147:1ff., *Ugaritica* VII pl. 29); El Amarna: one single example from Tyre, *lā i-lí-ú-nim ana ṣabāt*, "they were unable to take (the city)" (EA 149:66), beside the use of inf. in the acc. in *šumma ni-li-ú ṣa-bat GN*, (EA 93:19, Byblos). In a hymn to Nabû, *ana parā'a le-e-mu*, "unwilling (unable?) to cut" (*ZA* 4, 252:19)[19].

Two hybrid OB occurrences are difficult to classify: *ana PN ana* A.ŠÀ *šāti turram aqbi* (AbB 4, 68:10), where the editor assumes the omission of a name after the second *ana*, and *anāku ana anniātin ḫasāsam ūl e-le-i* (*RA* 62, 20, HE 191:15'), Birot: "I cannot understand anything of this" (does *ana* depend on *ḫasāsum*, cf. ARM 2, 29:12?).

3.2.3. With *infinitive in the accusative*.

3.2.3.1. *With infinitive alone*, very frequent in all periods (Aro 77ff.), e.g. *šaqālam lā imû* (OA), *alākam lemu* (OB Mari), *naparkâm ūl ele'i* (OB), *atmâ lā le'i* (*OIP* 2, 161:21). The auxiliary verb may govern more than one inf., *naparkâm u ittika nanmuram ūl eli* (TCL 18, 152:18). Note *ša marūtam ile'û*, "who knows the art of fattening" (ARM 5, 46:9), with abstract verbal noun as object, paralleled by *ša immerātim šūkulam ile'û* (ibid. 18). The inf. regularly precedes the auxiliary verb, but the reversed order is standard in EA and not infrequent in literary texts (*CAD* L 153f., 5'), for stylistic reasons (already OB lit., *JCS* 15, 8 iii:4 *ul ele'i k*[*ašāssa*]). With *lemûm* the inf. may follow (ABIM 19:14; UET 5, 6:9), as is the case with *lēmu* (Ur III) quoted under 3.2.1. In EA the construction is frequently recognizable from the case ending *-am* (88:21, 102:19, 105:30) or *-a* (81:21, 104:51, 114:37, etc.), but note simple *uššar* in 82:22. The subject may follow the auxiliary verb and precede the inf., [*lām*]*e tele'ūna amelūtum* [*dag*]*āla*, "the people cannot look at ..." (EA 249:13; cf. 79:39f.).Note in Sh. 911 + 922:6 (OB) the periphrastic *ša emūq šūkulišunu tele'û*, "those which you are able to feed", alternating with simple *ša šūkulam tele'û* (line 16).

3.2.3.2. *With infinitive and noun as object*, in all periods, in two constructions. a) *Verbal rection* (Aro 90ff.), very common, e.g. *našpertam ... ša šamā'am lā imûni* (CCT 6, 15b:11ff., OA), *ša ḫarranam alākam lā ile'û* (ARM 14, 70:7'). The noun regularly precedes the inf., but note with *lemû: kunukkātim... le-mu-ú nadānam* (AbB 8, 103:9'-12'). In EA, where the auxiliary verb comes first, the nominal rection (below, b) is predominant, but note perhaps *lā ala'e muššera* KASKAL (EA 287:58, Jerusalem), where *-a* is the accusative ending (cf. *lā ala'e erāba*, EA 286:42), but logographic KASKAL admits both *ḫarrāna* and *ḫarrāni*. The noun as object can have a pronominal suffix or be in the construct state, *ṣibūt bēlia kāta epēšam ele'i* (AbB 2, 86:29f.). In literary texts the word order may be different, e.g. *enšam ana danni tele'i turram* (prayer to Sin, *Handerhebung* 128:11), *ūl ile'i maḫārša* (En.El. III:53).

b) *Nominal rection* (Aro 98ff.), not infrequent in younger and literary texts, absent in OA and OB letters, and restricted to Mari: *ubbub ṣābim ūl tele'i*, "you cannot carry out a census of the troops" (ARM 1, 42:18); *wu'ur wardim u bī* <*t*>*ia... ūl ele'i*, "am I unable to govern my subjects and my household?" (108:16); *apāl bēlia ūl ele'i*, "I cannot answer my lord" (13, 125:3'f.); and *nadān neqētim ūl elê*, "I cannot offer the sacrifices" (2, 137:46). This construction may have been inspired by cases where the noun is the logical subject of the infinitive (Aro 89, 3.58-59) and especially where the inf. is subject of the sentence) (e.g. *wašāb ḫazannim ūl rittum*, "the presence of the mayor is not appropriate", 2, 137:47)[20]. The frequent West-Semitic use of the inf. in a construct state may provide an explanation. In EA the nominal rection is standard, cf. 93:20, 109:56,

114:44 (*laqi* ÌR-*ka*), 126:7, 211:9, 264:9f., 326:15, where the case of the noun is difficult to establish and theoretically a verbal rection is not excluded, since the inf. in the acc. may occur without case ending (82:21f.: *lā ili'u uššar*, "I cannot send"). But the spellings *ipēš mimmi* (89:43, 116:52), *uššar* LÚ-*lim* (113:29), *aṣi abulli* (244:16) seem to leave no doubt that the noun is in the genitive. In EA we have a rare example of substitution of such a construct state by infinitive + *ša*, *lā ile'e ezabi ša matāt GN*, "he cannot abandon the lands of GN" (287:62).

3.2.3.3. *With infinitive with suffixed pronominal object.* Examples occur in all periods (Aro 105ff.), e.g. *kullaša lā nile'û* "(since) we cannot keep it under control" (ARM 4, 25, 6), *mamman lá-qá-ú-šu lā imu'a*, "nobody wants to take it" (OIP 27, 13:13' , OA), *epēssu ūl nile'i*, "we cannot make it" (AbB 10, 41:13), note in EA *laqāia* (79:40, 82:7, 114:23?), *laqāši* (83:20), *naṣarši* (238:9) and *laqā [šina]* (124:53), following the auxiliary verb, but *uššaršunu... lā ili'u* (105:86) and *šaḫāṭši ili'ū u ṣabātši lā ili'ū* (106:12f.) preceding it. The (mistaken) use of -*ši* indicates the verbal rection. A problem arises when dative suffixes are called for, incompatible with the infinitive. One solution is to add them to the auxiliary verb instead, OB *ištiat epēšam i-le-i-kum*, "he is able to help you" (TCL 18, 94:17)[21], OA, with *mu'ā'um*, *tadānam lā i-mu-(a-)ni-a-ti*, "he refused to give it to us" (VAT 9251:6 // TC 2, 10 rev:11'). In UET 5, 6:9 adding a dative suffix to a 2nd pers. stative of *lemûm* may have been considered problematic, hence *jāšim leme'āti nadānam*, but there is also a contrast, "you gave copper to my principal(s), but to me you did not want to give (anything)!".

The transfer of the pron. suff., however, is also attested for accusative suffixes. With *mu'ā'um* (OA), *kaspam šašqulam lā ta-mu-a-šu*, "you refused to have him pay silver" (VAT 9226:17), *kīma mamman laqā'am lā i-mu-ú-šu*, "since nobody wanted to take it" (BIN 4, 151:23), *kīma magāram lā i-mu-a-ku-nu*, "since he refused to grant their wish" (CCT 6, 22b:22); with *le'ûm*, in Mari, *šumma šūṣâm ūl* (sic!) *te-le-e-en-ni*, "if you cannot get me out" (ARM 10, 101:17). Some of these constructions are optional, since we have comparable inf. with acc. suff.: *šūtubašina tele'i* (*Bagd. Mitt.* 2, 1963, 59 iv:25, OB), *laqā'ušu lā imu'a* (OA, quoted above), *gamālkunu ale'e* (CCT 4, 211b:15, OA) . The shift may have been due to hesitation to use an inf., basically a noun, with both a nominal and a pronominal (suffixed) object[22], and to the unacceptability of an inf. Š with pronominal object (*kaspam šašqulšu*).

Something similar is the case with *gamālum* "to oblige (somebody with regard to something)" in OA, with two accusatives *ṣibtam lā agammiluka*,

TC 3,87:18, in an oa h). We have a suffixed infinitive in *gamālka ale'e*, "I can oblige you" (TC 2,20:16), but when a nominal object has to be added this does not appear in the accusative (**kaspam gamālka ale'e*). Twice one uses *mala* + inf. and once *ina* instead of accusative: *mala šīm ṣubāti kilišunu gamālka ale'e*, "I can oblige you with regard to the price of all these textiles" (CCT 4,33a:18f.), *malama kaspim 5 mana gamālika ula alte'e* (CCT 4,26b:5-10; see 2.1.3.), and *ina annikim*(AN.NA) *gamālku[nu] ile'e*, "he is able to oblige you with regard to (by means of?) tin" (CCT 3,11:25f., correct Aro 106,3.124). Note in particular the hesitation between *mala ... gamālka* and *gamālika*.

A different problem with a pronominal suffix is presented by *apālum* in OB, "to answer (somebody for something)", also construed with two accusatives (AbB 5,92:30ff.). When used with *le'ûm* we meet a variety of constructions, simple accusative of the infinitive (*apālam tele'i*, AbB 3,28:29), infinitive and noun in the accusative (*bēlī apālam ūl ele'[i]*, AbB 10,68:4')[23], infinitive with nominal rection (*apāl bēlia ūl ele'i*, ARM 13,125 rev.: 4') and infinitive with pronominal accusative suffix (*apālšunu ūl ili*, ARM 2,94:21, cf. TCL 17,57:58). Most frequent in this latter category, however, is the form *apālia ūl tele'i* (AbB 3,37:13; 6,103:22f.; 7,172:18; 9,187:29f.; BM 96310:30, courtesy van Soldt), where we would expect **apālī*, " to answer me". There is no convincing explanation for the genitive form *apālīa*, cf. Frankena *SLB* 4, 1978, 128 f., but we note that there seems to be not a single occurrence of an inf. with an accusative 1st pers. sing. pronominal suffix denoting the *object* of the action expressed by the infinitive[24]. The unacceptability of such a form may provide an explanation and the form used may have been inspired by the use of the inf. in the terminative or with *ana* (above 3.2.1. and 3.2.2.) or the use of *mala* noted above (the alternation between *mala ... gamālka* and *gamālika*; cf. also *mala apālika ūl maṣiāku*, PBS 7,66:23f., OB).

3.3. *In subordinate clauses with mala and kīma (of le'ûm only)*

3.3.1. *Mala + verb in the subjunctive.*

Attested in two uses, a) with *mala* alone, and b) with *ana mala* (*ammala*). Both types of clauses qualify the action expressed by the main verb, *mala tale'āni awitī butqā*, "settle my affair as well as you can" (KTHahn 15:23), and *ammala talē'u awātia gumur*, "finish my case as well as you can" (ATHE 30:7), but the second seems to make the subordinate clause slightly more independent of the main verb. The first type may function as object of the main verb, *mala alē'u lalqe*,

"I will take whatever I can" (CCT 4,9a:8), but always refers back to the nominal object mentioned previously. We could supply an infinitive of the main verb, *mala laqā'am ale'u lalqe*, but such an infinitive is never written. In some cases the preposition *ana* may not belong to *mala* but depend on the main verb, in particular with *tadānum* + *ana*, "to sell for", *ammala ilē'u liddimma*, "let him sell (tin and textiles) for whatever he can" (*RA* 59,166:17f.). But since *tadānum* may occur alone we could also translate "sell as well as you can".
There is always agreement of subject between subordinate and main clause and the verb in the latter is normally in the imperative or precative. BIN 4,2:13 (quoted *CAD* L 154,d,1') is no exception since the quotation should end with the imperative *abkam*, "ship here", while *lušeribūnim* indicates how this should be done, "by having them bring it in".
See for two occurrences of *mala* + infinitive + *le'ûm* above 3.2.3.3. (with *gamālum*); *immala* is not used and attested only once in OA (Aro 68, 2.102).

3.3.2. *Kīma (kī) with le'ûm.*

Occurs in all periods, in younger texts also as *kī ša* (MB, NB) and *akī ša* (NA; see *CAD* L 155,2' for references). For OA and OB Stola (*WZKM* 63/4, 1972,95,e) defines its meaning as "restrictive" when used with *le'ûm* and he proposes translating "in wieweit, soweit wie". The restrictive notion actually seems to be inherent in *le'ûm*, and *kīma* is less specific ("according to, in agreement with"). In later texts, when kings and gods are the subject, their unlimited power and endless possibilities even suggest a meaning "to wish" for *le'ûm* and *kīma* (*akī ša*) implies free choice. This may obtain for OA and OB too, where we can translate "as well as possible", frequently with the implication that the person addressed is left a free hand. Comparison between *awātim kīma tale'āni gumrā* (BIN 4,220:9) and *ammala talē'u awātia gumur* (ATHE 30:7, both OA) shows that the difference in meaning can be nil. Occasionally *kīma tele'û*, when followed by the imperative of *epēšum*, can be considered the logical object of this main verb: "do whatever you can", as was the case with similar phrases introduced by *mala* (see above 3.3.1.). The number of OA occurrences with *kīma* should be increased by BIN 6,51:19 and ICK 1,63:18, both quoted *CAD* L 155a,e) with *šumma*. The use of the subjunctive, unknown with *šumma*, requires a reading [*ki-m*]*a* in the first and [*k*]*i*'-*ma* in the second reference (both confirmed by collations kindly made by V. Donbaz).

3.4. *Word order*

This subject has been repeatedly touched upon above, but a short survey is in order. The auxiliary verb regularly precedes the main verb in paratactic construction with two finite verbs (3.1.). With infinitive the auxiliary verb follows in "classical" Akkadian, but with the infinitive in the terminative there is variety, even in one dialect (OA; 3.2.1.). The same ambiquity exists with *ana* + inf. (3.2.2.), mainly in peripheral Akkadian. EA letters always have the auxiliary verb before the inf., with two exceptions 105:86 and 106:12f. In the second reference we may assume "foregrounding" due to emphasis, since two alternatives are contrasted (*šaḫātši ili'ū u ṣabātši lā ili'ū*, "they could attack her but not take her"). In OA and OB we have examples where the mention of two alternative possibilities results in the repetition of the main verb (*šumma pazzuršunu tale'ā pazzirāšunu*, "if you can smuggle them, smuggle them, if not..." KTHahn 13:6f., OA; *šumma tattaṭlama etēqam telte'a* «*tet*» *etqā*, "if you would observe that you can get through, get through...", AbB 8, 101:10-13), instead of simple *šumma tale'ā pazzirā* etc. as in *šumma tale'ā...eliā* (BIN 6,66:32f.). In literary and younger texts the auxiliary verb may precede the inf. for stylistic reasons. Note the same line of the Epic of Gilgamesh in the OB, *nuššašu ūl elte'e*, and younger version, *ūl ele'ia nūssu* (*CAD* L 153,5'). *Lēmu/lemû* precedes the inf. several times and twice when it follows it the inf. with added *-ma* may have been "foregrounded" (AbB 1,30:19; 36:7). Nominal object and subject regularly precede the infinitive (except with nominal rection, 3.2.3.2b), also in EA, with the subject accordingly between auxiliary verb and inf. (79:39; 249:13). In younger and literary texts there is again some variation. The position of the adverbial, frequently prepositional adjuncts is normally before the complex of inf. + auxiliary verb, but there are exceptions, not only in a legal record (*tēniq..nadānam ana PN ūl ili*, VAB 6,78:6-9), but also in letters (*alākam ana ṣērīka ulā nilê*, AbB 9,88:9ff., cf. OBTR 143:15ff.; *alākam ana maḫria ila'ā*, AbB 6,218:28, contrast AbB 10,73:11). In all cases the negation (*ūl*, *lā*, *ulā*) immediately precedes the finite verb and is accordingly repeated in parataxis (3.1.).

3.5. *Agreement and attraction.*

In general there is agreement of tense and mood. For tense see 3.1., where a late literary text provides an exception. Agreement is remarkable in AbB 8,101:10-13, quoted under 3.4., where the conditional perfect of the first verb is carried over to the auxiliary *le'ûm*, in consequence of what Kraus calls "Koppelung". Attraction or transfer of mood (*GAG* § 82c.) is in evidence in what seem to be ventive forms of the auxiliary: *mimma epēšam ūl* <*ė-*>*le-em* (ARM 13, 145:46f.), *šapāram ana ṣēr PN ūl e-le-em* (OBTR 143:15ff.), *alākam ūl e-le-em* (ARM 3,8:29), perhaps *awatam qabâm ūl e-le-a* (AbB 1,32:6), and certainly in *alākam lā im-tù-ú-nim* (CCT 3,49b:8), in several cases clearly caused by the ventive character of the main verb (*alākum*, *šapārum*). There is no need from the context to assume the transfer of the pronominal suffix to the auxiliary verb, discussed in 3.2.3.3., but the impossibility of adding a ventive ending to an infinitive may be the reason for adding it to the auxiliary verb. Lack of number agreement in *ila'i ikabbusū* in a NA text, discussed under 3.1. proves the use of *ila'i* as impersonal modal particle, "possibly".

Notes

* Cuneiform text editions are cited according to the sigla listed in *CAD*. Dialects/periods of the Akkadian language: OAkk - Old Akkadian, OA - Old Assyrian, OB - Old Babylonian, MA - Middle Assyrian, MB - Middle Babylonian, NA - Neo-Assyrian, NB - Neo-Babylonian, EA - El Amarna.

1) See for these forms below under 2.
2) Correct *CAD*, M, p. 436d and W. von Soden, *Akkadisches Handwörterbuch* (= *AHw*), Wiesbaden 1958-1981, p. 665a, under *mu'ā'um*, 2), since *lu gimillum* is a nominal sentence ("let it be a favour"), followed by "they refused" (*lā imû*).
3) The reason for the difference in spelling between singular and plural forms could be the quantity of the vowel contracting with the final *-e* of *tale'e*. Short vowels, such as the marker of the subjunctive *-u*, could cause a secondary lengthening of the first *-e*, which long vowels, such as the plural endings *-ā*, *-ū*, do not. Hence *talē'u* and *tale'ū*?
4) See E.E. Knudsen, "Stress in Akkadain" in *JCS* vol. 32, 1980, pp. 3-16, esp. p. 12, on plene writing before long suffixes.
5) *CAD*, L, p. 156a,b reads these forms as *el-te-'i*, but final *-e* is contradicted by the variant *el-te-'-e*. The syllabograms *IḪ* and *ḪI*, in the absence of a special sign *EḪ* for *'e* and because *ḪE* is not used for *'é*, render both *'i*, *'ì* and *'e*, *'è*.
6) Two further references for the preterite in K. Hecker, *Grammatik der Kültepe-Texte* (= *GKT*), Rom 1969, par. 98b, are difficult to accept. BIN 4, 229:16 is the subjunctive and ATHE 31:44 (*a-mu-ma*) is the only occurence without plene writing or final *-a*. The verb could well be in the subjunctive too, depending on *kīma* (after the oath) in line 42. The last lines probably have to be read: "... that K., while he was staying (*uš!-bu-ma*) in B., was not willing to accept".
7) *CAD*, M, p. 398a and p. 399b show that all occurrences of this verb, when not in a relative sentence introduced by *ša* or in combination with another verb (e.g. *amšima lā alput*), are in the perfect tense, since the reference is to the effect of the completed action, "I have forgotten". The rarity of forms with *t*-infix of *le'ā'um* and *mu'ā'um* in OA does not favour interpreting them along the same lines.
8) An OA verb *lamā'um*, "to refuse", listed *AHw*, p. 533b, which would be the exact counterpart of *lemû*, but spoil the complementary distribution of the latter with *lā mu'ā'um*, does not exist, since we have to read in BIN 4,85:10 *lá i-lá-mu-*[*du*], see *Studia et Documenta ad Iura Orientis Antiqui Pertinentia* (= *SD*), vol. 10, Leiden 1972, p. 417, l. 3.
9) Lexical references for *lēmu* are without context and note *CAD*'s emendation of unique *lemmia* into *lemnīja*.
10) See the references in *CAD*, L, p. 108b (as adjective in OA with final *-u*, genitive *lá-šu-im*) and p. 110a,b (stative, i.a. *lá-šu-a-ku*).
11) Final *-ū* in some OB form 3rd pers. sing. masc. could be due to compensatory lengthening after reduction of the long first vowel. In *laššu* the reduction of the long first vowel was compensated by the lengthening of the next consonant *š*, but there is no indication of a final long vowel in OA and OB (apart from occurrences in the plural or subjunctive).
12) Note West-Semitic *ykl* construed with second finite verb in Esther 8:6 (*'wkl wr'yty*), Elefantine, A. Cowley, *Aramaic Papyri of the Fifth Century B.C.*, Osnabrück 1967 (repr. of Oxford 1923), no. 1, l. 4 (*l'nkl ngrkj*), and Hebrew *'b'* in Is 1:19 (*'m-t'bw wšmᶜtm*).
13) In *AfO* vol. 18, p. 65, col. II, l. 6, quoted in *CAD*, *loc. cit.*, *le'ûm* is construed with inf. in the acc., but qualified by a second finite verb in the present tense.

14) *GKT*, p. 213, n. 6, "sehr auffällig"; H. Hirsch in *OrNS* vol. 41, 1972, p. 428 *ad loc.* "nicht recht möglich".
15) Inf. of verbs *tertiae infirmae* in the genitive in OA are written with *-i-*, *a-lá-qá-i-šu*, TC, vol. 3, p. 16, l. 8.
16) See J. Aro, *Die akkadischen Infinitivkonstruktionen* (*StOr*, vol. 26 (= *Aro*)), Helsinki 1961, p. 130, par. 6.11 and note CT, vol. 2, p. 47, l. 28 (*ana arna emēdišu iqbû*) beside numerous examples of *qabû* with inf. in the acc. quoted *CAD*, Q, pp. 35f., b)-c).
17) In Hebrew, we have *ykl* with simple inf., Gen 37:4 (*yklw dbrw*), Ps 78:20 (*ywkl tt*), Is 57:20 (*hšqṭ lʾ ywkl*, with inf. preceding auxiliary verb), and with *l*[e] + inf., passim, e.g. Gen 31:35 (*ʾwkl lqwm*).
18) *PN ana nakri alāki ūl i-el-ʾi*, KUB 3, 14:17, is ambiguous, since *ana* may depend on *alākum*, but the genitive *alāki* suggests haplography for **ana ana nakri alāki ul ilʾi*, "he was unable to meet the enemy".
19) Unlikely *AHw*, p. 36a, *alī/ēmu* and *ZA* vol. 61, 1971, p. 52, l. 51, *ana pa-ra-aʾ a-le-e-mu*, "das einen Gewaltigen 'abschneiden' konnte".
20) See for such constructions *Aro*, pp. 17ff., and R. Frankena in *Studia ad Tabulas Cuneiformes a F.M. Th. de Liagre Böhl collectas pertinentia*, vol. 4, 1978, pp. 8f.
21) The dative suff. normally goes with *epēšum*, cf. AbB vol. 3, p. 62, l. 20; vol. 4, p. 146, l. 9, where a translation "to cooperate with" for *ište/iat epēšum* + dative is used. But AbB vol. 6, p. 21, l. 17 shows that we may supply *ṣibūtum*, "wish", as nominal object. "To cooperate" seems to be rendered by *ištiat epēšum* without dative suffix, e.g. AbB vol. 5, p. 165, l. 5; vol. 8, p. 15, l. 28.
22) Cf. also *kaspam mahāram lā šaṭram*," (since) I had not been authorized to accept silver" (ARM vol. 5, p. 28, ll. 36f.), where one would expect **kaspam maḫārī lā šaṭir* and where the dative suffix added to the stative supplies the subject of the infinitive (but note OA *qabi* with inf. in the acc., *Aro*, p. 94, par. 3.77). Without added nominal object the inf. may occur with a pron. suffix as its subject, even in combination with a pronominal suffix added to the finite verbal form: *wašābka..šarrum išpurakkum*, "the king authorized you by letter to stay" (ARM vol. 4, p. 35, ll. 11f.). But note *mimma epēšam ūl ḫašḫassu*, "you don't wish to do him anything" (ARM vol. 2, p. 60, l. 22) where **mimma epēssu* was avoided.
23) Note *apālam anniam ...teleʾi* (AbB vol. 2, p. 125, l. 24), where we would expect **annītam apālam*, "to answer for this". The construction seems inspired by expressions like *epēšum/šapārum annûm* as subject of a sentence (cf. *Aro*, pp. 18ff. and ARM vol. 2, p. 5 55, l. 9), where, however, *annûm* is not the object of the infinitive, but cf. *anniam epēša* in Gilg. Yale l. 198 ("this action", or "doing this"?) and *Aro*, p. 299.
24) *Aro*, p. 17, par. 1.7 and p. 21, par. 1.14 gives examples of a first pers. sing. pron. suffix denoting the subject of the infinitive.

Scribes and Literacy in Ancient Egypt

H. te Velde, Groningen

The Ancient Egyptian scribe statues (Pl. I)* are well known and impressive. They are the visible remains of Ancient Egyptian culture, in which writing and literacy was cherished, was learned, was practised and was handed over to future generations for thousands of years. Ancient Egypt could not exist, as it was and as it still is to us, without scribes and literacy. Scribes were the core and backbone of Ancient Egyptian civilization. They were the elite. All state officials of a certain rank, including priests and military officers, were able to read and write the fairly intricate script and were trained in the art of drawing up written documents and to consult and study them. On the other hand there is no evidence of scribes without an office in state or temple. Just as in modern Egypt, the government provides a job for anyone who has had a university education. Scribes were not outsiders in Egyptian culture. They were and had to be in a leading position. Not birth by itself, or the ability to fight and to command brought Egyptians to high positions, as was sometimes the case in other cultures. The ability to read and write, i.e. literacy, was the first prerequisite for a career in the Egyptian bureaucracy[1]:

> One will do all you say
> If you are versed in writings.
> Study the writings, put them in your heart;
> Then all your words will be effective.
> Whatever office a scribe is given
> He can consult the writings.

Of course it was the children of magistrates who were send to school and learned to read and write. But nonetheless it was written[2]:

> The scribe is chosen for his ability (*ḏrt*);
> His office has no children.

Scribal education was not always and everywhere restricted to children of officials. Enough examples can be given to demonstrate that not only the sons of magistrates became magistrates[3]. Sometimes in Egypt-

ian history it was even fashionable to boast about one's humble descent. It was possible to rise socially, but for becoming a magistrate a scribal education was necessary. Examples of self-taught men are extremely exceptional and doubtful[4].
The story of the Hebrew slave Joseph, who became the highest official under pharaoh, is rather unlikely from the Egyptian point of view. This is not because Joseph was a foreigner or because he had been a slave, but in so far that it is not mentioned that he was versed in the writings of Ancient Egypt. One may presume that he learned to read and write in the house of Potiphar or somewhere else, so that he could become an official in the Egyptian bureaucracy. The bible, however, is reluctant to take a positive attitude not only towards Egyptian religion - another remarkable omission in the story of Joseph - but also towards Egyptian script and literacy. The Egyptian maxims in the Book of Proverbs were not recognized as such. Even of Moses it is not related that he learned to read and write and became an Egyptian literate. Only later it is vaguely indicated that he was instructed in all the wisdom of the Egyptians (Acts 7:22). When christianity came to Egypt the bible was translated into the native Egyptian language, in its Coptic form, written with Greek letters, but not in the traditional scripts and language-systems, which had been used for millennia. Obviously these were not felt to be free from ideology, but on the contrary, as expressions of the typical Egyptian, heathen, worldview[5].

Although the scribes and their literacy were the core and backbone of Egyptian civilization, numerically they were only a small group in Egyptian society. According to acceptable calculations no more than ten thousand out of a population of one million could read and write in the Egypt of the third millennium B.C.[6]. In the course of Egyptian history there was a considerable growth in the population density and certainly also a concomitant growth of literates, but until Greco-Roman times their percentage was hardly more than one to hundred. For many observers life in Ancient Egypt may therefore resemble life in any illiterate or primitive culture. But it cannot be denied that there are important differences. Even a small minority of one percent of literates influences life in any culture, especially when they are in a leading position[7]. Words and sentences of a written text differ from the stream of oral information. A written text abstracts from the emotion and the "context" of life of the here and now. A writer summarizes and orders oral information in a special way and can correct his text. Even oral information, learned by heart, ordered, and repeated in different situations differs from a written text. Visible information can be added to spoken words with a pictural script.

The act of writing itself is a training in logic. Writing and efficiency go hand in hand, or perhaps better, may go hand in hand more easily than speaking and efficiency. In the discussions between the Egyptian Wenamun and the prince of Byblos the latter acknowledges[8]:

> Indeed, Amun has founded all the lands. He founded them after having first founded the land of Egypt from which you have come. Thus efficiency came from it in order to reach the place where I am. Thus learning came from it in order to reach the place where I am.

The prince of Byblos thus specifies the cultural influence of Egypt on his country aptly as not only *sb3yt* i.e. 'learning' or 'written teaching'but also as *mnḫw* i.e.'efficiency'. At least the Egyptian scribe who drew up the vivid travel story of Wenamun, possibly Wenamun himself, who makes the prince say so. The Egyptian scribes were deeply conscious of the usefulness of schooling and literacy and its practical meaning for the wellfare of the land. Their pupils had to learn and write in school[9]:

> It is the scribe who assesses the taxes of Upper and Lower Egypt. It is he who receives the dues from them. It is he who accounts for them. All military troops are organized by him. It is he who conducts officials into the Presence (of pharaoh) and sets the pace for every man. It is he who commands the entire land. All business is under his control.

Indeed the scribes or state officials regulated and controlled the whole country. In literary works on the theme of social chaos, it is stated that in times of social upheavals, the rich became poor and the poor became rich and that also the privileged scribes suffered from the circumstances. But nowhere it is found that the illiterates actually replace the literates in their high positions. That was simply impossible. In the *Admonitions of Ipuwer* we read[10]:

> Lo, the archives, its books are stolen,
> The secrets in it are laid bare.
> Lo, magic spells are divulged,
> Spells are made worthless through being repeated by people.
> Lo, offices are opened,
> Their records stolen,
> The serf becomes an owner of serfs.
> Lo, [scribes] are slain,

Their writings stolen,
Woe is me for the grief of this time!
Lo, the scribes of the land-register,
Their books are destroyed,
The grain of Egypt is "I-go-get-it".

What strikes us is not so much the complaint that books are stolen or destroyed, but that *ḥk3w*-spells, *šmw*-spells and *sḫnw*-spells are divulged and made worthless through being repeated by people. Obviously some people who could read had made public the contents of certain books. The literates should, however, according to this scribe, hold on to their monopoly. The mandarinate should maintain control[11].

One might think that the scribe statues of Ancient Egypt, especially those who squat so humbly (Pl. I), do not look as if they are 'commanding the entire land'. Indeed the squatting attitude of these scribes is to be explained as signifying their position as servants[12]. This was the *decorum*: scribes were servants of pharaoh. Pharaoh himself was never represented as a squatting scribe or in reading or writing position. He embodied the highest authority on earth. His status was divine.Yet, however humble the squatting scribe statue might seem to be, he represents the intellectual governement official, who regulates and organizes the life of the people in Egypt. Scribe statues represent not just 'clercs', but influential persons. One of the oldest known scribe statues represents Kawab, the son of Cheops[13]. Only higher officials were eternized as intellectual scribes by means of these statues placed in tombs and later in temples. However, scribes depicted in tomb-reliefs in the execution of their work of writing were lower, subordinate officials[14]. The higher officials who had scribe statues were depicted as fishing and fowling or as overseeing the work of others, including the work of writing, in the tomb reliefs. The work of writing was delegated by the higher officials to the clercs or lower officials. The scribe statue indicates the high status of literacy and learning of its owner, not that his daily work consisted of writing on papyrus in an office. The squatting scribe statue shows on the one hand the intellectual background of the owner, on the other hand it shows his subservient attitude to pharaoh and state. The idea of intellectual freedom seems to have been unknown.

In fact, it is somewhat perplexing that the concept freedom did not seem to exist in Ancient Egypt, according to many egyptologists. It is indeed difficult to find the equivalent of the word "freedom" in the Egyptian language[15]. The nearest we come to "freedom" might be the verb *wstn* 'travel freely', 'be unhindered', which can also be used as

Photo: H. te Velde

an adverb[16]. It is interesting to note that this term is repeatedly used to characterize the relative freedom of the scribe in praises of his profession[17]:

> Apply yourself to being a scribe, a fine profession, that is your destination. You call to one and a thousand answer you. You stride freely (*wstn.tỉ*) upon the road and do not become like an ox to be handed over.

The life of the scribe is free and rich in comparison with the miserable life of the soldier. The soldier has many superiors who 'are after him like a donkey'. Moreover there are the enemies, surrounding him with arrows. In short, 'He is dead whilst yet alive'. It might be that this recurring theme of long enumerations of the miseries of the soldier's life is so often found in schoolbooks because to some children of the elite sports and the perspective of a military career seemed more attractive than literacy. In school they were taught to write but they were also exercised already in 'all the arts of war'[18]. An effective means of social advance for Egyptians as well as foreigners was the army. This may have sharpened scribal polemics against the military[19], for, as the scribe teaches his pupils[20]:

> Behold, I am teaching you and making sound your body to enable you to hold the palette freely (*m wstn*), to cause you to become a trusty one of the king, to cause you to open up treasuries and granaries... Be a scribe, so that you may be saved from being a soldier.

"To hold the palette freely" and "to be a trusty one of the king" are juxtaposed. That intellectual freedom can be a problem does not seem to have been perceived, or is smoothed over. Anyway, there are traces of the consciousness that the squatting scribe, who is subservient to pharaoh, is more free than others in Egyptian society. Another schoolbook, commonly called *The Satire of the Trades*, contains a derisive characterization of all kinds of illiterate trades. It does not contain polemics against the military, because it was written before the time of the New Kingdom, which was the imperialistic and militaristic period of Egyptian history[21]:

> There is nothing better than books.
> It is like a boat on water.
> .....
> See, there is no profession without a boss,
> Except for the scribe; he is the boss.
> Hence if you know writing,
> It will do better for you
> Than those professions I have set before you

Each more wretched than the other.
A peasant is not called a man,
Beware of it!

Here the officially subservient scribe shows that he feels himself to be the boss. This indicates that a certain way of indulging in the feelings of freedom may be equivalent to a feeling of superiority. If indeed the satirical exaggeration in this text were to be taken seriously, as has been done in recent research[22], then only the literate considers himself to be a real man. Such a narrow conception of what man is reminds us of Herodot[23], who tells that Egyptian priests showed to Hecataeus of Abdera 345 statues on his visit to the temple in Thebes. Each statue represented a *piroomis* son of a *piroomis*. In this word one can find an Egyptian word for man (*p3 rmṯ*), and Herodot adds that this Egyptian word means *kaloskagathos*.

That pharaoh was never represented in scribal position does not imply that he was illiterate[24]. The group of literate higher state officials, and the group next to these - the clercs - were not subjected to illiterate royalty. Princes learned to read and write together with children of high officials. A future king may be exhorted to surpass his ancestors[25]:

Surpass your fathers, your ancestors,
.....
See, their words endure in books,
Open, read them, surpass their knowledge,
He who is taught becomes skilled.

He is given the advice:

Do not kill a man whose virtues you know,
With whom you once chanted the writings.

The 'chanting' of the writings happened presumably at school when the texts to be written had also to be learned by heart.
A scene in the great temple of Abydos[26] shows us prince Ramses, the later king Ramses II, beside his father King Sethos I; the prince is acting as a *sem* priest, and holding a partly unrolled papyrus in his hand. On the wall there is a list of 76 names of kings from Menes down to Sethos himself, a conspectus of royalty over about 1800 years. Prince Ramses is described as 'reading out praises'. The king is in ritual attitude with his right hand raised and an incensor in his left hand. He is not reading himself, not because he cannot do so but because it is proper that the reading is done for him. The king should know the ritual texts by heart, but one can imagine that the recitation of an unusual ritual text, such as this long list with royal names to be

recited in the correct order, required some help. It is possible to translate the description of the activity of prince Ramses in a more neutral way as 'reciting praises' (*nǐs ḥknw*), but since he is holding the papyrus up to his face, he is unmistakably reading. So we must conclude that, according to iconographical rules, a prince may be depicted as reading, but not so the king himself.

Especially in representational art, the king is considered as a god. Egyptian gods are illiterate or better preliterate. The famous exceptions are Seshat, mistress of writing, and Thoth, the lord of the god's words (*mdw nṯr*). But on the whole Egyptian gods do not write or consult books. They do not need scribal education and leaning; they know. They are superhuman beings also in comparison with the narrow conception of humanity of the literate elite of the Egyptian people. Their pronouncements, their divine words, are more efficient and concise, more literate than written words. In the polytheistic religion of Ancient Egypt the gods do not write down pronouncements themselves, as did the God of Israel (Exodus 31:18). Egyptian gods delegate the work of writing to their special scribe Thoth, just as high Egyptian officials delegate the scribal work to their clercs. It goes without saying that one should not underestimate the work of the clerc of the gods. A pharaoh may be proud to act as such in the hereafter[27]:

> I am the scribe of the god's book, who says what is and brings into being what is not.

Nevertheless,there is some textual evidence for the king reading and writing himself, not only while he is still a youthful prince, but also later while he is in his royal office and still on earth. Sometimes officials, referring to letters they received from the king, add with pride that these were written by the king with his own fingers[28]. Such an expression sounds exaggerated, but it need not be so. An official would not lightly record such a gesture, which seems not to be in accordance with *decorum*, if it were completely untrue. Just as the king is a better warrior on the battlefield than his army, and a better strategist in the council of war than his generals, according to the *decorum*, so he may also surpass the scribes in research in the library. Such royal research is described as something of a *veni, vidi, vici*, as it should be[29].

> Then his majesty spoke to the nobles and the companions who are in his following, to the real scribes of the hieroglyphs (*mdw nṯr*), and the masters of all secrets: "My heart has desired to see the oldest writings (*sšw p3wt tpt*) concerning Atum. Open for me for a great investigation that I learn to know how god looks like (*nṯr m ḳm3f*)....." Then these companions said:"May happen what

> your *ka* commands. May your majesty go to the house of books and may your majesty see every hieroglyph." Then his majesty went to the house of books and his majesty spread out the bookrolls together with these courtiers. Then his majesty found bookrolls of the temple of Osiris...
> Now it was his majesty himself who has [found] these bookrolls. A scribe whosoever in the service of his majesty would never have found it!

The vexing question behind this text is: Who is the oldest and thus the most important god in Egypt? Tradition of long standing, admittedly even adhered to by pharaoh (see beginning of the quoted text), would say that it is Atum of Heliopolis. But priests in several towns in Egypt claimed that it was the local god of their temple, and so did the priests of the temple of Osiris in Abydos, where this text originated. But how to make acceptable the primacy of Osiris? The argument is a literary one: The oldest books in the royal library are not about Atum, but about Osiris. And to cut short a lengthy discussion in literary criticism, they used the authority of pharaoh. It is pharaoh himself who has discovered this during a special search in the library. The *rabies theologorum* for once neglected the *decorum* that pharaoh does not read books.

Even more striking is the introduction to the so-called *Prophecies of Neferti*. The famous king Snefru once wished to hear 'perfect words'. Then Neferti,'a scribe excellent with his fingers', is brought in[30]:

> His majesty said: "Come, Neferti, my friend, speak to me some perfect words, choice phrases, at the hearing of which my majesty may be entertained!" Said the lector-priest Neferti: "Of what has happened or of what will happen, O king, my lord?" (The king expresses his preference to hear more about the future and then the text goes on:) He stretched out his hand to a box of writing-equipment, took scroll and palette and began to put into writing the words of the lector-priest, that wise man of the East...

This text gives us what official representational art can not give: a writing pharaoh. The evidence, however, is not totally unequivocal. The official roles seem to be deliberately reversed here. A scribe is speaking and a king is writing! More examples, precisely about king Snefru, could be given in which he does what is not done by a pharaoh according to his divine status[31]. It is understandable that Egyptians liked those stories in which pharaoh appears out of his official role, and shows himself to be a human being, in this case someone who has literary interests and himself writes down 'perfect words' spoken by a literate. Although the *decorum* stressed the difference between the sacred king and the literary elite, it is evident that the Egyptians might imagine their pharaoh also as a human and literate being. In his youth, before becoming a pharaoh, he was taught to read and write and was instructed in literacy, and during kingship he may have practised it.

So the elite of the Egyptians, including pharaoh, was versed in literacy. Egypt was governed by intellectuals. The most famous culture heroes of Ancient Egypt are not the great warriors or commanders, but literates. The scribes Imhotep and Amenhotep, son of Hapu, were venerated as divine intermediaries[32]. Pharaoh and the higher officials of Ancient Egypt, though versed in literacy in their youth, did not spend all their active life reading and writing. Strictly speaking, the squatting scribe statue of Leiden is not reading nor writing. He has an intellectual attitude of listening attentively to what is coming to him from outside or from inside. This is the inner strength of the statue. A recurrent theme in Egyptian schoolbooks and wisdom literature - too many examples exist to enumerate here - is precisely listening. The wise king Solomon, during whose reign Egyptian influences were probably stronger than ever in Israel, asked from his God for "a hearing heart (1 Kings 3:9)." More than a thousand years before Solomon the connection between heart, hearing and wisdom was already made in Egypt[33]:

He who hears is beloved of god;
He whom god hates does not hear.
The heart makes of its owner a hearer or non-hearer.
Man's heart is his life-prosperity-health.
The hearer is one who hears what is said;
He who loves to hear is one who does what is said.

It would seem appropriate at the end of this contribution to observe this "hearing heart" not only in the statue of an Egyptian scribe. It could be found in a living person, who might be sitting at the head of the table, drinking a cup of coffee,smoking a cigar and enjoying the good things of life. May he live, prosper and be healthy!

Notes

* National Museum of Antiquities, Leiden. Inv.nr. AST 31. Grey granite. Height 32 cm.; ± 2400 B.C.

1) *Instructions of Ani*; see M. Lichtheim, *Ancient Egyptian Literature* (= *AEL*) vol. 2, Berkely-Los Angeles-London, 1976, p. 140.
2) See note 1; *ḏrt* literally means "hand".
3) P. Vernus, "Quelques exemples du type du parvenu dans l'Egypte ancienne" in *Bulletin de la Société Française d'Egyptologie* vol. 59, 1970, pp. 31-45; H. Brunner, *Altägyptische Erziehung*, Wiesbaden 1957, p. 42.
4) Vernus, *op. cit.*, p. 38.
5) H. te Velde, "Egyptian hieroglyphs as signs, symbols and gods" in *Visible Religion* vol. 4, 1986 (in the press).
6) J. Baines - C.J. Eyre, "Four notes on literacy" in *Göttinger Miszellen*, vol. 61, 1983, pp. 65-96.
7) J. Goody, *The Domestication of the Savage Mind*, Cambridge 1977; J. Goody - I. Watt, "The consequences of literacy" in *Literacy in Traditional Societies*, ed. J. Goody, Cambridge 1968, pp. 27-69.
8) *The Report of Wenamun* 2, 20-22, cf. Lichtheim, *AEL* vol. 2, p. 227.
9) *Pap. Chester Beatty* IV 4, 1-3; cf. A.H. Gardiner, *Hieratic Papyri in the British Museum. Third series*, London 1935, Pl. XIX, Text volume p. 41.
10) *The Admonitions of Ipuwer, Pap. Leiden* I 344, 6, 5-8; cf. Lichtheim, *AEL* vol. 1, p. 155.
11) A fascinating account of the problems of divulging written knowledge is given by U. Eco in a novel situated in the European medieval history: *The Name of the Rose.*
12) M. Eaton-Kraus, *The Representations of Statuary in Private Tombs of the Old Kingdom*, Wiesbaden 1984, p. 20.
13) W. Stevenson Smith, *A history of Egyptian sculpture and painting in the Old Kingdom* , Boston 1949, p. 31; W.K. Simpson, *The mastaba of Kawab, Khakhufu* vols 1 and 2, Boston 1978, p. 7 and fig. 17.
14) J. Baines, "Literacy and Ancient Egyptian society" in *Man* vol. 18, 1983, p. 580.
15) S. Morenz, *Ägyptische Religion*, Stuttgart 1960, p. 144, n. 1.
16) A. Theodorides, "Freiheit" in *Lexikon der Ägyptologie*, vol. 2, 1977, pp. 297-304.
17) *Pap. Lansing* 8, 1-2; cf. R.A. Caminos, *Late-Egyptian miscellanies*, London 1954, p. 396.
18) *Truth and Falsehood* 5, 1; cf. Lichtheim, *AEL* vol. 2, p. 212.
19) J. Baines, *op. cit.*, p. 595 n. 34.
20) *Pap. Lansing* 8, 8-9; cf. R.A. Caminos, *op. cit.*, pp. 400-402.
21) *Satire of Trades;* cf. Lichtheim, *AEL* vol. 1, pp. 185, 189-190.
22) W. Helck, *Die Lehre des Dw3-Ḫtjj*, Wiesbaden 1970, pp. 161-162.
23) Herodot, *Histories*, Book II, 143.
24) The material on kings and literacy is gathered by J. Baines - C. Eyre in *op. cit.*, pp. 77-81.
25) M. Lichtheim, *AEL* vol. 1, pp. 99, 100-101, and W. Helck, *Die Lehre für König Merikare*, Wiesbaden 1977, pp. 19, 29.
26) A. Mariette, *Abydos*, Paris 1869, pl. 43; K.A. Kitchen, *Ramesside Inscriptions*, vol. 1, Oxford 1975, pp. 177-179, cf. also T.G.H. James, *Pharaoh's people*, London-Sydney-Toronto 1984, p. 132.
27) *Pyramid-text 1146c*; R.O. Faulkner, *The Ancient Egyptian Pyramid-texts*, Oxford 1969, p. 186.
28) K. Sethe, *Urkunden des Alten Reiches*, Leipzig 1933, p. 60; cf. A. Roccati, *La littérature historique sous l'Ancien Empire Egyptien*, Paris 1982, p. 124; W. Helck, "Eine Stele des Vizekönigs Wšr-št.t" in *JNES* vol. 14, 1955, pp. 23, 25.
29) W. Helck, *Historisch-biographische Texte der 2. Zwischenzeit und neue Texte der 18. Dynastie*, Wiesbaden 1975, pp. 22, 25; cf. G.Roeder, *Mythen und Legenden um Ägyptische Gottheiten und Pharaonen*, Zürich 1960, pp. 286, 290.

30) W. Helck, *Die Prophezeiung des Nfr.tj*, Wiesbaden 1970; cf. Lichtheim, *AEL* vol. 1, p. 140.
31) G. Posener, *Littérature et politique dans l'Egypte de la XIIe dynastie*, Paris 1956, pp. 31-34.
32) D. Wildung, *Imhotep und Amenhotep. Gottwerdung im Alten Ägypten*, München-Berlin 1977.
33) *The Instruction of Ptahhotep* 545ff.; cf. Lichtheim, *AEL* vol. 1, p. 74; H. Brunner, "Das hörende Herz" in *ThLZ* vol. 79, 1954, pp. 697-700.

Meaning and Symbolism of Clothing in Ancient Near Eastern Texts

M.E. Vogelzang – W.J. van Bekkum, Groningen

> "Let my lord commander hear the case of his servant. As for your servant, your servant was harvesting at Ḥeṣar Asam and your servant had reaped and measured and stored (grain) for the days agreed before stopping. After your servant had measured his (quota of) grain and put it in store for the days agreed, along came Hoshaiah, son of Shobay, and took your servant's *mantle*. After I had measured my (quota of) grain over the aforementioned days, he took your servant's *mantle*.
> But all my companions can testify on my behalf - those who were harvesting with me in the heat (of the sun) - my companions can testify on my behalf, really, I am innocent, so please return my *mantle*, and I will be satisfied. It is up to the commander to return his servant's *mantle* and to show (him mercy). If you have heard the case of your servant, you will not be silent ..."

Thus the famous ostracon from Yavneh Yam found in 1960[1]. Professor Hospers made us familiar with the text of this inscription, dating from the 7th century B.C.E., during his lectures in Hebrew Epigraphics. Minutely he made us aware of every problem and pitfall in trying to read fragmentary texts such as this one. Concerning the manifold conjectures which have been made in connection with this ostracon, he would carefully give all the arguments for and against and try to figure out the most plausible ones. He used to put aside many suggestions for reading and translation, saying that there is no real proof for them. He showed therein his aversion of every exaggeration or a too imaginative exegesis[2], which in his eyes did no justice to the text al all. Characteristic is his remark that inscriptions like the one from Yavneh Yam are not at all destined for 20st-century scholars, but can only be understood against their historical setting, if at all.

Introduction

This inscription may serve as a starting point for this article. The following remarks will try to trace something of the meaning and symbolism of the concept of clothing in certain Mesopotamian and Ancient Hebrew texts.
The concept "clothing" may refer to three different things:

- The *representation* of a garment
- The *real* garment
- The *described* garment.

All three of them partake of the same reality; they may be equivalents but they are not identical. Thus for the same object three different structures may be perceived:

- The first reflects the plastic or iconic structure
- The second reflects the technological structure
- The third reflects the verbal structure[3)].

As appears from the title, we will occupy ourselves mainly with the *verbal structure*, the description of clothing. Only literature can transform an object into language. The *first* function of the word for cloth or garment in a literary text is the stiffening of the perception of a certain level of understanding. Language 'translates' a choice, and may impose the conception of "this particular garment"; it fixes the level of reading on this or that garment or on a detail of it. The described garment therefore is more or less a fragmentary garment. The *second* function of the word 'cloth/garment' is a function of knowledge. Language also provides information, which the plastic or iconic structure does not necessarily provide by itself.

Language not only adds knowledge: at the same time it assumes a certain knowledge. Thus the mention of a piece of clothing in a text may be an indication of:

- *necessity* - protection of the body
- *economy* - commercial value
- *legislation* - punishment, reward
- *elegance* - external ornamentation
- *affectivity* - mourning, submissiveness, joy
- *profession* - status.

Clothing can raise or reduce someone's personality or status; it is on the one hand an external expression of his inner identity, on the other hand a mark of his status in the society in which he moves. A garment is that object of material culture which takes the nearest position between man and his environment; it has therefore also an informative function. It informs us about the dignity and the function of a person in society.

Akkadian literature

Akkadian literature offers an abundance of descriptions of clothes in myths, epics, religious texts, hymns, letters, economical, juridical and historical texts. Particularly the aspects of affectivity, profession and elegance form points of interest in these texts. Meaning and symbolism of clothing depend of course also on the kind of text in which they are mentioned.

The most neutral indication in the Akkadian texts of the object 'garment' is *ṣubatu*, also often used as a determinative (TÚG). By use of certain adjectives or adverbial adscriptions this can be further specified. It seems to have been the term for the main, indispensable piece of apparel. The word *ṣubatu* disappears from general use after the Old Baylonian period and occurs later only in literary texts. It is replaced by forms of the verb *labašu*[4]. But there are also many specific terms for certain types of garments,notably in texts dealing with the ritual clothing of the images of gods in the Mesopotamian cult[5] and in economic or juridical documents. Although textile was one of the main industries for internal consumption as well as for export, garments were expensive in Mesopotamia, and a great proportion of the population possibly possessed just one garment[6]. A person with just one garment was considered poor, as one can read in the story of the so-called 'Poor Man of Nippur':

la-biš-ma ša la te-ni-e ṣu-ba-tú

'He was clad in a garment that had no change'[7].

Nudity meant socially the absolute low in a person's relative status, whether due to lack of finances or to negligence of the person to whom one was subordinated, or upon whom one depended[8].
Alternatively a person might have arrived at such a miserable situation that he has lost all possessions and his last dignity and has to go through life naked, literally and figuratively. An example of this situation is described by the Assyrian king Esarhaddon, when he boasts to have clothed the naked. It refers to freed prisoners which he 'made again into Babylonians'. He restored their stolen property and declared: 'I provided the naked with clothing and let them take the road to Babylon'[9]. By this act he gave them back their dignity (and ascertained himself of course of the loyalty of his subjects!)[10].

In Mesopotamian *myths and epics*, nudity is sometimes used as a literary motif, as a *device marking transition*. It then indicates the *thematic change* of oncoming evil that will befall the person in question because he took off his clothes or was stripped by accident. A example of this one finds in the Epic of Gilgamesh; Gilgamesh, on his way back with the rejuvenating plant after leaving Utanapishtim, sees a cool pond. He doffs his clothes and bathes. A serpent smells the plant which he had left behind with his clothes, and eats it. And so the snake, not Gilgamesh, obtains the power of rejuvenation and Gilgamesh is left with nothing to show for his great efforts[11]. Another example comes from the so-called Anzu-epic. The god Enlil used to bathe in the presence of the Anzu-bird whom he had appointed as a doorkeeper. Every day he takes off his tiara and divine garment, and lays aside the tablet-of-destinies. At last the bird is tempted by these symbols of power, and one morning when Enlil is bathing as usual, he steals the tablet and flies away, leaving Enlil helplessly behind[12]. It must be noted that the most dangerous moment for the god is when he takes off his tiara and divine garment, for both are the symbols of his divinity[13].

An example of the second situation is present in the myth of 'Ishtar's Descent to the Netherworld', where Ishtar, according to the rules of the netherworld, is successively deprived of her clothes and jewelry at each of the seven gates. By her nakedness she becomes assimilated with dead. Then Ereshkigal, the goddess of the netherworld, strikes her with sixty deadly diseases. When Ishtar is called to life again, she gets back her clothes and jewelry from all the gates in reverse order and is assimilated again to the living[14].
Clothing as *a mark of civilization*, in combination with anointments and hairdressing, also appears from the Epic of Gilgamesh as the mark of Enkidu's metamorphosis towards civilization. In the Old Babylonian text, IIiii, 22-27, one reads:

> 'He rubbed the shaggy growth, the hair of his body. He anointed himself with oil, became human. He put on clothing, he is like a man!'

Also the motif of *changing clothes* is used in certain myths and epics as a device marking transition, in order to indicate thematic changes[15]. Stripping off *clean* garments, putting on mourning clothes, wearing uncombed hair are used as a trick to appease the wrath of Anu, the god of heaven in the myth of Adapa. When he is out fishing one day for offerings, the south wind destroys his boat. The enraged Adapa utters a curse which breaks the wing of the south wind. Ea, in order to protect his servant, tells him to garb himself in mourning clothes to appease the vegetation gods who guard the door of heaven[16]. He instructs him not to accept the food and drink of heaven, but allows him to accept new clothes and anointing oil. Although Adapa rejects the food on the advice of Ea, he is given a change of clothing and is sent back to earth.
Stripping off *dirty and/or damaged* garments and putting on clean ones is again described in the Epic of Gilgamesh, where it brings about a positive transformation of Gilgamesh' appearance; at the same time it causes a negative development in the narrative. Gilgamesh, after his return from the battle against the monster Huwawa, attends to his toilet and polishes his weapons:

> 'He washed his grimy hair, polished his weapons,
> the braid of his hair he shook out against his back.

He cast off his soiled (things), put on clean ones,
wrapped a fringed cloak about and fastened his sash.
When Gilgamesh had put on his tiara,
glorious Ishtar raised an eye at the beauty of Gilgamesh'![17)]

The effect of his brilliant appearance is that the goddess Ishtar falls in love with him. Gilgamesh, however, scornfully rejects her, and this of course does inflame the anger of the goddess and disaster follows. *Putting on pure and clean garments* is not only important for the person in question; it also has or intends to have a positive effect on the surrounding. This positive effect was particularly important at certain religious or cultic actions as are described in the Akkadian *tamītu*'s, *ikribu*'s and *namburbu*'s[18)]. It is particularly seen in the oracle inquiries to the god Šamaš as they appear in the so-called Knudtzon/Klauber-collection[19)]. The *barû*-priest during the sacrificial ritual utters certain formulae to obtain the omina containing the gods' answers. Some of these so-called *ezib-lines*[20)] refer to the clothes to be worn at the ritual:

e-zib šá TAG-*it* SAG.KI UDU.TÚG *gi-ne-šú ár-šá-a-ti lab-ši*:
'neglect, that he who touches the forehead of the sheep, should be dressed in his (dirty) sacrificial garment'.

e-zib šá ana-ku DUMU.LÚ MAŠ ÌR-*ka*/TÚG *gi-ni-e-a ár-šá-a-ti lab-šá-ku*:
'neglect that I, the barû-priest, your servant, should be dressed in my (dirty) sacrificial garment'.

From this it appears that the priest was afraid that in spite of all his precautionary measures, he might have defiled himself unknowingly and would therefore influence the omen in a negative way. Dirt on a priestly garment - which should be clean - is obviously out of place; it is a threat to good order and thus objectionable and highly dangerous. "Dirt" may be unwanted bits of whatever it was it came from; especially at this stage it is dangerous to the cultic action, because the purity of the scene in which it obtrudes will be stained by its presence[21)].

On the other hand, stripping off clean and good clothes and *putting on dirty and torn clothes* brings about a negative transformation. It is a sign of mourning, sorrow, humility and meekness. The actual meaning of mourning is to place oneself symbolically and temporarily in the state of death[22)].

According to the twelfth tablet of the Epic of Gilgameš, the dead wore dirty clothes; according to the seventh tablet, the dead wore, like birds, a garment of feathers and was dust their food. Also in Western tradition we know a transformation code by means of clothing indicating the transition of one situation into another: the Christian-European custom has a bride veiled and dressed in white; a widow veiled and dressed in black[23].

On one of the two steles found in Harran, Adad-guppi, Nabonidus' mother, described what she did to appease the hearts of the gods:

> "..... In order to appease (the anger of) my personal god and goddess, I did not permit apparel made of fine wool, silver and gold jewelry, any new garment, perfumes and scented oil to touch my body. I was glad in a torn garment (*ṣubat naksu*) and when I left (my house) it was in silence ...."[24].

The postscriptum at the end of the stele forms a description of the empire-wide mourning over the death of Adad-guppi, where weeping was combined with symbolic rites concerning body and garment. Unfortunately the text is much damaged here, so that many details must remain obscure.

> '(...) He slaughtered fat rams and assembled into his presence [the inhabitants] of Babylon and Borsippa together with [people] from far off provinces, he [summoned even kings, princes] and governors from the [borders] of Egypt on the Upper Sea, to the Lower Sea, for the mourning and [...] and they made a great lament, scattered [dust] on their heads. For seven days and seven nights they walked about, heads hung low, [dust strewn], stripped off their attire.
>
> On the seventh day [...] all the people of the country shaved and cleaned themselves, [threw away] their (mourning) attire [...] [I had] chests with (new) [brought] for them to their living quarters, [treated them] with food [and drink], provided them richly with fine oil, poured scented oil over their heads, made them glad (again) and looking presentable. I provided them well for their [long] journey and they returned to their homes (....)'[25].

These mourning customs are also familiar from the Old Testament:

- Tearing clothes: Gen 37:34; 2 Sam 1:11; 3:31; 13:31; Job 1:20.
- Strewing earth on the head: Joz 7:6; 1 Sam 4:12; Neh 9:1; Job 2:12; Ez 27:30.
- No washing or anointing: 2 Sam 12:20; 14:2.
- A seven days mourning period: 1 Sam 31:13; Gen 50:10.

Interesting in this respect is also a letter of Esarhaddon to a recalcitrant vassal[26]:

> 'When he heard my royal message, which burns the enemy like

a flame, panic(?) befell him, his heart was touched, his legs trembled; he took off his royal dress and clothed his body in sackcloth (*bašamu*) as befits a penitent sinner. He assumed the appearance of a lowly person and (thus) came to look like a slave".

Stripping off one's garment as a mark of the deepest *humiliation* and *submission* is reported by Assurbanipal in one of his Annals:

"They (i.e. the king of Elam and family) fled from Indabigash and came to me in Niniveh, crawling naked on their bellies"[26a].

Taking away someone's clothes as a mark of *punishment* for serious offences is mentioned in Middle Assyrian law[27]. But garments could also be received as *rewards* (Sanherib for instance, in one of his building inscriptions, granted the responsable officials, besides jewelry, also multicolored and linen garments for the completion of an important canal)[28], or they could be part of the wages for seasonal workers hired for harvesting or irrigation[29].

Elegance must surely have been important in ancient Mesopotamia, although not many good examples can be found in the texts, at least if one tries to look for examples that would do justice to our sense of the word 'elegance'. Proper garments and jewelry alone are not enough to make a person elegant. It also needs physical and mental appeal. The passage from the Epic of Gilgamesh cited above[30], picturing the appearance of the hero after his return from the battle against Huwawa, is a nice example in that it reveals the admiration and recognition of "real elegance" according to the Mesopotamians: just look at the effect it has on Ishtar! Another example is a well-known and beautiful Old Babylonian Hymn to Ishtar[31]. In myths and epics, the description of the finely appointed hero contrasts sharply with the description of the opponent. The beauty of a hero or god or goddess is an important topic in the Mesopotamian literature. We may assume therefore, that external beauty was thought to go hand in hand with internal beauty, which principle is also present in the European fairytales, where the good one is in general beautiful, the wicked one ugly[32]. Letters sometimes particularly reflect everyday life, and give the impression that what mattered in the first place was the *possession* of clothes (quantity, value, colour): this was a token of someone's status and wealth, and thus much more important than being elegant. So kings sent each other valuable garments as appears from the El-Amarna archive: Tušratta sent Amenophis III together with many other gifts, a great number of garments as a wedding gift for his daughter Taduheba[33].
The Mesopotamians seem to have been aware that the technical level of

their produce was below that of the West, for the Assyrian kings in their reports on booty taken in the warfare against their western neighbours refer as often to multicoloured garments as they do to silver, gold and other precious objects, so that it becomes obvious that they prized these textiles higly[34]. The opposite, however, was apparently also true, because one can read in Jos 7:21:

"... I saw among the booty a beautiful mantle from Shinar"[35]

Sargon, in his eight campaign, mentions 130 multicoloured garments which he captured in the land of Urartu and Kulhu[36]. Yet in Mesopotamia too a flaunting way of dressing was not appreciated and could make one look foolish, as appears from the following proverb:

na-an-duq er-sú ṣu-bat bal-ti
nu-'u-ú ú-lap dame la-bis
"The wise man is girt with a loin-cloth
The fool is clad in a scarlet cloak"[37].

Of importance in this proverb is the translation of *ṣubat balti* and *dame*. The *ṣubat balti* in "Ishtar's Descent to the Netherworld" is the last piece of apparel that is taken from her body at the seventh gate of the netherworld. *Dame* need not be translated with "blood"; it can refer also to the red colour. Red or purple are the colours worn by kings and gods, and the important contrast in this proverb is the opposition wise/humble vs. foolish/arrogant[38].

The same meaning of the colours red and purple will be touched upon in the second part of our article[39], in which some of the concepts are explored with regard to the Old Testament and later Jewish literature. Also in Israelite society clothes had an important role. The Yavneh Yam letter shows us the preciousness of the mantle to the one who pleads for its return. The mantle certainly is his dearest possession; also, it is a sign of his personal dignity. Therefore the reaper repeats his plea to the magistrate[40]. We may very well interpret this case as a proceeding in law, and relate it to several passages in the Torah, where the taking away of garments is considered illegitimate within the social conditions of Israelite society[41]. These regulations are clearly meant for the protection of the poor, whose only property was their clothing and because of that of immeasurable value[42].

Concepts of nudity and clothing in Gen 3:21

The Hebrew word used in the Yavneh Yam inscription is *beged*, a common word for "mantle, garment", found many times in the Old Testament. A similar word is *l^{e}ḇūš*, from the stem *lḇš* - "to put on clothes, to dress"[43]. An even more general term is *k^{e}sūt* with its

verb *ksh* denoting something like *lbš*, but more in the sense of "covering nudity with clothes"[44]. It seems self-evident that the first function of clothes is to cover the naked body. Since the possession of clothes seems so important that even the Torah prescribes protective rules for it, the Hebrew must have repudiated public nudity quite strongly. This of course also applies to other Semitic peoples. Nudity became an equivalent of "shameful" and therefore it was "uncivilised"[45]. We can not discuss at length the anthropological and psychological factors implied. Still, one of the main reasons seems to be the idea that nakedness can be taken as a loss of identity. Identity in the widest sense of the word can in the first place be given expression by clothing and clothes.
Man is nothing without clothes, not only because the poor will be deprived of their dearest possessions, but also in a general sense, because nudity leaves a person "void, empty"[46].

The "origins" of clothing has everything to do with the consciousness of personal and communal existence; clothes are a part of the human soul, so to speak[47]. The psychological impact of clothes is far greater than a mere functional protection of the body. Clothes affect most individual and social aspects of human life[48]. In the story of Adam and Eve the motif of nudity and clothing is one of the intrinsic literary topics. Once Adam and Eve became aware of their nakedness (i.e., when this was recognised as such), two reactions follow: firstly, "they sewed fig leaves together and made themselves aprons" (Gen 3:7), an secondly, "God made for Adam and for his wife garments of skin, and clothed them" (Gen 3:21). Adding Gen 2:25, "and the man and his wife were both naked", one observes a reflection of the development of culture. First, the state of nakedness; second, the clothes made out of plant-materials; and third, clothes made from animal products (skins)[49]. These phases cleary express the appreciation of clothes in the march of cultural progress. It is interesting to point to the third phase: the garments of skins are made (*ᶜāśāh*, not created!) by God. In this "embarassing" situation, right at the moment of expulsion from the Paradise, God bestowed a blessing on Adam and Eve. The garments themselves and the wearing of them are part of an act of divine protection, while at the same instance the nearness of man to God is ended. The significance of clothing is profane *and* sacred; its function is cultural, social and religious[50].
The mythological background of clothing according to Genesis has led to a considerable number of traditions, laid down in Targumim and Midrashim and in other writings from the Rabbinical period and later on. It is striking to see the contrast between the divine character

of Adam's garments and their assumed history. Some traditions relate how these coats fell into the hands of Ham, the son of Noah, who in turn handed them as an inheritance to Nimrod. Nimrod then put them on and when all animals and birds saw the coats they came and prostrated themselves before him. When people saw this happen, they thought that this was because of his personal power and therefore made Nimrod king over themselves[51)].

How could the garments be passed on to Nimrod? In fact the picture of every kind of animal or cattle was engraved upon the coat, so that "a mighty hunter" (Gen 10:9) like Nimrod could show his power through it[52)]. From the one savage hunter they were passed on to the other, Esau[53)]. Esau wanted to be as great a hunter as Nimrod was, and this caused an enduring "strife between colleagues". Once during a hunt Esau ambushed Nimrod, killed him and stripped him of his garments[54)]. This tradition stands in some opposition to the stories about Jacob's involvement. Jacob warned his brother against the miraculous nature of Adam's garments. Esau could steal them only when Nimrod had removed them. Then he had to put them on to be able to fight Nimrod in single combat and kill him[55)]. It seems a paradox that Jacob for once supported his brother in acquiring the garments, and thus participated in the victory over Nimrod. However, this does not really differ from other traditions about Jacob and Esau. Generally a sharp opposition between the two is maintained. Here, Jacob's aid is in fact a humiliation of Esau, and once more Jacob's cunning and insight are shown up against Esau's impulsive and therefore dangerous attitude. The preference for Jacob is clear: only *he* is aware of the magic of Adam's garents. This magic is also indicated by the fact that Esau had to *wear* the garments before fighting Nimrod.

Traditions about the status of Adam's clothes also differ in the later stages of the Jacob story. Esau had lost his power by selling his birth-right to Jacob. This affected also his entitlement to Adam's garments. Rebekkah considered it justified to cover Jacob with them next to the skins of the two kids[56)]. And even so their magic function does not end: they enable Jacob ("Esau in disguise") to convince Isaac to give the blessing to him, because, according to some traditions, they spread the fragrance of the Paradise[57)]. Here the miracle of Adam's garments really ends. They are no longer to be worn by Jacob afterwards, i.e., after the deceit of Isaac which turned the natural blessing of the first-born into an "unheard-of" blessing of the younger and weaker son. The clothes, belonging to nature and its violence, are now buried by Jacob, the "pseudo-first-born", and thus they return to earth[58)].

Apart from these mythological interpretations of Gen 3:21, other legends also existed. Clothes of skins were also considered as high-priestly coats, belonging to primordial creation[59]. The descriptions of the *bigdēy k^e hūnāh* belong to mysticism rather than to mythology. They are defined as celestial clothing, created for Adam and worn by him until the original sin. In fact, Adam's state of nakedness was not different from the wearing of these garments. They were considered as transparant, so that no discrepancy existed between Adam's nudity and the high-priestly clothes he was wearing[60]. Connected with this is the matter of the substance of Adam's clothes. The commentaries on Gen 3:7 and Gen 3:21 at this point are parallel and at the same time divergent. The Midrash Haggadol adds the following to the exegesis of Gen 3:7: "and they made themselves aprons... and of what was the garment of the first man in the first place? A skin of nail was he wearing and the cloud of glory covered him, but when they ate of the fruits of the tree the cloud of glory departed and the nail skin was stripped off and they saw themselves naked and without covering; they immediately sewed fig leaves"[61]. In early sources like Apocrypha and Pseudepigrapha the garments of Adam are defined as garments of light on the basis of an interchange between ayin and aleph in the word *^cōr* (skin) vs. *'ōr* (light). The garments of light appear in the *Vita Adae et Evae* and in the *Apocalypse of Moses*. Here one gets the impression that the sheen of Adam's garments continues to exist even after the commitment of the first sin[62]. A certain contradiction exists in the traditions on this point. On the one hand there is the concept of luminous clothing; this is acceptable as long as Adam remained in a pure state in Paradise. Therefore the idea of this horny skin, alike to the substance of nail, again emphasizing his transparant ("naked") appearance, can be found in the interpretation of his garments of light[63]. But could this also be valid for the time after the fall? Most commentaries take the word *^cōr* (skin) in Gen 3:21 literally: Adam and Eve lost their celestial clothing and were dressed in skins. Some traditions say: "in the skin of the Leviathan which also sheds radiance of light"[64]. The Targumim prefer the idea that the skin of the snake was put on Adam and Eve[65]. The Fragment Targums opted for a more neutral interpretation of Gen 3:21: "and the *memra* of the Lord God created for Adam and his wife precious garments for the skin of their flesh, and He clothed them"[66]. In Genesis Rabbah 20:12 the divergent opinions on Gen 3:21 appear in one series of midrashim, thus reflecting several layers of traditions: firstly, the concept of the garments of light, described by Isaac the Elder as "smooth as a fingernail and as beautiful as a jewel"[67]; secondly, the garments of skin in the literal sense of the word, defined in two ways: one with the connotation: "near to the skin (of Adam)"; and the other: "produced from the skin"[68].

It is therefore clear that the Rabbinical tradition was familiar with the idea of the garments of light[69], yet there is a preference for the literal interpretation of *ᶜōr* as 'skin'. even with the awareness that it was God Himself who gave Adam and Eve these clothes.

Concepts of nation and religion - Num 15:37-41/Deut 22:12

The clothing of Adam has broad exegetical and mythological implications. In many places in the Old Testament one can discern the symbolism of clothes, in particular with regard to ritual acts or customs. Different layers in Israelite society are very much defined by clothes[70]. The ritual of mourning and fasting informs us about a clear preference system of well-defined types of garments[71].

As a point in case, the wearing of tasseled garments by the Hebrews in Biblical and post-Biblical times is an intriguing feature. It is one of the prescriptions in the Torah:

> "speak to the people of Israel and bid them to make tassels on the corners of their garments throughout their generations, and put upon the tassel of each corner a cord of blue-purple; and it shall be to you a tassel to look upon and remember all the commandments of the Lord, to do them, not to follow after your own heart and your own eyes, which you are inclined to go after wantonly" (Num 15:38-39).

Is the wearing of tasseled garments *exclusively* Hebrew or late Jewish? Certainly not; from stelae and paintings and from scarce literal material we know that in Syria and Palestine garments with fringes or tassels were very popular. We also have a wealth of evidence from Egypt and Greece that in Biblical times this kind of decoration of the borders of garments was very common[72]. Could it be that it was characteristic for Israel to wear the tassels as Deut 22:12 says: "on the four corners of your cloak with which you cover yourself"? This is more likely; the evidence on this restricted use of tassels is more limited, yet it is not completely absent[73]. The Hebrew word for tassel is *ẓīẓit*, derived from a stem which denotes: "to look upon", precisely in accordance with its cultic or liturgical function as described in the Torah. In Deut 22:12 the word *gᵉdīlīm* (threads) is used; this leads in Rabbinical tradition to the conclusion that one thread for a *ẓīẓit* is not sufficient[74]. The same is true of "the four corners" - and not another number - and "the cloak with which you cover yourself" (Hebr. *kᵉsut*). For the latter the *ṭallīt* was considered very appropriate. The *ṭallīt* is the upper coat par excellence and it is the garment which is mentioned most frequently in Rabbinical literature[75]. During the Biblical period the *ṭallīt* was preceded by the *śimlāh* as a cloak to which one could add tassels in order to fulfil the Torah prescription[76]. Actually the *ṭallīt* is a variant of the Roman *pallium* and its form and design survived in the synagogue until modern days. Already in Talmudic times *ṭallīt* became almost synonymous for *ẓīẓīt*[77].

Returning to our question whether it was typical for Hebrews to wear tassels on the corners of their garments according to the Torah prescription, we may say that one difference in detail can be observed, which has no parallel among non-Hebrews so far. This is the blue-purple thread prescribed as one of the eight threads which constitute a *ẓīẓīt*[78]. Although it is known that during the Biblical period dyeing garments with blue and purple was practised[79], particularly in the Palestinian-Phoenician area, there is no further proof for such a detailed distinction outside Israel. In this way the wearing of *ẓīẓīt* could develop in an early stage into a distinct mark for Hebrews. An additional difference could be the fixed numbers of corners to be tasseled[80], but here we have really to accept the verse in Deut 22 as congruent with Num 15:38[81]. It is probable that at the beginning of the Rabbinical period the *ṭallīt* with tassels was indeed exclusively Jewish. Greeks and Romans definitely did not wear fringes on their clothes in this way; it is very possible that it was old-fashioned in their eyes. In this period the discussion arises, whether the 'blue cord' in the *ẓīẓīt* is still a first prerequisite[82]. The only ones who followed the Jews in wearing tassels were the early Christians, but they left it after a very short period[83]. It was then that this feature established clearly the national and religious consciousness of the Judeans and later Jews. In Talmudic times it is even a means to identify a Jew[84]. Still, the *ṭallīt* was really a scholar's cloak and did therefore not maintain itself as common dress in daily life. The importance of the *ṭallīt* lies only in the *ẓīẓīt* and it was therefore possible to replace it by the *arba^c kanfōt* (the small fringed shawl), first mentioned in the 14th century. The *ṭallīt* became a purely ritual mantle, but in this way it remains an outstanding feature within the Jewish customs of prayer.

Still, the question remains what precisely the meaning of the tassel was. We think to have shown that their function as distinction mark was important. For Israel they are a reminder of the Torah and the special relation to God. The tassels inevitably became the strongest means for reminding Israel of its own characteristic position between the peoples of the world.

The tasseled garments, found in archeological material, seemed to be worn mostly by dignified persons as gods, kings and warriors. The colours red and in particular purple play a great role here. Purple was in the Ancient Near East an outstanding sign of royalty and dignity[85]. We saw already that this was also applicable to the Akkadian proverb (see above). In this proverb the contrast was shown between wise/humble vs. foolish/arrogant. In connection with this, we may conclude our article with an epigram of the Dutch poet Staring: " De meester in zijn wijsheid gist, de leerling in zijn waan beslist." The first truth Professor Hospers showed his students during his lessons, of which the Yavneh Yam-ostracon at the beginning of this article was an example. From the second truth he tried to refrain them.

Notes

1) J. Naveh, "A Hebrew Letter from the Seventh Century B.C." in *IEJ* vol. 10, 1960, pp. 129-139. H. Donner und W. Röllig, *Kanaanäische und aramäische Inschriften*, vol. 2, Wiesbaden 1968, pp. 199-201. J.B. Pritchard, *ANET*, p. 568. D. Pardee *et. al.*, *Handbook of Ancient Hebrew Letters* (= *HAHL*) Chicago 1982, pp. 20-23.
2) As in the articles by L. Delekat, "Ein Bittschriftentwurf eines Sabbatschänders" in *Bibl* vol. 51, 1970, pp. 453-470; A. Lemaire, "Le Sabbat à l'époque israélite" in *RB* vol. 80, 1964, pp. 161-185.
3) R. Barthes, *Système de la Mode*, Paris 1967, pp. 13-15.
4) *CAD*, Ṣ, p. 225b.
5) For a detailed study see A.L. Oppenheim, "The Golden Garments of the Gods" in *JNES* vol. 8, 1949, pp. 172-193.
6) Cf. H. Waetzoldt's article "Kleidung" in *Reallexikon der Assyriologie* (= *RLA*), vol. 6, p. 24.
7) O.R. Gurney, "The Tale of the Poor Man of Nippur" in *AnSt* vol. 6, 1956, pp. 145-164; J.S. Cooper, "Structure, Humor, and Satire in the Poor Man of Nippur" in *JCS* vol. 27, 1975, pp. 163-174.
8) Many examples can be found in the Mesopotamian letters through the ages. Cf. for instance *Textes cunéiformes du Louvre* (= *TCL*), vol. 18, p. 84, l. 6: *kima* TÚG *ṣubatama la labšaku ul tidê* "do you know that I have no garment to wear?"; *TCL*, vol. 18, p. 111, l. 7 and 10: TÚG *ṣubat ana šattim ana šattim idammiqu atti* TÚG *ṣubati šattam ana šattim tuqallali* "(other) people's garments get better from year to year, but you let my garment get worse from year to year!" See also A.L. Oppenheim, *Letters from Mesopotamia*, Chicago 1967, pp. 84-85; G. Dossin, *Correspondence feminine* (*Archives Royales de Mari*, vol. 10) Paris 1978, p. 36, ll. 14-26.
9) R. Borger, *Die Inschriften Asarhaddons* (*AfO Beiheft* vol. 9), Graz 1967, p. 25, Episode 37, ll. 18-28.
10) H. Waetzoldt's remark in *RLA*, vol. 2, p. 24: "Da Asarhaddon sich besonders rühmt, die Nackten bekleidet zu haben, muss es aber eine grössere Zahl unzureichend Bekleideter gegeben haben" - is a wrong citation of this passage in the context of his article.
11) A. Schott and W. von Soden, *Das Gilgamesch-Epos*, Stuttgart 1970, p. 97, ll. 285-296.
12) W. Hallo and W. Moran, "The First Tablet of the SB Recension of the Anzu-myth" in *JCS* vol. 31, 1979, pp. 81-83, ll.6-27.
13) That "putting off the lordly turban" could have serious consequences, may be seen from the Era-epic: cf. W.G. Lambert in *AfO* vol. 18, 1958, p. 399 (= Review of F. Gössmann, *Das Era Epos*, Würzburg 1956).
14) E.A. Speiser in *ANET*, pp. 80-85.
15) J. Sasson, "Some Literary Motifs in the Composition of the Gilgamesh Epic" in *Studies in Philology* vol. 69, 1972, pp. 259-279; P. Michalowski, "Adapa and the Ritual Proces" in *Rocznik Orientalistyczny* vol. 41, 1980, pp. 77-82.
16) Cf. G. Roux, "Adapa, le Vent et l'Eau" in *RA* vol. 55, 1961, pp. 13-33, who made valuable observations on the importance of the south wind in Mesopotamian agriculture which he uses as a basis for an interesting explanation of why these two vegetation gods were waiting at the doors of heaven.
17) E.A. Speiser, "The Epic of Gilgamesh", in *ANET*, p. 51, tablet VI, ll. 1-6.
18) H. Zimmern, *Beiträge zur Kenntnis der babylonische Religion*, Leipzig 1901.
19) E.G. Klauber, *Politisch Religiöse Texte aus der Sargonidenzeit*, Leipzig 1913; J.A. Knudtzon, *Assyrische Gebete an den Sonnengott für Staat und Königliches Haus*, Leipzig 1893.
20) These are lines spoken by the *barû*-priest during the ritual; they all start with the word *ezib*.
21) M. Douglas, *Purity and Danger*, London 1979 (repr. of London 1966), pp. 160.

22) F.M.Th.de Liagre Böhl, "Die Mythe vom weisen Adapa" in *WO* vol. 2, 1952, p. 426.
23) E. Leach, *Cultuur en Communicatie*, Baarn 1978, p. 25 (transl. of *id.*, *Culture and Communication*, Cambridge 1976).
24) C.J. Gadd, "The Harran Inscriptions of Nabonidus" in *AnSt* vol. 7, 1958, pp. 35-92; A.L. Oppenheim, "The Mother of Nabonidus" in *ANETSupp.*, pp. 560-562.
25) C.J. Gadd, *op. cit.*, p. 53, col. III, 11.16-43; A.L. Oppenheim, *op. cit.*, p. 108.
26) R. Borger, *op. cit.* , pp. 102-103, Gbr. II, 11.1-6.
26a) M. Streck, *Assurbanipal und die letzten assyrische könige bis zum Untergang Niniveh's,* vol. 2, Leipzig 1916, p. 34, IV, 1. 26; *ibid.* p. 48, V, 1. 112.
27) G.R. Driver and J.C. Miles, *The Assyrian Laws*, Oxford 1935, pp. 406-409, par. 40.
28) E. Klauber, *Assyrisches Beamtentum*,(*Leipziger semitistische Studien*, vol. 5, fasc. 3), Leipzig 1910, p. 51.
29) For a detailed study see J.G. Lautner, *Altbabylonische Personenmiete und Erntearbeiterverträge*, Leiden 1936.
30) See note 17.
31) F.J. Stephens, "Hymn to Ishtar" in *ANET*, pp. 231-233; M.J. Seux, *Hymnes et Prières aux Dieux de Babylonie et d'Assyrie*, Paris 1976, pp. 39-42.
32) For more information concerning clothes in Folktales, see K. Horn, "Das Kleid als Ausdruck der Persönlichkeit: Ein Beitrag zum Identitätsproblem im Volksmärchen" in *Fabula* vol. 18, 1977, pp. 75-104; *compare* the ancient Greek expression *kalokagathos*.
33) J.A. Knudtzon, *Die El-Amarna Tafeln*, vol. 1, Leipzig 1915, pp. 164-165, 170-171, 174-175, letter 22, col. II, 11. 36-42, col. III, 11. 24-25, col. IV, 11. 11-15; cf. also pp. 116-119, letter 14, col. III, 11. 11-33.
34) Cf. A.L. Oppenheim, *Ancient Mesopotamia*, Chicago 1972[5], p. 319.
35) Shinar is Babylonia; cf. Gen 10:10;cf. also *Genesis Rabbah* 85:14 and *Midrash Tanḵumā*, ed. S. Buber, Wilna 1913, mišpaṭīm 44a.
36) F. Thureau-Dangīn, *Huitième Campagne de Sargon*, Paris 1912, p. 57, 1.366; see also D.D. Luckenbill, *Ancient Records of Assyria and Babylonia,* vol. 1, New York 1975 (repr. Chicago 1926), where one can find many examples of booty and tributes.
37) W.G. Lambert, *Babylonian Wisdom Literature*, Oxford 1975[3], p. 228.
38) Cf. E. Cassin, *La Splendeur Divine*, Paris 1968, p. 106; see esp. ch. 8 "Couleur et éclat", pp. 103-119.
39) Cf. H.F. Lutz, *Textiles and Costumes among the Peoples of the Ancient Near East*, Leipzig 1923, pp. 73-101.
40) In *HAHL*,p. 23 the authors argue that the repetition of the plea to the governor for the return of the mantle is a sign of illiteracy, and implies that the reaper himself has dictated the petition. This is not characteristic for other Hebrew letters, found on ostraca. In our opinion the plea for the return of the mantle forms the kernel of the message and it is therefore not strange to stress it by repetition; the repetition is certainly not merely a matter of stylistics, but should also be judged in the light of its contents.
41) D. Pardee, "The Juridical Plea from Mesad Ḥashavyahu (Yavneh Yam). A New Philological Study" in *Maarav* vol. 1, 1978, pp. 33-66, esp. 55-57. See Ex 22:26-27: "if ever you take your neighbor's garment in pledge, you shall restore it to him before the sun goes down, for that is his only covering, it is his mantle for his body; in what else shall he sleep?". See also Deut 24:12-13,17, and Amos 2:8: "they lay themselves down beside every altar upon garments taken in pledge".
42) Clothes belong to the basic needs of life: when Jacob makes a vow at Bethel, he says: "if God will give me bread to eat and clothing to wear"(Gen 28:20). Also in Deut 10:18: "food and clothing". The importance of clothing and food can also be illustrated by Rabbi-

nical sources. In *Talm.B. Hullin* 84b, the verse: "It is well with the man who deals generously and lends, who conducts his affairs with justice" (Ps 112:5) is explained as follows: "a man should always eat and drink less than his means allow, but clothe himself in accordance with his means". This corresponds to a certain extent with the saying of R. Levi in *Genesis Rabbah* 20:12: "spend according to your means on food, but more than you can afford on clothing". The proverb in *Talm.B. Baba Meṣiᶜa* 52a: "dear for your body (clothes); cheap for your stomach (food)", apparently considers it all as a matter of balance in the expenses: buy for your body (clothes), even what is expensive, but for your stomach (food), what is reasonable. See also A. Rosenzweig, *Kleidung und Schmuck in biblischen und talmudischen Schrifttum*, Berlin 1905, p. 13.

43) Cf. A.S. Herschberg, *Ha-Halbāšāh ha-ᶜivrīt ha-qᵉdūmāh*, Warschau 1911; G. Dalman, *Arbeit und Sitte in Palästina*, Hildesheim 1964 (repr. of Hildesheim 1937), vol. 5, *Webstoff, Spinnen, Weben und Kleidung*; K. Galling, *Biblisches Reallexikon*, Tübingen 1977, pp. 185-188; M. Wäfler, *Nicht-Assyrer neuassyrischer Darstellungen*, (*AOAT*, vol. 26), Neukirchen 1975, pp. 42-67: Juda; pp. 68-76: Israel; S. Kraus, *Talmudische Archäologie*, vol. 1, Hildesheim 1966 (repr. of Leipzig 1910), pp. 127-207 and 516-666; Kraus treats about 100 different types of garments and decorations from Rabbinical sources; J. Rupert, *Le Costume juif, Edition documentaire*, Paris 1939; A. Rubens, *A History of Jewish Costume*, London 1967, pp. 1-32.

44) Cf. S. Kraus, *Talmudische Archäologie*, pp. 160-161; a popular etymology of the word *lᵉbūš* is *lō bōš* "without shame":*Talm.B. Shabbat* 77b. This joking etymology is not completely without sense! Also *ᶜtf* is very common in Rabbinical Hebrew in the meaning "to dress, to wrap oneself up". The stem occurs already in Classical Hebrew; also R.P.A. Dozy, *Dictionnaire détaillé des vêtements chez les Arabes*, Beirut n.d. (repr. of Amsterdam 1843), pp. 395-399.

45) Appearing nude in public is strongly different from being nude for sexual purposes, giving birth and the like. Sexual contact in clothes was forbidden, cf. *Talm.B. Kᵉtubot* 48a in the explanation of Ex 21:10: *šᵉ'ērāh* in the meaning of "nearness of her flesh": "that he (the husband) must not treat her as the Persians do, who perform their conjugal duties in their clothes- one gets a divorce for that". With the juridical regulation of sexual relations and the definition of the position of man and wife in society according to the rules of the Torah the concepts about nudity were strongly modified by the importance of ethical behaviour. For a reconstruction of the attitude of Judaism on nudity and clothing one can lean upon a wealth of opinions in Rabbinical sources, cf. A. Rosenzweig, *Kleidung und Schmuck*, pp. 11-12; E.Z. Melammed, "Lašon nᵉqīyyah wᵉ-kīnuyyīm ba-Mišnah" in *Lĕšonénu* vol. 47, 1982, pp. 3-17. A reflection of the position of man and wife concerning nudity can be found in Mishnah *Horayot* 3:7: "a woman's nakedness must be covered sooner than a man's"; also in *Talm.J. Kᵉtubot* 6:5, 30d: "the man says: let me be nude, only let my wife dress herself". The involvement of sexual and erotical aspects are obvious here, as can be illustrated by many other regulations or sayings, cf. L.M. Epstein, *Sex Laws and Customs in Judaism*, New York 1948, pp. 25-67.

46) "Naked" as a figure of speech for "without, not having, not being" in Deut 28:48: "in nakedness and in want of all things". Also *Sifrē Dᵉbārīm Wa-'etḥanan* 36: "woe is me, for I am 'denuded' from the commandments (*ᶜārom min ha-miẓwot* i.e. without *tᵉfillīn* and *ẓiẓit*).

47) See E. Haulotte, *Symbolique du vêtement selon la Bible*, Lyon 1966, pp. 72-113. Although this book gives some interesting thoughts on the significance of clothes in Biblical perspective, is it confusing and mystifying.

48) For a general introduction to the subject cf. J.C. Flügel, *The Psychology of Clothes*, London 1930; F. Kiener, *Kleidung, Mode und Mensch, Versuch einer psychologischen Deutung*, München-Basel 1956; M.S. Ryan, *Clothing. A Study of Human Behaviour*, New York 1966; A. Latzke, *The Wide World of Clothing. Economics, Social significance, Selection*, New York 1968.
49) Cf. C. Westermann, *Genesis 1-11 (Biblisches Kommentar, Altes Testament)*, Neukirchen 1976, p. 343.
50) In Sumerian and Akkadian mythology clothes are associated with numinous power, bringing vitality among gods and men; cf. Th. Jacobsen, *The Treasures of Darkness*, New Haven 1976, pp. 7-8, 199, 205.
51) L. Ginzberg, *The Legends of the Jews*, vol. 1, Philadelphia 1968, p. 177; for another version cf. *Pirkey d^e-Rabbi Eli^cezer* (*PRE*) 24, ed. G. Friedlander, London 1981 (repr. of London 1916) p. 175; Ham *stole* the garments of Adam and Eve and concealed them. Then his son Cush hid them for many years. He gave them to his son Nimrod at the age of twenty. When Nimrod appeared in these coats, beasts and birds fell down before him and men were defeated in combats.
52) *Talm.B. P^esāḥīm* 54b, commentary of the Tosaphists on the ten things which were created on the eve of the Sabbath at twilight.
53) Cf. *PRE* 24, ed. Friedlander, p. 178.
54) L. Ginzberg, *The Legends*, vol.1, pp. 318-319; vol. 5, p. 276, n. 38.
55) *Genesis Rabbah* 63:13.
56) L. Ginzberg, *The Legends*, vol. 1, p. 332; vol. 5, p. 283, n. 89.
57) Isaac recognised this fragrance from his stay in Paradise during the Aqedah, cf. also *Aggadat B^erešit*, ed. S. Buber, Cracau 1903, ch. 43; *Midrash Tanḥuma*, ed. S. Buber, Wilna 1913, *Tol^edot* 68a.
58) Cf. *PRE* 24, ed. Friedlander, p. 178.
59) See n. 52; on many places in Rabbinical literature, cf. L. Ginzberg, *The Legends*, vol. 5, pp. 103-104, n. 93. In *Midrash Haggadol*, ed. M. Margulies, Jerusalem 1975, p. 109 in the midrashim on Gen 3:21: "all this happened on the sixth day at the end of the day just before the Sabbath entered".
60) As we shall see, the shining, radiant quality of Adam's garment contains both elements: its transparency and its shining as a light. The difference is sometimes not clear. It is interesting to refer to the Havdalah ceremony at the end of the Sabbath, when one shows one's *nails* in the *light* of the fire or candle; cf. *PRE* 20.
61) *Midrash Haggadol*, ed. Margulies, pp. 96-97.
62) At least, that is a conclusion which one can draw from the suggestion by S.T. Lachs in his article "Some Textual Observations on the *Apocalypsis Mosis* and the *Vita Adae et Evae*" in *JSJ* vol. 13, 1982, on pp. 173-174. Lachs considers the Greek names of Cain and Abel, Adiaphotos and Amilabes, as denoting the opposition darkness vs. light by explaining the name of Cain, Adiaphotos, as "the one without lights", and of Abel, Amilabes, as a transliteration of *m^{ec}īley lābeš* and relating this term to the *k^otnōt 'ōr* (the garments of light). As a result of this interpretation Abel as the 'real' son of Adam (not conceived by Samael) was entitled to inherit the garments of light. Ginzberg remarks in his *Legends*, vol. 5, p. 135, n. 6, that the impression is just the opposite: in *Vita Adae* 21 Cain is described as a 'shining' person (*lucidus*), see ed. H.F.D. Sparks, *The Apocryphal Old Testament* Oxford 1984, p. 152. It is very doubtful, whether Lachs can maintain his suggestion for *Apocalypsis Mosis* as well. Moreover, in *Vita Adae* 20 it is made clear that Eve's nudity concerns the loss of righteousness and glory. As the text says: "I had been stripped (was naked) of the righteousness I had been clothed with"; see H.F.D. Sparks, p. 163. On the metaphorical use of clothing in glorious light, see G. Scholem, *Jewish Gnosticism Merkavah Mysticism*

and Talmudic Tradition, New York 1965, pp. 56-64.
63) L. Ginzberg, *The Legends*, vol. 5, p. 102, n. 87; p. 113, n. 104.
64) As the commentaries *Da^cat Z^eqenim* and *H^adar Z^eqenim* on Gen 3:21.
65) As in the *Targum Pseudo-Jonathan* on Gen 3:21; *Midrash Haggadol*, ed. Margulies, p. 109; S. Kraus, *Talmudische Archäologie*, p. 136, par. 76; p. 529, n. 80. Not only the skin of the snake, also the bark of the tree appears in the traditions as the new clothes of Adam and Eve (cf. *PRE* 20, ed. Friedlander, p. 144). E.A. Wallis Budge, *The Book of the Cave of Treasures*, London 1927, p. 65: "And God made for them tunics of skin which was stripped from the trees, that is to say, of the bark of the trees, because the trees that were in Paradise had soft barks, and they were softer than the byssus and silk wherefrom the garments worn by kings are made. And God dressed them in this soft skin, which was thus spread over a body of infirmities(!)" It is interesting to see that the motifs of sin, the snake and the tree are realised in the material of the garments of skin.
66) See M. Klein, *The Fragment- Targums of the Pentateuch According to their Extant Manuscripts*, vol. 2 (transl.), Rome 1980, p. 7.
67) Again the intrinsic relation between the substance of the fingernail with the concept of radiance of light is established.
68) *Genesis Rabbah* states explicitly (20:12): "garments of skin meaning those that are nearest to the skin... garments of skin meaning those which are produced from the skin"; also *Midrash Haggadol*, on Gen 3:21, ed. Margulies, p. 109, offers both aspects of the exegetical appraoch to the term 'skin'.
69) One should not confuse the garments of light with the concept of primordial light, cosmic light or light emanating from God or the Temple, which play a part in many traditions about the creation of the world; see P. Schäfer, *Studien zur Geschichte und Theologie des Rabbinischen Judentums*, Leiden 1978, p. 129 (Art. Tempel und Schöpfung); E.E. Urbach, *The Sages, Their Concepts and Beliefs*, Jerusalem 1975, esp. p. 164, 184-185 and bibliography.
70) Like priests; cf. Num 20:26: the high-priestly clothes are ordered to be transferred from Aaron to Elazar as office-clothes. Also prophets wore "professional" clothes, cf. 1 Kings 19:19; 2 Kings 2:12-14.
71) Cf. Gen 37:34, 2 Sam 3:31 and many other passages; see the present article.
72) G.E. Wright, "Israelite Daily Life" in *BiAr* vol. 18, 1955, pp. 61-62, section on dress.
73) S. Bertman, "Tasseled Garments in the Ancient East Mediterranean" in *BiAr* vol. 24, 1961, pp. 119-128.
74) *Sifrey Bamidbar*, ed. H.S. Horovitz, Jerusalem 1966, 115, pp. 124-125.
75) S. Kraus, *Talmudische Archäologie*, pp. 167-169, esp. his remarks on the *golta*.
76) *Genesis Rabbah* 70:5 "'cloak' means 'raiment'"; A. Rosenzweig, *Kleidung und Schmuck*, p. 84; A. Rubens, *A History*, p. 9.
77) To wrap oneself in a *tallit* was only done for one purpose: to fulfil the commandment of *zizit*. See the story of Naqdimon, *Talm.B. T^{ac}anit* 19b-20a, *Midrah T^ehillim* 30.
78) *Sifrey D^ebarim*, ed. L. Finkelstein, New York 1969, 234, pp. 266-267.
79) S. Kraus, *Talmudische Archäologie*, pp. 145-147; W.F. Albright, "The Excavation of Tell Beit Mirsim" in *AASOR* vol. 21-22, 1941-43, pp. 55-62.
80) About the choice of the corners and its symbolism in clothing cf. A. Jirku, *Die magische Bedeutung der Kleidung in Israel*, Rostock 1914, pp. 14-21.
81) S. Bertman, "Tasseled Garments" p. 119, is right in stating that it is difficult to decide, whether we have to do with two different prescriptions or that the verse in Deut 22 assumes the knowledge of Num 15:37-38.
82) *Mishnah M^enahot* 4:1; *Talm.B. M^enahot* 38a-39b; esp. *Numbers Rabbah* 17:5: "but that is a religious duty to get white wool and a blue

thread and make the fringes. When does this rule apply? When the thread is real blue. Now, however, we possess only white for the blue has been hidden (Hebr. *nignaz*)."

83) A. Rubens, *A History*, p. 15.

84) Like in *Talm.B. Ta^{c}anit* 22a.

85) S. Bertman, "Tasseled Garments", p. 128; cf. n. 39; A. Brenner, *Colour Terms in the Old Testament* (*JSOT. Supplement Series*, vol. 21), Sheffield 1982.

An 18th Century Hebrew Ode

G.J. Vos, Driebruggen

The eighteenth century produced an infinite variety of occasional verse, written not only in many European languages, but also in Hebrew. These Hebrew pieces were mostly intended for Jewish readers. Sometimes, however, Hebrew verse was written by Christian theologians, or by Jews having connections in the Christian world and whishing to impress their non-Jewish readers with their skill in Hebrew[1)].

Petrus Werner Neuman, 'former rabbi of the Jews in Leeuwarden' as he called himself, the author of the Hebrew ode published in this article, is an interesting example of the last sort. H. Beem has made a survey of what is known of his life[2)], which we will expand on some minor points. According to Beem P.W. Neuman and Hartog Leuwy, rabbi of the Jewish community of Leeuwarden sometime between 1735 and 1741, were the same man. The first time we come across the name Petrus Werner Neuman is in a booklet published in 1741, containing a translation of a Hebrew dialogue on the coming of the Messiah, with introduction and notes, by P.W. Neuman[3)]. Neuman dedicated this work to Willem Karel Hendrik Friso, Prince of Orange, Stadtholder of the province of Friesland, and from 1747 and onwards Stadtholder of the whole of the Dutch Republic, as William iv. In this work Neuman also included a Hebrew ode to the prince[4)], the first of several poems of this kind that he wrote.
Next we meet Petrus Werner Neuman in 1742, when he publishes a lament on the death of Hieronymus van Alphen, professor at the University of Utrecht, who died the 7th of November in that year[5)].
Towards the end of 1743 Neuman wrote the ode to Francina Catharina Roskam (for the text, see below p. 279). The subscript of this manuscript indicates that by then Neuman had connections in The Hague, that he provided for himself by giving Hebrew lessons, and that miss Roskam was one of his pupils. But it is not clear whether he lived in The Hague at the time, as most of his work suggests that he lived in Utrecht. This problem must remain unsolved as long as we do not find any data on miss Roskam and her domicile.

In 1745 Neuman writes another ode, this time for Abraham van Limburg, on the occasion of his promotion[6]. Van Limburg's dissertation dealt with a text from Isaiah; this interest in an Old Testament-subject, combined with the printing of Neuman's ode in the dissertation, suggests that van Limburg was also a (former) pupil of Neuman. Van Limburg's promotion took place in Utrecht, and we may assume that Neuman had connections in that town and at the university. This assumption is also supported by his lament on the death of van Alphen in 1742. Two years later these connections almost resulted in an appointment as 'lector in the oriental languages'. In October 1747 Neuman himself asked the municipal authorities for the appointment. The senate of the university intervened and despite pressure from William iv, who visited Utrecht and its university in July of the same year on the occasion of his inauguration as stadtholder also of the province of Utrecht, and to whom Neuman dedicated a book in 1741 (v. supra), he did not succeed in getting the appointment[7].
However, we know that Neuman remained in Utrecht from the title page of his Hebrew grammar, which has been preserved in manuscript. There he describes himself as 'former rabbi in Leeuwarden and at present teacher in the oriental languages in Utrecht'[8]. On the back this manuscript is dated 1750.
We last hear of Neuman in 1751, when he wrote a lament in Hebrew on the occasion of the death of William iv[9]. Here again he signs himself as teacher of oriental languages in Utrecht.

The manuscript of the ode to Francina Catharina Roskam is kept in the Municipal Archives of Leeuwarden[10]. It is first mentioned in the catalogue of the Municipal Art Collection, published in 1875, by W. Eekhoff[11], archivist of the town of Leeuwarden. He listed it under the acquisitions that were made after the first part of the catalogue had already been printed. The same work also includes a supplement to the catalogue of the Municipal Library (which is kept in the same archives). This supplement, recording the acquisitions made by the library during the years 1870-1874, contains the manuscript of Neuman's Hebrew Grammar. We may assume therefore, that both manuscripts entered the Leeuwarden collections in 1874[12].
The ode is written on parchment in pen with sepia. The manuscript measures 52.5 x 41.5 cm. Most of the text is written in an ashkenazic square letter measuring on the average 0.6 - 0.8 cm., letters indicating acrostics measuring 0.9 - 1.1 cm., and the letters forming the first line having an average height of 5.4 cm. The writing is clear, but not of any particularly high quality.

The language, full of borrowings from Biblical Hebrew, as is usual in a text of this kind, is rather pompous and sometimes one gets the impression that Neuman had difficulty in organizing his acrostics, especially in the latter part of the text.

The Hebrew text of the ode on Francina Catharina Roskam.

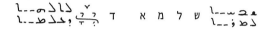

ש ל מ א ד

פ ה ראיתי אשה נבונה סוד יהוה נגלה אל

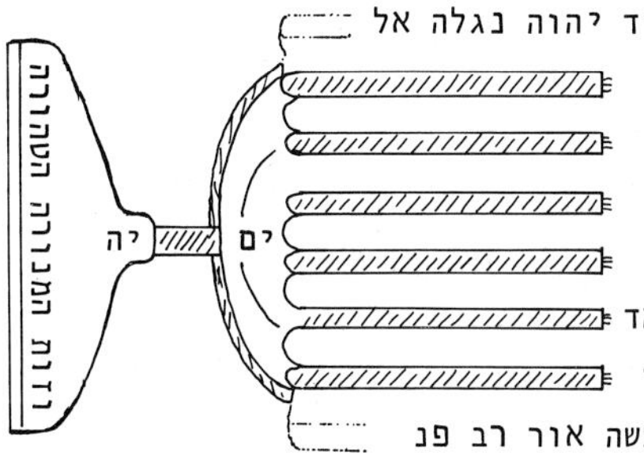

ר חב לבה בחכמת אלה

א מריה הן אמרי שפר

נ פשה חשקה בלשון עברי

ס חרה טוב מפנינים יקר

י דה רב לה בלשונות נחמד

נ רה לא יכבה יזרח לדור

א ל נורא יאיר סגולה נפשה אור רב פנ

כבודה בת מלך פנימה: אשת חיל ברוך טעמה: טעמה כי טוב הוא סחרה: אשר ערוכה ושמורה:
ראשית חכמה יראה טהורה: יש לתפרתה ואוצרה: נר מצוה ואור תורה: אשרי לה כי גדול שכרה:

ר או הגבירה אחזה בסנסנ
ו היא מדברת לשון גדול
ס פרי יונים כתבי חכמים בר
ק ראו נא זאת באהלי ישמעאל
א ם אין בקרבנו אל שוכן מעונ
מ ה לכם העבודה לשאול בתרפ

בסנסני החכמה לרעות בגנ
ובצחצחות דקדוק נחלת סגול
לשון אלוף לוטן ראש המדבר
ואדום אשר תהלתם פסיל
בראות בנותינו חלומות חזיונ
משובצי זהב ורצי כספ

ללקט בשושנ
שפת קדש הלול
בפיה הן שגור
קחו מוסר אויל
לאלהים פתרונ
עוברים וחולפ

ב חרו תבונה ה בינו בינה א זרו אמונה גדלו החכמה:

עשה פה האג הבירה יהיה לזכרון למורה על קליגרף הזה בחודש טבת שנת תקד לפרת ק עי ניימן יצו

Translation

a. Superscript (*line 1*; in Aramaic, flanked on right and left by four words in Syriac):
Aramaic: The peace of the Lord; Syriac: Glory to God, to the Lord of the Universe.

b. First register (*lines 2-9*; These lines give the name *Fransina* three times as an acrostic: the first letters 1° of these lines, 2° of the words in line 2, and 3° of the words in line 9, backwards. The lines 2 and 9 both end in *-yh*, whereas all the lines in between end in *-ym* (or possibly the lines 3, 5 and 7); this has been shown in a drawing of a menorah, characterized by a short line (9a) written on its base:

2: Here I see a sensible woman, the counsel of the Lord[a) has been revealed to her [b)];
3: her heart has enlarged[c)] in the wisdom of God[d)];
4: her words are pleasant words[e)];
5: her heart is longing for[f)] the tongue of the Hebrews;
6: her merchandise is better[g)] than precious pearls[h)];
7: great is her skill in languages of delightful people;
8: her light will not be extinguished[i)], it will shine for ever;
9: the awe-inspiring God lightens the treasure of her soul, a mighty light is her face;
9a: and this is the pure menorah.

c. Two *lines 10-11*, each consisting of four short sentences, spelling the name *Catarina* in an acrostic:

10a: A king's daughter is glorious within[k)];
b: a capable woman, blessed be her discernment;
c: she perceives that her merchandise is good[l)],
d: which is ordered and secured[m)];
11a: the beginning of wisdom is the real fear[n)];
b: that is to her a splendour and a treasure;
c: the commandment is a lamp, and a light is the Law[o)];
d: blessed is she, because her reward is great.

d. Second register (*lines 12-17*; these lines form the name *Roskam*; each line consists of three parts, all ending in *-ym*):

12: Behold, the lady, firmly holding on the palm-leaves[p)], palm-leaves of wisdom, to tend in the gardens, to gather lilies[q)];
13: and she speaks a language of the great, and in the clear words of grammar there is an inheritance of treasures, the language of holy exultations[r)];

14: the books of the Greek, clear writings of wise people, the language of the leader who speaks Latin - the foremost of those who speak - in her mouth they are fluent;

15: proclaim this in the tents of the Ishmaelites and Edom[s)] whose praise is for graven images[t)], accept discipline[u)], you fools[v)];

16: if God who dwells in heaven is not in our midst, when our daughters see visionary dreams[w)] - the explanations of which belong to God[x)] -

17: what sort of religion do you have, that you ask questions through the teraphim[y)] - set in gold[z)], with pieces of silver[aa)] - which are passing and changing?

e. The *last line* of the composition, consisting of four short exhortations, forming the acrostic *bh'g* "in The Hague" (line 18):

Choose understanding, perceive with intelligence[bb)], gird yourself with faith[cc)], glorify wisdom.

f. The text is finished off in *cursive* script with the following *subscription*:

He composed it here in The Hague, the capital, it will be as a remembrance of the teacher, by this calligraphy; in the month Teveth, the year 504 according to the short reckoning; by Neuman *y.ṣ.w*.

g. In the left-hand corner Neuman has *signed* in Dutch: by Petrus Werner Neuman C.j., former rabbi in Leeuwarden.

Remarks on the translation

a) Cf. e.g. Ps 24:14, Jer 23:18.

b) For the combination *swd* + *glh*, cf. Am 3:7.

c) Cf. Is 60:5.

d) Cf. 1 Kings 3:28.

e) Cf. Bamidbar Rabba xiv 11

f) Cf. Gen 34:8.

g) Cf. Prov 3:14.

h) Cf. Prov 3:15.

i) Cf. Prov 3:18.

k) Cf. Ps 45:14.

l) Cf. Prov 31:18.

m) Cf. for this combination of words 2 Sam 23:5.

n) Cf. Ps 111:10.

o) Cf. Prov 6:23.

p) Read probably *'aḥūzah*, and cf. *šyr lm^{c}lwt* for Abraham van Limburg[13)], first strophe, line h: *hm 'ḥwzym bsnsny hd^{c}t*; cf. however also Cant 7:9: *'oḥ^{a}zah b^{e}sansinnāw*.

q) Cf. Cant 6:2.

r) Cf. Lev 19:24.

s) Cf. Ps 83:7.

t) Cf. Is 42:8 (*ut*[e]*hillatī lapp*[e]*sīlīm*); the construction is awkward, however; or read *p*[e]*sillīm* (plural of *p*[e]*sillōs* "stammerer") and translate: whose praise is the praise of stammerers?

u) Cf. Prov 8:10.

v) Cf. also the combination *mūsar '*[a]*wilīm* "the discipline of the foolish ones" in Prov 16:22.

w) Cf. Joel 3:1.

x) Cf. Gen 40:8.

y) Cf. Ez 21:26.

z) Cf. Ex 28:20.

aa) Cf. Ps 68:31.

bb) Cf. Prov 1:2.

cc) Cf. Is 11:5.

Notes

1) Cf. Beem on Christiaan Meijer (see following note).
2) H. Beem, "Hartog Leuwy 'Geweesenen Rabbi der Jooden te Leeuwarden'" in *Nieuw Israelietisch Weekblad*, nos. 28/9, 5/10, 12/10, 19/10, 26/10, 1951; cf. also *id.*, *De Joden van Leeuwarden* (= *Joden*), Assen 1974, pp. 8f. The connection Hartog Leuwy = Petrus Werner Neuman first appeared in print in 1770. In the second printing of J. Koelman's *Historisch verhaal nopens de Labadische scheuring*, the publisher, Gerrit Tresling, mentions that J. Bosch' book *De ware Hope en verwachtinge Israels etc.*, which relates the conversion of Hartog Leuwy, may also be obtained from him, and he further remarks that the said rabbi after his conversion took the name of Petrus Werner Neuman.
3) *Het ligt ten Tijde des avonds Om te verligten de oogen Israëls, opdat zij mogen zien de trooster Zions, etc.* door Petrus Werner Nieuwman C.J., printed by Abraham Ferwerda, 1741.
4) See plate 1.
5) *Rouwklacht over het afsterven van den Hoogeerwaarden, Godzaligen en Hooggeleerden Heer Hieronymus van Alphen, in zijn Hoog Eerwaerde Leven Professor in de H. Godgeleerdheid in de Beroemde Hooge Schoole te Utrecht*, printed in Utrecht by Pieter Muntendam, text in Hebrew, with Dutch translation (Bibliotheca Rosenthaliana, Amsterdam, eenbladsdrukken B-28).
6) Abrahamus van Limburg, *Disputatio de instauratione Ecclesiae ad Jesaiae xxvi vs 19*; the promotion took place on 19 June 1745; see plates 2 and 3.
7) Cf. L. Miedema, *Resolutiën van de Vroedschap van Utrecht betreffende de Academie. Vervolg over 1693-1812* (*Werken van het Historisch Genootschap gevestigd te Utrecht*, *nova series*, vol. 52+), Utrecht 1900, pp. 302-303, and G.W. Kernkamp, *Acta et Decreta Senatus; Vroedschapsresolutiën en andere bescheiden betreffende de Utrechtse Academie* II, 1674-1766 (*Werken van het Historisch Genootschap gevestigd te Utrecht, tertia series*, no. 68), Utrecht 1938, pp. 431-432; on the visit of William iv to Utrecht cf. Miedema, *op. cit.*, pp. 300-301, Kernkamp, *op. cit.*, pp. 429-430; on this occasion Neuman is called Bernard, probably a misinterpretation of Werner, his middle name.
8) A reproduction of the title page is to be found in Beem, *Joden*, p. 8; for a description of this manuscript and some remarks on its contents, cf. K. Jongeling, "Petrus Werner Neuman, 18e-eeuws Hebraist" in *Studia Rosenthaliana* vol. 17, 1983, pp. 32-40.
9) *Rouwklacht op het zeer smartelijk afsterven van Willem Karel Hendrik Friso*, door P.W. Neuman, informator in de Oostersche Taalen te Utrecht, printed in The Hague by Anthoni de Groot and Sons, 1751; text in Hebrew, with Dutch translation (Bibliotheca Rosenthaliana, Amsterdam, eenbladsdrukken A-5).
10) Cat. no T.-H.A. B 60; under the same number as the MS. a description and translation of the ode can be found, copied from Frederik Muller, *Catalogue de Calligraphie*, 1873, no 116; both the description and the translation are incomplete.
11) W. Eekhoff, *Catalogus van de Kunstverzameling der stad Leeuwarden etc.* (= *Catalogus*), Leeuwarden 1875, pp. 195f.
12) W. Eekhoff, *Supplement op den Catalogus der Stedelijke Bibliotheek, 1870-1874*, in *Catalogus*, pp. 208f.
13) See above note 6.

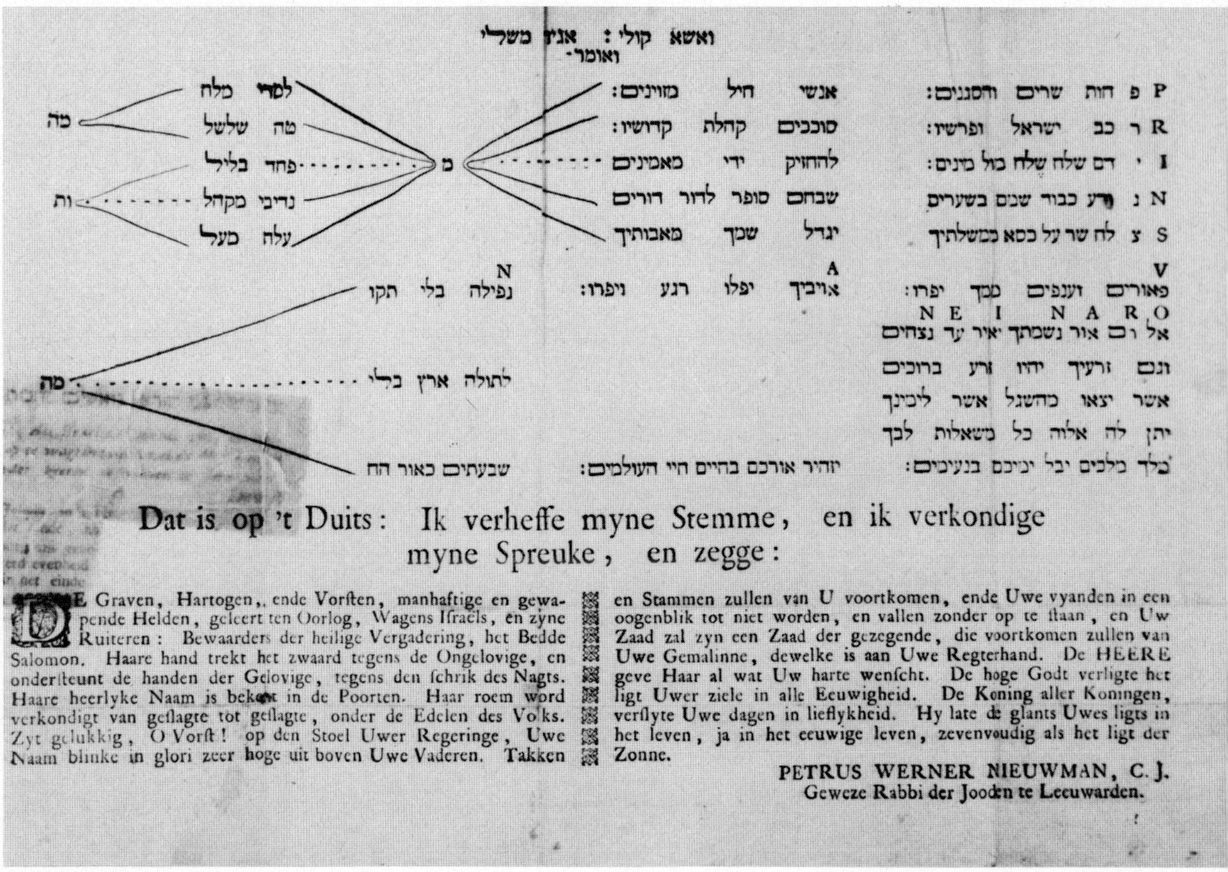

ואשא קולי : אניז משלי
ואומר׳

P פ חות שרים והסננים: — אנשי חיל מוינים: — לספרי מלח
R ר כב ישראל ופרשיו: — סוכבים קהלת קדושיו: — טה שלשל — מה
I י דם שלח שלח כול מינים: — להחויק ידי מאמינים — מ — פחד בליל
N נ רע כבוד שנם בשערים — שבחם סופר לדור דורים — נדיבי מקהל — ות
S צ לה שר על כסא ממשלתיך — יגדל שכך מאבותיך — עלה מעל

V
פאורים וענפים מכך יפרו: — A אויביך יפלו רגע ויפרו: — N נפילה בלי תקו
N E I N A R O
אל רם אור נשמתך יאיר עד נצחים
וגם זרעך יהיו זרע ברוכים — לתולה ארץ בלי — מה
אשר יצאו כהשגל אשר ליכינך
יתן לה אלוה כל משאלות לבך
מלך מלכים יבל ימיכם בנעימים: — יזהיר אורכם בחיים חיי העולמים: — שבעתים כאור החמה

Dat is op 't Duits : Ik verheffe myne Stemme, en ik verkondige myne Spreuke, en zegge :

DE Graven, Hartogen, ende Vorsten, manhaftige en gewapende Helden, geleert ten Oorlog, Wagens Israels, en zyne Ruiteren : Bewaarders der heilige Vergadering, het Bedde Salomon. Haare hand trekt het zwaard tegens de Ongelovige, en onderfteunt de handen der Gelovige, tegens den fchrik des Nagts. Haare heerlyke Naam is bekent in de Poorten. Haar roem word verkondigt van geflagte tot geflagte, onder de Edelen des Volks. Zyt gelukkig, O Vorft! op den Stoel Uwer Regeringe, Uwe Naam blinke in glori zeer hoge uit boven Uwe Vaderen. Takken en Stammen zullen van U voortkomen, ende Uwe vyanden in een oogenblik tot niet worden, en vallen zonder op te ftaan, en Uw Zaad zal zyn een Zaad der gezegende, die voortkomen zullen van Uwe Gemalinne, dewelke is aan Uwe Regterhand. De HEERE geve Haar al wat Uw harte wenfcht. De hoge Godt verligte het ligt Uwer ziele in alle Eeuwigheid. De Koning aller Koningen, verflyte Uwe dagen in lieflykheid. Hy late de glants Uwes ligts in het leven, ja in het eeuwige leven, zevenvoudig als het ligt der Zonne.

PETRUS WERNER NIEUWMAN, C. J.
Geweze Rabbi der Jooden te Leeuwarden.

שיר למעלות

הבחור הנחמד והמשכיל המלמד בתורה האלהות ושאר חכמתירא

אברהם פאן לימבורג

על ויכוחו אשר יתוכח בישעיהו הנביא סימן כו פסוק יש

תחת

המלמד הגדול/ וחכם הכולל/ אחד מראשי הישיבה/ בעיר איטרעכט/

אלבערטוס פוגעט

אשר כמוהו/ צח ויקר/ לא נתנו ויתנו/ האלהים וגורל הטבע/ אף
כי יהפכו הזמנים/ בזהב אופיר.

m h r b a

a א כבדך בחרווים ר חשתי ה יותן מ הנכב
b ב חור כארוים/ מבחורי חמד מזהב ומפז נחמ
r ר אשית בכורי שריגי שכלך/ אשר השרגת לפני נני — רים
h ה ס אחוזים בסנסני הדעת ועל ארני אמת מים
m מ רבדים ה לולים רברת בחכמתך/ אלי תידי

a b r h m

ואשא משלי ואומר

a א ין אשאף רוח לעצור כח למצא מנוח באלה הזמנים המסב
b ב וקה ומבוקה ומבלקה מכשול ופוקה בגד בוגדים בגדו בכל פ
r ר בו מלחמה והמהומה האף וחמה הבוק והבוז והבוז לגאיו
h ה שד ושבר חרב ודבר ובכל עבר בהלה וחלחלה כלו קמשו
m מ כנף ארץ שמענו פרץ גסבא הקורץ בשערי גוי צדיק שומר אמו — נים
v פ קו פרושים אשר מכחישים רעת קרושים מעשי עכביש הם מחסה לשפ
a א מרים זרים בלתי ישרים משתה שמרים מים הזדונים וטיט היו
m נ גד עינינו תלאותינו ואין טוב לנו כי אם להשען עלשוכן מעו

ואען G

ואען ואומר

ועתה יראי אלהים התנחמו/ l ל א אלכן עם אדוני התמים
עוד היום בא בהפיל ארץ רפאים/ i י ושר השיר/ עיר עז לנו אלה
וחפרה לבנה/ ובושה חמה/ m מ וסר תוא לא יחישו מאמינ
ואם כפירים ושועלים מחבלים/ b ב כרם אלהים צבאות חונ — ים
לא נכרת ער ועגה מאהלינו/ u ו עומד בין החיים והמת
הם החכמים/ מאורות הגדולים/ r ר כבי ישראל הרים הגבנונ
בי כרמנו סמדר/ בפרי עץ הדר/ g ג ן נעול וכו ילכו צדיק

וזאת ברכת אברהם

והנה גם אתה אברהם בן אברהם נצר מגזע ישר
נחלת נחלת אברהם אבין ליראה אדוני כל הים
דרכת בעקבות הורך ומורך הולך בארחות צדיק
אמריו אמרות טהורות צרופים רצופים ברצי כסף
אשפתך מלא חצים שנונים צרת ציד עשית מטעמ — ים
בפרושך על דברי הצחות מישעיהו יקר הנביא
רכב וצלח על מרכבת החכמה צמח בכתנות אלהי
היה גודר פרץ ועמוד כיכין ובועז בכנכת משיח
עד שבה טובה עד יאסף אברהם אל עמו לאור באור חי

P. W. NEUMAN,
geweesene Rabbi te
LEUWAARDEN.

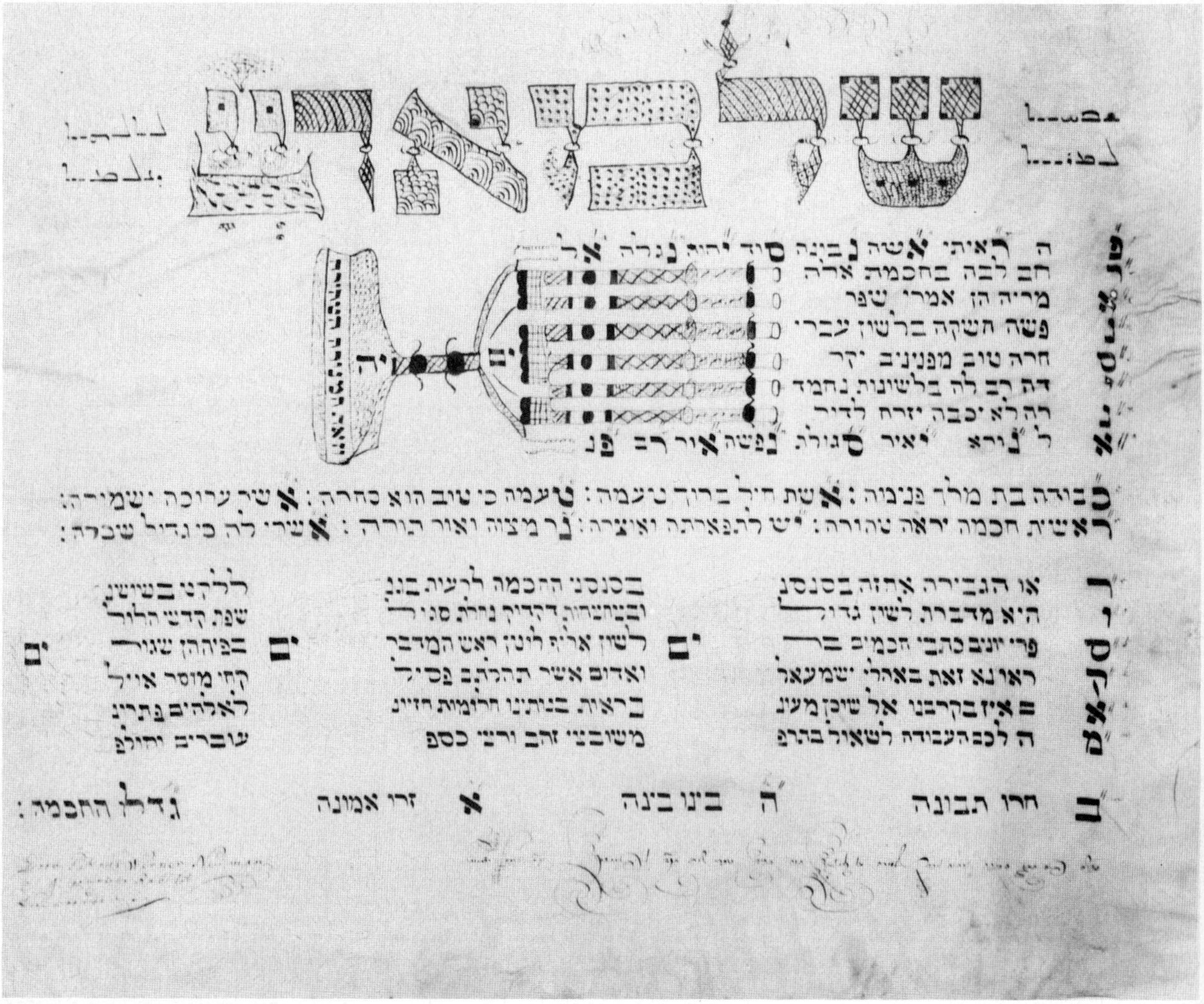
ה ראיתי אשה נבונה סיד יהיה נגרה אר
חב לבה בחכמה ארה
מריה הן אמרי שפר
פשה חשקה ברשון עברי
חרה טוב מפנינים יקר
דת רב לה בלשונות נחמד
רה רא יכבה יזרח לדיר
ר נורא יאיר סגולת נפשה איר רב פנ

כבודה בת מלך פנימה : אשת חיל ברוך טעמה : טעמה כי טוב הוא סחרה : אשר ערוכה ושמורה :
ראשית חכמה יראה טהורה : יש לתפארתה ואוצרה : נר מצוה ואור תורה : אשרי לה כי גדול שכרה :

או הגבירה אחזה בסנסנ
היא מדברת לשון גדול
פרי ינוב כתבי חכמים בר
ראו נא זאת באהלי ישמעאל
איז בקרבנו אל שוכן מעונ
ה לכה העבודה לשאול בתרפ

בסנסני החכמה לרעית בנג
ובצחצחות דקדוק נרות סני ר
לשון ארוך לונן ראש המדבר
ואדום אשר תהלתב פסיל
בראית בנותינו חרומות חזיונ
משובצי זהב ורשי כספ

לרקתי בשושנ
שפת קדשי הלור
בפיהן שגור
קחי מוסר איל
לאלהים פתרונ
עוברים יחלפ

חרו תבונה ה בינו בינה א זרו אמונה גדלו החכמה :

Translation and Canonicity

A Study in the Narrative Portions of the Greek Exodus

J. W. Wevers, Toronto

Translation as a branch of Applied Linguistics is often overlooked by professional linguists, but not by Hans Hospers the dedicatee[1)], for whom this study is written[2)].

0.1. The particular problem to be faced in this study is: Does canonicity affect the translation process, and if so, how? By canon I mean any writing which is viewed by the reader as having normative status for thought and practice, as containing more than human authority, as being "word of God." More specifically this study concentrates on the Torah, i.e. the Biblical Pentateuch. The presupposition underlying this paper is that the Jews of third century B.C.E. Alexandria accepted the Torah as canon.

0.2. It should be clear at the outset that the Torah was considered to be canon both in the original Hebrew format as well as in the Greek Translation. That the translation was itself viewed as the divine word is clear not only from the fact that it is cited as such in earliest times (such as in Philo and the N.T.), but from the Letter of Aristeas as well. The Letter quotes the verdict of the Jews as being accurate in all details (*katà pân ēkribōménōs*)[3)], and a curse on anyone who might alter the text in any way. This view of the translation as being canonical contrasts with the place of the Targums in Jewish thought. The Targums were not viewed as anything but aids to the understanding of the Hebrew text; they were not substitutes, they were not themselves canonical, but served as "cribs"[4)]. Since the Targums were intended as crutches they tend on the whole to be word for word translations (at least in theory), and seldom deviate greatly from their Hebrew parent text. In the discussion below it will be taken for granted that Tar[5)] in contrast to LXX equals MT unless otherwise stated.

1.0. It would seem reasonable to assume that canonicity would make some kind of impact on a translation. If one is producing the word of God one would expect an attempt at accuracy much greater than for some secular work. Thus at 4:6 MT states that "his hand was *mṣr^{c}t* as snow". LXX omits "leprous" since snow is not leprous but rather white. What MT really means to say is that his hand was white as snow. That this was intended is clear where LXX interprets the restoration of the hand as *eis tȇn chróan tē̂s sarkȍs autoû,* whereas MT simply has "like his flesh."

At 8:9 Moses in speaking to Pharaoh refers to the removal of frogs "from thee and from thy households." LXX inserts "and from thy servants" in agreement with v. 11, but changes the last phrase to the plural "your," i.e. reading "from thee and from thy servants and out of (*ek*) your households." That this is no lapsus calami is clear from the fact that the same distiction is made in vv. 11 and 21 although MT (and Tar) consistently read the 2nd masc. sing. suffix throughout.

1.1. This kind of pedantic exactness is often reflected when that which is implicit in the text is rendered explicit in LXX. I give but two examples of this very common phenomenon. At 16:3 MT reads "Would that we had died *byd yhwh*. Tar reads for the relevant phrase *qdm ywy*, whereas LXX understanding the phrase literally added a participle: *plēgéntes hupò kuríou*, i.e. "being smitten by the Lord." That death in Egypt would have been affected by Yahweh, i.e. a natural death rather than by famine, is implicit in MT (and in Tar?), but it is explicitly stated in LXX. At 24:1 Moses is commanded along with Aaron, Nadab, Abihu and seventy elders to ascend to Yahweh and "you shall worship from afar." It is of course clear who is to be the object of worship, but LXX makes this explicit by adding *tō̂i kuríōi*. From these examples it is obvious that every "i" must be dotted and every "t" crossed in the LXX in contrast to the practice of Tar.

2.0. The factor of canonicity also involves <u>clarity</u>, i.e. the word of God should be unambiguous. At 1:2-4 the names of Jacob's sons are given, and v. 5 continues with the number of the individuals coming from the loins of Jacob, and with the statement that Joseph was in Egypt. LXX inverts these two clauses of v. 5, thereby placing the gross total of descendants at the end, which makes for a more logical order. At 3:2-3 MT has the bush burning (*b^{c}r*) with fire but the bush is not burned up (*'kl*); then Moses wants to see why the bush is not burning (*yb^{c}r*). LXX uses *kaietai* (burn) for the first, *katekaieto* (burned up) for the second, and with better logic than MT *katakaietai* for the last. Tar also changes the root for the last verb to *mtwqd* (alongside *b^{c}r* and *mt'kyl* resp.).

On occasion pronominal referents are identified even though to a modern reader they would be perfectly obvious. For example at 4:6 it is said about Moses that "he brought his hand into his bosom." Then follows the clause "and he brought it out." This was not clear enough for the translator who wrote "and he brought his hand out from his bosom."

2.1. Clarity is sometimes achieved through a minor change which changes what MT has into a somewhat different statement, i.e. the change does not reflect accurately what MT says. Thus at 4:20 when Moses returned to Egypt he took the *mṭh h'lhym* (Tar has "the rod by which signs from before *ywy* were done"); this phrase is ambiguous - what does "God's rod" mean? LXX clarifies this by designating God as the source *tḕn rábdon tḕn parà toû theoû*.

At 18:23 verse a is not fully clear. "If you do this thing, *wṣwk 'lhym*, and you will be able to stand." Does "and God will command you" belong to the protasis or to the apodosis? Furthermore just what does it mean? LXX clarifies this neatly by its *katischúsei se ho theós*. By omitting the conjunction and rendering the verb by "shall strengthen" the matter is clear: it is part of the apodosis.

2.2. Clarity can often be achieved by identifying the subject of the verb. At 3:11 and at 3:13 MT has "And Moses said to God," but the intervening verse has simply "And he said." This was not clear enough for LXX which has "And God said to Moses." It really could hardly be interpreted as "Furthermore he said," since the context makes it fully clear that it is God who is promising Moses his continued presence and help, but LXX avoids even a momentary uncertainty on the part of the reader. This kind of clarification is particularly in evidence when a change of subject obtains. At 10:3 Moses and Aaron entered Pharaoh's presence and they proclaim a divine oracle. At the end of the oracle (v. 6) MT has "and he turned and left Pharaoh's presence." Since God had been speaking, the subject might theoretically be God; LXX avoids this possible reading by adding *mōusē̂s* as subject. Cf. also 11:8 for the same identification by LXX.

Such an identification for clarity's sake is particularly relevant at 13:19 where MT states that Moses took the bones of Joseph with him because *he* had made the Israelites swear on oath. But it was Joseph, not Moses, who had made the Israelites swear, and LXX adds *iōsḗph* after *hṓrkisen*. At 24:16 the subject of "And he summoned" is not stated in MT. Grammatically the possible antecedents might be the *kbwd yhwh* or *h^{c}nn*. Common sense tells us that it is of course *yhwh* who summoned Moses (or more particularly the glory of Yahweh), but LXX does not leave it to common sense; it adds *kúrios*. Similarly at 34:4 the subject of "took in his hand" has to be Moses. Since the immediately preceding clause read "as Yahweh had commanded him", the change of subject is shown by adding *mōusē̂s*.

2.3. Occasionally the translator adds an interpretative gloss in order to avoid any possible misunderstanding. At 2:11 "Moses went out to his brethern" to which LXX adds *toùs huioùs isra̅ḗl*, making sure that Moses, though the adopted son of the court, still recognized the Israelites, not the Egyptians, as his own race. So too at 4:15 MT has God saying to Moses in defining Aaron's role "and you shall put the words into his mouth." But what words? Not those of Moses but rather *tà r̄ḗmatá mou*.

3.0. If the translation is to be truly canonical it must also have inner consistency. Thus when the tense of MT does not seem to fit well into the context LXX levels it out. At 9:15 MT in a future context reads "*šlḥty* my hand *wʾk* you and your people with pestilence *wtkḥd* from the land." LXX "corrects" this by using resp. *aposteílas, patáxō* and *ektribḗsēi*. At 17:11 the opposite is the case; in a past context the statement occurs that when Moses *yrym* his hands, *wgbr* Israel, but when *ynyḥ* his hands *wgbr* Amalek. LXX uses the aorist and imperfect within the pairs with fine feeling for the narrative. Tar sensing an anomaly used participles. So too 18:26 is presented in MT in the future throughout even though vv. 25 and 27 are in the preterite. LXX removes all seeming inconsistencies by placing all the verbs in the aorist.

3.1. Inconsistency in number is often levelled out as well. At 10:17 *ś*' is rendered by the plural *prosdéxasthe* in LXX, since Pharaoh is addressing Moses and Aaron (v. 16), and the verse continues with the plural as well (*whᶜtyrw*). At 17:3 MT has "Why did you bring us up... to kill me and my children and my cattle...?" LXX interprets the verse as plural: "us... kill us and our children and cattle." And at 34:15b in referring to the indigenous populations, MT has "when they fornicate with their gods and sacrifice to their gods *wqrʾ* thee and thou wilt eat *mzbḥw*." Both LXX and Tar use plural references throughout, thereby making a consistent text.

3.2. Such a leveling of the text to fit its context manifests itself in various ways. At 6:13 Yahweh gave orders to Moses and Aaron for "*bny yśrʾl wʾl* Pharaoh ... to bring out the Israelites from the land of Egypt." But the Israelites are the object of the bringing out; they can hardly be the subjects as well. And according to vv. 11 and 12 Moses and Aaron were only ordered to appraoch Pharaoh, and so LXX leaves out this subject reference to the Israelites. At 18:1 LXX also shortens the text by omitting the reference to Moses in "what God had done to Moses and to Israel." Such mention is not only unnecessary, it also does not correspond to the rest of the verse: how Yahweh had brought Israel out of Egypt.

3.2.1. In 18:3-6 reference is made to Moses' wife and her (two) sons. This is rendered by his sons; so too when Moses is told about "her sons with her," LXX has "thy sons with him (i.e. Jethro)." Reference to Zipporah is kept to a minimum, not out of prejudice but rather to make a consistent narrative. In vv. 3 and 4 the popular etymologies for the sons' names are given and these are quotations from Moses not from his wife. Futhermore in the subsequent narrative only Moses and Jethro take part. Thus Moses' wife and sons are simply described as accompanying Jethro.

3.2.2. In vv. 8-10 reference is made in each verse to the fact that Yahweh delivered Israel. In v. 9 MT adds "from the land of Egypt" and in v.10, "from the hand of Egypt and from the hand of Pharaoh." LXX levels out the text by having the coordinate prepositional phrases in all three verses.

3.2.3. At 24:13-15 MT has an apparent inconsistency; it reads "And Moses and Joshua his servant arose ... and Moses went up ... and he said: wait here for us until we return ... and Moses went up." The part played by Joshua is most ambiguous. LXX makes a consistent plural narrative: "they went up", "they said", and "they went up." A similar inconsistency occurs in 32:4-6a. It is said of Aaron that "he took... fashioned ... made a golden calf and they said ... Then Aaron saw ... built ... called out and said ... and they rose up ... they sacrificed ... they brought peace offerings". In MT the action is divided between Aaron and the people, whereas LXX interprets all verbs as singular, with Aaron as the subject throughout the narrative.

3.2.4. At 33:1 LXX also makes a "correction", thereby showing how carefully the translator thought about his text. MT refers to the land which "I swore to Abraham, Isaac and Jacob saying *lzrᶜk* I will give it." LXX renders the word by *tôi spérmati humôn*, not "to thy seed" but "to your seed" because there are three fathers, not one, to whom the promise is directed.

4.0. Canonicity ought to involve the removal of apparent self-contradictions not only within the immediate context, but also within the larger context of the book as well as the full context of the Torah itself.

4.1. At 16:8 MT has an apparent discrepancy in the text. Verse a refers to "your murmurings against him (i.e. Yahweh)," but the verse goes on to say "but what are we? Your murmurings are not *kath hēmôn* but against Yahweh." LXX removes the apparent discrepancy by rendering "against him" by *kath hēmôn* as well. An apparent discrepancy is also removed in 24:1 and 24:2. Moses is told to come up to Yahweh along with Aaron, his two sons, and seventy elders and you shall worship at a distance. Then Moses alone shall draw near to Yahweh, but they (the others) shall not draw near nor shall the people go up with him. LXX, by changing you to "they" and him to "them", makes a more logical text. The others woship at a distance; Moses draws near to Yahweh.

Of course the people could not go up with Moses; what the narrative means is that they stayed behind the "others" as well.

4.2. Nor should there be discrepancies in the larger context of the book. At 7:7 the age of Moses and that of Aaron are given when they spoke (*bdbrm*) to Pharaoh. LXX, however, has *eláēsen*, with the verbal action involving only Aaron. This agrees with vv. 1 and 2 which state that only Aaron will be doing any speaking to Pharaoh. At 6:20 MT says that Amram's wife bore to him Aaron and Moses. But according to 2:4 there was also a daughter, and LXX adds after Moses "and Mariam their sister".

4.2.1. At times it is not so much anomalies that are being removed as the adoption of a rendering from the larger context. At 6:14 the manna is described as "fine, flaky, fine" (*dq mḥsps dq*), whereas LXX has *leptòn hōseì kórion leukón*. Only the first word equals MT, i.e. *dq*, but "like coriander seed white" is taken from v. 31. Similarly in v. 23 for MT *hwʾ* (is what Yahweh ordered), LXX seems to have a different text; it has *toûto tò rē̂má estin*, based on v. 32 where MT has *zh hdbr* in the same context.

4.2.2. The popular responses to the demands of Yahweh occur at 19:8 24:3,7. In each instance the people reply "All that Yahweh has spoken we will do," but at 24:7 MT adds "and we will obey". LXX makes the three exactly the same by adding *kaì akousómetha* each time. And at 19:10 Yahweh orders Moses: "Go (*lk*) to the people", for which LXX has "*katabàs diamárturai* to the people". Again the context supplies the source; in v. 21 Yahweh orders Moses: *rd hᶜd*, which LXX renders correctly by *katabàs diamárturai*.

4.3. Ideally the entire canon of the Torah should contain no discrepancies, and sometimes there is evidence in LXX of that ideal being present in the translator's mind. Occasionally the source of a plus in the text is to be located in some other part of the Torah. Thus at the end of 34:13 the clause *kaì tà gluptà tō̂n theō̂n autō̂n katakaúsete purí* has no support in MT; it is taken from Deut 7:5.

4.3.1. But of more consequence are instances of apparent contradictions. At 1:5 MT gives the number of people descended from Jacob as seventy, whereas LXX has seventy five. The difference in number probably has its source in the LXX of Gen 46:27 where the number coming down to Egypt is also given as seventy five (contra MT). It would then appear that the Gen LXX was known to the Exodus translator. According to 6:20 Amram married Jochebed his paternal aunt (*ddtw*). This, however, contravenes the laws of incest contained in Lev 18:12 and LXX therefore interprets the relationship as *thugatéra toû adelphoû toû patròs autoû*, i.e. a cousin.

At 13:6 the Israelites are ordered to eat unleavened bread (at Passover) for seven days, and the seventh day shall be a feast. LXX changes this to six days in accordance with Deut 16:8, i.e. first the six days (of unleavened bread), and then the seventh day (also one of unleavened bread! cf. v. 7), making a total of seven.
At 13:11 the promise of land is described in MT as being "as he swore to thee and to thy fathers". LXX simply has "as he swore to thy fathers". This then agrees with the patriarchal promises in Genesis. God's oath was with the fathers, not with the contemporary generation.

4.3.2. A list of the peoples occupying the promised land occurs at 3:8,17 13:5 23:23 33:2 34:11. The list is not always a complete list but in the LXX always includes the Girgashites, whereas MT never mentions them anywhere in Exodus. But the full list in Deut 7:1 does include the Girgashites, and LXX therefore includes them as well.

Above all, God's word must avoid that which is theologically infelicitous, or better said, it must be a theologically correct interpretation. This may simply mean a clarification as at 18:20 where Jethro says to Moses that he must teach them (i.e. the people) the statutes and the laws. This body of materials is divine in origin in the eyes of the Alexandrian translator who renders the coordinate nouns by *tà prostágmata toû theoû kaì tòn nómon autoû.*

5.1. At 33:13 the LXX interpretation may seem somewhat removed from MT. In the latter Moses pleads with God:"Make me know thy way (*hwdᶜny ʾt drkk*)", whereas LXX has *emphánisón moi ceautón*, "make thyself manifest to me". Scripture must be interpreted by Scripture, and in v. 18 Moses makes clear that he meant "Show me thy glory".

5.2. Sometimes LXX makes a statement which is stronger than MT, probably more in line with contemporary theological emphasés. Certainly this seems to be the case at 8:10 where the nominal clause "there is none like Yahweh our God" becomes a declaration of a monotheistic faith *ouk éstin állos plḕn kuríou*. In fact, the absoluteness is rendered even more starkly by the omission of "our God".
At v. 22 LXX also makes a much stronger statement than MT. Here too a nominal statement occurs in MT: "I am Yahweh in the midst of the land". Tar adds *šlyṭ* after Yahweh, and LXX represents such a tradition by its *egṓ eimi kúrios ho kúrios pásēs tē̂s gē̂s*[6)].

5.3. At times LXX avoids a so-called "literal" rendering, because such a rendering is according to LXX not what it really means. Thus at 3:6 Moses hid his face because he was afraid *mhbyṭ ʾl hʾlhym*, "of looking at God". - Tar has *yqrʾ dywy* for "God". - LXX interprets this as *katemblépsai enṓpion toû theoû*. After all, "looking at God" would result in death according to 33:20 (cf. 4.0. above).

At 4:16 MT says (about Aaron) "he will become a mouth for you (*yhyh lk lph*) and you will become God for him (*thyh lw l'lhym*)." Naturally this cannot mean that Moses will actually become God, and LXX interprets these to mean *stóma* and *tà pròs tòn theón* resp. Incidentally Tar interprets the two words as *mtwrgmn* "interpreter" and *rb* "master".

5.4. Finally there are two examples of statements in MT that the people "saw God" in 24:10 and 24:11 (in both cases Tar has *yqr' dywy* for "God"), which LXX interprets in a theologically correct fashion. Since 33:20 flatly states that this is impossible, the "literal" rendering cannont be correct. According v. 10 reads for the relevant clause *eîdon tòn tópon hoû heistḗkei ekeî ho theòs toû israḗl*, and in v. 11 *ṓphthēsan en tō̂i tópōi toû theoû*. What LXX says is that this is what those statements in MT really mean.

6. In summary it should be noted that the five characteristics of the Greek rendering of the narrative parts of Exodus are not necessarily due solely to the factor of canonicity. But it does seem noteworthy that over against the Targum which is not a canon the LXX which is such has such marked characteristics. The fact that a translator believed that his product was the word of God in the same sense that the Hebrew Torah was must have made a difference to the product. After all, the word of God should be exact, clear, consistent, without self-contradiction, and theologically correct.

Notes

1) For his most recent statement cf. J.H. Hospers, "Translating the Old Testament" in *Essays in honour of Rev. Chris MacKaay, contributed by colleagues, friends and students* (*Trinity Occasional Papers*, vol. 3,3), Brisbane 1984, pp. 9-15. Cf. pp. 13f. for a recent bibliography on the linguistics of translation. I am grateful for this opportunity of expressing my appreciation to the *ba^c^al haYovel* for 35 years of collegial friendship.
2) Recent studies of the linguistic phenomena involved in translation by the writer are J.W. Wevers, "The Use of Versions for Text Criticism: The Septuagint", in *La Septuaginta en la Investigacion Contemporanea* (V. Congreso de la IOSCS), ed. N. Fernández Marcos, Madrid 1985, pp. 15-24, and *id.* "An Apology for Septuagint Studies" in *Bulletin of the International Organization for Septuagint and Cognate Studies* vol. 18, 1986 (in the press).
3) *Letter of Aristeas*, 310f.
4) This fundamental difference between Septuagint and Targum is convincingly argued by R. Le Déaut in "La Septante, un Targum?" in *Etudes sur le Judaïsme hellénistique* (*Lectio Divina*, vol. 119), Paris 1984, pp. 147-195. Le Déaut gives a large number of examples to illustrate these differences from various parts of the O.T.
5) For this paper only the Targum Onkelos is cited. The edition used is A. Sperber, *The Bible in Aramaic Based on Old Manuscripts and Printed Texts*, vol. 1, Leiden 1959.
6) Possibly LXX's parent text read *'dn* after *yhwh*.

Erwägungen zur Doppelsprachigkeit des Buches Daniel

A.S. van der Woude, Groningen

In seiner am 9. Oktober 1948 gehaltenen Antrittsvorlesung erörterte Professor Hospers zwei Probleme betreffs des Aramäischen des Buches Daniel: die linguistische Datierung des in dieser biblischen Schrift verwendeten Aramäischen und die Doppelsprachigkeit des Buches[1)]. Es dürfte daher nicht unpassend sein, meinen verehrten Lehrer anlässlich der Niederlegung seines akademischen Amtes mit einem Aufsatz zu grüssen, in dem, obgleich hauptsächlich auf den Fragenkreis der Zweisprachigkeit beschränkt, die damals von ihm behandelte Thematik erneut aufgegriffen wird.

Unter Hinweis auf die Aktenstücke Esras hob Hospers in 1948 mit Recht hervor, dass für das Aramäische des Danielbuches mit einem *terminus a quo* um 400 v.Chr. gerechnet werden müsse, dass aber nach dieser Jahreszahl eine genauere Datierung mit sprachlichen Mitteln nicht möglich sei. Für die Bestimmung der Entstehungszeit der aramäischen Teile des Buches könnten deswegen nur inhaltliche Kriterien den Ausschlag geben[2)]. Tatsächlich lassen sich innerhalb des Reichsaramäischen sukzessive Sprachstufen nicht unterscheiden, nur dass seit etwa einem Jahrhundert nach dem Ende des persischen Reiches Schrift, Rechtschreibung und Sprache der einzelnen altorientalischen Länder sich verschieden entwickelten, wobei zunehmend die gesprochenen Sprachen auf das Reichsaramäische einwirkten[3)]. Solcher Einfluss lässt sich im Reichsaramäischen des Danielbuches nicht nachweisen[4)]. Hinzu kommt, dass in den aus vormakkabäischer Zeit stammenden aramäischen Fragmenten von I Henoch sowie im Hiobtargum weit weniger Parsismen begegnen als in den Erzählungen des Danielbuches[5)]. Beide Tatsachen zeigen, dass eine Verlegung des Danielaramäischen ins. 2. vorchristliche Jahrhundert unwahrscheinlich ist. Somit scheint die radikale Kritik mit ihrer Makkabäerthese auf dem sprachlichen Feld der aramäischen Kapitel des Danielbuches ihr Spiel eindeutig verloren zu haben[6)], allerdings ohne dass andererseits die Exilsthese gesiegt hätte[7)]. Erst recht liesse sich die Makkabäerthese nicht mehr behaupten, wenn Kutscher[8)] und Coxon[9)] darin recht habe, dass das Reichsaramäische des Buches bestimmte Spracheigentümlichkeiten des östlichen Typs zeigt, weil in dem Fall bei der nicht zu bezweifelnden palästinensischen Endverfassung der biblischen Schrift schon aus rein geographischen Gründen mit der Uebernahme einer älteren Vorlage aus dem babylonischen Bereich zu rechnen ist. Alles zusammengenommen befürworten die sprachlichen Indizien, die verhältnismässig zahlreichen akkadischen und persischen Lehnwörter, die Ergebnisse der Qumranforschung und die in den Osten weisenden Schauplätze der Danielerzählungen eine Datierung des Aramäischen des Buches in spätpersischer oder (wegen der griechischen Lehnwörter[10] und der Verwendung von 'Chaldäern' im Sinne von Astrologen)[11] wohl eher in frühhellenistischer Zeit. Obgleich linguistische Beobachtungen auf eine Entstehung der aramäischen Teile des Danielbuches im 3. vorchristlichen Jahrhundert hinweisen, dürfte es sich doch empfehlen, den Fragenkreis der Doppelsprachigkeit unabhängig von sprachlichen Schlussfolgerungen zu erörtern. Denn einmal ist die Verwendung des klassischen Reichsaramäischen in der Mitte des 2. Jahrhunderts nicht hundertprozentig auszuschliessen[12]. Zweitens hat die getrennte Behandlung des Problems der Doppelsprachigkeit den Vorteil, dass ihre Ergebnisse nachträglich mit den linguistischen Beobachtungen verglichen werden können, um zu sehen, ob jene mit diesen korrespondieren.

Es ist nicht meine Absicht, die seit 1948 veröffentlichte Literatur zum Problem der Doppelsprachigkeit Daniels aufzuführen und im einzelnen zu überprüfen. Diese Aufgabe erübrigt sich, nachdem Koch und zwei seiner Schüler eine kritische Uebersicht über die bisherige Danielforschung vorgelegt haben[13]. Unter Berücksichtigung älterer und neuerer Literatur möchte ich vielmehr eine These zur Zweisprachigkeit des Buches in Vorschlag bringen, die, wenn sie auch der früheren Forschung weitgehend verpflichtet ist, in dieser Form vielleicht noch nicht vorgetragen wurde.

Wenn man die Rede Hospers nach mehr als 35 Jahren nochmals durchnimmt, sieht man, dass die bis damals vorgeschlagenen Lösungen des Problems der Doppelsprachigkeit vielfach auch heute noch vertreten werden[14]. Wohl deswegen befürchtet P.R. Davies in seiner neulich veröffentlichten Einführung in das Buch Daniel, dass 'the presence, and the distribution, of the two languages in Daniel may be in the end inexplicable'[15]. Trotz aller Meinungsverschiedenheiten steht jedoch fest, dass das Problem sich - wenn überhaupt - nur auf redaktionskritischem Wege lösen lässt. Mit Recht stellt Koch fest, dass die Versuche, den Sprachwechsel zu erklären, in der neueren Zeit mit Beobachtungen zu Einheitlichkeit und Uneinheitlichkeit des Buches unter literarkritischen Aspekten zusammenhängen[16].

Fast bis zum Ueberdruss hat die Forschung darauf aufmerksam gemacht, dass die durch den Sprachwechsel bedingte Zweiteilung des Danielbuches (Aramäisch: 2:4b-7:28; Hebräisch: 1:1-2:4a; 8:1-12:13) nicht mit der Zweiteilung in Erzählungen (Kap. 1-6) und Visionen (Kap. 7-12) konform geht. Während Spinoza der Meinung was, dass Kapitel 1-7 'ex Chaldaeorum chronologiis' herrührten und dass Daniel die übrigen Kapitel geschrieben hatte[17)], haben seitdem bis heute viele Ausleger die Einheitlichkeit des Buches verfochten[18)], weil (wie Hospers[19)] richtig beobachtete) sich ihnen die formkritische Einteilung in Erzählungen und Visionen als zwingender erwies als die sprachliche. Aber auch diejenigen, die eine Zwei- oder Mehrquellentheorie vertreten[20)], scheinen in der Regel im Banne jener Einteilung zu stehen. Beek sagte sich jedoch in seiner Dissertation von ihr los[21)]. Er wies darauf hin, dass nur in Kap. 8-12 eine ausführliche Engellehre vorliegt, nicht aber in Kap. 7. Die Tiere als Symbole der in der Weltgeschichte auftretenden Weltmächte haben in Kap. 7 einen ganz anderen (u. zw. mythischen) Ursprung als in Kap. 8, wo Widder und Ziegenbock als Symbole für Persien und Griechenland seiner Meinung nach wahrscheinlich durch die astrologische Geographie des Altertums, nach der jedes Land einem Tierkreis unterstand, bedingt sind[22)]. Der wichtigste Unterschied zwischen Kap. 7 und 8-12 stellt nach Beek die verschiedene Beurteilung der sogenannten Endzeit dar, weil der hebräische Daniel vom Reich Gottes, so wie es in Kap. 2 und 7 geschildert wird, nichts weiss: 'mit dem Tode des verhassten Königs (Antiochos IV) ist anscheinend alles zu Ende'[23)]. Dequeker hat in 1960[24)] und noch einmal in 1973[25)] betont, dass nicht nur Kap. 7-12, sondern auch die danielischen Erzählungen apokalyptische Visionen enthalten (Dan 2: 31:45; 4:7-14.17-24), und dass Kap. 7 eine Traumvision ist wie die der Kap. 2 und 4, während in Kap. 8-12 der Visionär die Offenbarung im wachen Zustand erhält. Aehnlich wie Hölscher[26)] hebt er hervor, dass in Kap. 7 'the visionary's intention is to understand the secret of the myth', während in den folgenden Kapiteln 'a series of artificial allegories, largely invented and constructed by the author himself' vorliegen[27)]. Dieser aus inhaltlichen und formkritischen Gründen vorgenommenen, grundsätzlich mit der sprachlichen Einteilung konform gehenden Einteilung in Kap. 1-7 und 8-12 stimme ich zu, allerdings mit der Einschränkung, dass Kap. 7 nicht zum Grundbestand von Kap. 1-6 gehört[28)]. Denn in Kap. 7 erscheint ein ganz anderer Daniel als in dem vorangehenden Teil des Buches, noch ganz abgesehen davon, dass in Daniel 7 ursprünglich ein Ich-Bericht vorliegt, während Kap. 1-6 Er-Berichte bilden. In Kap. 1-6 zeigt sich Daniel, wenn auch von seinem Gott inspiriert, imstande, Traumvisionen und Rätselschrift zu deuten. Hingegen bedarf er in Kap. 7 der Hilfe eines *angelus interpres*, um die ihm gezeigte Vision zu erklären. In dieser Hinsicht entspricht der Daniel vom Kap. 7 dem der nachfolgenden Kapitel 8-12. Alles zusammengenommen zeigt Kap. 7 also nicht nur Unterschiede und Verbindungslinien in Bezug auf die Kapitel 1-6, sondern auch inbetreff 8-12. Diese Tatsache lässt sich nur dann befriedigend erklären, wenn wir Kap. 7 als Anhang zu Kap. 1-6 betrachten.

Wer könnte die ursprünglich separat überlieferte Vision von Kap. 7 diesen Kapiteln bzw. dem ganzen Buch hinzugefügt haben? In Betracht kommt wohl nur der makkabäische Verfasser von Kap. 8-12. Für diese These spricht erstens, dass dem ursprünglichen Ich-Bericht von Kap. 7 eingangs eine chronologische Notiz vorangeschickt worden ist (7:1). Die danielischen Erzählungen kennen derartige einleitende Datierungen der in ihnen geschilderten Ereignisse nicht (zu 1:1 und 2:1 s. unten), vgl. 3:1; 3:31; 5:1; 6:2. Sie sind jedoch für den makkabäischen Verfasser charakteristisch, vgl. abgesehen von 1:1 und und 2:1 die Stellen 8:1; 9:1 und 10:1. Durch diese chronologischen Notizen hat er das ganze Buch gegliedert, u.zw. in zeitlicher Abfolge: 3. Jahr des Jojakim (1:1); 2. Jahr des Nebukadnezzar (2:1); 1. Jahr des Belsazer (7:1); 3. Jahr des Belzaser (8:1). 1. Jahr des Darius (9:1) und 3. Jahr des Kyrus (10:1). Für die These, dass es der makkabäische Verfasser war, der Kap. 7 der aramäischen Vorlage von Kap. 1-6 hinzufügte, spricht auch, dass Kap. 7 inhaltlich Uebereinstimmungen mit den folgenden Kapiteln zeigt. Wie noch zu erklären sein wird (s. unten), erblickte der Endverfasser von Daniel 7 in den dort geschilderten Tieren, ähnlich wie in 8:8, wo auch das Bild des Horns zurückkehrt, die Diadochenreiche. Die Zeitangabe ^{c}*ad z*^{e}*man we*^{c}*iddān* in 7:12 und ^{c}*ad* ^{c}*iddān w*^{ec}*iddānīn uf*^{e}*lag* ^{c}*iddān* in 7:25 entspricht der von 12:7: *l*^{e}*mō*^{c}*ēd mō*^{ca}*dīm wāḥēṣī*. Das sich gegen den Himmel auflehnende Horn (Antiochos IV) sucht die Heiligen des Allerhöchsten (7:25) bzw. das Volk der Heiligen (8:24) zu vernichten. Dass diesem makkabäischen Endverfasser des Buches Daniel als Grundbestand eine aramäische Vorlage von Kap. 7 vorgelegen hat, dürfte auch aus den Worten der Ueberschrift *rē'š millīn '*^{a}*mar* von 7:1 und denen der Unterschrift ^{c}*ad kā sofā' dī mill*^{e}*tā'* von 7:28 hervorgehen, zumal ähnliche Formeln sonstwo weder in den Erzählungen noch in den Visionen begegnen. Die verwendete Vorlage lässt sich trotz der Ueberarbeitung noch ziemlich genau bestimmen, weil Kap. 7, so wie es uns jetzt vorliegt auffällige Unstimmigkeiten und sogar Widersprüche zeigt. Auf sprachlicher Ebene fallen (wie längst gesehen wurde)[29] in Vs. 8 die Wendung *miśtakkal h*^{a}*wēt* statt des sonst gebrauchten *ḥāzē h*^{a}*wēt* (VS. 2,6,7,9,13) und die Partikel *'*^{a}*lū* (der hier nicht, wie üblich, ein Partizip (vgl. Vs. 2,3, 5,7), sondern ein Perfekt folgt) statt *'*^{a}*rū* in Vs. 2,5,6,7 und 13 auf[30]. Zu beachten in diesem Vers ist auch die Hitpa^{c}al-Form *'et*^{ca}*qarā* statt einer Q^e^til- (vgl. Vs. 4,6,9,11,12,14) oder Hoph^c^al-Form (vgl. Vs. 4,5). Strukturell hat Noth[31] einen Unterschied gemacht zwischen dem durch *ḥāzē hᵃwēt waʾᵃrū* eingeleiteten Visionsbild und dem durch *ḥāzē hᵃwēt ᶜad dī* eingeführten Visionsvorgang. Er geriet dabei zu der Schlussfolgerung, dass in der ursprünglichen Vision Vs. 11b die Fortsetzung von Vs. 7 bilde, dass die Verse 9,10,13 und 14 sekundär seien, und dass von der Deutung, die die Vision von Daniel 7 in ihrer ursprünglichen Gestalt einmal gehabt haben muss, im jetzigen Bestand des Kapitels nur noch ein geringer Rest oder vielleicht überhaupt nichts mehr erhalten sei. Aber auch wenn man sich Noths Unterscheidung zwischen Visionsbild und Visionsvorgang anschliesst, lässt sich m.E. indessen nichts dagegen einwenden, in den Versen 9-10 und 11b eine zweigliedrige Beschreibung des nach dem Visionsbild von Vers 7 geschilderten Visionsvorgangs zu erblicken, zumal beide Stellen mit der für den Visionsvorgang bezeichnenden Formel *ḥāzē hᵃwēt ᶜad dī* anfangen und die aufgrund von den Versen 4 und 6 zu erwarteten Qᵉtil-Formen zeigen. Nicht die Stelle 9-10 oder Vers 11b dürfte daher die ursprüngliche Fortsetzung von Vers 7 bilden. Vielmehr waren es beide zugleich. Es ist sowieso verständlich, dass im Zusammenhang mit dem vierten Tier weiter ausgeholt wird als im Falle der anderen. Dass beide Stellen (Vs. 9-10 und 11b) als Schilderung des Visionsvorgangs betrachtet werden müssen, wird auch durch die Verse 19 und 22 nahegelegt, die sich leicht nacheinander lesen lassen und wohl beide (anders als Vs. 20-21) zum Grundbestand von Kap. 7 gehören[32]. Denn Vs. 22 setzt nicht nur die Verse 9-10, sondern auch 13-14 voraus, die ihrerseits eine Erwähnung der Vernichtung des vierten Tieres voraussetzen. Wenn aber die Verse 9-10 und 13-14 zum Grundbestand von Kap. 7 gehören, wird die These Noths, dass von der Deutung der ursprünglichen Vision nur noch ein geringer Rest oder überhaupt nichts mehr erhalten sei, hinfällig. Damit soll nicht verneint werden, dass der aramäische Urverfasser von Kap. 7 den poetischen Text von 9-10 und 13-14 einem ihm zur Verfügung stehenden Text entnommen haben kann.

Wenn, wie allgemein angenommen wird, mit den vier Tieren von Kap. 7 die vier Weltreiche (das babylonische, medische, persische und griechische) gemeint sind, vertragen sich Vs. 8 und Vs. 12 nicht mit dieser Deutung. Denn dass Vs. 8 sich auf Antiochos IV. bezieht, ist fast unbestritten[33]. Er aber war nicht das elfte Horn des griechisch-makedonischen Reiches, sondern des seleukidischen, eines der Diadochenreiche. Anders als der Autor der Vorlage erblickte der makkabäische Verfasser im vierten Tier das Seleukidenreich[34], vgl. auch 8:8. Diese Tatsache geht mit aller gewünschten Deutlichkeit auch aus Vs. 12 hervor. Dort heisst es, dass nach der Vernichtung des vierten Tieres den drei anderen Tieren noch für eine bestimmte Zeit 'Länge des Lebens' gewährt wird. Diese Bemerkung reimt sich nicht mit einer Weiterexistenz des babylonischen, medischen und persischen Reiches nach dem Fall des griechischen. Es kann nur daran gedacht sein, dass nach dem Ende des seleukidischen Reiches den anderen Diadochenreichen noch eine bestimmte Frist verliehen wird[35]. Es lässt sich daher folgern, dass der makkabäische Verfasser eine ihm zur Verfügung stehende aramäische Vorlage aktualisierte, indem er das vierte Tier auf das seleukidische Reich und das elfte Horn auf Antiochos IV. bezog. Somit dürfte die schon längst von manchen Forschern befürwortete These, dass Kap. 7 in seiner jetzigen Gestalt eine Ueberarbeitung einer aramäischen Vorlage ist, das Richtige treffen. Dann aber sind die Verse, die in diesem Kapitel auf das Seleukidenreich und auf Antiochos IV. Bezug nehmen, als spätere Zusätze des makkabäischen Verfassers zu betrachten. Es handelt sich dabei um die Verse 8,11a,12,20-21 und 24-25, die dementsprechend stellenweise Elemente enthalten, welche in den folgenden Kapiteln zurückkehren.

Weil der makkabäische Verfasser von Kap. 7 offenbar bestrebt war, seine Vorlage möglichst getreu zu behalten, hatte er die Wahl, entweder diese aus dem Aramäischen ins Hebräische zu übersetzen oder ihr seine Ergänzungen in aramäischer Sprache hinzuzufügen. Er entschied sich für die letzte Alternative, weil seine Ergänzungen bei weitem nicht so umfangreich waren wie der von ihm übernommene aramäische Text. Er konnte sich auch deswegen die Mühe einer Uebersetzung der Vorlage ersparen, weil er die vorangehenden Kapitel (mit Ausnahme von 1:1-2:4a, dazu s. unten) ebenfalls in ihrer Ursprache belassen hatte. Seine Ergänzungen auf Hebräisch dem aramäischen Text hinzuzufügen, dürfte er wohl nie ernsthaft erwogen haben!

Lässt sich so die Redaktionsgeschichte von Kap. 7 und dessen Ueberlieferung in aramäischer Sprache relativ leicht erklären, grössere Schwierigkeiten scheint die Frage zu bereiten, weshalf Kap. 1:1-2:4a in der heutigen Gestalt im Hebräischen vorliegt. Denn dass die auf Aramäisch geschriebenen Erzählungen, die uns in Kap. 2-6 erhalten geblieben sind, unbedingt einer Einleitung bedürfen, ist unbestritten. Diese bietet 1:1-2:4a, nur ist sie nicht in aramäischer (wie zu erwarten wäre), sondern in hebräischer Sprache überliefert worden. Zur Lösung des Problems hat wiederum Beek[36] vieles beigetragen, indem er voraussetzte, dass die ursprünglich aramäische Einleitung zu den folgenden Erzählungen von Kap. 2-6 inhaltlich grösstenteils in 1:3-7, 17-20 und 2-1aβ-4a vorhanden ist.

Mit Recht betrachtete er den Abschnitt 1:8-16 als Ergänzung des makkabäischen Endverfassers des Buches. Hatte die aramäische Urschrift harmlos mitgeteilt, dass die vier Jünglinge vom königlichen Tisch zu essen bekamen, eben an diesem Punkt lag für den späteren

Leser, besonders in der Zeit Antiochos IV. und seiner Religionsverfolgung, wo das Speisegesetz ein *articulus stantis aut cadentis ecclesiae* war, ein Anstoss, der behoben werden musste. Daher fügte er nach Vs. 7 in erbaulicher Paränese die weithin für sich stehende Geschichte der Frömmigkeitsbewährung Daniels und seiner drei Freunde hinzu. Dass wir tatsächlich mit einem Zusatz zu tun haben, wird nicht nur durch den sich von einleitenden Notizen abhebenden Erzählungsstil nahegelegt, sondern lässt sich auch daran erkennen, dass Vs. 17 lückenlos an Vs. 7 anschliesst. Dass hier der makkabäische Verfasser das Wort führt, geht auch daraus hervor, dass er die Wendung *'ākal ēt patbag* im Anschluss an Vs. 5 nicht nur in 1:8,13,15 und 16, sondern auch in 11:26 gebraucht, während Parsismen bei ihm sonstwo selten zu finden sind.
Die Verse 1-3 des 1. Kapitels greifen offensichtlich auf 2. Chronik 36:6-7 zurück und lassen ausserdem die Neigung des makkabäischen Verfassers zur Datierung zutage treten. Wie immer man auch das Problem der Datierung der Eroberung Jerusalems im dritten Jahr Jojakims zu lösen gedenkt, diese chronologische Ansetzung scheint doch in irgendeiner Weise durch die 70 Jahre der jeremianischen Voraussage der Dauer des Exils (Jer 25:11ff.; 29-10), auf die in Kap. 9 Bezug genommen wird, beeinflusst gewesen zu sein. Es lässt sich daher kaum verneinen, dass gleich am Anfang des Danielbuches die Hand des makkabäischen Verfassers zu erkennen ist, der sich wie in Kap. 9 auf ältere, 'kanonische' Ueberlieferung stützt.
Die dritte Spur des makkabäischen Autoren hat Beek in der chronologischen Notiz 'im dritten Jahr Nebukadnezzars' in 2:1 gefunden. Diese Angabe steht nicht nur im Widerspruch zu der dreijährigen Pagenerziehung, von der 1:5 redet (vgl. auch 1:18), sondern lässt sich m.E. auch deswegen als Zusatz erkennen, weil nach den Worten 'im 2. Jahr Nebukadnezzars' die Fortsetzung 'hatte Nebukadnezzar einen Traum' mit der ausdrücklichen Wiederholung des Eigennamens nicht zu erwarten ist.

Wenn diese Beobachtungen das Richtige treffen, lässt sich folgern, dass von den insgesamt 25 Versen von Dan 1:1-2:4a mindestens ungefähr die Hälfte unmittelbar vom makkabäischen Verfasser herrührt. Wegen dieser umfangreichen Ergänzungen stand im nichts im Wege sich zu entschliessen, den Anfang des von ihm mit Hilfe seiner aramäischen Vorlagen verfassten Buches in der Sprache zu schreiben, die zu seiner Zeit aus nationalistischen Gründen ohnehin die nächstliegende war und die er nach Ausweis von Kap. 8-12 auch selber bevorzog. So schuf er inzwischen auch eine sprachliche *inclusio*!

Nichtsdestoweniger sah er sich nicht genötigt, die von ihm verwendeten aramäischen Vorlagen insgesamt ins Hebräische zu übersetzen. Denn seinen Lesern war das Aramäische nicht nur mindestens so geläufig wie das Hebräische, sondern er fand auch in seiner Vorlage einen besonders geeigneten Punkt, wo er anfangen konnte, diese im Prinzip ungeändert zu übernehmen. Weil er, anders als der Autor der ursprünglichen Sammlung der Danielerzählungen, der noch davon gewusst hatte, dass man die vier Jünglinge in der babylonischen Sprache und Literatur unterrichtet hatte (1:4), der Meinung war, dass am babylonischen Hof Reichsaramäisch, die *lingua franca* der vorangehenden Jahrhunderte, gesprochen wurde, sah er sich imstande, seine Vorlage ab der Stelle zu kopieren, wo die Diener Nebukadnezzars zu reden anfingen, nachdem der König sie aufgefordert hatte, ihm seinen Traum mitzuteilen und zu erklären (2:4b).

Aus obigen Erwägungen hat sich ergeben, dass der Gesichtspunkt des makkabäischen Verfassers des Danielbuches für die Lösung des Problems der Doppelsprachigkeit von entscheidender Bedeutung ist. Dass das Buch ursprünglich ganz in aramäischer Sprache verfasst und aus bestimmten Gründen nachher teilweise ins Hebräische übersetzt wurde, konnte ich dabei nicht annehmen, geschweige denn, dass das Buch ursprünglich in hebräischer Sprache vorgelegen hat. Denn die These, dass der hebräische Teil des Buches, abgesehen von 1:1-2-4a, auf einer aramäischen Vorlage beruht, hat sich weder durch die Qumranfunde noch aus sprachlichen Gründen bestätigt. Dass der Text von Kap. 8-12 bei einer Rückübersetzung ins Aramäische verständlicher wäre, hat sich mir nirgends als zwingend erwiesen. Aramäischer Einfluss auf das Hebräische dieser Kapitel wird oft zu voreilig angenommen. Auch wenn sich zeigen sollte, dass es Aramaismen enthält, wäre dies kein Beweisgrund für einen ursprünglichen aramäischen Text, nachdem das Aramäische Volkssprache geworden war und deswegen auf das Hebräische jener Zeit einwirken musste[37]. Die These, dass das Danielbuch einst ganz auf Aramäisch verfasst wurde, ist auch deswegen unwahrscheinlich, weil in den hebräischen Teilen die für die aramäischen Erzählungen bezeichnende Wendung *ᶜānē wᵉ'āmar*, 'er hob an und sprach' (vgl. auch 7:2), niemals in hebräischer Form erscheint. Die von mir in Vorschlag gebrachte Erklärung der Doppelsprachigkeit des Buches bedarf jedenfalls der erwähnten These nicht. Noch weniger sollte man behaupten, dass das Danielbuch als ganzes ursprünglich in hebräischer Sprache geschrieben wurde, weil kein überzeugender Grund vorliegt, der erklären könnte, weshalb man später Teile des Buches ins Aramäische übersetzt oder in aramäischer Sprache tradiert hätte. Dass der makkabäische Verfasser sich im Hinblick auf die von ihm vorgenommenen Ergänzungen im Fall von Kap. 7 für das Aramäische, im Fall von 1:1-2:4a hingegen für das Hebräische entschieden hat, hängt nach meiner Auffassung mit dem Ausmass seiner Aktualisierung zusammen. Die Frage der

Einheitlichkeit oder Uneinheitlichkeit des Danielbuches lässt sich nicht mit einem einfachen Entweder-Oder lösen. Ihre Endgestalt verdankt die Schrift als ganze dem in makkabäischer Zeit lebenden Autoren, der vorzugsweise in hebräischer Sprache schrieb. Er verwendete jedoch aramäische Vorlagen, die er, abgesehen von der Einleitung zu den Erzählungen und von den Ergänzungen zu dem ursprünglich separat tradierten Visionsbericht vom Kap. 7, in der Sprache beliess, in der sie in frühhellenistischer Zeit verfasst worden waren. Dass ihn bei der Endgestaltung seines Werkes kanonische Erwägungen geleitet hätten, braucht man dabei nicht anzunehmen und ist im Hinblick auf die Qumranfunde auch recht unwahrscheinlich.

Kehren wir noch einmal zu den eingangs gemachten linguistischen Beobachtungen betreffs des Aramäischen des Danielbuches zurück, so ergibt sich, dass die redaktionskritische Analyse, so wie sie in diesem Aufsatz vorgetragen worden ist, völlig den sprachlichen Indizien entspricht. Mit dieser Feststellung dürfte sich der Ring schliessen.

1) J.H. Hospers, *Twee problemen betreffende het Aramees van het boek Daniël*, Groningen-Batavia 1948.
2) *ibid.*, p. 12.
3) Cf. K. Beyer, *Die aramäischen Texte vom Toten Meer samt den Inschriften aus Palästina, dem Testament Levis aus der Kairoer Genisa, der Fastenrolle und den alten talmudischen Zitaten*, Göttingen 1984, p. 32.
4) K. Beyer, *op. cit.*, p. 33, nimmt an, dass bei der endgültigen Festsetzung des Konsonantentextes im 1. nachchristlichen Jahrhundert spätere Schreibungen und Formen eingedrungen sind.
5) In den aramäischen Fragmenten von 1 Henoch habe ich drei persische Lehnwörter gezählt (*pardēs; paršègèn, rāz*) und im Hiobtargum ebenfals drei (*pitgāmā; dāt; dḥšt*), cf. die Wörterverzeichnisse in J.T. Milik, *The Books of Enoch*, Oxford 1976, pp. 367-397, und J.P.M. van der Ploeg-A.S. van der Woude, *Le targum de Job de la grotte XI de Qumrân*, Leiden 1971, pp. 89-98.
6) Cf. K. Koch, *et. al.*, *Das Buch Daniel* (*Erträge der Forschung*, vol. 144), Darmstadt 1980, pp. 45f.
7) Gegen die Exilsthese sprechen eindeutig die persischen und griechischen Lehnwörter und die Anspielungen auf die gegenseitigen Beziehungen zwischen Ptolemäer und Seleukidenreich in Dan 2.43. Auch der gründliche Aufsatz von K.A. Kitchen, "The Aramaic of Daniel" in *Notes on Some Problems in the Book of Daniel*, ed. D.J. Wiseman, London 1965, pp. 31-79, der die Sprachstufe des Danielaramäischen noch einmal untersuchte, kann die Exilsthese nicht unterstützen.
8) Cf. E.Y. Kutscher, "Biblical Aramaic - Eastern Aramaic or Western Aramaic?" in *Proceedings of the First World Congress of Jewish Studies, Jerusalem 1947*, Jerusalem 1952, pp. 123-127; *id.*, "Aramaic", in *Current Trends in Linguistics*, vol. 6, The Hague-Paris 1970, p. 347-412.
9) P.W. Coxon, "A Philological Note on Dan 5,3f.", in *ZAW* vol. 89, 1977, pp. 275f.
10) Die drei griechischen Lehnwörter finden sich in Dan 3:5.
11) Zwar hat sich die Entwicklung von Gentilicium (noch Dan 1:14) zum Standesnamen und Sammelbegriff für Fachleute in Magie und esoterischer Weisheit (Dan 2:2,4,5,10; 4:4; 5:7,11) anscheinend schon früh vollzogen. Herodot kennt Chaldäer als Priesterklasse (I,181, 183), cf. auch Ktesias, *Persika* 15. J.T. Nelis zufolge in *Daniel* (*De Boeken van het Oude Testament*), Roermond-Maaseik 1954, p. 31, war schon im 4. Jh. v. Chr. in Aegypten die Rede von chaldäischen Horoskopen. Aus babylonischen Quellen ist die Verwendung von 'Chaldäern' als Standesnamen aber nicht bekannt.
12) Auf Reichsaramäisch wurden noch in der ersten Hälfte des 3. vorchristlichen Jahrhunderts die Ostraka aus el-Kōm, Samaria und Gaza und die Inschrift aus Kerak geschrieben, cf. K. Beyer, *op. cit.*, pp. 51f. Diese Tatsache macht klar, dass Reichsaramäisch im 3. Jahrhundert noch im judäischen Bereich gesprochen wurde. Der Endverfasser von Daniel konnte diese Sprachstufe nachgeahmt haben.
13) Koch, *op. cit.*, pp. 45f.
14) Cf. jetzt K. Koch, *op. cit.*, pp. 49ff.
15) P.R. Davies, *Daniel* (*Old Testament Guides*), Sheffield 1985, p. 35.
16) Koch, *op. cit.*, pp. 51f.
17) *Tractatus theologico-politicus*, ed. 1674, p. 189.
18) Unter den neueren Forschern plädieren für einen einheitlichen Verfasser, der älteres Material verwendete: O. Plöger, *Das Buch Daniel* (*Kommentar zum Alten Testament*, vol. 18), Gütersloh 1965, p. 28; A. Lacocque, *The Book of Daniel*, London 1979, p. 9f.; H. Lusseau in *Einleitung in die heilige Schrift I: Altes Testament*, ed. A. Robert-A. Feuillet, Wien 1963, p. 687, sowie konservative Kommentatoren, cf. G.Ch. Aalders, *Daniel* (*Commentaar op het Oude Testament*), Kampen 1962, pp. 13ff. und J.G. Baldwin, *Daniel*, Leicester-Downers Grove, Ill. 1978, pp. 38ff.

19) Hospers, *op. cit.*, p. 23
20) Unter den neueren Auslegern unterscheidet M. Delcor, *Le livre de Daniel* (*Sources Bibliques*), Paris 1971, pp. 10-13, mindestens zwei Autoren und eine aus frühhellenistischer Zeit stammende Schrift, die Kap. 2-6 umfasste. H.L. Ginsberg, *Studies on the Book of Daniel*, New York 1948 (vgl. auch *id.*, "The Composition of the Book of Daniel" in *VT* vol. 4, 1954, pp. 246-275) hingegen unterscheidet einen Dan A (Das Buch der Hofgeschichten) aus der Zeit vor Antiochos IV. und einen Dan B (Das Buch der Apokalypsen) aus makkabäischer Zeit. In Dan B gäbe es vier Schichten (Apoc 1-4), die vom Endredaktor zusammengestellt worden seien. Cf. auch L.F. Hartman-A.A. di Lella, *The Book of Daniel* (*The Anchor Bible*, vol. 23), Garden City, N.Y. 1983, pp. 11-18.
21) M.A. Beek, *Das Danielbuch. Sein historischer Hintergrund und seine literarische Entwicklung*, Leiden 1935, pp. 8f.
22) *ibid.*, p. 8.
23) *ibid.*, p. 9.
24) L. Dequeker, "Daniel 7 et les Saints du Très-Haut" in *ETL* vol. 36, 1960, pp. 353-392.
25) L. Dequeker, "The 'Saints of the Most High' in Qumran and Daniel" in *OTS* vol. 18, 1975, pp. 108ff.
26) G. Hölscher, "Die Entstehung des Buches Daniel" in *Theologische Studien und Kritiken*, vol. 92, 1919, pp. 111-138.
27) Dequeker, *op. cit.*, in *OTS*, pp. 112f.
28) Dass Kap. 7 als Anhang zu Kap. 1-6 zu betrachten sei, wies Hölscher, *op. cit.*, überzeugend nach. Ihm folgten M. Haller, "Das Alter von Daniel 7" in *Theologische Studien und Kritiken* vol.93, 1920-1921, pp. 83-87, und M. Noth, "Zur Komposition des Buches Daniel" in *ibid.* vol. 98-99, 1926, pp. 143-163. (auch veröffentlich in *Gesammelte Studien zum Alten Testament*, vol. 2 (*Theol. Bücherei*, vol. 39), München 1969, pp. 11-28).
29) Cf. Dequeker, *op. cit.* in *OTS*, pp. 115f.
30) Die Partikel *'ᵃlū* begegnet zwar auch einige Male in den Erzählungen. Deswegen ist öfters hervorgehoben worden, dass man in Kap. 7 auf sie keine Quellenscheidung stützen könne. Abgesehen von anderen Tatsachen, die auf eine Ueberarbeitung des Kapitels hinweisen, bleibt die Verwendung von *'ᵃlū* zwischen *'ᵃrū* in den Versen 2,5,6 und 7 einerseits und Vers 13 andererseits doch merkwürdig.
31) Noth, *op. cit.*, pp. 144f.; s. dazu Dequeker, *op. cit.* in *OTS*, pp. 118ff.
32) Cf. auch Dequeker, *ibid.*, pp. 127ff.
33) Aalders, *op. cit.*, p. 163, sieht im vierten Tier das römische Reich und in den zehn Hörnern die daraus hervorgegangenen Staaten und Mächte, so dass er im elften Horn den Antichrist erblickt. J.-C. Lebram, *Das Buch Daniel* (*Zürcher Bibelkommentare AT*, vol. 23), Zürich 1984, p. 84, identifiziert das elfte Horn nicht mit Antiochos IV., sondern mit Antiochos III. und lehnt eine Ueberarbeitung von Kap. 7 ab. Er sieht sich daher gezwungen, in Kap. 8 eine erweiterungsschicht anzunehmen, die von einem Redaktor herrühre, der die ursprünglich auf Antiochos III. bezogene Vision durch Hinweise auf Antiochos IV. (vv. 11, 12a, 13, 14, 16, 18, 19, 24-26a, 27b) ergänzt habe. Ich vermag Lebram bei dieser literarischen Analyse von Kap. 7 und 8 nicht zu folgen.
34) Schon H. Gressman, *Der Messias*, Göttingen 1929, p. 344, identifizierte die vier Tiere mit den Diadochenreichen, machte aber keinen Unterschied zwischen der Deutung des Verfassers der Vorlage und der des makkabäischen Autoren.
35) Die Kommentatoren, die die vier Tiere mit den vier Weltreichen (dem babylonischen, medischen, persischen und griechischen Reich) identifizieren, und nicht eine Neuinterpretation des makkabäischen Verfassers annehmen, geraten bei v. 12 in grosse Schwierigkeiten, cf. z.B. die nicht überzeugenden Deutungen des Textes bei Plöger, *op. cit.*, p. 111; Aalders, *op. cit.*, p. 145; und Lebram, *op. cit.*, p. 90.
36) Beek, *op. cit.*, pp. 96ff.

37) Cf. auch M. Delcor, *op. cit.*, p. 11: "les arguments linguistiques avancés ne nous contraignent pas à admettre l'existence d'un traducteur opérant sur un texte araméen. On peut songer aussi à quelqu'un de plus familier avec l'araméen qu'avec l'hébreu mais écrivant directement en hébreu".

The Cushitic Article

A. Zaborski, Warszawa

It is impossible to postulate a Proto-Cushitic form of the definite - and, consequently, also the indefinite - article because there are, as also in the Semitic group, considerable differences between the particular branches as far as the exponents of the category "definite/indefinite" are concerned. There are also good reasons to consider some of the Cushitic articles as later, i.e. secondary developments. This note has only a provisional character, mainly because we lack exhaustive descriptions of several Cushitic languages. The emphasis will be on the Beja language which provides interesting parallels with Berber and to some extent also with Egyptian. This does not surprise, since Beja, with its isolated location as a north Cushitic language, shares with Afar-Saho, which itself is east Cushitic, the distinction of being among the most conservative or archaic Cushitic languages. Unfortunately, for many years the Beja language, notwithstanding its being one of the most important Hamito-Semitic languages generally, has been neglected by linguists, so that we lack a detailed reference grammar and comparative studies of Beja dialects. Extant sources are incomplete, and it is not always clear whether authors are dealing only with a particular Beja dialect, or whether they are presenting elements from different dialects. Therefore a synopsis of what we already know about the article in Beja is necessary if we want to explore its prehistory.

There is no doubt that the Beja definite article goes back, as was indicateted by Almkvist (1881, p.112) to the demonstrative pronoun. This means that the category of case which is marked in the definite article appeared there at a relatively later stage, i.e. the marking of case before possessive suffixes - most probably a survival of the old Hamito-Semitic phenomenon - and in the demonstrative pronouns is primary, while its marking in the definite article is secondary[1].

Beja demonstratives in Beni Amer, which is spoken in the south, and in Bishari, a northern dialect, are as follows (Almkvist 1881, p. 113; Reinisch 1893, par. 177):

Near (English: "this, these")

	Subject	Absolute		Subject	Absolute
sing. m.	*ū-n*	*o-n*	plur. m.	*ā-n*	*ē-n*
f.	*t-ū-n*	*t-o-n*	f.	*t-ā-n*	*t-ē-n*

In the Hadendiwa (more precisely the Imera) dialect described by Roper, there is a neutralisation of the opposition of case in the plural, so that we have only *ā-n* (masc.) and *t-ā-n* (fem.) corresponding to subject *and* absolute in the singular.

Remote (English: "that, those") demonstratives in Beja show a different system of case and number marking (Almkvist 1881, p.113; Reinisch 1893, par.178; Roper 1928, par.83):

	Subject	Absolute		Subject	Absolute
sing. m.	*b-e-n*	*b-e-b*	plur. m.	*b-a-l-ī́-n*	*b-a-l-ī́-b*
f.	*b-e-t*		f.	*b-a-l-ī́-t*	

Here we see a neutralisation of the case opposition in the feminine. Final absolutive *-b* and *-t* have their counterparts in the indefinite forms.

It is not clear whether the near and remote demonstrative pronouns have anything in common at all - apart from *-t* which is a general morpheme of the feminine and appears also elsewhere. It is difficult to say whether *-e-* has anything in common with *-i-*, which itself occurs as a variant of the definite article before non-monosyllabic words (see below); the same must be said about *-ī-*.

Beja demonstratives are clearly similar to Egyptian demonstratives:

Near	m. *pw*	f. *tw*	pl. *nw*
	p-n	*t-n*	*n-n*
	p-ʼ	*t-ʼ*	*n-ʼ*
Remote	*p-f*	*t-f*	*n-f*

It is well known that the demonstratives *p-ʼ* etc. were later used as definite articles in Late Egyptian and Coptic (Callender 1978, p.15; Zaborski, forthcoming).

The definite article in the Bishari dialect of Beja has the following forms (Almkvist 1881, p.64):

	Subject	Absolute		Subject	Absolute
sing. m.	*ū́-*	*ṓ-*	plur. m.	*ā́-*	*ḗ-*
f.	*t-ū́-*	*t-ṓ-*	f.	*t-ā́-*	*t-ḗ-*
e.g.	*ū́-tak*	*ṓ-tek*		*ā́-nda*	*ḗ-nda*
	"the man"			"the men"	
	tū́-tak-at	*tṓ-tak-at*		*tā́-ma*	*tḗ-ma*
	"the woman"			"the women"	

Almkvist (1881, pp.64-65) mentions only one variant, namely *te-*, which occurs with verbal nouns (abstracts) like *te-náye*, *te-háusō*, "milking" and "dreaming" respectively. It is remarkable that in all the examples the *te-* variant is unstressed, while long variants always are in this dialect. Almkvist was inclined to consider *te-* "as a weakening" (eine Schwächung) of *tō-*. He also mentions a tendency to use more and more the absolute forms instead of the subject forms, even though the forms with the subject variants were still considered as correct or even more correct.

It is not clear whether the forms provided by Reinisch are exclusively from the Beni Amer dialect - Reinisch also investigated Halenga and a variety of Hadendiwa to some extent - but in any case his forms can be taken as representative of southern Beja:

	Subject	Absolute		Subject	Absolute
sing. m.	*w-ū-, ū-*	*w-ō-, ō-*	plur. m.	*y-ā-, ā-*	*y-ē-, ē-*
f.	*t-ū-*	*t-ō-*	f.	*t-ā-*	*t-ē-*

The *w/y* masculine variants occur before pharyngeal consonants /'/ and /h/; *ū-, ō-, ā-* and *ē-* before non-pharyngeals.

According to Reinisch there are other variants typical for normal colloquial speech ("die gewöhnliche Konversationssprache"); there is also a tendency to use absolute forms instead of subject forms. These 'short' variants are:

sing. m.	*wo-, o-*	plur. m.	*ye-, e-; yi-, i-*
f.	*to-*		*te- ; ti-*

While in these forms there is a neutralisation of the category of case, there is also a neutralisation of the category of number in the most reduced variants:

m. *e-* :f. *t-e-*

Reinisch does not mention any other conditioning for his shorter variants apart from the socio-stylistic constraints mentioned above. It is remarkable that neither Almkvist nor Reinisch mention any variants conditioned by the number of syllables of the following word or its accentuation (cf. below). Reinisch emphasises also that in the southern dialects the definite article is accentuated only when "er an Quantität das Uebergewicht über den Vokal des Nennwortes besitzt", e.g. *ū-mḗk* "the donkey", but *ā́-mak* "the donkeys", although the latter word is usually stressed also on the last syllabe (i.e. *ā-mák*) so that in general in the southern dialects the definite article is usually not accentuated. Here are some examples taken from Reinisch:

wū-háḍḍa	"the lion"	*wu-hā́*	"the jackal"
ū-ták	"the man"	*û-mḗk u-wī́n*	"the big donkey"
û-kām-ū̃	"my camel"	*a-gaw-ā́-k*	"your(f.) houses"
wō-'ōrṓk	"your son"(abs.)	*yi-'árū*	"my children"
u-bā́'no	"the vulture"	*wṓ-ha*	"the beer"(abs.)
wū-ankʷána	"(the)god"	*wō-hawā́d-īb*	"in the night"(abs.)
ê-yām-ḗb	"into(the)water"	*û-dháy*	"the people"
tū́-nde	"the mother"	*wū-'ṓr*	"the boy"
tō-'ōt tu-bar-y-ū́k	"your daughter"	*tō-tak át*	"the woman"(abs.)
tō-tak at-ṓs	"his woman"(abs.)	*tā-má'*	"the women"
t-yamēt-hatā́y	"the frog"	*wū-hárrū*	"(the)corn"
u-kʷárkʷar	"the snake"	*ū́-mha*	"the morning"
â-mak-ā́n	"our donkey"	*te-tak at-ū́k-wa*	"and your woman"

And from Reinisch' <u>Halenga</u> texts:

ū-kʷasanayūn	"(the)god"	*wō-'ṓr*	"the boy"(abs.)
yā-'ar-ā́k	"your sons"(abs.)	*tō-'or*	"the girl"(abs.)
tā-m'a	"the women"	*tē-mháy ar*	"the three girls"
tā-'art-ā́k	"your daughters"(abs.)	*ū-ragad-ū́k*	"your leg"
û-zībha	"the morning"	*wū-hád'a*	"the chief"

The short forms are found practically only in Reinisch'Grammar (1893, par.113), e.g.:

e-dī́rfin	"the he-goat"	*te-dī́rfin*	"the she-goat"
plur.:*e-dī́rfin-a*		plur.: *-dī́rfin-a*	

In the <u>Hadendiwa</u>, or perhaps better, the <u>Imera</u> subdialect of Hadendiwa as described by Roper, the situation is as follows:

1. Always before /h/, and at least sometimes before /'/[2)], there is a neutralisation of case distinction and moreover a neutralisation of number in the feminine:

sing. m. *ū-*   plur. m. *yi-*

f. *te-*, *t-*

ū-hó-yi "my lambkin": *t -'a-té* "his milk"(abs.)

See e.g.:

ū-háḍa	"the lion"	*u-had'ai-y-ūk*	"your sheikh"
u-'or-wa	"and the boy"(abs.)	*t-hawi yé-wa*	"and the pack-saddles"
ū-'arabi náy	"the hillman"	*u-'ĭmi r*	"the affair"(short *u-'*.)
u-hášī-da	"on the ground"		

But there is also *tū-'or* "the girl", although it is *tə-ót-i bāba* "the girl's father"(Roper 1928 p.127) and *te-'ót-i* "my daughter".

2. Before bisyllabic and longer polysyllabic words, i.e. before:
   a. monosyllabics with a suffix, (Roper does not specify whether all suffixes or only some specific suffixes are involved; in any case the possessive suffixes are included), and
   b. bisyllabics with either a long vowel or an accented short vowel in the first syllable,

   there is also neutralisation of case, and, moreover, neutralisation of number in the feminine, while the neutralisation of number in the masculine is optional.

sing. m. *i-*   plur. m. *i-/ e-*

f. *t-e-*

See e.g. (from Roper's Texts and Vocabulary):

i-kam-ūk	"your camel"	*te-takát-ti*	"my woman"
te-másse	"the year"	*i-ragád-i*	"my foot"
e-kam-é	"their camels"	*i-lága*	"the calf"
i-súg-ī-b	"in the market"		

But there is also *i-k^w ák^w ar* "the snake"(ibid. p.128), and *u-k^w ák^w ar* (ibid. p.129).

3. Before other polysyllabics there is total neutralisation of case and number:

m. *i-*   f. *t-e-/t-i-*

See e.g.:

i-ǧammāl	"the camelman"	*ti-wi nna-y-t-ú-k-na*	"and your big things"
te-gabīlát-úk	"your tribe"		

See f.i. *i-tim-īkte ū-adum-tī-ka hanyīs*: "silence is better than talk" (Roper 1928, p. 143). *tū-beḍáwie*, abs. *to-beḍáwie*, is probably an archaism.

4. Before monosyllables - but excluding words with initial laryngeal - and before all bisyllables with a short unstressed vowel in the first syllable, the system of gender, case and number is

still preserved:

	Subject	Absolute	Subject	Absolute
sing. m.	*ū-*	*o-*	*ā-*	*e-3*
f.	*t-ū-*	*t-o-*	*t-ā-*	*t-e-3*

See e.g.:

ū́-bire	"the rain"	*o-sū́k*	"the market"(abs.)
tū-kām	"the she-camel"	*tō-kām*	id.(abs.)
tū́-sā'	"the hour"	*ū-tǻk*	"the man"
tū-n'é	"the fire"	*ū́-rba*[2)]	"the hill"
ó-sīb	"the direction" (abs.)	*ū-dhéy*	"the people"
ā́-kam	"the camels"	*tā́-kam*	"the she-camels"

The stress is usually, but not always, on the article.

5. The masculine variants with initial *w-* and *y-* are preserved in the dialect described by Roper, but only under the double condition that a) the definite article has the function of a relative pronoun, and b) it is immediately followed by a vowel. The forms are the following:

   sing. m. *wi-*, *wa-* plur. m. *yi-*

   but "*u-* often remains before initial *-a-*" (Roper 1928,par. 289). Roper adds (*loc. cit.*) "In some dialects, e.g. Suakin, the masculine article is always *wi-* even before a consonant" in relative clauses. I have not been able to find any example of *wa-* in a relative clause in Roper's texts or in his vocabulary.
6. Only Roper mentions variants which have been disregarded so far by other scholars who have dealt with the origin of the Beja article. These are variants with *-n-* occurring before *d-*, *ḍ-*, and *g-*, as well as *-m-* before *b-*. These variants seem not always to occur in this position, however, but other conditioning factors - if any - remain unknown (Roper 1928,par. 30).

See e.g. (from Roper's texts):

ā́n-da	"the men"	*én-da*	"the men"(abs.)
tū́n-de	"the mother"	*tā́n-de*	"the mothers"(abs.)
tón-dï	"the iron"(abs.)	*ū́n-ḍa*	"the newly born calf"

ān-ḍiwa	"the family, the people"	*en-ḍiwa*	id. (abs.)
un-ga'	"the back"	*ten-gináf*	"the camp"
en-geraba	"the evenings"	*im-bi', en-bi'*	"the day(s)"
um-baḍáḍ	"the sword"	*im-baḍáḍa*	"the swords"
em-bakw	"the place of shelter"	*tem-birát*	"termites"

But there are also the following attestations:

tū-dīn	"thorn"	*ū-dín*	"silence"
i-gin'-ok	"your heart" (abs.)	*tú-bire*	"the sky"
i-bhále	"the words"	*te-bút-tī-da*	"on the ground"

Hudson, whose study deals with the Arteiga dialect, provides the following forms and rules (Hudson 1976, p.108):

1. With monosyllabic nouns and adjectives there is a full set distinguishing case, number and gender:

	Subject	Absolute	Subject	Absolute
sing. m.	*ū-*	*o-*	*ā-*	*ē-*
f.	*t-ū-*	*t-o-*	*t-ā-*	*t-ē-*

2. Otherwise, there is *-i-* for all cases:
   m. *i-* f. *t-i-*
3. If the following word starts with *'-* or *h-*, there are variant forms:
   sing. *wi-* plur. *yi-*
   which shows that presumably distinctions of number are preserved. Hudson adds some notes (notes 12 and 13 to pp. 130-131) explaining that in Arteiga the shortening of the vowel in the article is obligatory, and that "When the vowel is shortened, it may be either /i/ or /u/ for the singular and just /i/ for the plural depending on the dialect ... In the transcription used here it is always given as /i/". The latter transcription convention is based on the fact that:

   "In Arteiga, and also in Hadendiwa, only two short vowels are distinguished, one corresponding morphophonemically to /ā/, the second to all other long vowels respectively; the close short vowel (corresponding to all long vowels but /ā/ is pronounced either [I] or [U] according to sub-dialect and linguistic environment, and the open one is pronounced [ʌ] before /y/, otherwise [a]".

Therefore it is not clear whether in Arteiga only *wi-haḍa* "the lion" or also *wu-haḍa*, as in other dialects, is possible as singular for *yi-haḍa* "the lions".

On the basis of dialect variations known so far, and on the basis of Berber parallels, it is possible to reconstruct provisionally the following Proto-Beja forms for the definite article:

	Subject	Absolute		Subject	Absolute
sing. m.	**w-ū-n*	**w-ō-n*	plur. m.	**y-ā-n*	**y-ē-n*
f.	**t-ū-n*	**t-ō-n*	f.	**t-ā-n*	**t-ē-n*

The parallels with the <u>Berber</u> demonstrative pronoun (as already indicated by Reinisch and Vycichl) are striking. See for instance the following examples taken from the most important dialect synopsis by E. Destaing (1921):

	m. sing.	f. sing.	m. plur.	f. plur.
Beni Iznasen	*wu*	*ṯu*	*yīnu*	*ṯīnu*
Beni Snus	*wu*	*ṯu*	*yūnu*	*ṯūnu*
Wargla	*u*	*ṯu*	*i ni*	*ti ni*
Ait Uriaġel	*wa*	*ṯa*	*yī n*	*ṯī n*
Zwawa	*wa*	*ṯa*	*wi*	*ṯi*
Ahaggar	*wa-reġ*	*ta-reġ*	*wi-reġ*	*ti-reġ*

It is particularly interesting that the prefixed markers of case in Berber probably also go back to the original definite article having its origin in the demonstrative pronoun (see Vycichl 1957, pp. 139-146, and a criticism by Prasse 1974, p. 12), so that we have e.g. (from Basset 1959, p. 85):

	Subject	Absolute		Subject	Absolute	
sing.	*u-funas*	*a-funas*	plur.	*i-funas-ən*		"bull"
	t-funas-t	*t-a-funas-t*		*t-funas-in*	*ti-funas-in*	"cow"
	wu-ššən	*u-ššən*		*wu-ššan-ən*	*u-ššan-ən*	"jackal"

On the relation between Berber and Cushitic, see Sasse 1983, pp. 120-122. While Beja Subject case *-ū-* has good cognates in Berber and Semitic, it is possible that Absolute case goes back to **wa-* (Sasse 1983, p. 118). It is remarkable however, that there is an *i-* in the Berber plural "préfixe d'état", as there is in Beja. This raises the question whether the Beja plural *(y)i-* may not be an archaism (see below).

The reconstruction of the Beja definite article as proposed by Vycichl (1953, pp. 373-379, and 1960, p. 257 and 254) *viz.*:

	Subject	Absolute		Subject	Absolute
sing. m.	**woi*	**wa*	plur. m.	**yei /wēi*	**wi*
f.	**toi*	**ta*	f.	**tēi*	**ti*

is less probable. Though there is as Ablaut series /ō/:/a/ as in *bōk* "he-goat", plur. *bak*, this does not mean that Beja Absolute sing. *-ō-* has to go back to **-a*. The same objection can be made to the alleged origin of *ā* from **ē* or **ei*, or from **i*, since a relation to the Ablaut *dibil*: *dābil* does not necessarily follow. The notion that there may be traces of the Cushitic Subject case morpheme *i-* in Beja, as suggested by Vycichl, merits attention. He does not mention, however, the Beja variant *i-* which occurs in Hadendiwa and Arteiga.

There has been another attempt to reconstruct the Proto-Beja definite article by Hetzron in his very important study "The Limits of Cushitic" (Hetzron 1980, pp. 88-90). Hetzron practically takes for granted that the situation in Arteiga and in Hadendiwa (he does not mention the Bishari or Beni Amer dialects), specifically the occurrence of the variant *i-* before non-monosyllabic words (including suffixes), is relatively the oldest, so that *i-* should be considered as the original definite article. He disregards somehow the connection between the definite article and demonstratives for the near object. On p. 89 he states:

> "We may very well conjecture that originally there was *u/u?/-i-ták* 'Case-Article-Noun', where *i* was either deleted or assimilated to the initial vocalic case-marker. As pointed out above, before /'/ and /h/, the *i* remains intact (see Hudson 1976, note 12: this happens only in Arteiga but *not* in Hadendiwa which has *ū-*, not in Bishari and not in Beni Amar, see above. A.Z.), but there is number-marking in the masculine: *wi-háḍa* (*wū-haḍa* or *ū-haḍa* in other dialects. A.Z) "the lion", *yi-háḍa* "the lions". This may be a case

of neutralisation: nominative **u-i-haḍa* and oblique (or Absolute. A.Z.) **o-i-haḍa* both yielding *w-i-haḍa*, and nominative **a-i-haḍa* with oblique **ay-i-háḍa* converging into *y-i-haḍa*. For the feminine, after an introductory *t-*, the immediately subsequent vowels, the case markers, must have dropped (Why? A.Z.), leading to *t-i-*."

In order to account for the occurrence of 'long vowel' variants with full case and number with gender distinction Hetzron further remarks (p. 89):

"It is possible to conceive that mono- or asyllabic units like demonstratives and articles have better resisted erosion than phonetically more substantial nouns. For the former, losing something may have meant losing everything and disappearing completely. That length is a relevant factor is shown even by the present distribution rules, as exposed obove. The long vowel case-markers *ū*, etc. tolerate only one subsequent syllable after them."

In my opinion the situation in <u>Beni Amer</u> and <u>Bishari</u> is probably older in relative terms. The following factors were decisive in the disintegration of the originally highly symmetric system:

1. The redundancy of the case marking in the article when possessive suffixes, containing the <u>same</u> case morphemes, have been added. The use of the definite article with nominals having possessive pronouns suffixed to them is obligatory with some exceptions (such as a few kinship terms) (see Roper 1928, pp. 32-33). While in the southern dialects we have many examples of 'long' case marking variants, such as *w-Ū-ašō-y-Ū́-k* "your enemy", *w-Ō-ašō-y-Ṓ-k* "your enemy"(abs.), *y-Ā-ašō-y-Ā́-k* "your enemies", *y-Ē-ašō-y-Ḗ-k* "your enemies"(abs.) (see Reinisch 1893, par. 168), are normal. In <u>Hadendiwa</u> there is already a neutralisation of case distinction and partially also of number (see above) so that we have e.g. *i-k ām-Ū́-k-na* "your (pl.) camel" instead of **Ū-k ām-Ū́-k-na* (see Roper, par. 102).
2. The syntactically conditioned tendency to use Absolute case for Subject case, so that gradually the latter is ousted in some positions in <u>Arteiga</u> and in <u>Hadendiwa</u>. This process has typological parallels on other languages, even in Indo-European.
3. Phonological processes not fully explained so far, yielding in the masculine plur. Absolute *yi-* from *yē-* over *ye-*, and similarly *ti-* from *tē-*.
4. The shift of stress from the definite article - where it still remains in <u>Bishari</u> - to the stem. This resulted in vowel shortening and vowel change (reduction).
5. In connection with stress also syllabic (or mora) length of a word plays a part in the change of the vowel.

6. Laryngeal /'/ and /h/ also play their role[3]: see Reinisch (1893, par. 179) who assumes that *yi-'ár* "the boys" goes back to *yā-'ár* because of the influence of the laryngeal.

Another possibility or hypothesis would be that the Hadendiwa situation is original, and that the neat system in Beni Amer and Bishari - notwithstanding the fact that these are peripheric and therefore probably archaic dialects - are a result of analogic regularisation. The *i-* and *yi-* variants might be connected to the Berber 'état d'annexion' *i-* and *y(i)-*, and even to the Semitic *-ī-* in the plural oblique (i.e. genitive-accusative) *-ī-na*. The problem is however that there is no trace of *i-* or *yi-* in demonstrative pronouns in Beja. A hypothetical regularisation of the demonstratives is not impossible, but would need some proof. In Somali there is a system of suffixed definite articles (also genetically connected to demonstratives and, as suggested a.o. by Hetzron 1980, pp. 19-20 with note 107, also to Beja; *w-* would go back to Proto-Hamito-Semitic $^*k^w$-, like Egyptian *p-*) with three variants as well, and both *-u* and *-i* for Subject case: *wîl-ka* "the boy" (abs.) *wîl-ku* and *wîl-ki* "the boy" as subject (Lamberti 1983, pp. 570-572; Moreno 1955, pp. 31-33; see Sasse 1983, p. 117), although the Somali definite article is still largely related to the distinction near: remote (see Heine 1978, pp. 27-29; he states that in the Sam group comprising Somali, Boni and Rendille, only Somali developed a definite article). That the situation in Somali may have an eastern Cushitic origin is suggested by the evidence of Highland eastern Cushitic. In this branch we have e.g. in Sidamo a Subject case *-hu* (*ex* *-*ku*), Absolute *-ha* (*ex* *-*ka*) and *-ti* (Subject) and *-ta* (Absolute) for fem. singular (Moreno 1940, par. 14; see also pars. 13 and 60 and also Tucker and Bryan 1966, p. 529 for relative *-n-k-u, -n-k-i, -n-k-a, -n-t-u, n-t-i, -n-t-a)*.There are more parallels in other Highland eastern Cushitic languages (see Plazimowsky-Brauner 1958, pp. 128-129) and also the Dullay languages have a similar system of what Sasse (Amborn, Minker, Sasse 1980, p. 89) calls 'connectors', e.g. m. sing. *k-u*, f. sing. *t-i*, plur. *k-i* in Tsammay; cf. also Yaaku (Heine 1974, p. 37 and 41).

In the Oromoid branch (Oromo, Konso with Dirayta or Gidole) the original suffix of the singulative has a function partially corresponding to the definite article. See e.g. *mōt-iččā* "the king" (abs.), *mōt-ičči* "the king" (subj.), where *-ič-či* may go back to *-*it-ki* since the feminine form has *mōt-it-ti* "the queen" (abs.), and *mōt-itti̋n* (subj.) (Moreno 1939, p. 46). Compare also Dirayta *inant-in-i̋tt/inant-i̋n* "the girl" and *appat-in-ĭtt/appat-ĭn* "the man" (see Hayward 1981, pp. 140-142), with a neutralisation of gender. Another definite suffix has a morpheme *-s-* which is found also in Konso (Black MS, V-25), in Dullay (Amborn, Minker, Sasse 1980, p. 94) and in Iraqw (Whiteley 1958, p. 59). Also the Sam languages and Yaaku could be compared here.

In Arbore we find a suffix *-ló* denoting proximity but

> "there are very clear indications that *-ló* also functions rather like a definite article" (Hayward 1984, p. 191).

This has a cognate in the closely related Elmolo (demonstrative *-lu*, f. *a-lu*; Heine 1980, pp. 184-185) and in Dasenech (*-la*: Sasse 1976, p. 207) which Hayward (1984, p. 44) even connects with Boni. In any case, this definite article is an innovation in the Cushitic system.

The otherwise very archaic languages Afar and Saho do not have a real definite article though demonstrative pronouns are frequently used in functions corresponding to the definite article in other languages (see e.g. Bliese 1981, p. 15). It is interesting that while the originally feminine morpheme *-t-* appears with both feminine and masculine nouns, there is *-o* and *-a* (i.e. *-to*, *-ta* for the masculine and *-tó* and *-tá* for the masculine singular) and *-i-* (i.e. *-t-i-t*) in the plural in Saho as a 'Particularizing Determinative' (Tucker and Bryan 1966, p. 526).

In the Agaw or Central Cushitic languages

> "Definiteness of noun phrases can be clearly expressed for the object only in Bilin and Kemant, the accusative case being reserved for definite objects" (Hetzron 1976, p. 69 and 46).

This system has *-s* for the masculine and *-t* for the feminine.

In Iraqw, usually classified as a member of the alleged "southern Cushitic" group, there is a particle

> "with little 'demonstrative' significance; and in some contexts it is difficult to associate it with any particular meaning " (Whiteley 1958, p. 60):

masculine *wó* or *kó*, feminine *ró*. The masculine variants may both be related to $*k^{w}$*-u*, but the problem needs further data and special research. It is most interesting that the masculine demonstrative is *kwi* after adjectives (otherwise *wĭ*). In the closely related Alagwa and Burunge the demonstrative is *wĭ* (Alagwa) but *kĭ* (Burunge) for the masculine and *tĭ* for the feminine in both languages. Also in Dahalo, the position of which is still to be explained, there is a masculine demonstrative *úkwà* corresponding to feminine *íta*.

In spite of all the diversity it is possible that the Beja prefixed definite article and the eastern Cushitic suffixed article

(But note that the demostrative in Afar precedes the noun!), probably even the Iraqw particle, contain the m. *ku-*, f. *ti-*, as postulated by Hetzron (1980, pp. 18-21).

Notes

This article has been written during my stay in the Institute of African Studies, University of Cologne, on a research grant of the Humboldt Foundation.

1) The use of the demonstrative as a definite article is relatively old, since now they occur together; i.e. the use of the definite article is obligatory when the noun is preceded (or, for emphasis, followed - an even stronger emphasis is present when a noun with the definite article is both preceded and followed by a demonstrative pronoun); e.g. *un ū-lák* "this man", *tū́n te-takat* "this woman".
2) This is a case of ellipsis of a short accentuate vowel - "hill".
3) In Arteiga short vowels are deleted before /'/ and /h/ (Hudson 1976 1976, 100).

References

Almkvist 1881: H. Almkvist, *Die Bischari-Sprache*, Uppsala 1881.
Amborn, Minker, Sasse 1980: H. Amborn, G. Minker and H.-J. Sasse, *Das Dullay*, Berlin 1980.
Basset 1959: A. Basset, "Sur la voyelle initiale en berbère" in *Articles de dialectologie berbère*, Paris 1959, pp. 83-89.
Bender 1976: *The Non-semitic Languages in Ethiopia*, ed. M.L. Bender, East Lansing 1976.
Black MS: P. Black, *Konso Phonology, Morphology and Syntax*, Manuscript (1973).
Bliese 1981: L. Bliese, *A Generative Grammar of Afar*, Arlington 1981.
Callender 1978: J.B. Callender, *Middle Egyptian*, Malibu 1978.
Destaing 1921: E. Destaing, "Note sur le pronom démonstratif en berbère" in *Mémoires de la société de linguistique de Paris* vol. 22, 1921, pp. 186-200.
Hayward 1981: R.J. Hayward,"Nominal Suffixes in Dirayta (Gidole)" in *BSOAS* vol. 44, 1981, pp. 126-144.
Hayward 1984: R.J. Hayward, *The Arbore Language*, Hamburg 1984.
Heine 1975: B. Heine, "Notes on the Yaaku Language" in *Afrika und Uebersee* vol. 58, 1975, pp. 27-61 and 119-138.
Heine 1978: B. Heine, "The Sam Languages" in *Afroasiatic Linguistics* vol. 6, 1978, pp. 1-93.
Hetzron 1976: R. Hetzron, "The Agaw Languages" in *Afroasiatic Languages* vol. 3, 1976, pp. 31-75.
Hetzron 1980: R. Hetzron, "The Limits of Cushitic" in *Sprache und Geschichte in Afrika* vol. 2, 1980, pp. 7-126.
Hudson 1964: R.A. Hudson, *A Grammatical Study of Beja*, London 1964 (diss.).
Hudson 1976: R.A. Hudson, "Beja" in Bender 1976, pp. 97-132.
Lamberti 1983: M. Lamberti, *Die Somali-Dialekte. Eine vergleichende Untersuchung*, Köln 1983 (diss.).
Moreno 1939: M.M. Moreno, *Grammatica teorico-pratica della lingua galla*, Milano 1939.
Moreno 1940: M.M. Moreno, *Manuale di Sidamo*, Milano 1940.
Moreno 1955: M.M. Moreno, *Il Somalo della Somalia*, Roma 1955.
Plazikowsky-Brauner 1958: H. Plazikowsky-Brauner, "Die Determinativen Elemente der kuschitischen Sprachen" in *MIO* vol. 6, 1958, pp. 121-141.
Prasse 1972-1974: K.-G. Prasse, *Manuel de grammaire touarègue* 1-3, Copenhague 1972-1974.
Roper 1928: E.M. Roper, *Tu Bedawie*, Hertford 1928.
Sasse 1983: H.-J. Sasse, "Case in Cushitic, Semitic and Berber" in *Current Progress in Afro-Asiatic Linguistics*, ed. J. Bynon, Amsterdam 1983, pp. 111-126.
Reinisch 1893: J. Reinisch, *Die Bedauye-Sprache*, Wien 1893.
Tucker - Bryan 1966: A.N. Tucker and A.M. Bryan, *Linguistic Analyses - The Non-Bantu Languages of North-Eastern Africa*, London 1966.

Vycichl 1953: W. Vycichl,"Der bestimmte Artikel in der Beija-Sprache. Seine Beziehungen zum Aegyptischen und Berberischen" in *MUS* vol. 66, 1953, pp. 373-379.
Vycichl 1957: W. Vycichl, "L'article défini du Berbère" in *Mémorial André Basset*, Paris 1957, pp. 139-146.
Vycichl 1960: W. Vycichl, "The Beja Language Tū Bedawiye. Its Relationship with Old Egyptian" in *Ks* vol. 8, 1960, pp. 252-264.
Whiteley 1958: W.H. Whiteley, *A Short Description of Item Categories in Iraqw*, Kampala 1958.
Zaborski (forthc.): A. Zaborski, "A Note on Cushitic Demonstrative Pronouns" in *Festschrift Rundgren* (forthcoming).